EXPLORING
MEDIA
CULTURE

COMMUNICATION AND HUMAN VALUES

*Communication
————— and
Human Values*

EXPLORING MEDIA CULTURE

A Guide

Michael R. Real

SAGE Publications
International Educational and Professional Publisher
Thousand Oaks   London   New Delhi

For information address:

SAGE Publications, Inc.
2455 Teller Road
Thousand Oaks, California 91320
E-mail: order@sagepub.com

SAGE Publications Ltd.
6 Bonhill Street
London EC2A 4PU
United Kingdom

SAGE Publications India Pvt. Ltd.
M-32 Market
Greater Kailash I
New Delhi 110 048 India

Printed in the United States of America

Library of Congress Cataloging-in-Publication Data

Real, Michael R.
    Exploring media culture: a guide / Michael R. Real.
        p.   cm.   —(Communication and human values)
    Includes bibliographical references and index.
        ISBN 0-8039-5876-5 (alk. paper).   —   ISBN 0-8039-5877-3 (pbk. :
    alk. paper)
        1. Mass media and culture—United States.   2. Popular culture—
    United States.   I. Title.   II. Series: Communication and human
    values (Newbury Park, Calif.)
    P94.65.U6R4   1996
    302.23′0973—dc20   96-10043

This book is printed on acid-free paper.

96 97 98 99 10 9 8 7 6 5 4 3 2 1

Production Editor: Astrid Virding
Typesetter: Christina Hill
Cover Designer: Candice Harman

Contents

List of Figures

Acknowledgments

All media today are collective enterprises, and I am indebted to countless individuals for their assistance and collaboration in the making of this book. Acknowledgments are due especially to Robert White, the series editor, and to Sophy Craze, Margaret Seawell, and Sara Miller McCune of Sage. Without their thoughtful assistance, this work would not have come about or, at a minimum, its failings would be much more apparent.

Thanks are due also to an immense number of authors, scattered throughout the English-speaking world and beyond, who have led the way in the exploration of media and cultural studies. The reference list at the end of this book is only a hint of the huge intellectual indebtedness that provides the base of any work of this kind.

The stimulation and support of faculty from the new School of Communications at San Diego State University and my other colleagues past and present at SDSU, the University of California at San Diego, the University of Illinois, and elsewhere are deeply appreciated. They have always been there to share the burdens of learning and teaching and, importantly, to make bearing the burdens so pleasant. I am also grateful for the stimulation and friendship of those in our Binational Association of Schools of Communication and other scholarly organizations throughout the world.

Specifically, I wish also to thank James Lull, James Curran, Herbert Schiller, Richard Pack, Arthur Lyons, Lorna Francis, Manuel Alvarado, Carroll Blue, Jeffrey Segrave, Stephen Barr, Marlene Cuthbert, Martha Lauzen, Robert Mechikoff, Kim Reinemuth, Jonathan Jerald, Avis Anderson, Michael Shubert, Loren Kling, Anita Michetti, Diana Fowler, Kevin Pearce, Kelley Reilly, Ariella Kaye, Lisa Katz, Manuel Gomez, Lisa Nava, Pavanee and Pakavadee Tamsakal, James Wilson, Julie Dillon, Shane Hope, Deanna Russo, Brian Liberto, Adreana Langston, Kristin Ferguson, and undoubtedly a couple of others who I am forgetting. Each made a significant and generous contribution to these pages. Kathy Hines did the figure artwork. I also must thank my crazy two brothers and three sisters, my incredibly patient and funny and wonderful wife and daughter, Paula and Marisa, and especially all my students for their generous inspiration and assistance.

Here's to media culture and all it offers. As we explore its highways and byways, may we drink deeply of its essence but never fall victim to its poisons. May its "terrible beauty," to borrow from Yeats, be ours to possess, correct, and appreciate.

Introduction:
A Guidebook for Media Study

A child sits in front of a television set. Look more closely. You recognize the child, the clothes, the setting. It is you, as a child, sitting absorbed in the television program. It is as if you the child have climbed inside the television set to inhabit its imagined world, as you would climb into a closet or a bathtub. What is going on in this unique, continuous experience as you enter and inhabit the space of media culture?

These pages introduce methods for examining the particular discourse that is media culture, especially as it is found in the English-speaking world today.

The goal is not to give answers but, at the risk of sounding trite, to *empower* readers to find their own answers with the assistance of tools suggested here. Each chapter introduces a technique, or set of tools, for analyzing culture and media as they are experienced in daily life. Applying these techniques empowers the reader to cope better with media culture, that is, to understand and take charge of that crucial point of intersection between communication technologies and the meanings we make from them. To accomplish this, the book is addressed to students, professors, and the public alike.

Understanding Media: Getting Inside Our Culture

Like the child absorbed by the television set, we have come to inhabit media culture as a space rich in stories, information, and meanings. Research on media culture has shifted away from a focus on one obvious mass medium, television, coming from "out there" to affect us, toward examining a range of media that we enter into in our daily life, a shift from sociological mass communication to personal media experience. Media invade our living space, shape the taste of those around us, inform and persuade us on products and policies, intrude into our private dreams and public fears, and, in turn, invite us to inhabit them. Notice how children watch television, how they become oblivious to the rest of the world. Later the same happens with movies, popular music, books, the Internet, and the range of media we become absorbed into. What is this "media culture," and how can we explore it with appreciation and critical understanding?

The first task of this introductory text is to provide a digest or overview of *critical techniques,* a synthesis of the most important and useful approaches to understanding media culture today. In this, the book is eclectic, drawing from a wide range of authors, concepts, and theories, particularly from works in recent years in the cultural studies tradition. The book's sources are wide-ranging but its focus is selective and unique, zeroing in on the relation between media and identity. The original contribution of these pages is the distinct road map blended from multiple traditions. Media literacy, critical theory, social science research, formalism, industry data, popular journalism, phenomenology—these and other creative sources combine with cultural studies to provide the critical techniques suggested and applied here.

The second task is to identify *commonly shared experiences* of media culture. Modern media make it possible for people living continents apart to know and experience the same cultural products: the Olympics, Disney, film noir, Madonna, video games, aerobics, quiz shows, and the other goodies spilling out of the cornucopia of media. The cases explored here are international in their availability to all of us, although there is some emphasis on "the heart of the beast," Hollywood, as cultural producer. In these explorations of commonly shared cultural experiences, the purpose is different than the normative study of classical culture where one is led upward to "better" cultural products. These explorations instead call us to reexamine and come to terms with what we already share experientially as our given culture. The goal is to attain not so much new knowledge as self-knowledge.

The third task is to present a *case study* approach that combines the techniques and insights developed by critical media studies with the everyday experience that we have of our media environment. Ideas are fleshed out with examples; examples propel us to new syntheses of understanding. Each chapter takes a familiar example (or several examples), examines it with developed techniques of analysis, and makes of it a case study of media culture. In the process, we both critically understand our media culture in more depth and develop our abilities for interpreting other cases. The book uses multiple case studies because the size and complexity of media culture prevent one from extracting a single test tube sample of our culture and measuring it with the intent of generalizing to the totality with scientific certitude. Instead, we more modestly select significant typical cases of cultural products and practices to clarify the basic general outlines, dynamics, and tendencies of the larger culture and our relationship to it. In the process, we hone techniques for exploring, evaluating, and enjoying our media experiences and meanings in context.

The organizational structure of each chapter is simple.

- An imaginative scenario sets the tone for the chapter's topic and method.
- The investigative method introduces interrelated concepts, ideas, and theories and the questions they suggest.
- A case study, in the form of a prominent example, takes us inside the cultural practices and products.
- Interpretations, ethnography, criticism, and meanings are suggested and evaluated.
- Major points are summarized.
- A series of exercises is suggested to apply this method of study to the reader's own experience of media culture.

This book provides an introductory exploration of media but it is not a traditional mass communication textbook. Such texts have been aimed primarily at those planning professional careers in journalism, television, and mass media. In the United States, they typically present a historical review of the development of media with a chapter on early American newspapers and magazines, other chapters on the history of radio and television, and perhaps one on film. They present the professional codes of journalists, broadcasters, and filmmakers, and they review a selection of findings of social science research on media effects and audience gratifications. Those are useful to know, but they are typically couched in such a way as to serve primarily the interests of media professionals and media industries, rather than the interests of media users and the public at large.

Exploring Media Culture concerns the experience of users of media, not producers or researchers. This is a guide for those who expect to attend to film, television, popular music, and similar media whether or not they may also actively produce such media culture or conduct formal research on media. As a handbook for media consumers, the presentation of "methods" of study is quite distinct from the usual methodology text for media research. Those methods are the formal methods of science with requirements for research instruments, funded personnel, sampling methods, stringent controls, limited questions, and empirical measures. Those methods contribute to the growth of an academic discipline but are not accessible to the average person. Instead, instruments of "research" are proposed here that borrow from the humanities, arts, and sciences but in ways that are available to anyone willing to think and pay attention. These methods both enhance appreciation and provide critical understandings. These are, in effect, research methods for the "lay" person encountering everyday media and creating meaning from cultural products and practices.

Four factors especially motivate this exploration of media culture. First, requests for a second edition of *Super Media: A Cultural Studies Approach* (and not all requests were from my blood relatives!) brought home how quickly this field of study is developing. Too much had happened to merely revise that earlier book. A new book would be necessary to focus and integrate the current explosion of insights into media study and to present tools for exploring it. A second factor shaping the book came from the opportunity to teach film courses and media aesthetics in addition to courses with a more social science approach to mass communication. Film is art, broadcasting is commerce, or so one might conclude from reviewing the polarized literature on each. Film study forces certain reconceptualizations of what media theory and methods are all about and reconfirms the necessity of cultural studies as a balance to social science research. A third motivation for this exploration of media culture came from the challenge of incorporating the extensive development of feminist media theory and criticism. A fourth motivation concerned the numerous contributions of "postmodernism" to cultural criticism and the necessity to incorporate these into any analysis of contemporary media. For better or for worse, the issues in postmodern theory engage many of the conditions we live in more directly than any other critical perspective today.

Still, the underlying motivation for creating this book is the same as for most who read and use it—a sense of the importance of media culture and its pleasures and dangers, coupled with a desire to grasp and appreciate it better. Media culture today is significant both because of its size and invasiveness and because of its "signifying" power. Other significant institutions today—the family, economics, education, religion, politics, the arts, and the rest—are sometimes set against media, as if each exercises power separately. Yet in the media age it is clear that all power is exercised, not independently, but in interaction with and through media culture. Media incorporate and standardize the sign systems available to us with which we can grasp and change the world. Media culture plays a personally invasive and culturally decisive role in the contemporary world.

Media Culture, Identity, and Difference

But are there not insurmountable distances and differences between what people experience as media culture around the world, differences that preclude a common examination of even one nation's experience today?

Amazingly, given the distances between them, there is more than the English language shared among the cultures of Canberra, Wellington, Ottawa, New Delhi, London, Washington, Lagos, and others in the English-speaking world and beyond. We all know broadcast sports, rock 'n' roll music, Anthony Hopkins and Holly Hunter, CNN and live war coverage, Guess jeans, and fish and chips (even if we call them "fries"). We follow similar news, hear simplistic sound bites, worry about crime and family life, gripe about taxes and television—whether we call it the tube or the telly, a sacred national trust or the idiot box.

Yet perhaps more amazing than the commonalities that make us alike are the differences that distinguish us—not so much the huge historical or geographical differences but the differences within a single locality. In one neighborhood, even one family, we find side-by-side a person whose tastes are relentlessly classical, from preset radio stations to art films and literature, and a person whose tastes are aggressively alternative, from low-hanging skater clothes to gangster rap to heavy metal magazines. Next door a country western line dancer shares a roof with a video game whiz and a football fanatic. Very often each such taste entails a range of associated media habits, cultural preferences, lifestyles, and worldviews, making these individuals seem as different as people from separate centuries and continents.

Still more amazing, and confusing above all, is how any one of us contains within us simultaneously a similarly jumbled set of contradictory tastes and associations. We change from nylons to jeans, from reggae to oldies, from homemade meat pies to apple pie, from fast food tacos to Indian carryout. We shift unthinkingly at warp speed among a postmodern pastiche of taste cultures, negotiating among the schizophrenia of multiple split personalities without thinking twice about it.

Who are we, at once so similar and so different as groups and within ourselves?

Critical Analysis and Co-Authorship of Media Culture

As we see cumulatively in these pages, we share central tendencies, a kind of "dominant culture," through our global media, and here we tease out the meaning of its dominant tendencies not to prove a single thesis but to suggest interrelated insights. Our media culture also displays awesome variety, a "cultural pastiche," and exploring that too is our task here.

What we seek most of all here, though, is to propose techniques of analysis through which we can come to understand all that is at work in our lives as constructed by media culture, as mainstream or oddball as our choices may be. To put it pedantically, what have years of collective scholarship discovered to be effective concepts and methods for exploring and comprehending media culture? More mundanely, how do people go about uncovering the glories and depravities of our personal experience of pop media? We inhabit our media culture like a virtual home and whether we resist or celebrate its dominant ideology, we find "fun" in the culture and even fun in the analysis of it!

In academic terms, the approach here is phenomenological, employing "thick description" and grounded theory. We seek an "ethnography of practices" and an "exegesis of texts" that connect our experience of media with the best of cultural theory and media studies. The phenomenology and existentialism of our approach appears not in abstract debates over Husserl or Merleau-Ponty but in our concrete emphasis on "the immediate experience" of media culture. This approach attempts to work through points of convergence with British cultural studies, American popular culture analysis, social science research, film studies, and the many theoretical and methodological approaches cited throughout the following chapters. These sources cannot be simply combined, for their differences and even disagreements are many. But their divergences are most extreme in the abstract theoretical range and less so in the phenomenological range, grounded close to our immediate experience of media culture. A goal here is the development of theory itself, but more emphasis is given to how theory relates to experience, to clarifying and shedding light on our lived experience. By staying close to texts, narratives, interpretations, and rituals of actual people, we can "lay open" great ranges of media culture without getting lost in the most esoteric, though important, of scholarly debates today. This is, after all, an introduction to media studies, not a conclusion.

A somewhat unusual emphasis in these pages is on *co-authorship.* Each of us, as what is inadequately labeled an audience-member or media consumer or user or reader or net surfer, is a co-author of our media culture. The co-author theme rejects the notion of audience members as cultural boobs, as couch potatoes passively receiving whatever is injected into them by the hypodermic needle of mass media. Rather as a media *user* co-author, you or I select from what is given by our media *creator* co-author(s) and work up from that our own "meaning." Extending the idea of the active audience, the "co-author" thesis places responsibility squarely on the shoulders of both media producers and consumers. Our co-authors who create media content bear great responsibility—they are public agenda-setters, celebrity-makers, and enforcers of social norms—but each of us also bears responsibility for our selection and use, our "creation," of media culture as well.

To repeat, our central purpose here is to provide tools—in the form of concepts, methods, theories, and applications— for analyzing media and culture, tools that move us closer to comprehending the meanings, purposes, and ideologies infusing our media-saturated lives. The result sought is a reader who is empowered to create, sustain, or change that very media culture in his or her own best interest and the best interest of all.

Chapter Sequence:
A Guide to Exploring Media Culture

The concepts in these pages and their sequencing are meant to build cumulatively an improved ability to explore with awareness, understanding, and critical facility the world of media culture. The techniques and concepts presented focus successively on distinct "moments" in cultural analysis or on specific "problematics." These include the following:

1. "Culture, Media, and Identity" are defined in the opening chapter as we experience them today. What are the issues in the wars raging around culture and media today, and how do popular music and culture theory help to explain each other and our personal identity?
2. "Participation" examines how we *ritually* participate in media activities from sporting events to aerobic exercise to video games. Far from being detached and passive, we enter into, inhabit, and interact with our experiences of media culture in daily life. What can ritual theory explain about our relationship to media culture?
3. "Reception" asks how we receive, interpret, and apply what is presented in media. Different people may take the same media message in quite different ways. Can media make us violent, sexually indulgent, and Madonna wannabes? How does reception theory account for the peculiar dynamics of media culture?
4. "Text" concerns the message *content* itself in the media experience. The text is the organized content of images, sounds, and words in the form of narrative, genre, signs, and intertextuality that we encounter at the point of intersection between media production and media reception. Why do

Disney and film noir engage our attention so differently? What has been put into a television program, film, book, advertisement, web site, or other cultural product that elicits attention, understanding, and involvement?

5. "Production/Hegemony" looks at how social power is exercised through media. What difference does it make that dominant cultural products and practices are produced and distributed by large commercial institutions within the capitalist system? How does the dominance by Hollywood of world movie screens exercise hegemony over the values and ideology of film viewers?

6. "Gender," like "ethnicity," considers how group identity is represented in media culture. How do patriarchy and the male gaze structure our media messages and reception? The historic exclusion, stereotyping, and under-representation of females in media illustrate how unequal power in sex, race, or class groups affects media culture.

7. "History and Ethics" asks how a (mis?)reading of the past is used to configure right and wrong in the present. Media reconstruct historical events, persons, and controversies, such as the American quiz show scandal in the early days of television. How are views of history, evolution, and current ethical choices influenced by media reconstructions?

8. "Postmodernism" foregrounds the unique characteristics of where current media culture has come from, is, and is going. How are aesthetics and self-identity renegotiated in the new age of pastiche, fragmentation, excess, and consumption under late capitalism? What characteristics of MTV, the modern Olympic Games, and the films of David Lynch and Quentin Tarantino distinguish the postmodern condition?

9. "Constructing the Self" considers how we co-author our media and ourselves as we select and respond to cultural products and practices. The way Navajos react each year to a drive-in screening of *Cheyenne Autumn* clarifies issues of media, culture, and identity that carry throughout this book. How do we become and express our self within the world of contemporary media culture?

In addition to the preceding, there are, of course, other methods and tools for examining media culture. Many of these—structuralism, poststructuralism, political economy, experimentalism, ethnography, ethnomethodology, and so forth—are incorporated at least implicitly in the preceding methods, but there is no claim that it is an exhaustive list of analytic tools.

As a whole, these chapters suggest guideposts in our journey through contemporary culture. The encoding-decoding model of Stuart Hall (1980) suggests the relations between production, encoding, text, decoding, and

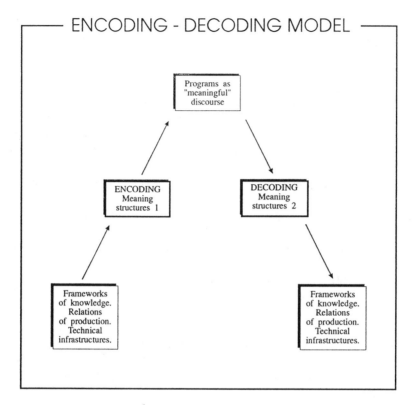

Figure 0.1. Relationship of text, its production, and its consumption with infrastructural elements in Stuart Hall's (1980) "Encoding-Decoding" model.

reception. The model (Figure 0.1) underscores how the moments and problematics of media culture are embedded in historical and contextual relations of knowledge, production, and technology.

Many of the terms and relationships in Hall's model are applied in the following pages. The model has an attractive self-explanatory quality. Everyone today has lived with media all her or his life and has a gut-level sense of meanings produced by oneself (meaning structures 2) and others (meaning structures 1). There is also a sense that these meanings develop within a larger social context, dependent on what many people already know, how they work together, and how technology is being employed. The less obvious meanings have been explained by Hall himself (1980, 1994) and others. Among the wide variety of books that have used Hall's schema are *The*

"Nationwide" Audience (Morley, 1980), *Fields in Vision: Television Sport and Cultural Transformation* (Whannel, 1992), and *Feminist Media Studies* (Van Zoonen, 1994).

Hall's model and the work of many others have inspired the organizational structure of this book, a structure that is portrayed in Figure 0.2.

The first chapter maps the basic terrain and the next four chapters explore fundamental components or "moments" in our experience of media: our ritual participation in media, our differential reception and interpretation of media, the text itself of the media product, and the industry that produced it.

The order of presentation of these concepts (chapters) starts with the experience of the receiver of media and works backwards toward its origins. As a consequence, the numbering of concepts is the reverse of the direction of the solid arrows that represent the order of media transmission. In traditional chronological order, the first five, the "moments" of media culture, would be first production, next text, and finally reception and participation and their effects on identity. The music video is produced, it appears on television as a text, we view and interpret it, and we participate by dancing to it, memorizing it, buying the CD, playing air guitar with it, singing it as karaoke, fantasizing our own stardom, or otherwise. Here we have chosen not to present the moments in that order because that would evoke too much of the old bullet, one-way effects model of mass communication. Instead, we begin with our decoding of texts as we watch, listen, or read, and work back toward the encoding of those texts by creative, commercial teams.

The next four concepts (chapters), the "problematics" of gender and ethnicity, history and ethics, postmodernism, and co-authorship occur across all stages in the communication sequence. For example, racism and sexism in media employment patterns are paralleled by biased images in the media and by bias in the reception and interpretation of audience members. The concepts are "problematic" because they are among the major sources of injustice, confusion, and power manipulation in our media culture.

The entire process of media making and receiving occurs within a larger shaping context. This context, as Hall insisted, includes the inherited frameworks of knowledge we employ, the relations of production that determine who does what in creating meaning, and the technical infrastructure of equipment and procedures that further constrain what meanings are possible and likely.

If all this appears impossibly dense at this point, be assured that the model is really one that should be appreciated *after* reading the chapters, at which time the applications and implications of the concepts and their interrelationships should be clear. For now, it may be enough to merely see a sequencing

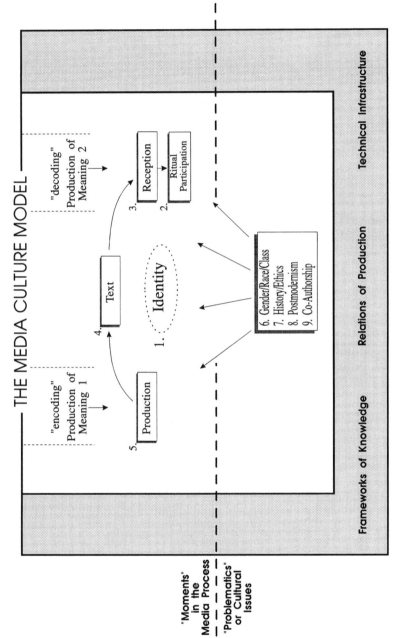

Figure 0.2. Chapter sequence and model for exploring the many aspects of media culture.

in the concepts and chapters and to sense what one hopes is there, an underlying logic in the sequencing.

The "Mystery" of Media Culture

Be forewarned—there is a narrative plotline running through these pages. As a story carries a film, novel, play, video game, or television drama, so an argument runs through this book. As a mystery story is propelled by an unsolved crime that occurs early on, so a scholarly book starts with a problem or series of problems. And, just as the challenge of the mystery is to solve it, so the challenge of scholarship is to unearth solutions. The problem or "mystery" here is the distinct problematic of contemporary culture and communication. Who, or what, is the ultimate *mysterium* in media culture today and how do we uncover it? Be patient in the search. Many clues and suspects will emerge along the way, but you may have to wait till the end to find out "who done it."

1

Culture, Media, and Identity:
My Music

A lonely flute rasps quietly on the soundtrack. The rainy street dimly reflects streetlights in the darkness of the alleys. A lone figure shuffles along with collar turned up and hands jammed in pockets. A shot rings out. Feet scurry off. A body lies motionless awaiting the dawn and the coroner. The camera pulls back and up in a slow crane shot. Eerie music fills in the dark scene.

"Media culture" is replete with scenes like the preceding. Metaphorically one can imagine the current state of media culture as a mystery story which opens on an unsolved crime much like the film noir murder described. Who has created this mystery? What is the mystery? Who can solve it?

In this opening chapter we explore the nature of our present predicament by defining central concepts, particularly "culture" and "media." These fundamental concepts are illustrated by examples drawn from contemporary music, noting how these play a role in our sense of personal identity. The emphasis is on how media and culture interact in reciprocal causality, a "system" perspective rather than the disputed "causal" perspective often applied to media's relation to culture. System reciprocity provides a context for exploring the development of personal and social identity. Exactly what is it we are exploring when we explore "media culture"?

Experiencing "CULTURE":
Music as Expression and Social Bond

Three teenagers ride in a car with the music blaring. The contemporary rock station plays an oldie. The song is Pearl Jam's "Jeremy." As Eddie Vedder's agonized vocals fill the interior of the car, each teen is flooded with a series of associations from years earlier . . . the person I had a crush on at the time, my friend who talked of suicide, the too-familiar classroom of the music video of "Jeremy," the political eccentricities of Pearl Jam, associated memories of Kurt Cobain's self-destructiveness at that time. . . . Each occupant's mind and emotions are absorbed into different but parallel worlds of association. They talk about some of them. They ride on, radio blaring.

When we listen to our favorite music, whatever our tastes may be, we are engaging in a cultural experience of great resonance. The joy of music may be the simplest and most immediate of pleasures but the experience is also complex and many-layered. For example, accessing music today connects us with the creators of music through a series of very sophisticated, if transparent, technologies of recording, storage, and playback. Our choice of music is influenced by our past musical choices and what our friends like. The music is structured and shaped in historically and socially established cultural forms of melodies, lyrics, and instrumentation, and is delivered through an industrial system that manages, distributes, promotes, and sells. The lyrics may concern love or heartbreak, joy or sadness, the world outside or our feelings inside. The musicians may be superstars known to all or an obscure local group or singer; they have managers, contracts, and technology to work with. We do not think about these elements as we listen, no matter how dependent we are on them. All we know is the way the music seems to reach inside and express what we feel and care about. We are experiencing "the meaning of culture."

In describing the carload of teens listening to music we have created a crude "ethnography," a grounded description of actual people experiencing and expressing culture in a particular case. In the spirit of the anthropology of Clifford Geertz and others, we are looking over the shoulders of natives to discover the meaning the text of their culture has for them. As we discover the meanings particular experiences have for the subjects—the carload, a popular concert, a rock party, individual listening, background music, and so on—we begin to discover the outlines of the larger culture that these experiences are drawn from and recreate.

When we explore the cultural experiences of others—and of ourselves— we sense that "culture" may be defined simply, but it is not a simple concept. Culture is the shorthand label for everything that sets us apart as humans. Culture is the way we mentally structure our interactions with other people and our environment. At once so close we can hardly see it and so encompassing that we can scarcely imagine it, culture is the way we collectively express ourselves as human beings. Culture is meaning constantly being created. Like sound, culture is observed as it is emerging and disappearing from existence.

The basic anthropological definition runs something like *culture is "the systematic way of construing reality that a people acquires as a consequence of living in a group."* But culture is not vague or abstract; it is our lived experience shared with others. Culture is the peak emotion when music hits us just right and carries us along with power and strength and awareness. Such cultural experiences we have access to "as a consequence of living in a group," and they relate to our "systematic way of construing reality."

Cultures Large and Small. The cultural group can be any size, from those teens riding in a car to the entire population of the planet. On a *global scale,* we can talk of a consumer culture of capitalism and the multinational music industry that markets pop stars and hit songs. On a *national* scale, there are "God Save the Queen," "The Star-Spangled Banner," and other national anthems, together with less official rock anthems, reggae classics, or sitar solos. On a *regional* scale, we have the culture of Yorkshire puddings and heath and folk songs or the Beach Boys celebrating California coastal culture. On a *local* scale, one can point to the club scene of Pearl Jam's Seattle or the Beatles' Liverpool replete with favored bands, musical styles, clothing, hair length, and attitude.

As we explore musical culture, we often discover ourselves occupying local expressions of larger trends. The levels of culture interact in complex patterns. Our local pop music may be, for the most part, just one small market within international hype, but at the same time, global cultural trends are often the outgrowth of local cultures. Memphis blues and New Orleans Dixieland jazz were first local, then regional, and finally international musical styles. Pearl Jam came from Seattle and the Beatles from Liverpool, but both groups produced, and themselves became, international cultural products. "Subcultures" may refer to a rural bluegrass style in West Virginia or a punk style among unemployed youth in Glasgow or widely scattered individuals who share a set of values and tastes associated with heavy metal or hip-hop or salsa. Most of us occupy at least one, and usually several, subcultures of music and values. Our musical choices are part of our subculture's systematic way of construing and expressing our reality. Because of media access to once distant expressions, geography no longer restricts cultural groupings to specific places. Teens listening to music in a car are one rich specific point in a huge array of disparate but somehow interconnnected cultural expressions.

Each individual today is a unique blend of cultural forces. Culture exists in our head like a Walkman implant, and our heads are filled from many sources, both individually and as groups. The external expression can be seen in cultural artifacts of T-shirts or neckties, paintings or posters, a room in a tenement or suburbia, in art, architecture, clothing, dance, or any other expression of style. Beneath these external expressions, the internal knowledge, values, myths, fears, and ideals define and express the internal consciousness and identity of members of that culture or subculture. Each of us finds and creates meaning in our life in and through culture. The way we understand and feel about our relationship with our family, our friends, our work, our play, our politics, our music, and all the rest occurs in and through the culture we share. The better we understand our culture and culture in general, the better we understand ourselves—and others.

In our preceding example of culture, when Eddie Vedder sings that Jeremy spoke in school today, anyone who knows the music video of that song recalls the horrible image of a preteen carrying his father's gun to school and killing himself in front of his classmates. The silent, unloved boy "spoke." Based on a true incident, the song is the sixth cut, 5 minutes and 19 seconds long, on Pearl Jam's 1991 CD *Ten*. The song is most powerful and unsettling, close to home for many because the boy, the school, the classmates seem so familiar. What does it say of a culture when such a problematic expression becomes widely dispersed and popular? A media system that allows such a challenging expression, in an MTV forum widely followed by teens and preteens, can be admired for its openness and honesty at the same time as the alienation and cultural disintegration thus portrayed can be deplored. The music video is clear about what is happening but never quite shows it explicitly on screen, restrained perhaps by both a fear of censorship and a concern for role modeling and copycat viewers. Exploring our media culture brings us face-to-face with loaded cultural expressions and tough choices.

Cultural Stability Versus Change. A music video like *Jeremy*, just as our culture in general, can be both order-maintaining and order-transforming. Those who would exclude such troublesome videos favor order-mainte-nance; the creators of *Jeremy* would seem to favor order-transformation. Cultural expressions are a source of both stability and change. The degree to which culture maintains either one is a source of great controversy.

What is the relationship between culture, individuals, and change? S. N. Eisenstadt (1992) describes three distinct ways of characterizing the rela-tionship. One approach, popular in American sociology, is the "structural-functionalist" approach. This approach emphasizes the place of established norms and values as givens to which we conform. This emphasis says in effect: We fit into our culture. Another approach, the "structuralist," was developed largely in France and among linguists. The structuralist approach reads culture in reference to the programmatic codes and deep structure of human behavior and language: We decipher and apply the binary codes of our culture. A third and somewhat similar approach, that of "symbolic anthropologists," sees culture as a set of expressive symbols that create a worldview through human action and interaction: We interactively express and create culture. In this last view there is increased room for change because it envisions individuals selecting from a range of options and fabricating new options. Culture is no longer a given map for behavior that the individual or group must accept passively. In general, all three agree on the centrality of culture as a determining human system. If children grow up in a culture where the alienation of the character Jeremy is normative, the culture is in trouble. On the other hand, if children grow up in a culture so restrictive that the music video *Jeremy* cannot be made or seen, the culture is also in trouble. Whatever its character, individuals exist in and through their culture.

When the cultural order is transformed, the guardians of the established order are frustrated because they cannot prevent cultural change. For example, when Little Richard and Elvis and others first threatened traditional pop music standards with the initial rock and roll invasion, there was a widespread outcry from both classicists who heard it as junk and traditionalists who found it threatening. Punk rock in Britain in the early 1980s negotiated a fascinating mixture of accommodation with the big business distribution system and radically outrageous rejection of establishment values, as David Rowe chronicles in *Popular Cultures: Rock Music, Sport, and the Politics of Pleasure* (1995). In Rowe's sophisticated historical and theoretical analysis, small independent music labels and major music distribution companies cooperate and feed off each other as much as they represent opposite alternatives. When we select our personal and group musical preferences, we take an implicit stand on competing interests of taste, control, and power. Of course, we can also listen to "Jeremy" or any music and remain oblivious to any meanings or cultural associations connected to it. But such lack of individual self-consciousness does not mean that the individual's cultural choices are not in themselves significant and consequential, only that that individual is unfortunately lacking in awareness.

Music is "central to the cultural practices of all societies," as Garth Jowett notes (Jones, 1992, p. ix), and has both order-maintaining and order-transforming dimensions. Music's power extends beyond physical pitches and words; it creates an entire aural environment. For example, many young people may not have a clear-cut physical space of their own, but they can at least have a clear-cut aural space in the form of a, usually loud, sound system (Eisenberg, 1987, p. 251). A boombox or home entertainment center can superimpose its own space on the space people live in. Music can overcome the limits of time and space and give "what youth discovers and desires in popular music—freedom and oneself" (Jones, 1992, p. 183). Teens on the road listening to a car stereo are a classic illustration of mid- to late-twentieth century ideals of independence. Yet music's freedom has enemies. Steve Jones notes that the development of recording technology is "biased toward control" whereas popular music relies on spontaneity, inspiration, and creativity. The conflict is eased however, by multitrack recording which allows musicians, in his words, "to *work* on their spontaneity" (Jones, 1992, p. 185). To quite different degrees, each of us is open to music that is familiar to us—order-maintaining —and music that is different for us—order-transforming.

Similarly, the commercial structure of the transnational music industry favors stability and uniformity but cannot afford to eliminate variety and change. Large-scale international research indicates how new local versions of punk or rap or reggae or other trends are stimulated by the spread of large musical markets and not merely overwhelmed and eliminated by them (Robinson, Buck, & Cuthbert, 1991).

Exploring musical culture means examining both how we *receive* culture as a given, by accepting meanings shared by a group, and how we *create* culture, by expressing anew those meanings. Each new performance by Whitney Houston expresses culture, each replaying of her CD reexpresses culture, and each mangling of it by us in the shower expresses culture as well. We learn the language that is our culture and we speak it. The proportion between what is imposed and what is chosen, however, remains hotly contested, especially by cultural studies, as we see in the following sections. Are the car's occupants who hear "Jeremy" freely expressing their unique individuality or are they passive pawns in a global media chess game for corporate profit? And how do the vehicles through which we access culture, the media of communication, operate as we enter the third millennium?

Experiencing "MEDIA":
How Music Reaches Us

> One of the teens from the car, a young Toronto sporting goods clerk named Hester Prine, hears a new U2 song on the radio. Two days later she catches the same song on MTV. She checks out the Bono and U2 home pages on the World Wide Web, likes what she finds, and decides she wants the CD with this song on it. The next morning Hester sees in the newspaper that the CD is on sale at a local music store. She calls the store for their hours and stops by after work to buy the CD. The store has sold out, but the salesperson checks the computer and refers Hester to their sister store close to Hester's home. Hester buys the CD and immediately goes home to listen to it and tape it so she can also play it in her car and lend it to her girlfriend.

Eight media were employed by the young woman from Toronto in the preceding process, five mass media—television, radio, a newspaper, a compact disc, and a cassette tape—and three interpersonal media—a telephone, the Internet, and a computer network. And she has most likely not thought twice about any of it. Media, both mass and interpersonal, are deeply embedded in our daily lives today, and they interact with each other abundantly. The net effect for Hester is that she can cruise along in her car totally lost in her favorite music, an intensely personal experience and, yet by traditional definitions, a supposedly nonsocial experience because she is sharing it with no one else, only the electronic ghost of U2.

"Media" are any *extensions of the human sensory apparatus,* any technologies that enable communication. They mediate interpersonal or mass communication as the go-between. Each of Hester's means for connecting with U2 is a medium of communication.

Media as Transmission. The nature of "mediating" recalls Harry Lime in *The Third Man,* a mediator between the hidden underworld and the proper society of his friend Rollo Martins. In Michael Curtiz's film noir classic, *The Third Man* (1949), and in Graham Greene's novelized version of his own screenplay of it (1971), the setting is rubble-strewn, post-World War II Vienna. One famous scene takes place in a large, closed cabin high up inside a giant Ferris wheel. Played charmingly by Orson Welles, Harry Lime is a black marketeer responsible for killing and deforming countless children by selling diluted penicillin. He has been hiding out and getting around through the sewer system underneath Vienna. Speaking for his underground world, Harry attempts to draw his old school chum, Rollo, into his scheme.

> "Victims?" he asked. "Don't be melodramatic, Rollo. Look down there," he went on, pointing through the window at the people moving like black flies at the base of the Wheel. "Would you really feel any pity if one of those dots stopped moving—for ever? If I said you can have twenty thousand pounds for every dot that stops, would you really, old man, tell me to keep my money without hesitation? Or would you calculate how many dots you could afford to spare?" (Greene, 1971, p. 104)

Like any medium, Harry Lime is the link between two entities, in this case the subterranean criminal world and the aboveground proper world of social rules and propriety.

In the transmission view of communication, the medium transmits messages from a source to a receiver. Harry speaks for the underworld of cynicism but conveys it to the upper world of order. The process has historically been described through a "bullet" or "transmission" model of communication as pictured in Figure 1.1: source—message—medium—receiver—effect.

Media as Ritual. Yet Harry and Rollo are here also engaging in a ritual, the ritual of conversation high above the "black flies at the base of the Wheel." This *ritual* view conceives of communication as a process through which a shared culture is created, modified, and transformed. The ritual view concerns not the extension of messages in space, the transmission view, but the maintenance of society in time. This view concerns less the imparting of information than the creation and representation of shared beliefs. Harry and Rollo are reestablishing their boyhood relationship; they are testing each

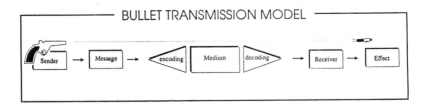

Figure 1.1. One-directional flow in the transmission effects model known as the "bullet theory."

other, finding what they share and no longer share, at the same time as they are transmitting information back and forth. The ritual view of communication, as articulated by James Carey and others, opens the exploration of media to the full range of cultural questions. This view takes media operations well beyond the merely technical transmission model that once dominated media analysis. In the ritual model, all dimensions of culture and media interact with all other dimensions, as in Figure 1.2.

In the ritual view, the relationship between media and culture is integral and dynamic. Media are not merely neutral technical instruments but are shaped by and themselves shape the culture. New media technologies constantly arise and influence cultural life—in turn, books, newspapers, movies, radio, television, satellites, computers, on-line networks, multimedia, and more. Many fall by the wayside—quadrophonic sound, beta home video—at least partially because they do not work culturally and economically at that time and place. Some find their identity only 20 or 40 years after their introduction, as in the case of FM radio and teletext. Some blend with other technologies to make a third entity—computers and video combining to make interactive games, or satellites and television joining to create cable movies.

Technologies have ritual dimensions in their very social uses, structuring, and consequences. Successful technologies have unanticipated social effects—television's domination of domestic life beginning in the 1950s, film's creation of stars in the World War I era, or television's multiplication of sports salaries since the 1960s. New technologies or combinations of technologies often stimulate transcendent visions of a utopian or dystopian future, which are often seen in retrospect as naive or cynical.

Mass communication is a restricted category of media, one that includes one-to-many transmissions with large-scale dimensions like film or television but excludes person-to-person media like telephones, faxes, electronic mail, or CB radio. Mass communication is generally defined as a process in which professional communicators through an institution use mechanical or

Figure 1.2: Ritual view conceives of communication as a process through which a shared culture is created, modified, and transformed. What we know as "real" is not planted in us but emerges with experience.
SOURCE: Carey, 1989.

electronic reproduction to disseminate messages widely to relatively hetero-geneous and anonymous audience members, in the process generating meaning and influence but offering only limited opportunities for feed-back. Tracy Chapman or the Berlin Symphony create music that their recording label distributes as music videos, CDs, or tapes to music stores where we buy them. The source and message may be artistic but the medium and effect must also be commercial to be successful within capitalist mass media markets. Mass media play a decisive role in both transmitting cultural products and ritually structuring our cultural environment.

Specialized communication refers to one-to-one or one-to-few interaction or data transmission that lacks the large-scale, one-way distribution of mass communication. On-line computer interaction and telephone conversations are examples. This two-way communication, in which the service provider provides the channel but not the content, has historically been labeled "common-carrier." Using this distinction, federal regulation of communica-tion in the twentieth century has generally been divided into mass media regulation and common-carrier regulation. But in the transition into the twenty-first century, that dividing line has largely disappeared. Telephones, computer networks, broadcast television, cable television, movie distribu-tion, and other media have converged into inseparable combinations of mass and specialized media.

The term *media* refers to all communication relays and technologies. Media can be either mass or specialized communication or, more likely, a combination of both. Any device that relays messages is a medium. Any technology that ritually structures culture is a medium in the broadest sense. Practically speaking, it is nearly impossible today to exclusively explore

Television: a medium. So called because it is neither rare nor well done.

Ernie Kovacs

"mass communication" because such mass media are interrelated with specialized, non-mass technologies and a broader media culture expressed in both mass and specialized communication. Exploring "interpersonal communication" is also difficult without recognition of the media culture that surrounds and, increasingly, shapes the way we interact as individuals and groups (see Real, 1989, chapter 1).

Media as New Technology. Predicting the future direction of media technology and culture is one of the most popular and difficult aspects of exploring media culture.

Global networking, the race to rewire, the information superhighway, data till you drop—the titles in the popular and trade press hint at further expansions of the place of media in public and private life in the twenty-first century. Technologies that are already available drive these visions. The translation of audio and video signals into digital information, digitized storage and compression of signals, fiber-optic wiring with virtually limitless capacity, and new switching and control techniques all come together in predicted vast, interactive, user-friendly systems. These systems are popularly portrayed as providing new access to and delivery of movies, shopping catalogs, travel services, concerts, sports, video games, financial transactions, news and information, classified ads, television archives, recorded music, and other services and diversions, many of them unimagined yet today.

The development of this form of advanced information infrastructure began over 30 years ago and is increasingly making the distinction between mass and specialized media obsolete. The first step involved replacing analog technology with digital, according to a typical report, *Vision for a 21st Century Information Infrastructure* by the United States Council on Competitiveness (1993). The second step is currently underway and deploys high-capacity, digital transport media such as wireless, ISDN (Integrated Services Digital Network), and fiber optics, all aided by developments in data communication and computing. The third step is on the way with substantial upgrades in the intelligence of the telecommunication networks and movement toward open computer systems. The goal is, in the words of the Council on Competitiveness (1993), "an advanced information infrastructure which will reduce costs, enhance services and create an astonishing array of new applications" (p. 2).

Ironically, the best preparation for such dreams of the future of media is often a sense of the past. In this case, an awareness of media history and a sense of media theory help to place futuristic predictions in comprehensible (and more restrained) contexts. Defining technology and media more broadly than the engineers and assessing their benefits more skeptically than the marketers is especially useful. The application of a technology and its social uses are not separate from and unrelated to the technology itself. From the moment we develop and attempt to apply an invention, it begins to take on additional meaning, and as soon as it is accepted in regular use, it takes on a specific social and human meaning relative to that use. To use the most obvious example, because of the way television has been used, "television" now implies certain types of content, certain distribution systems, and certain human applications, even particular living room arrangements, that go well beyond the electronics involved in transmitting moving visual images. Because technology does not float free above its actual uses, technology is never "value-free." As social critics have stressed (Christians, 1989), normative theories of how media should be used are essential for allocating resources and determining public and private policy for media use. The unfettered development and application of media technology has never by itself ensured open and democratic systems rather than monopolies, despite the arguments of new media utopians like George Gilder (see Kline & Burstein, 1996).

In defining media, we should remember that, when we listen to popular music on the car radio or buy a U2 CD, we are participants in what John Thompson (1990) has called "the mediazation of modern culture." By this he means the general process by which the transmission of symbolic forms becomes increasingly mediated by the technical and institutional apparatuses of the media industries. Once music culture meant listening to live, local musicians from the community. Now music culture and other symbolic forms are "increasingly mediated by a complex, trans-national network of institutional concerns" (Thompson, 1990, p. 4). This, Thompson argues persuasively, has implications for theories of ideology, technology, and culture; it also has implications for our personal sense of identity and consciousness.

Developing "Identity" and "Consciousness": What Music Means

Rock and roll is implicated in a struggle, not only for the money of its fans, but for their minds as well. By communicating certain meanings, or structures of meanings, it offers its audiences ways of seeing the world, of interpreting experiences; it offers them values that have a profound impact on the ways they respond to particular situations and challenges. We can refer to this relationship of music, meaning, and reality as the domain of ideological struggle. (Grossberg, 1992, p. 154)

Our personal identity and consciousness today are constructed in interaction with media and culture. Face-to-face human interaction without the intervention of media is terribly important: The child is largely shaped by interaction with family, neighborhood, schoolmates. But that child is also influenced directly and indirectly by interaction with and through media (see Real, 1989, chapter 1). A father soothes the child with a lullaby, a face-to-face experience, and then babysits the growing child with television cartoons, a mediated experience. Does one influence the child and the other not? No, of course not. We are influenced by person-to-person interaction and we are influenced by mediated interaction.

What connects the individual person to media and culture is *consciousness*. We direct our consciousness to media texts and the texts impress our consciousness. We pay attention to the movie screen, the stereo speakers, the newsmagazine page. Those texts in turn input their software into our memory storage, to put it in the language of computerese. But, as we shall see in later chapters, we are not passive recipients; we are active, receiving and interpreting with preformed screens and interior discourses. Our consciousness attends to, receives, and interconnects within itself the varied multitude of messages pressing on it from outside.

In this process our sense of personal identity is formed. Personal *identity* is who we are. That is related to, but not the same as, who we *think* we are. Our total, complex, even at times self-contradictory sense of what constitutes our personal existence is what we mean by identity. Consciousness is that which enables us to be aware of who we are and who we are not: within their consciousness children progressively develop a sense of separateness and individuation, a sense of personal identity. The music I participate in through life adds up to the song that is my life. In classical terms, consciousness is existence and identity is essence. In visual representation, consciousness is internal space and identity is internal meaning. Together, and fleshed out in our physical existence, consciousness and identity distinguish who each one of us is as a person. We select music that we feel comfortable with, that confirms who we are, and the music further reinforces that identity. Listening to Pearl Jam or U2 or the Toronto Symphony or jingles from *Sesame Street* is one of the bricks that helps build the structure of our personal identity and consciousness.

Aesthetic Experience. Cultural experiences have formative influences on us, but the more immediate question is not what a cultural experience does to us but what it is in itself. In reality, most of the time we select our media not because we want the experience to shape us in a particular way but because we enjoy the experience for its own sake, whatever its consequences. The experience is a source of pleasure, as when the carload of teenagers liked hearing "Jeremy." In this, media culture recalls the classical concept of "aesthetic experience," an artistically inspired experience that is moving and satisfying (see Farber, 1982). Personally and emotionally connecting with a great symphony, a profound novel, a moving drama, a striking painting—these are the kinds of aesthetic experiences that great art has classically been able to inspire.

Everyday media experiences are not usually at the level of a major aesthetic experience, but for many persons *the most moving* cultural experience will be through popular media rather than classical art. A powerful emotional experience can be triggered by an otherwise trivial song floating out of an alley and awakening rich associations. The important quality in the aesthetic experience, whether it is an emotional, earthshaking, life-changing encounter or a quiet, simple, weightless sense of deep appreciation, is *your subjective response*. Seeing a captivating movie, hearing the right popular song at the right time, interacting electronically at maximum capability, getting caught up in a popular novel's sweeping narrative—these are sources of aesthetic experience shorn of artistic pretentiousness. By inspiring such moments, media culture can take on exceptional power, meaning, and importance.

When asked to describe an important, moving, and memorable aesthetic experience, university students today select an amazing variety. My collection of several hundred of these includes watching a favorite team win a title, enjoying a children's show with one's family, attending a historic live concert, meeting a celebrity, seeing the Star Wars trilogy, and enjoying an extreme variety of cultural products and practices, only a few of which have associations with classical art in the form of ballet, sculpture, opera, and other high arts. Some describe a primal experience: giving birth to a child, experiencing the death of a relative, learning one's parents are divorcing, surviving a car crash. Others identify an exciting, firsthand experience: snowboarding in the Alps, surfing in Baja, winning a school award. Still others have aesthetic experiences associated with travel in Europe or being in nature. But many describe an experience of media culture as the most impressive personal experience they can recall: attending a concert by Metallica or U2 or 10,000 Maniacs, seeing a World Cup soccer game, going as a child to Disneyland or a first Indiana Jones movie, attending a rave.

The importance of media culture should not be underestimated, even as a source of the classical aesthetic experience.

Cultural Differences. Especially important to keep in mind is that consciousness and identity are both capable of very different formulations in different cultural contexts. The aborigine, isolated in the Australian Outback, differs dramatically from the Sydney banker, immersed in accounts and high-tech living style. Each envisions environment and self in quite distinct ways.

Culturally, perhaps the greatest differences can be found in "oral" versus "literate" cultures. Cultures of orality and literacy contrast with each other by almost any measure. They tend toward opposite forms of internal consciousness and external social order. Following McLuhan, Innis, Carpenter, Teilhard de Chardin, and others, Walter Ong (see especially 1982) has developed an extended cultural analysis of orality and literacy.

In Ong's view, it is a mistake to conceive of media and communication as simply ways of moving information. Each medium does far more than that: "it makes possible thought processes inconceivable before" (Gronbeck, Farrell, & Soukup, 1991, p. 13). For Ong, communication strikes deep into the "consciousness" (in Gronbeck, Farrell, & Soukup, p. 18). Communication is not surface contact but part of life's substance. The consciousness at stake is defined by Ong (1981) as "reflective self-possession expressed in the saying of 'I'" (p. 199), whereas culture is a kind of collective consciousness that characterizes a people at a particular time (p. 20). To unpack these dense phrases and see them in action, it may be helpful to consider the dramatic changes in music resulting from the historical evolution of media forms.

Popular Music and Oral Cultural Identity

When our carload of teens cranks up the bass and pounds along with the rhythm, the scene suggests answers to the question, why has the music of the electronic age, rock and roll in all its variations, been so frequently compared to the music of the preliterate era, so-called primitive music? Why are the Red Hot Chili Peppers or Stone Temple Pilots sometimes portrayed as prehistoric barbarians? The answer lies in the recognition that music is essentially an oral-aural experience based in the human ear and is, therefore, most comfortable in an oral rather than a visual culture where the eye and visual stimuli dominate. In other words, the high print culture of many nineteenth and twentieth century intellectuals is visual and not aural, and therefore is far removed from the expressiveness of preliterate or postliterate music. Elite critics contend that both early and late popular music is inferior and barbaric, but they do so at the risk of revealing their own cultural myopia.

To place ourselves historically, we can recall the now standard breakdown of cultural eras (Real, 1989, p. 25):

- oral preliterate: from first human origins (4 million B.C.?)
- print: from first writing (4000 B.C.) and printing press (1456 A.D.)
- electronic: from first telegraph (1844 A.D.)

The change is not only technological; we find a shift in *sensory balance* and in *consciousness* between the preliterate and print periods, plus a partial shift back during the present transition from print to electronic media. Rock and other strains of popular music capture the continuity between preliterate and electronic culture.

Music in oral, preliterate cultures plays a central role in expressing the collective memory and aspirations of the tribe. Music is closely associated with storytelling, and both are crucial to the instruction of youths learning the ways of the people and imitating ideals and behaviors that have worked in the past. The centralized, traditionalist authority structure of the village is supported by music. The people are welded together in unity through music, dance, storytelling, and related mythic rituals.

Music and Written Language. With the evolution of a phonetic, vowelized written language in the first half of the first millennium B.C., music began to contend with a new force, the power of written language. Writing made possible a quasi-permanent record of song lyrics or notation, one extending in time, in contrast to the performed song which extends itself in space only. Exact records of folk songs, written descriptions of music, and written musical scores for performers all emerged to enrich music. With the first technology of industrialization, the printing press in 1456, the mass reproduction of printed music became possible (see Inglis, 1990, pp. 8-15). Eventually, elaborate systems of notation with scales and keys and note-lengths, written with mathematical precision, made possible the complex performances of classical symphonies, marching bands, dance orchestras, and any performance where many musicians played independent, complex lines of composition together. At the same time, print played its essential role in spreading European empires, private property, and capitalism. Books, writing, and textuality played a formative role in fashioning imperial control and colonial worldviews (see Tiffin & Lawson, 1994).

There was a downside to the intrusion of print into music culture, however, as there was to the spread of European empires. Written forms, when exercising dominance over music, removed improvisation and the uniqueness of any given performance by restricting a song to a single uniform version based on sheet music or the written score. Writing and attendant rational classifications contributed to a general consensus on the quasi-official "canon" of good music centered around European court culture; this provided a narrow central criterion for music and marginalized many popular and authentic musical forms. Linear reasoning, similar to the sequence of printed letters and pages, and individualism, the privatized way we decode writing, came to dominate print culture. Print contributed to more "mental" appreciation of music, detaching music from the kinetic, expressive forms of tribal music. The tactile dance culture identified with folk music was replaced by cognitive processing of music. Those who clung to nonliterate music styles were judged "savages" by the literati. Jazz fought for legitimization against this, but by the middle of the twentieth century, most popular and classical music was first written and orchestrated and then performed. But at mid-century, the development of electronic amplification began to reverse all of the preceding.

Music in the Electronic Age. Reactions against rock 'n' roll in the 1950s rightly sensed that the music represented more than just one more popular musical fad in the tradition of maybe the Charleston or swing music. If it seemed to threaten a whole way of life as ministers led mass record burnings and Elvis was censored from the waist down on national television, it was because a larger cultural shift from print to electronic and even from modern to postmodern was being ushered in, however indecorously.

Today many styles such as rap, reggae, metal, alternative, or country clearly reflect the turn back toward oral, preliterate forms in the electronic postindustrial age, but one older song, "Johnny B. Goode" by Chuck Berry, makes a particularly useful milestone for assessing changes in media culture. "Johnny B. Goode" is significant here not so much for what it is but for what it is associated with: the explosion of electronics in popular music in the form of rock 'n' roll; the reassertion of African-American creative dominance in popular music; the new niche marketing for teen youth audiences; the expansion of popular music markets toward a transnational mega-industry; the complex resonance of the "star" phenomenon in cultural industries; and other qualities not excluding story quality, guitar playing, infectious rhythm, and performance style. All these changes were new when Chuck Berry unleashed this 2 minutes and 35 seconds of hard-driving rock in 1958.

Although "Johnny B. Goode" climbed only to number eight on the Billboard chart in its day, it is ranked number two *all-time* by prominent rock critic Dave Marsh (1989), surpassed only by Marvin Gaye's "I Heard It Through the Grapevine," a 1968 hit. The author of "Johnny B. Goode," Chuck Berry, was among the 11 initial inductees into the Rock and Roll Hall of Fame in its first year. "Johnny B. Goode" represents the first generation of rock 'n' rollers with roots in urban blues, gospel expressiveness, and exuberant performance styles. For the first time, sheer volume was available to an individual instrument, the guitar, without having to include an entire section of guitars playing in unison off a written score, the big band method, to create loudness. Rock music was a revolution not in a political sense but in a subtler cultural sense, primarily by marking the turn away from an older print, industrial culture toward an oral, electronic culture.

We can admit that "Johnny B. Goode" has all the qualities that make rock music culturally suspect. The story is simplistic, some phrasings awkward, the musical structure is repetitious, the performance lacks subtlety or variety, the beat is incessant, everything is loud and perhaps overdone; it has all the failings of the popular song attacked by Theodor Adorno in 1941 (reprinted in Adorno, 1993).

But, turning the standards on their head, those are also the qualities that give the song power. "Johnny B. Goode" is not calm, distant, impersonal, rational, individualistic, and sober, as "good" print-era music was. What, in fact, ultimately distinguishes "Johnny B. Goode" from classical music is everything that makes Chuck Berry's single work. More particularly, the traumatic cultural transition from print to electronic media unleashed the attraction of powerful emotions, throbbing rhythms, expressive exuberance, ear-splitting volume, mass frenzy, sensate excess, Dionysian ecstasy, and liminal rites which had been suppressed when "civilization" in the literate European sense spread across the world in the modern era. Rock's break with traditional print sensibilities includes the volume distortions of Jimi Hendrix and heavy metal, the multitrack mixing of *Sgt. Pepper's Lonely Hearts Club Band,* the sampling and remixing of Grandmaster Flash or Salt N Pepper, and countless other electronic sound manipulations. Listen to the amazing progression of rhythmic patterns in "I Heard It Through the Grapevine" and appreciate how much oral *feel* for music extends beyond what the printed page can convey.

Also marking the rediscovery of aural culture, rap music clearly reflects oral traditions among urban African Americans. In anticipation of discussions of postmodernism to follow, let us say here that rap is a form of postmodern discourse shaped and made possible by our consumption-based, technologically advanced society which simultaneously tells the story of oppression that has come from that society. Rap is personalized and fragmented in the "pastiche" style characteristic of postmodernism. Rap's "sampling" of mixed and remixed sounds reflects the breakdown of standard frames of knowledge and even traditional ethics in the postmodern era. The flexible language game that is rap captures the beauty of oral improvisation within the technologies of electronic culture. Deplorable as its sexism and violence may be, it is as much a new art form born outside the status quo as it is a popular music form identified with industrial capitalism. In terms of classical film theory, rap's content has the realism loved by film critics such as André Bazin and Jean Mitry, whereas its form has the complex manipulations preferred by formalist critics such as Rudolf Arnheim and Hugo Munsterberg.

The dialectical tension in rap music illustrates well how personal identity and consciousness are not simple, uniform qualities today even for residents of one community or one household, as we mentioned in the introduction. Yet nothing is more fundamental to human life than one's identity and consciousness. Those internal characteristics reflect and direct everything about us. "Johnny B. Goode" ultimately exists inside us. For now, in the postmodern era, identity is considered to be fragmented and our consciousness multilayered. Yet media culture is not without dominant tendencies on a broad scale and intellectual tools with which to explore those tendencies. The spirit of this most modern enterprise was summed up almost three centuries ago by the Scottish balladeer Andrew Fletcher. In 1703 he proclaimed, "Give me the makings of the songs of a nation and I care not who makes the Laws" (Perris, 1985, p. 5).

In the following section, we move away from the definitions of culture, media, and identity and their shifting dynamics in musical culture. Now we ask: What are the vantage points and vehicles for approaching media culture most meaningfully?

"Cultural Studies" and the Exploration of Media Culture

> The point of cultural studies is to empower ordinary people to take control over their own lives . . . . (Aronowitz, 1994, p. 180)

The phrase *cultural studies* refers to the examination of contemporary culture based in the definitions of "culture" (and "media") already given and drawing from recent anthropology, literature, history, arts, and humanities, coupled with social and psychoanalytic theory. In scattered centers of cultural studies (Milner, 1994, pp. 1-2), in journals, conferences, and extensive literature, a consensus has emerged concerning the central orientation of cultural studies, if not a specific methodology. Milner (1994) and Storey (1993) stress the following roots and categories for cultural studies. The chapters that follow work out details of their dense but useful summary:

Culturalism accents that "culture is a whole way of life" in the work of the Birmingham School by Richard Hoggart, Raymond Williams, and Stuart Hall.

Structuralism concerns "signifying practices" from language to movies and *poststructuralism* as a skepticism toward totalizing theories. Both schools are dominated by the French: Ferdinand de Saussure, Claude Lévi-Strauss, Roland Barthes, Jacques Derrida, Jacques Lacan, Michel Foucault, and Edward Said.

Marxism explains economic power in versions developed by classical Marxism, the Frankfurt School, Louis Althusser, Antonio Gramsci, E. P. Thompson, and others.

Feminism explores domination by gendered, patriarchal culture in works by Virginia Woolf, Simone de Beauvoir, Kate Millett, Laura Mulvey, Janice Radway, and many others.

Postmodernism characterizes the present time as without the intellectual moorings of recent centuries, particularly as argued by Jean-François Lyotard, Fredric Jameson, and Jean Baudrillard.

The consensus on cultural studies extends further. Five recent anthologies[1] all feature at least one selection by Stuart Hall and offer sections on theoretical foundations, identity, media representation, meaning, power, pleasure, and consumption. *The Polity Reader in Cultural Theory* (1994) notes, "the domain of cultural studies covers the social processes involved in the production, transmission and reception of symbolic or cultural forms" (p. 1). From initial concern with the powerlessness of the underclass against the state, cultural studies has moved to foreground issues of feminism, racism, homophobia, and others (During, 1993). Cultural studies is especially concerned with "everyday life" (de Certeau, 1984) in pubs, ballparks, family rooms, schools, shopping malls, factories, and especially the world of media.

The summary in the introduction to the historic collection titled *Cultural Studies* (Grossberg, Nelson, & Treichler, 1992) is worth quoting at length:

> . . . One may begin by saying that cultural studies is an interdisciplinary, transdisciplinary, and sometimes counter-disciplinary field that operates in the tension between its tendencies to embrace both a broad, anthropological and a more narrowly humanistic conception of culture. Unlike traditional anthropology, however, it has grown out of analyses of modern industrial societies. It is typically interpretive and evaluative in its methodologies, but unlike traditional humanism it rejects the exclusive equation of culture with high culture and argues that all forms of cultural production need to be studied in relation to other cultural practices and to social and historical structures. Cultural studies is thus committed to the study of the entire range of a society's arts, beliefs, institutions, and communicative practices. (p. 4)

In addition, cultural studies develops theory *and* improved cultural practices, yet not with any sense of preordained solutions. "Cultural studies thus believes that its practice does matter, that its own intellectual work is supposed to—can—make a difference. But its interventions are not guaranteed; they are not meant to stand forever" (Grossberg, Nelson, & Treichler, 1992, p. 6). Cultural studies also resists the temptation to proclaim totalizing permanent formulations. "There is little attempt at the sort of grand theorizing that imagines it can define the politics and semiotics of representation, gender, race, or textuality for all time. You can draw much out of these essays [on cultural studies] for use in other contexts and to answer new challenges, but not, ideally, without asking how their theoretical work needs to be rethought" (p. 7). A thesaurus of terminology, *Key Concepts in Communication and Cultural Studies* (O'Sullivan, Hartley, Saunders, Montgomery, & Fiske, 1994), notes that in cultural studies "the aim was to understand how culture (the social production of sense and consciousness) should be specified in itself and in relation to economics (production) and politics (social relations)" (p. 72). Cultural studies makes explicit "that the production of knowledge is always done either in the interests of those who hold power or of those who contest that hold" (p. 73).

Taken together, the concerns of cultural studies give direction to anyone exploring popular music as culture and media and as an aspect of our identity. Cultural studies, in its varying manifestations, is the principal source for the case-study explorations in the chapters in this book.

The Case-Study Method of "Cultural Exegesis"

Suppose we want to understand what is going on in that carload of teenagers. Are they men or women? Are they people of color or Caucasian? Are they affluent or poor? Do they prefer Coolio and L.L. Cool J or Clint Black or Bob Marley? The case-study method suggests ways of getting under the surface of that small group of young people listening to music on a car stereo.

The case-study method provides a particularly useful methodology for raising and answering questions about our experience of media culture today. Case-study methodology does not eliminate real-world contexts as laboratory science does, nor does it eliminate symbolic and communitarian dimensions as behaviorism does. Fundamentally, the case-study method provides a series of structured steps built around central concepts and concerns of cultural studies.

Selection. The case-study method in cultural studies begins with a specific experience of culture, such as a carload of teens reacting to a popular song. This concrete experience, or "problematic," must then be situated historically and contextually in relation to cultural, ideological, economic, political, or other questions. The selection of the case or cases is crucial. The most productive cases are those that influence and represent many other aspects of culture and in which ideology and hegemony are especially operative. Any popular musical song ("Stand By Me"), artist (Cranberries),

CD (*Frogstomp*), music video (*Express Yourself*), musical style (gangster rap), or any combination of these is likely to meet these criteria for a case study.

The classic case study resembles Clifford Geertz's famous study of what the cockfight in the country of Bali means to its residents, as we discuss in the next chapter. What is equivalent in our own media culture to the rich texture, meanings, and centrality that cockfights possess for the Balinese? For some, it is cruising with the music on.

Text. For the carload of teens, the text of media culture is "Jeremy" or "Johnny B. Goode" *and* it is the discourse among the car occupants generated by the songs or other influences.

The case-study method identifies a singular "text" by selecting a very specific example, illustration, or experience of a cultural product or practice. The method identifies this specific point-of-impact text in the form of a social practice or a media message through which the culture expresses itself and from which we create interpretations. The text may take the form of image, sound, and words transmitted by media, or it may be a set of social practices, such as the working routines of a recording studio. The text may be an advertisement, a television program, a film, a music video, an on-line chat group, a superstar, or some other concrete cultural expression. The text has messsages in it and generates meaning for persons accessing it. For example, the lyrics, arrangement, and video of a song constitute a text, and that text generates multiple levels of meanings to be examined in the following steps.

Ethnography. Ethnography precisely names what is going on in a cultural product or practice. Are the car's occupants crowded or spaced out, are they mature teens or totally adolescent, are they well-educated or uninformed, were they raised in this neighborhood or elsewhere? What exactly are they doing and saying as they cruise in the vehicle?

An exact account must be provided of the facts of the case, just as an anthropologist obtains the facts of an unknown rite and its uses within the group that practices it *before* setting about to interpret the rite. Geertz had to find out why Balinese attended cockfights, when and where they took place, what family and clan patterns played a role in them, how economic status and daring fit into cockfights, and all the other specifics of the case before he could begin to explain and interpret their role in Balinese culture. The immediate origins, characters, plots, practices, and interpretations of a case within media culture require careful definition. Here, questionnaires, surveys, in-depth interviews, audio or video records of respondents, experiments, quantitative content analysis, detailed logs, audience ratings, marketing analysis, and other empirical instruments may be employed as a step toward understanding the case. For example, for a music video it is useful to know factual background on the artist, the director of the video, the production of the video and the CD it is part of, the recording label and its parent company, the frequency of play on MTV or elsewhere, the song's ranking in the top 100 on specific dates, the demographics of its target audience, and related contextual information, in addition to the interpretations and meanings assigned to it by specific viewers/listeners.

To conduct effective ethnography, it is generally necessary to "pitch your tent among the natives," as Christians and Carey (1981) recommend. This means that the exact experience of the primary subjects of this cultural expression is to be identified, rather than what an outsider's literary deconstruction of it might come up with. For example, a professor of English might find rich interpretations of the lyrics of a song by the Australian group Silverchair, but what does the typical popular music fan understand in that song? Only when the precise, articulated meanings of the case as experienced by its primary audience have been identified can the observer step back and attempt more general exegesis and criticism.

Exegesis. Ethnography considers the immediate situation, whereas exegesis examines the larger context, intent, and meaning. Ethnography describes what is going on in the car, and exegesis extends the interpretation of its meaning. Just as biblical scholars examine the rich denotations and connotations of "the Word" in the fourth Gospel, the Gospel according to John, so exegesis might find especially rich interpretations of what the label "rad" or "cool" or "it sucks" means to teenagers enjoying music in a car.

The traditional scriptural technique of textual exegesis goes beyond the immediate ethnography to identify precisely the literary genre of a work, the comparative life situation from which it emerged, and the intention of the original author. For example, what did the biblical passage describing the Creation or the Flood mean in its original time, place, and language and what was it attempting to say or teach? Scriptural exegesis answers this by comparing the work with closely parallel works from inside and outside the Scriptures and situating it carefully with regard to time, place, language, and purpose. Exegesis is the opposite of arbitrary interpretation, which simply makes up what the text is supposed to mean to fit a different time and place. Exegesis is also not the practical application of a text to other circumstances and needs distant from those of its origins. Rather, it is a careful, expanded analysis of exactly what was intended by the text's creator.

The case-study method identifies explicit and implicit meaning in a text or practice. What do the images, lyrics, and feelings of a particular music video literally mean in themselves? What specific cues and suggestions can be identified? How do similar music videos relate to this one through artist, director, visual cues, imagery, lyrics, message, and so forth? What is the video meant to evoke and remind us of outside itself? How do others interpret it? How do these aspects relate to the larger cultural and historical context of the time? From such direct parallels, what interpretation of the text seems most true to its origins and intentions?

Because cultural studies has been especially concerned with how culture relates to unequal distributions of power, the case study of media culture should normally examine issues of race, class, and gender, in addition to whatever else it examines. Are non-whites excluded or stereotyped? Do women initiate action? Are wealthy white men shown to be in control and to be admired? There are innumerable explicit and implicit representations of gender, race and ethnicity, and socioeconomic class embedded in cultural products and practices. Teasing out the implications of these representations may reveal a great deal about the product, its creators, it audiences, and the cultural system.

Criticism. How do we then "evaluate" what is going in connection with the auto or boombox music being shared by a group of young people?

Together with the foregoing sociological, historical, and analytic practices, the case-study method in cultural studies engages in direct criticism. Here the questions of aesthetic judgment, of social power and conflict, of ideology and hegemony, of human values and bias, of what should and should not be, all enter explicitly into the case. What do you and others like and dislike in this video? Overall, is it good or bad, and as judged by what standards? Does it seem to serve reactionary or progressive causes? Is it escapist or confrontational? Has it received the distribution and recognition that it deserves? More than it deserves? Whose vested interests are most served and protected by this? What alternatives were excluded by doing the video in this way? In total, what are the meanings and implications of this music video?

In brief, the case-study method selects a problematic expressed in a received text or practice and then subjects it to ethnographic description, exegetical clarification, and critical examination in the search for a full understanding of its social origins, meanings, and consequences.

Clues to the Study of Media Culture

The approach in these pages emphasizes certain "clues" to the understanding of media culture.

The first clue is to consider media culture as *a world that we inhabit,* as a world of "make believe" that can be as real in its meanings and consequences as the material world of everyday life. Horace Newcomb (1983, chapter 1) suggests that media culture holds out various possible worlds that we can enter into, try out, embellish, and use in themselves and in relation to everyday life—it is human to first imagine the world we want to create and then to create it. The media world is symbolic and imagined; it is a future we can escape into and then, if we choose, make real. We live in the media world in constant dialectical interaction with the nonmedia world. Each conditions the other.

The second clue is to *gain knowing access* to this world of media culture, to appreciate the popular culture as an ethnographer with fresh eyes making sense of the media world. This is close to the Birmingham School sense of "subcultures" where we listen to people who hang out on street corners or read teen magazines in their struggle with hegemony. Culture is not an ideology; it is a site of struggle over meaning. Cultural anthropologists immerse themselves in the culture, pitch a tent there, participate, observe rituals, and respect the culture for having a logic and serious meaning of its own.

The third clue is to *achieve a certain critical distance* so that, even as we experience the culture as the natives do, we note that everything in it is an arbitrary construction and a choice. The ethnographer seeks to articulate, as the natives do not, how and why this world is constructed the way it is.

A fourth clue is to *carry over this "double hermeneutic"* into our analysis of our own culture. We experience culture and we know that we experience it. We know that the media world is a constructed world related to the everyday world. We talk about it and think about it. And that talking and thinking are part of the culture as well. Every time we discuss a newspaper article, a shopping center, a film we have seen, a game we went to, we are engaging in this double hermeneutic that both reflects and builds the culture. This self-consciousness and our ability to reconsider our habitation of the media world are part of the attraction of media culture.

A fifth clue is to *relish the pleasure* of media culture. We enhance the fun of the world of media by accepting and consciously appreciating what it offers. Contrary to classical puritan or elitist attitudes, here we are exploring media culture with an awareness of it as pleasurable, fun, and useful in abundance. What many have attempted to put down, despise, consider in need of reform, and question, we want to first legitimate and endorse, not unthinkingly but before any qualifications and attacks are mounted.

A sixth clue to the approach here is to know that media culture is *about us and our identity*. We select media genres of comedy or science fiction or history because we want to inhabit that world; it is a place we choose to identify with. We begin with the choices of our friends, our age group, our socioeconomic class, our ethnic identification, not the imposed classics of another time or place or taste. We modify the group choices and make them our own.

A seventh clue is to *distinguish different dimensions* of the experience of media culture, as each chapter in this book attempts to do. There are very important distinct dimensions to the world of media culture that we inhabit and shape for ourselves. We ritually participate in media culture, we receive and interpret its highly developed texts, we know the corporate production of it, and we appreciate the gender, ethnicity, history, and ethics embedded in it. By distinguishing these different dimensions, each of these areas becomes a special invitation to explore afresh what we know only in part. Our self-conscious understanding of our habitation of the world of media culture enhances the pleasure and meaning offered by it.

These clues distinguish our approach from those that would treat media only as manipulative ideologies or only as marketing tools or only as troublesome social forces. None of these crucial concerns is excluded, but they are taken up only after the fundamental experience of inhabiting the worlds of media culture is explored in its own right. This is what media education aims at.

With the case-study methodology and these clues in mind, we can begin to confront the arguments that would have media culture at once controlling and lowering our human potential through the commercial incentives so obvious in the production, marketing, and consumption of cultural products and practices accessed through media.

How Free Is the Individual Within Modern Media Culture?

There are extreme disagreements about what value the experience of media culture has for the individual. Around this question, the once "great debates" over media culture have largely given way to the more specific questions and approaches of current methods outlined in future chapters. But, initially, what are the larger, complex value questions underlying the specific questions of text, reception, ritual, production/hegemony, gender, history, or postmodernism that we explore in future chapters? Directly stated, how free is the individual in media culture? More elaborately, can I hear and make whatever music I choose and find most relevant to me, obtaining from it the meanings that serve my best interests within my particular class, gender, race, and other points of identity?

Two long-standing debates on the question of social control and freedom have shifted ground in the past generation. The first debate concerns the extent to which the political economy restricts and dictates culture, or, to rephrase it, the extent to which infrastructure directs consciousness. For example, does selecting Pearl Jam or U2 or Chuck Berry automatically incorporate us into ideological manipulation and brainwashing by the capitalist media industries? The argument from political economy suggests that the structured relations of power prevent me from being exposed to a full range of musical choices and encourage me to restrict my choices to predictable, heavily marketed, escapist bubblegum music. The argument also suggests that powerful centers of cultural production exercise cultural imperialism and domination over other countries, cultures, and markets.

The second debate concerns the relationship between high culture and mass culture, between elite tastes and "the popular." Does a steady diet of Eddie Vedder and Bono represent an unhealthy dumbing down of the potential of truly rich and expressive culture? The argument from high culture implies that I should instead favor the more sophisticated and elevated qualities of classical music, even, or especially, in the face of an onslaught of mass-marketed kitsch.

How relevant are these debates to my actual experience of musical culture, media, and identity? What variations on these "great debates" of the past are useful today?

Who's in Charge: Does Political Economy Dictate Popular Consciousness?

Most people experience some frustration in finding a desirable television program or theatrical film when they wish. Everyone has problems with the phone company at times or with the electronic world of credit cards and bank accounts. We surf the Internet, coming across much of interest but cannot locate what we went searching for. Our newspaper has biases that drive us crazy, as do local talk radio and television chat shows. Many media offerings are offensive in their blandness or their crudeness. Other people we know have more horror stories of their dealings with media. Yet we keep paying large amounts of our time and attention, not to mention money, to support our media access and usage. Why does the system not serve us better?

The first so-called great debate concerns whether commercial profitmakers have preconditioned our musical and cultural taste to favor and protect their interests at the expense of our own best interests. Is not my acceptance of popular music, whether Public Enemy or k. d. lang, Barbra Streisand or Gregorian chant, a conversion of my personal consciousness into a convenient tool of the mass music industry?

Political economy refers to the structured distribution of political and economic power into separate classes, a dominant and privileged class of owners and their management over and against the subordinate worker/consumer classes exploited by the system. This debate was born in charges that the material infrastructure of society, here the commercial base of popular music, determines the superstructural expressions of the culture, in this case the ideologically stunted consciousness of popular music consumers. The first directly causes the second, in the argument from political economy: Consciousness is falsified in its manipulation by the political economy behind music. The political economy of the music industry maintains the massive, structured relations of economic power and political control at the service of a small, privileged elite. The billions of dollars made each year by the music industry create profits for stockholders without regard for the welfare of the general public. This power advantage creates the cultural domination of the advantaged over the marginalized populations, with "marginalized" including everyone but the corporate elite who control media conglomerates and the capitalist system. Such criticism cannot be lightly dismissed. As we explore media culture in future chapters, an implicit question is, how does this specific case study reflect larger arrangements of media production and cultural power?

In the critique from political economy, the "industrialization" of music in the twentieth century changed music as expression into music as commodity. The original formulations of this critique came from the Frankfurt School, an influential group of expatriate social critics who came from that German city to the United States to escape Nazism in the 1930s. Simon Frith (1992) describes this position as it applies to music:

> The industrialization of music means a shift from active musical production to passive pop consumption, the decline of folk or community or subcultural traditions, and a general musical deskilling—the only instruments people like me can play today are their record players and tape decks. The rise of multinational leisure corporations means, inevitably, the efficient manipulation of a new, global pop taste that reaches into every first, second, and Third World household like Coca Cola (and with the same irrelevance to real needs). (p. 69)

Fans trapped in the four-bar and eight-bar structure of popular songs were portrayed as colonial victims of cultural imperialism (Adorno, 1941/1993).

The actual development of popular music in this century, however, indicates that music "machines" have not been "as dehumanizing as mass media critics from both left and right perspectives have suggested" (Frith, 1992, p. 71). The commercial music industry has preserved previously unreproducible aspects of performance such as spontaneity and improvisation. The industry has enabled African-American music to replace European art and folk music as the foundation of Western popular culture; it has provided new means of self-definition for majorities and for minority cultures and subcultures. After such closer examination, "more nuanced theories of the relation between infrastructure and superstructure" have redrawn our picture of these power relationships, thanks to the work of Gramsci, Bakhtin, Jameson, and others (Wuthnow, 1992, p. 168). Rather than conceiving of the material base as mechanically causing ideology and consciousness, the base and ideology are seen to be interactive; they generate a discursive practice in which text and context are related but not homogeneous. Gangster rap, expressing the rage of inner-city streets, may be suppressed or distorted by the powers that be, but it is not entirely eliminated or completely drained of its revolutionary potential.

Incorporating these modifications of the Frankfurt position, the so-called "Birmingham School" in the United Kingdom produced a more nuanced portrayal of power in media culture through the work of the Centre for Contemporary Cultural Studies. Popular music does not mechanically reproduce patterns of domination, yet music is limited by the social context in the way that it constructs the text through genre, narrative, redundancy, voice, and signification. Voices of authentic protest can perform in small venues and at rallies and can record on smaller, independent labels. But if they are to sign with a major label, they must conform to 3-minute song lengths, commercial tours, and the hype of pop-music merchandising. Bono of U2 underscored the resulting conflicts at the 1994 Grammies when he accepted one of the Irish group's many awards with an obscenity-laced promise that, despite such acceptance, they would continue to "bleep" the establishment. Reebee Garofalo (1992) extensively documents how popular music is controlled by massive commercial structures but still, on specific occasions such as celebrity megaevents—Live Aid, Farm Aid, Mandela tributes, AIDS fundraisers, and so forth—manages to effectively support progressive change around racism, human rights, women's issues, and political and economic restructuring. Rock music was long a center of underground political resistance in Eastern Europe (Garofalo, 1992) and the former Soviet Union (Cushman, 1995). Contemporary theorists such as David Rowe (1995) and Angela McRobbie (1994) actually like popular culture, as Adorno and the Frankfurt School did not, and can therefore incorporate the subtleties and contradictions of its pleasures with tough-minded critiques of its failings.

Arguing even more vigorously against simple conceptions of media domination and manipulation of audiences, Fiske (1989a and 1989b) claims that the popular audience is active and necessarily resists the imposed meanings from the obvious white, patriarchal, dominant structure. In the process of receiving and making meaning, people create a "resistant interpretation" of the popular. The resilience of the popular classes enables even the oppressed to develop antiestablishment interpretations of the musical pap spooned out to them by commercial media. In Latin America there is a long tradition of such subtle popular resistance and reinterpretation (Martin-Barbero, 1993).

Hegemony. The key term in more recent years is "hegemony," a term that defines a space between direct corporate domination and complete individual autonomy (see Gramsci, Hall, Bennett, and others). The well-known original Frankfurt School formulations made it appear that, for example, popular musical taste was simply dictated by the capitalist commercial apparatus and then exploited. Songs and styles could be imposed willy-nilly on musical audiences. Liberal theory, equally simplistic in the opposite direction, countered that citizens and consumers exercised total freedom in selecting their music from a complete array of cultural and political choices of all kinds; the music industry readily provided whatever the public might want. Writing from a prison cell in fascist Italy, Antonio Gramsci suggested an attractive alternative between these extremes. He argued that "hegemony" is that forceful but not automatic persuasion emanating from the dominant controllers of culture to the less powerful masses of society. Consent rather than coercion persuades the marginalized to accept the status quo. Hegemony is "the power or dominance that one social group holds over another" (Lull, 1995, p. 31). Hegemony creates an "asymmetrical interdependence" (Straubhaar, 1991) and results in "dominance and subordination in the field of relations structured by power" (Hall, 1985). Crudely put, under conditions of hegemony others may profit more from media culture than we do, but we learn to live with it. This media of abundance, with *lots* of channels, does not necessarily offer a culture of true diversity.

Curiously, in the 1990s a simplistic modification of the argument about cultural domination shifted the blame from corporate control to government interference. This argument charged that government regulators and old-style liberal media had fostered a big government monopoly that constrained the natural freedoms that would emerge if only media could be freed of its regulatory shackles. Touted self-servingly by broadcasters, cable operators, telephone companies, and other industry-friendly voices, this argument lacked the historical and theoretical sophistication of the Frankfurt or Birmingham Schools but enjoyed considerable popular play. Whereas the Frankfurt critique suggested public control of media was desirable, the newer critique argued that private marketplace control was preferable and, in its extreme versions, that public sector protections had no place in society.

Later chapters in this book suggest ways of clarifying these questions of power and control, particularly by closer examination of the actual workings of media culture built around Hall's model of media and hegemony. A closer understanding of how we receive texts in different ways, of how Hollywood both dominates and responds to markets, and of how groups are represented differently in media, in addition to other clarifications, all help to explain the ways base and superstructure operate in media culture.

These arguments about control and freedom are actually the same questions that each of us as an individual in media culture faces in daily life. Do
we have genuine choices and alternatives? Are we free in the sense of being
self-actualized and self-determined in cultural matters? Is the system we
participate in balanced and fair? Are we, obviously or subtly, limited and
coerced into choosing and thinking in certain ways? In a similar way, the
following argument about high culture versus popular culture is a large
system debate that can also apply to an individual, personal level as well.

What Is Best: Is High Culture
Superior to Popular Culture?

The second great debate about culture, the individual, and the system
ultimately implied unequivocally that one *should* listen to classical music
rather than popular music. The so-called "great debate" (Rosenberg & White,
1957) argued over whether high culture was absolutely better than mass or
popular culture. Traditionally in English-speaking scholarly circles, only
culture with a capital C deserved to be called (preferably with an arching of
the eyebrow) "Culture." Ironically, this argument aligned on the same side
marxists from the left and elitist cultural conservatives from the right, all of
whom charged that popular culture and popular music pandered to and
debased the taste of the masses (see Real, 1977). They were opposed by
liberal apologists, who saw no detrimental effects in popular culture and
who, in fact, found in it a genuinely democratic expression of the tastes of
the average person. Once a source of considerable argumentation, "today the
high culture/mass culture debate arouses little passion in academic life"
(Featherstone, 1992, p. 271).

As working class representatives entered this debate (Hoggart, 1957;
Williams, 1958), *culture* was redefined, jettisoning the capital C. Culture
became "inclusive and common—as contrasted with exclusive and carried
by elite cultural agents" (Smelser, 1992, p. 5). Many developments contributed to this change. Informed, intelligent critics were finding as much to
appreciate in the Beatles as in Schoenberg; in Warhol as in Rembrandt.
Detailed examination of the creation, content, and reception of music found
similar mechanisms at work in the classical and popular arenas. Michael
Schudson (1991) has concluded, "In all three dimensions—the study of the
production of culture, the study of texts, and the study of audiences—the
intellectual developments of the past generation have provided a new validation for the study of popular culture" (p. 50). The Museum of Modern Art
ultimately combined the once-competing levels of culture for a famous
exhibit that traveled across the United States and was published under the
title *High and Low: Modern Art, Popular Culture* (Varnedoe & Gopnik,

1990). This exhibit vividly illustrated how the interaction between once classical forms and popular forms now allows little real distinction between them. Scholars who previously dismissed popular media as eye candy for cultural boobs began to admit that media did not work that way in their own lives. Those conducting ethnographic studies of how people really understood, talked about, and used popular media found that "reception" and "interpretation" were active, complex processes involving class, race, gender, and taste, even among less-articulate working-class cultures (Morley, 1980).

Popular Culture. The "popular" now receives serious cultural analysis as once only high culture did. David Rowe (1995) defines *popular culture* as "an ensemble of pleasurable forms, meanings and practices, whose constituents are neither static nor unambiguous, and which cannot be insulated from the social processes and structures in which they are imbedded" (p. 7). Popular music was not mindless, tasteless, and useless but was capable of complex, sophisticated, subtle, popular expression within its social context.

This recognition of the richness of popular culture led in turn to the application of analytic methods from high culture to the works of popular media and culture; Chapters 3 and 4 illustrate this by applying literary standards to how popular texts are structured and interpreted. There are still many attempts to enforce cultural judgments, but they do not break down into the high and mass culture debate.

A related debate asks, does social *class* determine my selection of culture? If I am wealthy, privileged, and well-educated, will I then condescend to listen to only the finest of classical composers and performers? If I am blue-collar or homeless, will I automatically accept only predictable country western, blues, and top-40 hits? How closely does social class correlate with cultural taste?

In many general ways, high, middle, and lower classes do have corresponding levels of taste, even when one argues that "high" is not necessarily better (see Gans, 1974). But closer examination of groupings of musical taste reveals that variables of age, race, and sex compete with class in determining musical taste: "we pretty much listen to, and enjoy, the same music listened to by other people we like or identify with" (Lewis, 1992, p. 200). Our identity groups only partially coincide with high, middle, and lower class. We also pick our friends by age affinity, racial grouping, and gender identity, sometimes across class lines. Group identity, however formed, is crucial. Surveys of British youth found that popular music is, on the one hand, a means by which groups define themselves and, on the other hand, a source of in-group status (Lewis, 1992, p. 201). This echoes the larger point that culture provides both group boundaries and prescribed roles and that either the boundaries or the roles may be strong or weak in a given culture (Thompson,

Ellis, & Wildavsky, 1990). Even the influence of "race, class, and gender" (the so-called mantra of cultural studies), although considerable in the aggregate, are no longer considered to automatically predict individual tastes. In general, social class and other groupings may condition but not dictate one's musical tastes.

The debate about high culture versus popular culture has largely broken apart on newer questions of intertextual sophistication, postmodern relativism, and other issues addressed in the following chapters.

Who Should Decide: Why Fight Culture Wars?

Despite the preceding complication of once simple notions of who controls the culture and how, many are still tempted today to wage war against those whose culture differs significantly from their own. Although this conflicts with the pluralism inherent in democratic societies, it has not deterred militants from attempting to impose their culture and their political and economic ideology and system on others. The centrality of culture and media to public policies and personal identity leads to "culture wars" that lack the armaments but not the passion of military wars. Religious fundamentalists in, for example, the Middle East and North America, have urged war on the presence of cultural values that they see threatening a desired way of life. In many contexts and locations, traditionalists and progressives do battle over the choices and directions of religious expression, moral codes, censorship, drugs and alcohol, weapons and violence, care for the poor, sexual preferences, abortion, family structures, and other issues that are cultural and also political, economic, ethical, legal, or social.[2]

Shifting group identities related to cultural choices lie at the heart of these current conflicts, in the view of James Davison Hunter. In *Culture Wars: The Struggle to Define America* (1991), he redefines cultural categories that once separated Catholic, Protestant, and Jew:

> At the heart of the new cultural realignment are the pragmatic alliances being formed across faith traditions. Because of common points of vision and concern, the orthodox wings of Protestantism, Catholicism, and Judaism are forming associations with each other, as are the progressive wings of each faith community—and each set of alliances takes form in opposition to the influence the other seeks to exert in public culture. (p. 47)

Taking advantage of these conflicts, politicians love to push the "culture" button of blame. In his study of that subject, Michael Bérubé (1994) notes that the "PC Wars" of the 1990s remind us "about the difficulty of sustaining legitimate intellectual exchange in a culture more accustomed to waging mass-media smear campaigns than to fostering substantive debates. . . ." (p. ix). Those accusing campuses of leftist oppressive censorship, in Bérubé's view, mistake opposition for oppression and confuse criticism with censorship. He concludes:

> Conservative attacks on academic life, then, should be understood as the consequence of conservatism's failure to achieve among the academic American intelligentsia the kind of hegemony it has enjoyed in American economic and social policy, not to mention the federal judiciary. (p. 67)

Domestically and internationally, many conflicts center in cultural issues, from American or British welfare and tax reform to conflicts in the former Yugoslavia, South Africa, Ireland, Israel, Iran, India, Peru, Quebec, and elsewhere, and conflicts concerning aboriginal populations in Australia, Canada, the United States, and many other countries. Culture must be thought of as practices and not only as products, and, as a consequence "the cultural realm often expresses antagonisms, both deep-rooted and more casual" (O'Connor, 1990, p. 31). As actual wars remind us, far more than musical taste is at stake in our relationship to "culture."

The fragmentation of the social order through culture wars especially concerns Todd Gitlin in *The Twilight of Common Dreams: Why America Is Wracked by Culture Wars* (1995). The identity politics of blacks, women, youth, and other demographic groups have emerged as a necessary antidote to the marginalizing of such groups. But a political agenda that confines itself to only the self-interest of one such identity group may ultimately splinter society rather than better distribute the common good. Identity politics fret about diversity in faculty hiring and school curriculum but may fail to connect with the larger impoverishment of the cities and "all the dying out there." Instead, identity politics pit groups against each other and focus on narrow gains when these groups' goals can only be achieved by forming alliances with other groups and struggling to persuade others without giving up their own identity. In Gitlin's view as an experienced political activist, activist groups that cannot rise to this level will finally contribute to the destruction of progress and common social ideals as much as if they were opposed to progressive change.

Current cultural wars tend to conduct debate at a more superficial level than the two preceding classical debates. The first debate, the argument about ownership constraining cultural products, built on philosophical and sociological studies indicating that structured relations of power established in the political economy generally direct and constrain choices for the public. In contrast, pop declarations of cultural war suggest that specific individuals or groups act arbitrarily and with questionable motives against the preferences of good people. The second debate drew from classical literary and artistic debates about quality, integrity, complexity, and evaluation, wondering if these were adequately present in mass culture. In contrast, those who wage cultural wars tend to argue from a partisan ideological position without critical self-awareness or broad historical and intellectual foundations.

Less superficially, critical theory proposes that an overriding commercial incentive encourages catering to mass tastes and sensationalism, tastes that have been sustained for generations by commercialism. In this, the classical debates appear closer to commonsense observation than do the more strident cultural warriors. The capitalist media protected by the First Amendment are generally interested in making a profit and maintaining the established order rather than agitating in a partisan way for particular social change. This commercial structural analysis, developed in the great debates over culture, seems a far more plausible account than the socialist bias alleged by cultural warriors. Why was Time Warner willing to market inflammatory rap artists for years? Because they made money. Why did they finally drop them after Republican presidential candidates attacked Time Warner? Because they feared loss of money in the long run.

Any sustained critique of popular music—or television news or the entertainment industry or other aspects of media culture—cannot ignore the profit-driven commercial context in which it exists.

This may be the most overarching message of all the debates on culture: the influence of the commercial context in which a cultural product resides. The theory of hegemony argues that the political economy and ideology "exert pressure" and "set limits" but in large systemic ways rather than in obvious partisan political ways. At the same time, hegemony recognizes that the link between social structure, textual configuration, and popular reception creates a negotiated "space" and not stimulus-response causality. Individuals live somewhere between the extremes of being independent agents free from culture and passive victims of culture. Although conservatives charge leftists with pushing oppressive political correctness, it is ironically those conservative forces waging cultural warfare—as opposed to engaging in cultural debates—who generally offer fewer rather than more choices in the long run. The following chapters in this book suggest that closer examination of the specifics of how we receive, interpret, and participate with media texts, and how hegemony, gender, and history condition these practices, will both clarify and qualify what the cultural wars fight over.

All debates on culture involve issues of "symbols" and "structures," and adequate definitions of culture must relate to this. With this in mind and following Clifford Geertz, John Thompson (1990) suggests a definition of culture that refers to "the symbolic character of social life, to the patterns of meaning embodied in the symbolic forms exchanged in social interaction" (p. 12). But Thompson's definition would go beyond Geertz by stressing also "that symbolic forms are embedded in structured social contexts involving relations of power, forms of conflict, inequalities in terms of the distribution of resources, and so on" (p. 12). His suggestion is to understand culture as *"symbolic forms in structured contexts"* (p. 12).

The carload of teenagers listening to "Jeremy," Hester Prine ordering U2 in Toronto, and Chuck Berry pounding out "Johnny B. Goode," like music participants anywhere, are enjoying "symbolic forms in structured contexts," that is, culture. John Shepherd (1994) captures the power of musical culture:

> Music as a socially constructed symbolic medium speaks immediately, con-cretely and globally to the experiential world of different individuals. There is in other words little or no disjunction between people and music. Within a particular cultural context, both are in intense dialectical relationship with the same social structure. . . . What is common to the social-musical reality of . . . rock music is an emphasis on the experiential richness of the here and now, on the inherent potential of people to exist fully in the world. . . . (p. 235)

Summary of Culture, Media, Identity, and Cultural Debates

We initiate our exploration of media culture by laying out a map of its basic terrain with "culture," "media," "identity," and "cultural debates" set in high relief. Culture is our life made up of symbolic forms in structured contexts. Media are the technologies that carry culture. Identity is who we are today in the context of media culture. Cultural debates argue the pros and cons of media control, content, and influence. Popular music illustrates the forms, contexts, technologies, and issues that we experience through media culture.

Turning now to the question of media culture as a "mystery" for these pages to solve, Paul Schrader, in his famous 1972 article on film noir, argues that in its brief heyday in the 1950s film noir "was able to create artistic solutions to sociological problems" (p. 13). He describes his favorite noir film this way:

> Appropriately the masterpiece of *film noir* was a straggler, *Kiss Me Deadly,* produced in 1955. . . . The private eye hero, Mike Hammer, undergoes the final stages of degradation. He is a small-time "bedroom dick," and makes no qualms about it because the world around him isn't much better. Ralph Meeker, in his

best performance, plays Hammer, a midget among dwarfs. Robert Aldrich's teasing direction carries *noir* to its sleaziest and most perversely erotic. Hammer overturns the underworld in search of the "great whatsit," and when he finally finds it, it turns out to be—joke of jokes— . . . . (p. 13)

Sorry to interrupt the quotation before the punchline, but no self-respecting narrative names the culprit in the first chapter. The resolution of *Kiss Me Deadly*, like the clues and solution to the mystery of media culture, waits in its proper place—ahead.

Notes

1. A number of anthologies of cultural studies have been issued in recent years sharing similar sources, key concepts, and applications. The British tradition of cultural studies is especially well-represented in a group of five recent anthologies.

In 1990, Manuel Alvarado and John O. Thompson gave us *The Media Reader*, with its emphasis on critical media theory. The selections emphasize the nature of the current market economy and Enlightenment ideals as opposed to self-denigration, contempt for others, or the deskilling that leaves audience-members with less know-how, sensitivity, and liberty.

Ann Gray and Jim McGuigan, in their reader, *Studying Culture: An Introductory Reader* (1993), offer a selection of "classic" readings to introduce cultural studies. They trace the path of cultural studies from its Birmingham origins into sociology, linguistics, and literature and back again. They reflect the institutional spread of cultural studies from the academic margins, accompanied by communication, film, and media studies into a central place in many curricula. In addition, they follow the steady internationalization of cultural studies in Australia, North America and other places. Their selections highlight the role of feminism, black politics, and discourses of "the other" in broadening the range of cultural studies. The Gray and McGuigan reader favors ethnographies over textual analyses and accepts a necessary openness in defining cultural studies. The reader's resistance to disciplinarity and policing the boundaries of knowledge leaves it by intent "peculiarly boundless. . . . Cultural studies, broadly speaking, can still be said, however, to be concerned with anything that is meaningful, usually seen in connection to power relations" (p. ix). Anthony Easthope and Kate McGowan's *A Critical and Cultural Theory Reader* (1992) is a similar, sound collection. *The Polity Reader in Cultural Theory* (1994) particularly concerns media and mass communication.

Simon During traces the roots of cultural studies in the selections and introduction in *The Cultural Studies Reader* (1993). Cultural studies' origins are affected by studies of the British working class, French theory, ethnographic methods and findings, and a privileging of otherness and marginalized populations. From an initial concern with the powerlessness of the underclass against the state, cultural studies has moved to foreground issues of feminism, racism, homophobia, and others; cultural studies also foregrounds suppressed theories that promise to confront inequalities and initiate practices for correcting them. Cultural studies sifts through the structure and meanings in popular culture as a "problematic" reflecting and resisting dominant patterns of culture.

Many other works have moved cultural studies forward in the 1990s and reflect increased clarity, maturity, and varied applications. The decisive and voluminous collection by Lawrence Grossberg, Cary Nelson, and Paula Treichler, *Cultural Studies* (1992), in 788 tightly packed pages reports the proceedings of a historic conference at the University of Illinois in 1990. This collection's topics cover cultural policy, technology, postcolonialism, audiences, Chicanas, AIDS, ethnicity, gender, crime fiction, popular music, aesthetics, pornography, psychoanalysis, commodification, technoculture, ethics, Shakespeare, historians, national trends, pleasure, and postmodernism. Despite that amazing diversity, the collection suggests a bibliography that traces the evolution and terrain of cultural studies (p. 15).

One finds the insights of cultural studies fleshed out in innumerable other works, including Fred Inglis's nicely historicized *Media Theory: An Introduction* (1990), Ben Agger's focused *Cultural Studies as Critical Theory* (1992), and James Lull's excellent summary *Media, Communication, Culture* (1995).

2. Cultural debates have also played a role in many actual wars. The American Secretary of Defense who managed the war in Vietnam from 1963 until 1968 admitted decades later that a huge culture gap helped make that war effort disastrous. Robert McNamara acknowledged,

> I had never visited Indochina, nor did I understand or appreciate its history, language, culture, or values. The same must be said, to varying degrees, about President Kennedy, Secretary of State Dean Rusk, National Security Adviser McGeorge Bundy, military advisor Maxwell Taylor, and many others. When it came to Vietnam, we found ourselves setting policy for a region that was terra incognita.
>
> Worse, our government lacked experts for us to consult to compensate for our ignorance about Southeast Asia. The irony of this gap was that it existed largely because the top East Asian and China experts in the State Department . . . had been purged during the McCarthy hysteria of the 1950s. (McNamara, 1995, p. 31)

In this case, one destructive cultural-ideological war in the 1950s handicapped the following military war in the 1960s.

EXERCISES

Chapter One

Exercise A. MUSIC. Select a specific piece of music you like, of whatever type, and explain why that piece has a particular personal meaning for you. Why do you like it and what do you associate with it?

Exercise B. MUSICAL IDENTITY. Now play that song for a group. What does the group now guess about you based on that song? We tend to assume different things about listeners to classics, to country, to rock, to alternative, to heavy metal, to jazz, to other culturally disparate sources. What might one infer about you and your friends based on your choice of song?

Exercise C. CULTURE. Drawing from the preceding choices of music, define your own culture in terms of geography, population size, gender, race and ethnicity, class, and shifting boundaries. What definition of culture do you prefer from among the many suggested?

Exercise D. MEDIA. What definition of "media" do you prefer? What elements should be present in any description of what a communication medium is? How many different kinds of media technologies can you name?

Exercise E. MEDIA AND IDENTITY. Why do we say that media culture relates to our identity as a person? What social forces shape our sense of identity and consciousness, and where do communication media fit in this picture? Do you find that media collectively are major factors in society today or in your life?

Exercise F. AESTHETIC EXPERIENCE. Describe a specific significant experience that you have had in your life in connection with media culture, an "aesthetic experience" as it is traditionally called. The range of types of experiences is potentially infinite. You may even describe an experience that occurs separately from the media work itself, that is, you may flash on a movie scene as you meet a friend or camp in the woods, and it may take on special meaning for you. Your aesthetic experience may be a grand, earth-shaking, life-changing encounter or it may be a quiet, simple weightless sense of appreciation. But it must have real importance *for you.* Yours may be high-minded and noble or earthy and socially suspect. Be honest, but also be expansive and elaborate in your explanation, an explanation that you may wish to put in the form of a short story, screenplay, poem, or other medium. You may wish to compare your aesthetic experience to those of others that you have read of, heard described, or seen in films or video or on stage. Many great artists like Joyce or Dostoyevski describe such experiences of their own. There are also normally "permanent lessons" that one takes away from such experiences.

Exercise G. ORALITY. Summarize ways in which popular music relates to an "oral" cultural tradition. Why are printed writing and performed music in some conflict with each other?

Exercise H. CULTURAL SELF-DETERMINATION. Which side do you favor in the debate over cultural manipulation and dominance? Explain what you find true and false about the argument that the political-economic infrastructure automatically dictates the culture and popular music of the masses. Explain what you find true or false about the opposite position, the argument that media culture is a free and balanced forum expressing and satisfying everyone's preferences.

Exercise I. HIGH VS. LOW. Take a position on the high culture versus popular culture debate. Do you believe one is absolutely better than the other? If so, which one and why? Do you believe they are equivalent, even indistinguishable from each other? An examination of the history of this "great debate" (going back to original sources) will, of course, enable you to discuss this question more knowledgeably.

Exercise J. CULTURAL CONFLICT. Examine issues and positions in a "culture war" that you have noticed. What issues are talked about, what issues seem to be hidden between the lines, and who are the people on the contending sides? Are your impressions of this culture war dependent solely on media information or do you have additional resources to draw from?

Exercise K. CASE STUDY. Conduct a case study of one group watching a music video or listening to music, using the steps identified for such "cultural exegesis."

Exercise L. MYSTERY. From the description of the mystery of media culture, what do you anticipate will be the solution to this mystery? What clues and evidence do you suspect will prove most important?

2

Ritual Participation:
Toward an Ethnography
of Fans, Hackers, and Jumpers

Tribal ritual requires preparation. The adult male in the clan prepares to watch the ritual game. The adult female joins others in a ritual dance with rhythmic music. The adolescent clan member gathers tokens for a trial challenge with peers.

The tribe's rituals this day break into stereotypes: males watch the televised game, females do aerobics, and youths play video games. The presence of the most advanced technologies in human history only superficially distinguish today's rites from their ancient forebears.

Ritual behaviors precede, interact with, and issue from the encounter with media texts. The teen mastering a video game, the aerobics instructor working out a class, the football fan with friends screaming at the screen—these are forms of ritual participation in media. The *mythic* and *ritual,* that is, our analogic reasoning and our patterned behaviors, condition our relationship with texts and interpretations and are conditioned by them as well. Ritual interweaves with production, text, reception, and interpretation.

Can "ritual interpretation" of how people participate in media culture solve the mystery of media culture today? Does an ethnography of media participation explain our relationship with media culture?

Beyond Reading: The Active Media User

This chapter looks at the pervasive dimensions of myth and ritual that operate in current media activities. What kinds of play and "deep play" do media users engage in? How has close ethnographic description opened up new dimensions of our relationship to media culture?

The chapter is illustrated by an examination of ritual participation on three levels: social, physical, and interactive. The *social* participation of sports fans in mediated sports exhibits a feeling of involvement and an emotional relationship to the game and its outcome. The *physical* participation of a person doing aerobics, complete with intense movement, music, and mirrors, makes the person the subject and the body the outcome of a mediated aerobic

Right: Tammilee Webb,
president of Webb
International, has created
scores of bestselling exercise
videos, including "Buns of
Steel" and "Perfect Abs."
SOURCE: Webb International,
Del Mar, CA.

Below: An unidentified
Manchester United fan at
Wembley Stadium also wears
an Oakland Raiders cap.

These photos suggest
interrelated problematics
of sex and gender, sports,
exercise, transnationalism,
history, hegemony, and
postmodernism within media
culture.

experience. The *interactive* participation of a video game player creates immersion in the experience and even personal control of its outcome.

These cases of active participation in media are noteworthy because they especially belie the old stereotype of media users as passive cultural dopes, as undifferentiated couch potatoes dully receiving the bullet messages targeted at them by media. These cases also highlight the weakness of the term *reader* for subjects interacting with media texts. *Reader* implies a mentally active but physically passive subject. We do not normally cheer, dance, or frantically push buttons while we read.

In fact, none of the usual labels is adequate as a name for the subject who participates in the media text. *Reader* misses the excitement of live involvement in media events while they happen and the physical participation in media experiences. *Receiver* likewise implies a passive subject. Calling the media receiver a *user* adds some receiver activity but implies an addictive relationship to media. *Audience* and *spectator* add the collective dimension and possible affective responses but retain the sense of passivity in receiving an already finished product. *Consumer* is problematic because it accepts what many consider questionable, that media exist for commercial purposes only, that the consumer culture is and should be the totalizing center within culture. *Decoder* implies someone sitting with telegraph keys or secret symbol systems. All these limitations may be why Jon Cruz and Justin Lewis, whose book is subtitled *Audiences and Culture Reception,* make the main title simply *Viewing, Reading, Listening* (1994). Yet, although those three terms together describe media reception, each singly refers to access through only one sense, either eye or ear. On the World Wide Web, however, we can view, read, listen, *and* write to inquire, respond, interact, or whatever.

Given the inadequate options, I suggest the label *co-author* to insert the receiver actively into the process of media culture. *Co-authors* are active participants with concomitant responsibilities and abundant rewards. But linguistically, we cannot easily use *co-author* in all those cases where reader, receiver, user, audience, or consumer of media might otherwise be used. No single label is adequate, especially for conveying the active, dynamic, interpretive interface between media and persons or the passive, manipulative dependence on media that may also exist.

Henry Jenkins has proposed a new label in *Textual Poachers: Television Fans and Participatory Culture* (1992). *Textual poachers,* taken from de Certeau (1984), characterizes how media receivers appropriate texts for their own purposes, as backwoods poachers might steal a rabbit or mink from another's trap and use it for their own purposes. Media poaching can especially be identified in the way fans use a cult film or a television series such as *Star Trek* or *Twin Peaks.* Such textual poaching encompasses five levels of activity.

First, the fan's "particular mode of reception" entails watching the show closely with undivided attention, multiple times, within a framework of social interaction with like-minded fans. *Star Trek* fans *know Star Trek* and other Trekkies. Second, "a particular set of critical and interpretive practices" includes learning the community's preferred reading practices, interpretations that are playful, speculative, and subjective, finding parallels with their own lives, and constructing a metatext that is larger, richer, more complex and interesting than the original series of which they are fans. Trekkies move way beyond passive acceptance of the shows as given. Third, "a base for consumer activism" enables fans to organize and lobby for changes in a show or against cancellation, learn about and respond to spin-off products, and assert their desires for alternative development. Trekkies are the authorities on *Star Trek* and they use their authority. Fourth, "particular forms of cultural production and artwork" generate from fans a range of folk songs, reworked stories, videos, and other creations that circulate through word-of-mouth, reciprocity, and loyalty. Being a Trekkie encourages self-expression. Fifth, "an alternative social community" emerges where interaction with like-minded fans offers a utopian dimension and empowerment. Being a Trekkie can mean enjoying a sense of belonging and happiness.

The textual poachers described by Jenkins are neither passive nor escapist. In this, they contradict much of the sociology written about fans and the popular stereotype of the fan as misfit. Instead, Jenkins proposes a model of the relationship between spectators and text "in which textual materials are appropriated and fit to personal experience" (p. 287). When we appropriate a text and fit it to our personal experience, we make it our own and take on ownership and control of it. No longer is it the flat text as presented by media, and no longer are we isolated receivers able only to accept or reject it as given. We become ritually united with and through the textual experience.

Media receivers, like dancers around a campfire, can be decisively active at times. "Poachers" aggressively take animals not originally theirs. Elvis Presley supposedly expressed his disgust with the passionless singing of Robert Goulet on television by shooting out his television screen with a handgun. In February, 1994, a 65-year-old woman in Newark, New Jersey, was convicted of shooting her husband to death with a shotgun during a fight over where the television remote control was. These shootings illustrate how much more than "receive" the poachers of media texts often do. Such actions were once characterized simply as "effects" of media, but they are not psychologically or even physiologically separated from reception enough to be set off as "effects" created by a *separate* "cause." The viewer *interacts* with the media text, and the interaction incorporates both text and viewer to generate meaning and immediate experience. Fans cheering for their team to do well at home or in the pub are acting from a concern for the future as much as in response to a past media message. They are not only responding to something as an "effect"; they are hoping to cause improvement, however absurd that hope may be in practical rather than psychological terms. The video game player's button pushing, knob twisting, and joystick maneuvering all serve to direct and change the action on the screen, clearly behavior that is more a cause than an effect. Dancing to recorded or amplified music is likewise more a simultaneous participation with the medium than an effect of it. The next chapter describes studies of measurable "effects" of media exposure, but there is far more to media experience than those behavioral effects.

Past terminology and conceptualizations of "audiences" and "effects" are increasingly recognized as inadequate for characterizing the interaction between humans and media texts. Anthropologists studying distant cultures sought to understand the meaning of the experiences of the culture far more than they sought to measure the behavioral effects of its public messages. Media culture today stimulates the same curiosity.

Ritual Participation:
The Human/Other Interface

How does "ritual analysis" explore our media reception and the human-machine interface? To begin, it clarifies what we mean by ritual.

The notion of *ritual* is valuable because it denotes activity that has a pattern, is simultaneous with other concerns, and is continuous. Weeping over a soap opera or cheering a team is ritual. This simultaneity of participation is a major addition by ritual theory to the older, mechanical, bullet model of communications. As we saw in Chapter 1, the bullet model is unidirectional, singular, and automatic in the way it represents the communication process. The bullet model is useful for engineers measuring the transmission of bits of information, but it is inadequate for capturing the multiple directions and dimensions of human communication. The bullet model appears in much of traditional communication research: information theory, influence and persuasion theory, functionalism, uses and gratifications, and media effects. As Carey notes (1989), these views "reduce the extraordinary phenomenological diversity of communication into an arena in which people alternatively pursue power or flee anxiety" (p. 32). The experience of media is reduced to motives that precede it or effects that follow it. "In contrast, a ritual view conceives communication as a process through which a shared culture is created, modified, and transformed" (Carey, 1989, p. 43). Our perception and structuring of what the world is and what our experience of it means is not a given but something developed as our perceptions and mind develop; what we know as "real" is not planted in us but emerges with experience. Rather than a bullet, "communication is a symbolic process whereby reality is produced, maintained, repaired, and transformed" (Carey, 1989, p. 23).

In the ritual act—the tribal campfire, the video game, the live ball game, the aerobic dance—the receiver acts simultaneously with the transmission and text, interacting with it in anything but a passive way. A ritual approach to media culture offers a dynamic sense of how we construct and carry on our interactions with the world around us (see Figure 2.1).

Yet a sense of ritual's power can be difficult to achieve today. Individualism, rationalism, and scientism reduce our sense of evidence, proof, and causality to singular physical causes and effects. This "modern" worldview contrasts with a sense of how common and rich ritual experience is in everyday life. The Renaissance, Reformation, and Enlightenment moved us away from the sense of fundamental human unity so common in traditional preliterate, oral societies. As W. H. Auden noted, Luther denied any intelligible relation between faith and works, Machiavelli denied any intelligible relation between private and public morality, and Descartes denied any intelligible relation between matter and mind. As a result, it is easy to also deny any intelligible relation between male and female, between people of color and others, between individuals and collectives, between one nation and another. Yet without these connections, media culture would mean nothing.

Myth and ritual reverse these separations by stressing a fundamental unity. In ritual, the participant feels and expresses a unity with the ritual story and meaning, with others in the ritual, and with the origins and purposes of human life. In ancient societies, myth and ritual are not untrue fables and arbitrary rites; they are absolute truth expressed in action and narrative (Eliade, 1961). When Australian aborigines reenact their relationship with a sacred time in a sacred place, they are expressing their perception of existence, their deepest feelings, their collective experience. This mythical perception contrasts with empirical-scientific thought. Mythical perception knows nothing of scientific categories and theoretical distinctions that we come to believe are, as it were, a part of objective reality. In mythical perception, "nature" is not "existents determined by general laws" but a dramatic world, a world of actions, of forces, of uniquely individual things and powers. And the human relationship to these is expressed not in abstract symbols but in concrete and immediate ways. When confronted with death and other imponderables, mythic perception is not content to apprehend the individual event as nothing more than a specific instance of a general law and ask no further "why." The scientific explanation of death does not satisfy our anxiety about why this family member died at this time. Myth is concerned with the why of the individual act, event, or thing (Cassirer, 1958). Myth is my story, and ritual is the acting out of it.

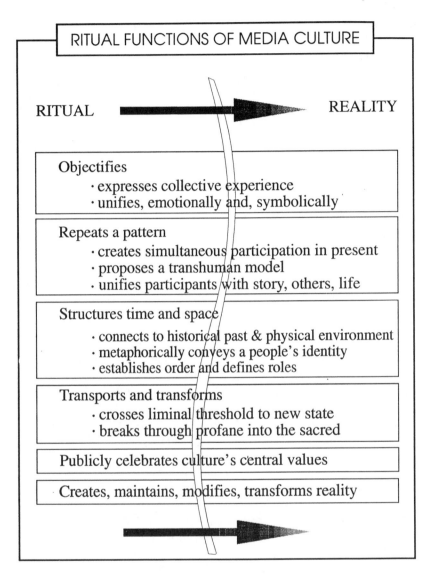

RITUAL FUNCTIONS OF MEDIA CULTURE

RITUAL ➤ REALITY

Objectifies
- expresses collective experience
- unifies, emotionally and, symbolically

Repeats a pattern
- creates simultaneous participation in present
- proposes a transhuman model
- unifies participants with story, others, life

Structures time and space
- connects to historical past & physical environment
- metaphorically conveys a people's identity
- establishes order and defines roles

Transports and transforms
- crosses liminal threshold to new state
- breaks through profane into the sacred

Publicly celebrates culture's central values

Creates, maintains, modifies, transforms reality

Figure 2.1. Ritual participation operates in a variety of ways to express and shape our relations with society and the environment.

Media culture connects us to screen dramas, star personas, other fans, data sources, and the global village; it unifies us ritually and reawakens our sense of drama and the uniqueness of individual events. We join other fans in cheering our athletes in the televised Olympics and we sense the unique magic of a world-class single Olympic performance, whether in gymnastics, soccer, skiing, running, or any other event.

Ritual has the power to connect the participant to richer meanings and larger forces. In the classical mythology of Greece or China, myth breaks through the profane and reaches the sacred. The ritual participant is transported. In African rites of initiation, the participant crosses a threshold to a new level of existence by going into the forest alone for a period of time. He or she passes through a liminal stage that separates youth from adult, nonmember from member. In this rite of passage, there is a ritual of separation, then entry into a liminal period of trials and teachings, and finally return to normal society in a newly assumed role (Dayan & Katz, 1992; Turner, 1969). For the collective, a ritual marks a suspension of normal activities and structure and a transformation toward a better community. In classical mythology and ritual, there is a transhuman model, the repetition of an exemplary scenario, and the breaking away from mere profane time through a moment that opens out into the Great Time, making possible participation in the very source of existence in the myth (Eliade, 1961). On an everyday level today, going to the ballpark, the gym, or the video arcade brings us into the experience of an exemplary pattern, its repetition, a break with profane duration, and an entrance into special time.

Rituals and myths, then, take specific forms. Slotkin (1973) points out that "a mythology is a complex of narratives that dramatizes the world vision and historical sense of a people or culture, reducing centuries of experience into a constellation of compelling metaphors" (p. 6). The predominant myth in the United States, according to Slotkin, is contained in the title of his book *Regeneration Through Violence.* Rebirth and redemption are made possible through intense physical conflict with forces of evil, leading ideally to their destruction. Stories of superheroes from *Star Wars* to *Mortal Kombat,* or Disney stories from *Snow White* to *The Lion King* retell this myth. Television, movies, and video games celebrate this mythical tale in an immense variety of versions.

Mythic rituals, whether in classical stories or contemporary media, celebrate unifying, emotional, symbolic objectifications of collective experience. In traditional society, these were confined to tribal members gathered physically together. In modern media, these can be as large as a national celebration such as the FA Cup Final or the Super Bowl, or an international celebration such as the Olympics or World Cup. Mythic rituals connect us with the historical past and our physical environment. They establish order and define roles. They restructure time and space for our era. They celebrate the central tendencies and values in a culture. They are security blankets against the terror or boredom of mere profane existence.

All this can today be found in the dynamic ritual interface between human subjects and the technology and texts of media culture.

Ritual Interaction With Media Texts and Technology

How do we interact with our culture and our media? Close ethnographic descriptions of subjects in shopping malls (Fiske, 1989a, pp. 13-42; Morris, 1993), surfing in Australia (Fiske, 1989a, pp. 43-76), and reading romance novels (Radway, 1984) find subjects actively expressing themselves in ritualized ways. Enough viewers of entertainment television are also involved in discussions on electronic bulletin board services that Denise Bielby and C. Lee Harrington (1994) have developed an elaborate analysis of the meaning of the televisual experience based on these electronic discussions. David Morley (1994), Roger Silverstone (1991), and Shaun Moores (1993) have examined in detail the role of domestic media technologies in personal and family life. The television set, the video recorder, the computer, the telephone, and the satellite receiver interact with gender roles and other structures of daily life, and recent years have brought us authoritative accounts of these interactions.

A medium often overlooked, perhaps because it is neither mass nor electronic communication, is the family photo album. Fred Inglis (1990) reminds us that photography is "the nearest thing we have to a universal popular art" (p. 159). Inexpensive cameras bring it within reach of almost every household, which then "keeps its archive in snapshot albums" (pp. 159-160). The subject matter is uppermost and recalls family members to the viewer. The favorite photo brings together the way things were at that moment and our valuation of it now. The experience and the art-object carry an equal charge. As an example, when French semiologist Roland Barthes grew older, he tempered his formalism with deeper respect for the felt truths of experience and discussed his own photos. He describes (1984) the frustration of searching family photos after his mother's death to find her true likeness. He struggled among photos that were almost like her or not at all like her:

> There I was, alone in the apartment where she had died, looking at these pictures of my mother, one by one, under the lamp, gradually moving back in time with her, looking for the truth of the face I had loved. And I found it.
>
> The photograph was very old. . . . My mother was five at the time. . . . [There was] the kindness that had formed her being immediately and forever. (pp. 66-67)

Rituals around family photo albums illustrate how media can have the most personal of meanings.

On a larger, public level, in their ground-breaking study *Media Events: The Live Broadcasting of History,* Daniel Dayan and Elihu Katz (1992) vividly describe the ritual power of royal weddings, presidential funerals, diplomatic summits, global sporting events, space conquests, and other live, preplanned, enthralling televised public events. These events invite ritual participation by offering wide public access, creating a liminal space, re-hearsing the ritual order, and positioning viewers so that they can both identify as observers and respond as participants. For the funeral of assassi-nated Indian head-of-state Indira Gandhi, a home viewer reported,

> About an hour before the ceremony began, we were ready, washed and dressed, as if we were going to be physically present at the scene. My mother insisted that we wear long clothes and cover our heads as a mark of respect. A large group of people congregated at my house as they did around most television sets in the country. (Dayan & Katz, 1992, p. 123)

When the King or Queen of England, beginning in 1932, offered a Christmas greeting over BBC radio, many at home stood up for it (Dayan & Katz, 1992, p. 129). The funeral of President Kennedy in 1963 culminated three days of national ritual around the television set (Real, 1989). The funeral of Israeli Prime Minister Yitzak Rabin in 1995 initiated similar ritual participation.

To say that we use media in ritualized and interactive ways does not, however, imply a global uniformity in usage. An important collection of qualitative empirical studies of television and family life in various world cultures (Lull, 1988) found many similarities and many differences among the active audiences. The studies, in Great Britain, Venezuela, West Germany, India, the United States, and China, led Lull to draw the following conclu-sions. In terms of gender, in many countries "television reinforces and extends the 'patriarchal constitution of women' and this discrimination can be observed in family television viewing activity" (Lull, 1988, p. 257). The studies found television is not just a technical medium transmitting bits of information; "it is a social medium, too—a means by which audience members communicate and construct strategies to achieve a wide range of personal and social objectives" (p. 258). The general summary is especially interesting.

> It is clear that audience members do not live in a "free field" at home or anywhere else, uninfluenced by textual and technological factors and the ideological agenda and force they contain and impose. However, viewers also are not "constructed by the text," nor are their experiences "determined" by the

technological, economic, or ideological structures that are associated with mass media. Television viewing in family settings throughout the world occurs along the lines of cultural, household, and personal extensions of audience members that represent the interest of viewers but are also influenced by factors external and internal to the home that are not under their control. . . . While certain homogenizing tendencies of television and video appear throughout the world, world families also watch television distinctively within their own cultures. (Lull, 1988, pp. 258-259)

The clearest way to grasp the actual role of ritual in modern media culture is through specific ethnographic analyses of actual media culture, here in the form of sports fandom, aerobic dance, and video games.

Case One: Mediated Sports and the "Deep Fan"

While many fans attend sporting events each week, many million more watch sports on television, listen on radio, and read about events in the sports page. Those who do so are doing much more than merely finding out who won the big game or what the strategy is for the next one. We have chosen to celebrate sports culture, immerse ourselves in its values, and share its fruits with others. (Wenner, 1989b, p. 7)

Although it is illegal and occasionally gets raided, the cockfight in the Balinese village attracts great interest as fighting cocks are pitted against each other amid considerable excitement, side taking, and betting. As one cock slices another to death with the razor sharp blade attached to his claw, much is revealed about culture. The Balinese cockfight reveals and reinforces group alliances within the village, relative positions of status, willingness to risk often unwise bets, and, more than any other event, how villagers interact and understand themselves. They are engaged in "deep play." (Geertz, 1973)

The most intense involvement of a viewer in an event has been labeled "deep play" by Clifford Geertz (1973). He developed the theory of deep play in his descriptions of the involvement of Balinese spectators in the popular ritual cockfight, an event in which social order and large bets are often at stake. Historically and culturally, the involvement of the sports fan in a mediated sporting event closely parallels this deep play. The sports fan has many conscious motives (Wenner & Gantz, 1989) but also less-conscious mythic goals. Watching sports on television illustrates how ritual participation today occurs in a technological, fully commercialized wonderland. The obvious difference between a Balinese cockfight and a televised ball game is in the array of technology and advertising that mediates between the subject and the event. Is the media sports participation really deep play, and what does it mean?

This question has been examined by implication in early studies of football on television in the form of British soccer (Buscombe, 1975) or the American Super Bowl (Real, 1975) and, more recently, in intense international work. Studies of media and sport in Australia by Geoffrey Lawrence and David Rowe (1986; also Rowe & Lawrence, 1990) and by John Goldlust (1987); in Canada by Richard Gruneau (1983) and Hart Cantelon and Jean Harvey (1987; also Harvey & Cantelon, 1988); in Great Britain by Jennifer Hargreaves (1982), John Hargreaves (1986), Alan Tomlinson and Garry Whannel (1984; also Whannel, 1983, 1992), and Steve Barnett (1990); and in the United States by Benjamin Rader (1984), Lawrence Wenner (1989a), and Allen Guttman (1978, 1986, 1988), all examine distinct issues, but taken together they document the awareness that sport is a powerful ritual force in these societies when wedded with the expressive potential of media.

On a global scale, mediated sports are as massive a ritual as exists today. More than half a billion people watched as the 24 qualifying World Cup soccer teams fought it out in Mexico in 1986, in Italy in 1990, in the United States in 1994, and will in France in 1998. The World Cup, like the modern Olympic games, now estimates that it reaches a billion or more people; it reaches them immediately and on every continent through a vast array of communication technology. More than 100 countries purchase television rights to these games, with radio and print media accounts blanketing the world alongside television.

As a consequence, when Roberto Baggio's penalty kick sailed over the goal to end Italy's hope of defeating Brazil for the World Cup in Pasadena in 1994, it ignited an explosion of emotion felt around the world. Brazil and other countries featured the game on giant screens in large stadium settings. Television coverage of World Cup victories sparked countrywide, long-lasting street parties in Nigeria, Cameroon, Mexico, Ireland, Bulgaria, Italy, Germany, and other competing countries. Less happy fans have rioted, fought, and even killed in the frenzy inspired by sports in our mass-mediated culture. Who was not appalled by the tragedy of 95 fans crushed to death in the terraces at Hillsborough, Great Britain, in 1989, or by the assassination of Colombian player Andres Escobar during the 1994 World Cup? Escobar, a 27-year-old defender, accidentally deflected in an "own goal" that let the United States eliminate Colombia from the 1994 World Cup; he was gunned down 9 days later, shot 12 times, outside a nightclub in his hometown of Medellin. The fan feels so plugged into major sporting events through television and other media that strong emotions and strange behaviors can result.

The Obsessed Football Fan. A particularly colorful and engaging account of fandom is available as *Fever Pitch* by Nick Hornby (1992, quotes used by permission). This is a detailed ethnographic account of his tragic and occasionally triumphant life as a diehard, completely *obsessed* fan of the Arsenal team in the British "football" league (what is called "soccer" in the States). Fans of other sports in other countries will recognize the symptoms, despite differences in stadium arrangements and other details. Followers of the Dallas Cowboys or Toronto Bluejays or Chicago Bulls or any other team will relate easily to Hornby's obsession with his precious "football" team.

Attempting to gain some kind of an angle on his obsessions, Hornby asks, "Why has the relationship that began as a schoolboy crush endured for nearly a quarter of a century, longer than any other relationship I have made of my own free will?" (p. 11). Taken in adolescence to a game by his divorced father, Hornby was immediately struck by "the overwhelming maleness of it all—cigar and pipe smoke, foul language" (p. 19). Moreover, every man appeared to hate being there, beginning with anger that turned later into outrage, "and then seemed to curdle into sullen, silent discontent . . . The natural state of the football fan is bitter disappointment" (p. 20). Entertainment as pain proved to be "something I'd been waiting for" (p. 21). Being a football fan gave him "a place where unfocused unhappiness could thrive, where I could be still and worry and mope; I had the blues, and when I watched my team I could unwrap them and let them breathe a little" (p. 43).

In his brutal, funny self-examination, Hornby makes interesting distinctions. He is "an Arsenal fan first and a football fan second" (p. 135). His obsession is not to be entertained but to experience "an alternative universe, as serious and stressful as work . . . and when I look around me on a Saturday and see those panicky, glum faces, I see that others feel the same" (pp. 135-136). Now living within walking distance of his team's home field, Highbury, Hornby suspects his relationship is with Highbury rather than the team. Good luck rituals are, of course, essential.

> I know I am particularly stupid about rituals, and have been ever since I started going to football matches, and I know also that I am not alone. I can remember when I was young having to take with me to Highbury a piece of putty . . . which I pulled on nervously all afternoon. . . . I can also remember having to buy a programme from the same programme seller, and having to enter the stadium through the same turnstile.
>
> There have been hundreds of similar bits of nonsense, all designed to guarantee victories. . . .
>
> I have tried "smoking" goals in (Arsenal once scored as three of us were lighting cigarettes), and eating cheese-and-onion crisps at a certain point in the first half; I have tried not setting the video for live games. . . . I have tried lucky

socks, and lucky shirts, and lucky hats, and lucky friends, and have attempted to exclude others who I feel bring with them nothing but trouble for the team. . . .

We are reduced to creating ingenious but bizarre liturgies designed to give us the illusion that we are powerful after all, just as every other primitive community has done when faced with a deep and apparently impenetrable mystery. (pp. 110-111)

With typical obsession, Hornby argues that being a fan "is not vicarious pleasure" because "football is a context where watching becomes doing," not in the aerobic exercise sense, but "when there is some kind of triumph, the pleasure does not radiate from the players outward. . . . The joy we feel on occasions like this is not a celebration of others' good fortune, but a celebration of our own" (p. 187). The players are Hornby's representatives and he is a part of the club. He had worked every bit as hard for a remembered victory as the players had. "The only difference between me and them is that I have put in more hours, more years, more decades than them, and so had a better understanding of the afternoon, a sweeter appreciation of why the sun still shines when I remember it" (p. 187).

After 18 years of Hornby's vain efforts, Arsenal finally beat Liverpool in 1989 for the championship in what Hornby titles "the greatest moment ever" (p. 217). When the winning goal was scored at the very end, Hornby's hardened skepticism vanished "and I was flat out on the floor, and everybody in the living room jumped on top of me. Eighteen years, all forgotten in a second" (p. 229). Such moments are beyond comparison for the truly obsessed fan. Childbirth, promotions, awards, huge gambling wins, even sex are inadequate analogues.

Even though there is no question that sex is a nicer activity than watching football (no nil-nil draws, no offside traps, no cup upsets, *and* you're warm), in the normal run of things, the feelings it engenders are simply not as intense as those brought about by a once-in-a-lifetime last-minute Championship winner. (p. 230)

So please, be tolerant of those who describe a sporting moment as their best ever. We do not lack imagination, nor have we had sad and barren lives; it is just that real life is paler, duller, and contains less potential for unexpected delerium. (p. 240)

Hornby's account both decries and helps explain the tragedies associated with big-time soccer. On May 29, 1985, 39 people were killed and 437 injured in a fan confrontation prior to the European Cup Final between Liverpool and the Italian team Juventus. Provocations on both sides led up to the Liverpool fans charging the protective fence and, just as Italian fans were forced against a high concrete wall, it collapsed on them. When 95 died at the Heysel Stadium football ground in Hillsborough near Sheffield on Saturday, April 15, 1989, it was again a case of crowd violence, poor policing, inadequate facilities, and bad judgment. Hornby acknowledges that these were part of an organic culture that British football fans were part of, even with his own antiviolence, antiracist, and antisexist opinions setting him apart from vocal fans near him at many games. Hillsborough forced some perspective-seeking: "Over the years we have come to confuse football with something else, something more *necessary.* . . . We view everything from the top of this mountain of partisan passion; it is no wonder that all our perspectives are wrong. Perhaps it was time to climb down, and see what everyone else in the outside world sees" (p. 223).

Emotion in the Sports Stadium. Another striking ethnographic account of the mythical power of sport appears in a scholarly study of the closing of several old time baseball stadiums in the United States. Nick Trujillo and Bob Krizek in "Emotionality in the Stands and in the Field: Expressing Self Through Baseball" (1994) captured the subjective associations that can make sport viewing—or other experiences of media culture—so moving.

Krizek interviewed fans in the final days of Comiskey Park in Chicago as Trujillo did with Arlington Stadium in Texas. Both were being torn down and replaced, and the authors wanted ethnographic records of what that meant to people. They found many fond personal memories connected to the ballparks. One subject told Krizek: "My father passed away about 10 years ago, and I have my fondest memories of my father in this ballpark. He used to take me out here frequently . . . I'm here to reconnect one more time with those memories while I still can" (p. 316). This led Krizek to his own ethnographic "confessional" account:

I, too, have my fondest memories of my father, George, in Old Comiskey Park. Whether real or imaginary, I have very vivid recollections of my father at my very first Sox game. I was 6 years old that summer of 1954, and the White Sox played the New York Yankees. I remember the smell of hot dogs and the cool dampness of the park's inner caverns. I remember wearing a Sox cap atop my head and holding a bag of peanuts in one hand and my father's reassuring grip in my other hand as we traveled to our assigned seats. We—my father and I—sat in section 213, seats 21 and 22, in the upper deck far down the right field line—not very good seats. As I attended games at Comiskey Park during subsequent years as an adult, I often would take the time to sit in those seats and enjoy the strong feelings of warmth and contentment that would come over me.

. . . [This] marked my first return to Comiskey Park since my father's death. . . . I arrived winded. I paused, took a few deep breaths, and then held one large mouthful of Comiskey Park air as I sank into the chair closest to the aisle. For one brief moment, the confidence of adulthood drifted away, replaced by feelings of a lost 6-year-old boy. I began to cry. This may have been the first time I truly missed my dad and genuinely mourned his passing.

. . . To other fans, these still were not very good seats; to me, they were "sacred." I removed my Sox cap from the equipment bag, slipped it on my head, settled back in my chair, and thought about my father.

I remembered how he used to show me the "proper way" to open salted peanuts in the shell with one hand. I tried one but failed. I remembered how he used to hold two fingers to his mouth and whistle when the Sox rallied. I tried to whistle but could not. That technique had always been beyond me. We cheered long and hard as the visiting Seattle Mariners failed to tie the score in the top of the ninth, but the jubilation of the Sox victory soon gave way to the fears of a small boy about to be separated from his father. Like a confused and frightened child, I reached for his hand. Perhaps out of habit or perhaps due to the pain of being alone, I honestly reached out to hold my father's hand. I believe I succeeded.

When the game ended at 4:23 p.m., we, my dad and I, stayed for almost an hour. I sat there locked in an emotional embrace with him until the public address announcer pleaded for the park to be vacated and an usher, almost apologetically, asked me to leave. I knew that usher felt my grief. I sat there the entire time replaying memories of the park and of my dad, overcome with feelings about a relationship both "wild and controlled," as Donald Hall . . . described it. For the final time in Old Comiskey, I touched the arm of my chair, I touched my father, and I left.

As I backed out of the front entrance of the park, treasuring every glimpse, where Comiskey curves from Shields into 35th Street, an elderly man played "Auld Lang Syne" on his saxophone directly to the park. I stood mesmerized by the sounds and sights of that scene. That song always ignites an emotional reaction in me no matter where I am; on that Sunday, more than ever, it pumped me full of sadness. When the man paused to wipe the perspiration from his face, I complimented his work. He responded simply and eloquently, "I'm saying goodbye to an old friend the only way I know how." Finding the best way to say goodbye seemed to be the task at hand for many of us that sad day.

When Old Comiskey closed that autumn day in 1990, I lost something. (pp. 316-317)

The mythic experience of the sport spectator takes place through live attendance in the stadium or arena, the ballpark, or via television or another medium (Wenner, 1989b). These are related but distinct experiences. The television camera isolates action around the ball, focusing on what is considered important but eliminating larger pictures of team positioning and overall field strategy. Announcers add to this tighter focus by emphasizing specific players and actions. The technology of instant replays further isolates specific parts of the action for slow-motion scrutiny. The score, time, and other performance details are added to the screen.

In contrast to this highly focused and informed presentation, the stadium experience is almost vague and unclear. Fans often make up for this by combining the two, listening to broadcasts in the stadium, using binoculars for close-ups, and carrying newspapers and programs for additional information. Fans in the stands are often more expressive than those at home, with cheering, clapping, jeering, high-fives, waves, pennants, and team colors. But those at home and, even more commonly, in pubs, restaurants, sports bars, dormitories, and other group viewing sites, may also indulge in stadium-style behavior. The stadium viewer is spared the television commercials but increasingly the stadium itself has commercials posted throughout and features advertisements on scoreboards and anywhere else they fit. Players' uniforms in bike racing, skiing, auto racing, and other sports become crowded with commercial logos and names, as do automobiles, racing boats, and other equipment.

This postmodern consumerism is deeply embedded in media sports and throughout media culture today, raising fundamental questions and distinguishing modern consumerist rituals from traditional rites.

Sports, Technology, and
Ritual in the "Commercial" Context

The mass popularity and resulting economic bonanza of media sports spurs technological innovations. Technologies of graphics storage and recall, of special effects generation, of visual and audial manipulation, of electronic amplified relays, of virtually every aspect of television have been spurred on by the demands of speed, scale, and complexity in media sports. The Olympics and World Cup events were the first to use stereo transmission, cordless on-field cameras, mechanically shuttered slow- and stop-motion cameras, and uniform graphics fonts. NHK in Japan first squeezed two simultaneous video pictures into one frame for satellite transmission for the 1984 Los Angeles Games, and provided the first high-definition television (HDTV) to 200 public monitors in Tokyo for the 1988 Seoul Games. Developments in communication technology in the twentieth century have enabled the fan to become vicariously immersed in the experience of sporting events to a depth and breadth previously unimaginable.

As in other areas of media culture, a decisive element in the new experience is the increasing commercialization and commodification of the sport experience. The financial linkage between the sports events and the media transmission is paid for by on-air advertising in many cases. As a result, the sports media complex has become a crossroads through which billions of dollars pass each year, most of that money generated by commercial sponsors paying for advertising time. What does this do to the sporting event?

In a typical year, the largest sponsors in the United States may spend $50-$100 million or more on sports; they include Chrysler, General Motors, Philip Morris, Anheuser Busch, Ford, AT&T, Sears, the U.S. Armed Forces, McDonald's, and American Express (Real & Mechikoff, 1992). As a result, sports telecasts are intertwined with shots of new cars, beer consumption, fast food, consumer goods, and military recruitment. Especially controversial is the involvement of tobacco companies in placing tobacco signs prominently in American stadiums, in sponsoring women's tennis tournaments, and in getting plugged during stock car and drag racing competitions—in a country with more than 400,000 tobacco-related deaths per year, almost seven times the 58,000 American deaths during the whole of the Vietnam War (Oates, 1994). Similar concerns have been raised about the deep association between alcohol and sports through incessant beer advertising and sponsorship. "Official sponsors" of Olympic Games and the World Cup, and even of specific teams such as the U.S. ski or volleyball teams, spread commercialism beyond ads and into the events and dynamics of the sports world itself.

Media sports contracts have grown steadily in size and effect. By the start of the 1990s the three commercial United States networks had contracts in place for professional football, baseball, basketball, and three Olympics that totaled more than $6 billion. Olympic television rights payments now provide the majority of the operating budgets of the International Olympic Committee and the international sports governing bodies. Team operating budgets and escalating player salaries in many cases receive less than half their support from ticket sales; the rest is from broadcasting. Player endorsement contracts for shoe companies and others are now even larger than superstar salaries because of the star's commercial media value. The scandal of athlete loyalty to salary over the team has become obvious, as recorded in *The Global Sports Arena: Athletic Talent Migration in an Interdependent World* (Bale & Maguire, 1994). Even once-noncommercial university teams now compete for television money so ambitiously as to tempt them to cut corners in recruiting players, overseeing their academic advancement, and reporting problems with drug abuse or crime; Gary D. Funk has studied this in *Major Violation: The Unbalanced Priorities in Athletics and Academics* (1991). Television has led the way to a thorough commercialization of sports. This has been documented in *The Name of the Game: The Business of Sports* (Gorman & Calhoun, 1994) and criticized in *Sports for Sale: Television, Money, and the Fans* (Katell & Marcus, 1988).

Television has also directly affected the sports themselves. In 1972, the Olympic basketball final in Munich was played at 11:30 p.m. to put it in early evening prime time in the States. In 1988, the Seoul Games were dubbed "the breakfast games" when more than half the track and field finals were held in the morning to fit U.S. television schedules. The Winter Olympics have been stretched from 12 to 16 days and spread over three weekends to maximize television appeal. Lengthened time-outs have brought an additional $43 million in to the National Basketball Association. In the early 1990s, the National Football League added time for five more 30-second commercials per game and added two more teams to the playoffs and two more weeks to the season, primarily to benefit television income.

The "symbiotic" (McChesney, 1989; Ruttle, 1989), or mutually beneficial, relationship between sport and media has paid off for both but has also brought commercial media concerns into the center of major sports decision making. This relationship has thoroughly "commodified" the experience of media sports for the viewer. Games are packaged and promoted as products. The viewer buys them by investing time and attention. The advertiser pays the television producer for access to that audience's time and attention. The viewer's experience results in a commodified super fan who drinks beer, wears Nike shoes and a Raiders hat or Bulls jacket, and consumes whatever other commodities successfully embed themselves in the commodified text of media sports.

Are We "Deep Fans"?

Do media sports qualify as "deep play" in Geertz's meaning of the term?

Geertz (1973, p. 432) borrows the phrase from Jeremy Bentham to characterize "play in which the stakes are so high that it is . . . irrational for men to engage in it at all." If a man wagers half his life's savings on an even bet, the disadvantage of his potential loss is greater than the advantage of his potential gain. In deep play, both parties are "in over their heads" (p. 432) and the participants stand collectively to reap net pain rather than net pleasure. Bentham considered such activity immoral and preferably illegal. Geertz, however, notes that there are symbolic and utilitarian issues in deep play: "Much more is at stake than material gain: namely esteem, honor, dignity, respect . . . status" (p. 433). Psychological and financial stakes increase the meaningfulness of it all, and Geertz calls on Max Weber to remind us that "the imposition of meaning on life is the major and primary condition of human existence" (p. 434).

The deep fan of contemporary media sports bears remarkable similarities to the participant in Geertz's Balinese cockfight. First, both the cockfight and sports provide double meanings and metaphors that reach out to other aspects of social life. Second, both are elaborately organized with written rules and umpires, although one might grant that presenting Wimbledon tennis to the world considerably outstrips organizing a local cockfight. Third, betting plays a major role in each; the Balinese wager serious amounts, and American sports attract an estimated $41 billion a year in gambling (Wilstein, 1993). Fourth, violence heightens the drama of each. Fifth, the presence of status hierarchies surpasses money in importance at the event, with corporate and political elites assuming central roles; competition between high-status individuals makes the game "deeper" to Geertz. Sixth, each of the two, the cockfight and the media sporting event, "makes nothing happen"; neither produces goods or directly affects the welfare of the people.

The big game on television works almost exactly like the cockfight: "The cockfight renders ordinary, everyday experience comprehensible by presenting it in terms of acts and objects which have had their practical consequences removed and been reduced (or, if one prefers, raised) to the level of sheer appearances, where their meaning can be more powerfully articulated and more exactly perceived" (Geertz, 1973, p. 443). A close Olympic finals competition, a well-matched World Cup game, a British Cup final between Liverpool and Arsenal (Barnett, 1990, p. 139; Hornby, 1992), a college or professional season-ending championship game in your favorite sport—many of these imitate the way the cockfight presents "death, masculinity, rage, pride, loss, beneficence, chance—and, ordering them into an encompassing structure" (Geertz, 1973, p. 443). These events ironically become real in an ideational sense. The deep fan learns what the Balinese learns from the cockfight, "what his culture's ethos and his private sensibility . . . look like when spelled out externally in a collective text" (p. 449).

Symbolically, then, the deep play of the participant in a Balinese cockfight has become diffused in a pluralistic society into the varied spectator sports available for live or mediated participation by today's deep fan. Sports activities create between 1% and 2% of the gross national product of the United States (Samuelson, 1989, p. 49). But their symbolic or expressive importance is far greater than that for many Americans because they provide a language or interpretive structure that at once reflects, explains, and interprets social life. Media sports today operate in a specific historical arrangement of technology, advertising, and consumerism. These mass-mediated sports give the deep fan crucial expressive, liminal, cathartic, ideational mechanisms and experiences. They represent, celebrate, and interpret contemporary social life, warts and all.

Understanding the ritual dimensions of media culture is essential to understanding how humans act as they encounter texts and technology.

Case Two: At the Gym—
With Aerobic Movement, Music, and Mirrors

This gym is one of 66 Family Fitness Centers spread throughout Southern California, with a total of some 200,000 members. Park the car, grab your workout towel, join in the fast-walking parade into the club. Sign in and show your membership card. (This is not an indulgence available to the indigent.) Select an activity. Mostly males in the free weight area. Mixed groups working the Nautilus machines. Mostly females in the aerobics room. As Four Non-Blonds ask over the sound system spread throughout the facility, "What's Going On?"

The most *physically* participatory form of media available makes the ritual participant jump, stretch, and sweat. This media subject follows the directions of the aerobics instructor, moves with the musical aerobics tape, and critically improves performance by feedback from enough mirrors to rival Versailles. What does this "mean" and how does it relate to media culture?[1] Unlike football and major media sports, aerobics is a sport dominated by women. Feminist debate over aerobics asks whether the motivation and goals of women doing aerobics has been subtly co-opted by patriarchal culture telling women they must have "the look" that men like. Susan Willis (1991) asserts that recuperative pressure on aerobics takes "women's positive desires for strength, agility, and the physical affirmation of self and transforms these into competition over style and rivalry for a particular body look and performance" (p. 70). Cheryl Cole (1994) and Jennifer Hargreaves (1994) echo Willis' charge. But Mary Duffy and Maura Rhodes (1993) claim the reverse, that motivation has changed in recent years: "The aesthetic payoffs took a back seat to the pragmatic . . . away from the emphasis on how we look to how we feel" (p. 17). Are aerobic exercise classes liberating and self-determining for women or confining and determined by the male gaze? Can an ethnographic description of aerobic workouts resolve this question?

Workout routines, fitness clubs, and a new generation of exercise styles evolved in the second half of the twentieth century, particularly among the more privileged in affluent urban and suburban areas. On television this emerged with Jack LaLanne and Richard Simmons. On video the trend came in the form of workout tapes by Jane Fonda and, it seems, every celebrity short of Orson Welles. By 1985, an estimated 22 million people were participating in aerobic dance exercise. The once-generic "gym shoes" became a high-tech commodity with infinite variations: running, tennis, walking, basketball, soccer, crosstraining—specializations for every leisure activity except bingo. Running became a status symbol as much as golf remained a business bonding routine. New workout clubs emerged as privatized heirs to the YMCA, public parks, and school recreation facilities. Higher status than the working class boxing gym but lower status than the private country club with its leisurely golf, swimming, tennis, and social life, fitness clubs have become a haven especially for upwardly mobile, fitness-freak yuppies.

Patterns of exercise and fitness, like styles in food or architecture, are cultural indicators. Yoga represents a peaceful, self-controlled, disciplined form of workout and mind-body integration; it goes with a nonexploitive, nonviolent lifestyle and culture. Yoga is especially associated with gentle Hindu culture in India, with echoes of Gandhi as its symbol. Martial arts can be either aggressive or used only defensively. In the 1970s, the introduction of "Chairman Mao's Four-Minute Exercise Plan" to the West gave Westerners access to an unusual combination of stretching and martial movement blended for mass health in the People's Republic of China. That exercise system would be unlikely to be developed anywhere else but in that collective culture. Popular forms of exercise and fitness, especially when they incorporate media, relate to larger cultural and ideological trends in curious ways.

But is aerobics not a face-to-face, *unmediated* experience in which technologies of communication do not intervene? After all, a live instructor is leading an exercise class. How is this media culture? Is it not simply small group interpersonal interaction? On close examination, both the technologies and mystique of aerobics make such classes reliant on the pulsating power of amplified prerecorded music, the instructor's microphone, the visual feedback of extensive mirror arrangements, lighting and air movement technology, and the public awareness that comes from popular media exposure. Take away modern forms of media technology and aerobics would not happen. There would be no vehicles through which aerobics could promote itself and the public could be attracted to it except word of mouth. Take away media technology in the activity itself and you have a boring school gym class or football calisthenics workout. (Research indicates that compelling music significantly increases the length and rigor of workouts.) Aerobics exists at least as much within media culture as outside it. In fact, it is doubtful that a better example can be found to counter the myth that media audiences are passive.

This chapter explores exercise and culture in the age of media culture by combining an examination of gender issues in sport and fitness with an ethnographic description of aerobic workouts based on numerous brief interviews with aerobics instructors and students and some 350 to 400 hours of participant observation spread over 7 years.

Sports, Feminism, Violence, and Male Hegemony

> Many young women today do not realize that exercise for women as a widely available and socially acceptable endeavor represents a recent victory in women's struggle for equality with men.
>
> I want to look at women's exercise, bearing in mind its narrowly defined constituency, but realizing at the same time that middle-class white America defines the model and the look of consumer capitalism. I also want to maintain a sense of all the positive features that exercise for women generates, including the development of independence and the opportunity for bonding between women; but I want particularly to scrutinize the way exercise has evolved in a commodified society so as to contain or limit these positive features. (Willis, 1991, p. 65)

Sport and exercise form one of the more heavily contested terrains today in the struggle by women for self-determination. Inherited gender-based attitudes and practices around developing and working out "the body" are complex and subtle and have tremendous influence. Feminist critiques have uncovered multiple dimensions of the conflict. The project that Susan Willis assigned herself, to assess women's exercise, has many levels.

"Sports remains a bunch of boys observing what a bunch of boys do together," according to Sally Jenkins, senior writer for *Sports Illustrated* (Cramer, 1994, p. 159). Against this contemporary cultural norm, Pamela J. Creedon poses the figure of Artemis, the ancient Greek goddess of physicality and the hunt, often portrayed with a bow stretched to shoot. Artemis is distanced from male society because she can protect and hunt and because her femininity is not defined in relationship to a lover, child, father, or husband (Creedon, 1994a, p. 278). As Christine Downing (1988) says, "Artemis embodies a profound denial of the world of patriarchy, the world where some persons have power over others, the world of dominance and submission . . . ." (p. 176). *Patriarchy,* in this sense, is defined as the institutionalized system of male dominance over women and children in the family and society in general (pp. 277-278).

Despite various matriarchal societies earlier and elsewhere, the history of the West is a long, one-sided patriarchal tale. Gerda Lerner in *The Creation of Patriarchy* (1986) notes how profound the embedding of male domination has been:

> We should note the way in which inequality among men and women was built not only into the language, thought, and philosophy of Western civilization, but the way in which gender itself became a metaphor defining power relations in such a way as to mystify them and render them invisible. (p. 211)

The documented history of women's sports (Guttmann, 1991) and masculine responses (Messner & Sabo, 1990) finds them operating in an environment of patriarchal domination. Michael Messner has summarized the modern Western history of gender and sport in "Sports and Male Domination: The Female Athlete as Contested Ideological Terrain" (1994). Patriarchal ideology presents the division between the sexes as being of biological, natural, or divine essence, instead of being historically constructed. The first "crisis of masculinity" occurred from 1890 to 1920, when fewer men owned their own business or controlled their own labor. Organized sports became increasingly important as a primary masculinity-validating experience (p. 68).

The second "crisis of masculinity" followed World War II, as traditional means of male expression eroded with the bureaucratization of work, an increasingly service-oriented economy, and increased structural unemployment, at the same time as women continued to move into public life. Messner concludes, "Sports in the postwar era have become increasingly important to males precisely because they link men to a more patriarchal past" (p. 70). This works especially well with North American football: "Football, based as it is upon the most extreme possibilities of the male body (muscular bulk, explosive power and aggression) is a world apart from women, who are relegated to the role of cheerleader/sex objects on the sidelines rooting their men on" (p. 71). Messner observes finally,

> The current wave of women's athleticism expresses a genuine quest by women for equality, control of their own bodies, and self-definition, but within historical limits and constraints imposed by a consumption-oriented corporate capitalism and men's continued attempts to retain power and privilege over women. (p. 77)

In "Sport and the Maintenance of Masculine Hegemony," Lois Bryson (1994) asserts that sports support male dominance by "linking maleness with highly valued and visible skills and with the positively sanctioned use of aggression/force/violence" (p. 59). This linkage is made by the types of sports men play—in Australia, football and cricket, according to Bryson—and by the celebration of men's sports in the public arena and media. Ritual elements of sports strengthen the male hegemony and male solidarity, not just for teams but for men in general. She warns, "Sport needs to be analyzed along with rape, pornography, and domestic violence as one of the means through which men monopolize physical force" (p. 60).

These concerns motivated Mariah Burton Nelson to write *The Stronger Women Get, the More Men Love Football: Sexism and the American Culture of Sports* (1994a). A former Stanford and professional basketball player herself, Nelson asserts,

Many women are angry at football, basketball, baseball, boxing, ice hockey, wrestling, soccer—sports that I call the manly sports; sports that men use to define masculinity. . . .

Women seem to intuit that football and other manly sports hurt women. There's something about the way certain games are played and the way they're worshipped that's injurious to women's mental and physical health. When Patricia Bowman testified that William Kennedy Smith "tackled" her on the lawn, we cringed. When Desiree Washington testified that boxer Mike Tyson "pinned" her to the bed, then raped her, we were furious but not surprised. When a new "sports bar" opens in New York and it features topless dancers, we understand that this seems natural to the bar's owners and enthusiastic patrons. We sense a connection: there's something about male sports privilege that contributes to the sexual objectification and abuse of women. Given how pervasive and what cultural icons men's sports are, that's a scary thought. (pp. 4-5)

Nelson is concerned by an American culture in which more than 2 million women each year are beaten by husbands or boyfriends, where 1,400 women each year die at the hands of their "lovers." Following Catherine MacKinnon, Nelson notes how sports to men are a form of combat. You assert yourself against an object, a person, a standard. Physicality for men has meant male dominance, force, coercion, and the ability to subdue and subject the natural world, one central part of which has been women. Locker room talk feeds this and the whole sports ethos today exudes it. Nelson quotes quarterback Tim Rosenbach when he quit professional football after the 1992 season:

I thought I was turning into some kind of animal. You go through a week getting yourself up for a game by hating the other team, the other players. You're so mean and hateful, you want to kill somebody. Football's so aggressive. Things get done by force. And then you come home, you're supposed to turn it off? "Oh, here's your lovin' daddy." It's not that easy.

It was like I was an idiot. I felt programmed. I had become a machine. (Nelson, 1994b, p. B5)

Women's interest in sports is not only driven by a belief in a woman being able to do what she wants; it is also self-defense. As a consequence, the "F" word in sports is not a four-letter word but an eight-letter word. Feminism is the "F" word today in sports. Why? The four-letter word means business as usual; the eight-letter word threatens to change things (Creedon, 1994b, p. 7). Why are sports a women's issue? Mariah Burton Nelson (1994a) answers emphatically,

Sport is a women's issue because on playing fields, male athletes learn to talk about and think about women and women's bodies with contempt . . . It's a women's issue because the media itself cheers for men's sports and rarely covers women's, thereby reinforcing the notion that men are naturally more athletic. . . . And it's a women's issue because female sport participation empowers women, thereby inexorably changing everything. (p. 9)

Aerobic Exercise Classes:
"With Every Beat of My Heart"

Given the force of feminist interest in sports, what might turn up in a detailed analysis of a fitness activity dominated by women, namely, aerobic exercise classes? In a cultural sense, what is the typical experience and meaning to those who participate in aerobic workouts? "Thick description" in the form of ethnography has revealed a great deal about media and ritual. In-depth interviews and focus group discussions have been used by David Morley, Janice Radway, James Lull, Shaun Moores, Annette Kuhn, and others to probe the "meaning" of actually participating in media activity, of interacting with media technology and texts.

In ethnography, the terminology and interpretations become those of the participants rather than a priori analytic categories. This follows Geertz' model in examining the Balinese cockfight. In ethnography we "pitch our tent with the natives" (Christians & Carey, 1981) and "interpret the interpretations" (Geertz, 1973). We avoid deductive over-generalizations. Getting in among the people has opened important avenues for cultural studies. Richard Hoggart (1957) pioneered the break from elitist literary studies by going back to his own roots and exploring the working class culture of music halls and popular recreations. Dick Hebdige's work with the subculture of unemployed working class youths (1979) did not find them inarticulate and uncomprehending in the manner of traditional sociological caricatures. Instead, the alienated punks were consciously using shopping malls and popular music to articulate resistance and opposition to the dominant but rejected culture. Only by "reading the text of the culture over their shoulders" (Geertz, 1973) can we discover what it means to the people who express themselves in it.

The subjects of most ethnographies, members of pretechnological societies studied by anthropologists, would be amazed to observe a modern workout club. Physical effort is expended at intense levels for no external result. A traditional labor-intensive society would build bridges, buildings, or roads with the kind of physical effort expended in a health club. A poor society would rig up the exercycles and other machines to produce electricity or some other outcome from all the muscle force exerted. But the health club uses physical effort for internal, personal benefit, not for external accomplishments. In the framework of human evolution, workout clubs seem to occupy a compensation niche for a species that has evolved many forms of work that are mentally but not physically demanding and has surrounded those jobs with labor-saving, creature-comfort devices that eliminate physical exertion.

The aerobics classes at the Family Fitness Center are typical of those around the world. The growth and structure of aerobics is reflected in the development of the International Dance Exercise Association (IDEA), active in 50 countries and attracting more than 5,000 instructors to its conventions. Likewise the American Council on Exercise (ACE) International certifies organizations in different countries and has certified more than 19,000 instructors internationally. The American Aerobics Association International (AAAI) has 80,000 members and has provided conferences and certification for instructors in Argentina, Colombia, Brazil, India, and numerous locations around the world. The Aerobics and Fitness Association of America (AFAA), founded in 1983, has more than 80,000 members in 73 countries and more than 70,000 certified instructors, and claims to be "the world's largest fitness educator." Such organizations offer certification in primary aerobic instruction, step instruction, fitness practitioner training, personal training, fitness counseling, weight room/ resistance training, and first-aid and emergency response in addition to specialty workshops, extension programs, continuing education, home study courses, educational publications, and national and international special events.

What does an ethnography of aerobics uncover about the media culture experience of an aerobics class?

At the La Jolla Family Fitness Center, there are 51 aerobics classes scheduled each week, plus 4 yoga classes and 1 "kidz danz" class. The schedule is almost identical to that of clubs such as the Club Montmartrois in Paris, which offers 47 classes per week in categories similar to those of the La Jolla Center, though with more labeling by muscle groups—abs, glutes, and so forth. Clubs of this type exist in major cities in many countries. The typical LaJolla FFC aerobics class has perhaps 30 participants ranging from people in their late teens to the active elderly, but with the majority in their twenties and thirties. Asian, Latino, and black participants comprise typically 20 percent of participants, overrepresenting Asians from the general population and underrepresenting the other two groups. Women typically make up 80 to 90 percent of the classes and the instructors. Members of the club typically pay $100 to $150 to join, depending on various membership packages, and $10 to $15 dollars in monthly fees, depending on length of membership. Although the club was remodeled only a few years ago and is in an upscale shopping mall, the rich have finer clubs available and the poor are not represented.

Many activities are aerobic, that is, highly oxygen consuming, but the "aerobic exercise class" is a group activity in which an instructor leads a group in rapid, organized movement accompanied by music for the purpose of conditioning and cardiovascular improvement. The leader calls out the moves rather choppily in 4/4 cadence devoid of the verbal stylizations of square dance calling, and illustrates them too. Members of the group, spaced in rows around the room, follow the instructions and copy the moves of the leader. Aerobics is a thoroughly centralized activity in which the leader has total control over the music, the sequence of moves and routines, and the manner in which movements are performed. Leadership can be passed around during a class, but this happens less than 3 percent of the time. The style is authoritarian within a context of voluntary participation.

The sound system is operated by the instructor and feeds 14 speakers planted in the ceiling. The music is normally pop with a very strong, repetitious beat. The volume is normally loud but not overwhelming because of a museum upstairs that "feels" overly loud music despite the baffling insulation in the ceiling. The musical style may be technopop, mainstream rock, Motown funk, rap, salsa, or even heavy metal or country western. The *sine qua non* of the music is a strong, consistent rhythm. Lyric content is clearly nonessential, as becomes obvious if one notes the words: "Work that body, work that body, work that body," "Push it, push it real good," "You take me up the mountain," "Get up, get up, get moving." Instructors are prevented by copyright law, enforced by ASCAP and BMI, from preparing or trading their own compilations of pop songs. However, legally licensed compilations are continuously available from more than a dozen companies. The warm-up in the beginning is often done to songs with a moderate but brisk beat, then stronger, more aggressive music carries the middle or peak workout and slower songs, even ballads, lower the exercise heart rate during the ending cool-down.

As in other exercise and self-improvement programs, aerobic activities are carefully graded for ability level, age, and personal preferences. Aerobic instructors excel in particular categories and are identified on the wall schedule by their first names, "Michelle, 8 a.m., Beginning Step," "Norm, 5:30 p.m., High Impact." The low-impact class eases participants through physiologically vigorous routines with the impact on the muscular-skeletal structure diminished. "Fat-burner" instruction offers low impact combined with more exacting form, concentration, and attention to tightening specific muscle groups. High-impact instructors resemble dance ensemble leaders and may show the effects of formal training in jazz dance, ballet, or gymnastics. Step aerobics instructors also may teach low impact, fat burner, or high impact but are often classified as simply "advanced" or "basic step."

Advanced step classes not only may be demanding and rapid but also may feature complex routines. Whereas basic classes often repeat movements to counts of four or eight with many repetitions at each number, the advanced step instructor may have the class doing combinations that extend into two-, four-, or eight-part sequences that each include four- and eight-count routines within each part of the sequence. A single sequence may move from basic step-up-step-down to alternating knee lifts with a T movement off the front and end of the step, straddling steps up and down, lunges up and down, and then a cross over the board to repeat all those movements in a mirror pattern on the other side of the step board. Such complex patterns hold the concentration of advanced students and drive away the unpolished, who quickly become hopelessly lost and, in a crowded room, may fear crashing into others.

The ability to concentrate on and lead such intricate, complex patterns counters the bubble-head stereotype of aerobics instructors. The most rigorous advanced instructors are not only superbly conditioned athletes but also rigorously self-disciplined and intelligent goal achievers. The ability to continue a movement while cueing the next movement for the group is especially demanding. The instructors at the La Jolla FFC include accountants, flower shop owners, college students, waiters, journalists, and others. A not-atypical instructor at this gym is Michelle Mazzoni. A native of Minnesota, she completed a PhD in bioengineering with a 4.0 average and works as a research scientist in addition to leading aerobics classes at varying levels each day of the week.

The entire environment of the workout gym is systematic, technological, industrial, and methodical. Nautilus machines and free weights isolate muscle groups and require methodical repetitions in sets. Members tend to appear serious and intent, breathing deeply and exerting effort as they move through their personal routines. There may be only three or four small conversations in rooms of 40 and 50 people. Men may gaze around the room from time to time, but the concentration in general is "internal" as members focus on effort, feel, and completeness. Some members may succumb to excesses of self-preoccupation in the gym and beyond, but for others the mirrors may be less a narcissistic flatterer than a nasty reminder of imperfection, to be ignored if possible but capable of motivating by guilt as needed. This issue of motivation is the focus of the debate among feminists discussed on the following pages.

Aerobic means "in the presence of oxygen," as opposed to *anaerobic,* which means "in the absence of oxygen." Aerobic fitness results from at least a minimal degree of training in such endurance activities as distance running, cycling, exercise walking, distance swimming, or aerobic dance. The one-hour class is a classic aerobic activity with exercise heart rate measured during several pauses in each class.

What are the health benefits of aerobics? McDonald and Hodgdon (1991) have summarized the results of numerous empirical studies of the effects of aerobic fitness. They report that successful aerobic exercise programs protect against coronary heart disease, increase oxygen capacity, reduce total body mass and fat weight, decrease blood pressure, improve carbohydrate metabolism, improve bone density in women, improve slow wave sleep, create higher levels of energy for longer periods, improve digestion, control constipation, improve intellectual capacity and productivity, and, at least temporarily, modify other health habits such as diet intake (pp. 17, 25). In addition, 90 studies of the psychological effects of aerobic exercise find that it is effective in combating, in decreasing order of effect, depression, anxiety, low self-esteem, and social maladjustment (pp. 182-186). Effects were similar for men and women except that women showed slightly less effect for certain forms of depression and anxiety. Results were virtually identical for young adults (<30) and middle-aged adults (30-60), and were similar but less complete for older adults (>60).

Gender and Aerobic Exercise:
Is It Liberating or Regressive?

Are aerobics classes that are developed for women's use entirely self-determined by independent female concerns or do patriarchal influences distort the motivation and participation into something else?

Aerobics has a strong female orientation that contrasts with many men's sports activities. Unlike traditional men's body-building gyms, clubs catering to women often include a nursery for young children and pay greater attention to brighter colors, lighting, and acoustics. There is no score keeping and no winners and losers in aerobics, common ingredients of competitive men's sports. There is little value in a spectator relationship to aerobics; it is something to *do,* not to watch, despite loiterers (most commonly male) occasionally hanging around the entranceways to the aerobics room or passively watching aerobics on television. As previously explained, women have historically been excluded and stereotyped by the sports world. Yet women engage in the demanding participation of aerobic workout classes far more often than men, in a ratio of 8 or 10 to 1. Aerobics is one area of exercise that women have in many respects carved out for themselves.

Studies in Great Britain indicate that women are less likely to engage in regular exercise despite organized programs to increase their numbers. In 1986, 56.9 percent of men participated and 37.2 percent of women were involved, making a total of roughly 10 million men and 7 million women (Hargreaves, 1994, p. 240). A 1991 survey found interesting differences in men's and women's sports activities:

39 percent of active sportsmen take their sport seriously or quite seriously, compared to only 17 percent of sportswomen. And 33 percent of the women questioned never take part in any sport, compared with 17 percent of the men. And in the traditional male sports such as football and rugby, men still massively outnumber women. In golf, male players outnumber female players by seven to one, though in athletics and jogging the ratio drops to three to one. Squash has seen a fall-off in female players over recent years and tennis, traditionally enjoyed by both sexes, has more male players. Only keep-fit and aerobics appeal almost exclusively to women, and, interestingly, weight training has gained popularity with women (6 percent of women compared to 14 percent of men). Marginally more women are still taking a dip, and swimming is by far the most popular sport enjoyed by both sexes. (Hargreaves, 1994, p. 240)

Susan Willis (1991) puts such trends in perspective by noting how different the context for women was as recently as 1971, when the Boston Women's Health Collective published its historic resource book for women, *Our Bodies, Ourselves.* Recently rereading that book, Willis writes: "I was amazed by the book's comparatively mild chapter on exercise. It urges women to get into exercise, investigate a YMCA program, or consider taking up a sport such as swimming, tennis, perhaps jogging. How tame these suggestions seem by comparison to the exercise standards many women set for themselves today" (p. 65). Sixty-minute aerobic workouts four or five times a week or jogging 25 miles a week have replaced the simple exercise class for women at the Y. Those older community recreation programs, however, often promoted bonding between women, conversation, and a sense of community that cut across generations and socioeconomic class; participants reported "they most appreciate getting to know, and to laugh and sweat with other women" (p. 70). For Willis, those social benefits are lost when the experience becomes individualized, privatized, and commodified by reducing it to a workout tape on television or typically silent attendance at a commercial health club, with some participants even wearing the privatizing earplugs of an individualized Walkman-style music system. Willis sees emerging in women's workouts a "body rivalry" that was long a feature of men's exercise. As previously noted, Willis perceives a trend that takes "women's positive desires for strength, agility, and the physical affirmation of self and transforms these into competition over style and rivalry for a particular body look and performance" (p. 70).

Rivalry and competition are vaguely evident within the aerobic workouts at the La Jolla FFC even in the absence of competitive score keeping. One can observe an elevated status among those who can perform at or near the front of an aerobics class without making mistakes or wearing down. One aerobics respondent explained how nervous she gets on the way to a class because she is afraid of not doing well. She suspects other women are noticing whether she is as good as she should be. Another respondent finds aerobics relaxing because she is doing it for herself and honestly does not care how she looks to anyone else as she does it. Unlike the "competitor," this "relaxer" stays toward the back of the aerobics room. When asked what aerobics means to her, one instructor responded typically: "It gets the heart pumped up. Fun. A cardiovascular workout. I like teaching better than taking it. At least I know the music's good."

A female interest is sometimes reflected in the introductory explanations by aerobics instructors; they convey concern for *trimming* specific body areas—the abdomen, referred to as "abs" or "tummy tucking"; the gluteus maximus, called "glutes" or "buns" as in Tammilee Webb's *Buns of Steel* (1992); quads; hips; shoulders; arms, and so forth. In contrast, more male-dominated weight training tends to "bulk up" muscles. Given that distinction, women in body building and men in aerobics are resisting sex typing, often with a degree of explicit awareness. The woman wants to be strong, the man trim, both against standard sex typing. There are specific aerobic activities that women protest—the announcement of push-ups occasionally brings groans and complaints from females. And there are others that men find awkward—hip flexors and wide-legged floor stretches that even male aerobics instructors do not excel in.

Willis (1991) finds an excess of exaggerated female sexuality in such workouts. She is particularly concerned with the "gendered look" produced by the workout: "long Barbie-doll legs, strikingly accentuated by irides-cent hot pink tights, offset by a pair of not too floppy purple legwarmers . . . and finally a color coordinated headband (or wristbands)" (p. 72). More recently, the de rigueur attire included crop tops and thong leotards or biking shorts. When workout clothes are worn doing errands to and from the gym, Willis finds their implied liberatory statement about seizing control over the making and shaping of a woman's body becomes instead a defensive over-gendering of the female. Thus, the gendered look of successful workouts for women contains the contradiction of asserting control and self-definition but conforming to cultural image norms defined primarily by the male gaze. The healthy utopian dimensions of realizing an ideal as defined by and for oneself and as experienced internally fight in dialectical tension with the stereotype of perfection driven home in the body types of health spa ads and commodity advertising in general.

What agreements are present in feminist critiques of aerobics? Cheryl L. Cole (1994) repeats Willis' charges that privatized workouts in commercial clubs and on video isolate women from one another and promote rivalry based on "the look." Jennifer Hargreaves (1994) also echoes Willis:

Although there are aerobics classes, for example, that take place in community facilities rather than commercial venues, and cater for women who are more interested in the enjoyment of exercise and the social interaction with other women than with the ideal of a beautiful body, they are in the minority. Aerobics has been successfully packaged to persuade women, specifically, to participate in order to lose weight and improve their sex-appeal, rather than for reasons of fitness and enjoyment or for competition. . . . The focus of publicity is on appearance (the athletic looking body), fashion (the trendy-looking image) and physique (the sexy-looking shape); rather than on movement (the active-looking woman). The idea of exercise is blurred with sexuality. . . . (p. 160)

The last point about publicity and media coverage is certainly true. Horne and Bentley (1989, p. 4) argue that "Fitness Chic" magazines promise fitness but are really built around "the look." Even the publicity for the Family Fitness Centers studied here often present images of attractive young men and women who look more like professional models than athletes.

The televised forms of aerobics raise particular problems. Margaret Mac-Neill (1994) has studied in detail the presentation of aerobics in the popular Canadian program *20 Minute Workout* and compared this with presentation of a women's bodybuilding competition. She is specifically concerned with how television presentations have hegemonic effects. "The everyday practice of sending young girls to figure-skating lessons while their brothers go to the arenas to play hockey is an example of hegemonic relations" (p. 274). For aerobic participation, MacNeill notes that the camera aimed directly at the instructor with a full body shot is ideal as a standard frame for the active viewer. However, the *20 Minute Workout* used this view for only 36.63% of the shots. Another 18.28% of the shots were aerial shots from above, accentuating " 'cleavage' shots of the women, in their low-cut leotards, exercising on a rotating stage" (p. 276). The largest number of shots, 47.08%, were from an upwardly tilting angle, usually when participants were bent over from the waist. In addition, 62.57% of all shots were close-ups and medium shots rather than full-body shots. Predominantly, the hips, thighs, and buttocks were emphasized. Also, 32.79% of all shots zoomed in or out. The rotating stage and camera angles and movement thus "titillated by the constant visual caressing of the female body" (p. 278). In other studies of sports media production, MacNeill has specified the ways in which the gendered tastes of the male production crew affect such shot and camera movement selections.

Evaluating the television coverage, MacNeill acknowledges that aerobics is "counterhegemonic to the notion that intense physical activity for women is harmful" and symbolizes "the increased opportunities for physical activity which are opening to women," but this occurs "in a form that stresses a preoccupation with beauty, glamour, and sex appeal as status symbols" (p. 281). As a consequence, aerobics on television "caters to the voyeur through the sexualization of the images," and the objectification of body parts "tends to fabricate pornographic and erotic myths" (p. 284). The presentational mode, then, of aerobics on television aligns it with dominant hegemonic relations and recuperates its liberating potential back into conformity with patriarchal culture.

Qualifying the Feminist Critique

But what of aerobics classes themselves in a feminist context? There are reasons to question the charges that commercialized facilities isolate women from each other and that participants are motivated by goals having to do with appearance rather than fitness. Some feminist criticisms may be based on an earlier, less mature generation of aerobics. A report by Mary Duffy and Maura Rhodes (1993) in *Women's Health and Fitness* is more consistent with our ethnographic observations and reports than are some of the charges by Willis, Cole, and Hargreaves. Duffy and Rhodes report,

> Ten years ago, many women donned form-fitting leotards and pranced and puffed their way through an hour-long aerobics class for the *express purpose of looking good* in said garment. Spurred by vanity and a diehard crash-dieting mentality, dance exercisers faced the music and the mirror in hopes of sweating off—fast—what flab they couldn't diet off. (p. 17, italics added)

In contrast, Duffy and Rhodes report that more recently "the aesthetic payoffs took a back seat to the pragmatic" (p. 17). Aerobics participants found they felt better between workouts and had more stamina for work days and chore-packed weekends. They find this important change in motive has contributed to a slow but sure change in the mode and mood of aerobics classes. A 14-year veteran of teaching aerobics, Molly Fox, told Duffy and Rhodes, "It's been a gradual evolution of awareness away from the emphasis on how we look to how we feel" (p. 17). The health benefits, longer experience with the rigors and effects of aerobics, learning from injuries, and a practical desire to maximize the payoff in quality of life have made current aerobics instructors and students wiser than the first generation. Familiarity with exercise physiology and biomechanics has greatly increased. Duffy and Rhodes report, "what it all boils down to is a more holistic approach to exercise. The concern is not just how strong, toned, and well-developed certain muscles are, but how well all the major muscle groups work together as a team" (p. 18).

This sophistication, which one finds frequently reflected in random comments of aerobics participants, conflicts with the implication that aerobics has been irrevocably "recuperated" by male hegemony and patriarchal culture. Women still predominate in aerobics and there is little hard evidence that all of them, or even most of them, are driven by the goal of achieving the sexualized image of "the look" to please others. Aerobics participants are happy to look good, but many express motivations well beyond that. When asked why participants take or teach aerobic classes, responses cluster around "I enjoy it," "It makes me feel good," "I'm healthier," "It gives me energy," and so on. They may also add, "it keeps me looking better" but even that may reflect a concern for visible healthiness as much as sexual attractiveness. Based on my interviews with participants and until there is ethnographic evidence to the contrary, there seems little reason to generalize broadly that aerobics students are motivated exclusively or even principally by the hegemonic demands of "the look."

The conflict between internal and external motivation, however, is real and continuous. The exercise industry appears to be slowly moving away from the external emphasis on "the look," but the vast majority of persons first attracted to aerobics may well be motivated by the look. Instructors discuss the limits of aerobics and warn, for example, that one cannot change body fat in particular spots through aerobics, but they find participants wanting to do just that. But as the exercising population ages, it tends to shift from external motives to more internal, health-oriented goals. The baby-boom generation that jumped into high-impact classes in their 20s turned toward lower impact in their 30s, and now are shifting toward yoga and more functional goals in exercise. This shift is not consistent across the board, however, and does meet resistance.

The assertion that aerobics in commercial clubs isolates women from each other and prevents the solidarity alleged to occur in the older community centers and YMCAs also requires further documentation. Participants in the classes studied often hustled into and out of the club and classes without speaking with others, but the overriding impression is that they want their workout to be "efficient," with maximum benefits and minimum time. Their social life is clearly elsewhere. Often conversations arise after classes, particularly around the instructor. These constitute about as much social interaction as takes place anywhere in these clubs, between men or women. Two-person conversations between people working on stationary machines sometimes take place, and conversations are slightly more common in the male-dominated free weights area than around the Nautilus machines. But it is quite evident that the lifestyles of the vast majority of members of the Family Fitness Center include the gym for physical fitness purposes and not for other affective concerns. This may, however, be less true in many other aerobics settings, where the search for friends and affective relationships combines with the search for health and fitness. Less yuppie-dominated clubs sometimes feature large groups of women participants moving to a health bar to chat for an hour following exercise.

Still, it appears that for most participants aerobics retains the liberating, self-actualizing female potential originally ascribed to it, without being completely victimized by the recuperative forces that exercise great influence over the mediated presentations of these activities on television and in magazines.

At the same time, it should be acknowledged that the utopian potential of aerobics for women is greatly reduced by its current practice, in contrast to the male bonding and ideology generated around traditional men's sports activities. The centuries-old, established male sports culture serves a wide range of psychological, sociological, and hegemonic functions that bind men in an aggressive, interactive solidarity. There is no sports equivalent to that for women in aerobics or elsewhere. The culture of female bonding is built around less physically active recreational pursuits. But if Morley, Gray, Moores, Lull, and other ethnographers of media experience are correct, there is no reason to think that women are not active, critical readers of the culture, including the recuperated aspects of aerobics. If Mary Ellen Brown (1994) can rightly find so much "reactive pleasure" available to women in talk around soap operas, then aerobics and fitness activities will certainly continue to be seized and used effectively by and for women: "Feminist ethnographic work has dealt with resistive pleasure—Radway's (1984) study of romance novels, Ang's (1985) analysis of *Dallas* viewers, Walkerdine's (1986) observation of family television viewing, or McRobbie's (1984) theorization of the resistive position of dance for young women" (Brown, 1994, p. 182-183). In aerobics, feminist ethnography has a subject offering more than resistive potential without losing the strength of what Brown calls "emancipation through the constant awareness of contradiction and the struggle to secure a space for the voice of the female spectator who speaks as well as sees" (p. 182).

Aerobics offers genuine utopian possibilities because it combines exercise, fitness, solidarity, and dance art forms. On an experiential level, aerobics can initiate meaningful aesthetic experience. Like any demanding activity, it can make possible reaching "the zone," as elite athletes refer to the experience of peak performance. This utopian aspect appears in the experience of achieving personal goals as part of a communitarian activity; it is an extreme example of the "participatory culture" of Jenkins' (1992) textual poachers. The person and the group become a danced unity, an experience that may or may not spill over beyond that moment. The musical beat is working on participants, the instructor has everyone involved and challenged, and visual feedback from the mirrors cues and displays the unity. When everything is clicking for participants who relish aerobics or similar fitness and sports activities, they experience a "natural high." Endorphins pump through the system, stimulated by exertion and an elevated exercise heart rate, and this experience is shared. Subjects shift from participating in aerobics initially as a laborious task performed to achieve health benefits and improved appearance; over time they begin to enjoy "the pleasure of the text" of aerobics for its own sake and for its integral part in a healthy life. Aerobics then offers not merely fitness, but a kind of aesthetic experience.

Sport and exercise tend all too often to replicate the worst of the dominant patriarchal culture. Patriarchal hegemony can distort the healthful, self-determining qualities of aerobics into an other-directed search for "the look" that pleases the male gaze and into a gendered commodification of the participating subject. These antidemocratic pressures contradict self-determination and instead place control in the hands of others. Such pressures reduce the collective, healthful experience of feminine solidarity to competitive and individualistic regression into the dysfunctional modes of late capitalism. Yet the actual experience of aerobics participants shows considerable evidence that all is not lost. The emancipatory potential of aerobics may be limited but not eliminated by the patriarchal commodity form it can take on. Participants find considerable benefits in aerobics, both as women and as embodied humans. They experience satisfaction and self-determination in aerobics, even though the effects of its commodification and privatization cannot be denied.

Case Three: Electronic Participation
in Video Games and Cyberculture

A long time ago there were no toys and everyone was bored. Then they had TV, but they were bored again. They wanted control. So they invented video games. (Victor Aurelio Bautista, age 8, in Kinder, 1991, p. 1)

Media culture is especially important to trends associated with "cyberculture." New technologies of personal computing, the Internet, virtual reality, the interactive CD-ROM, video games, faxes, pagers, cellular communication, fiber optics, and the information superhighway combine with older technologies of television, video, film, radio, magazines, books, cable, microwave, and satellite to create a multidimensional, interactive, random access environment. The generation born from 1961 to 1981, "Generation X," especially knows life framed by these media realities. A variety of current subcultures dip in and out of the cyberculture of Generation X. The roots of cyberstyle, more or less, in music were punk rock, heavy metal, techno-industrial, and alternative; in clothing were Doc Martens, black leather, flannel shirts, or "skater"; and in visuals were pop art, MTV, and cyberpunk. Cyberculture may be euphoric about surfing technological frontiers but it is also skeptical, if not cynical, about human nature and easy happiness. The generation that knows the convenience and potential of information technology also knows life can be reduced and packaged, that McJobs do not offer a future worthy of major sacrifices, that "virtual" lives may be boring or even tragic.

William Gibson's *Neuromancer* and Douglas Coupland's *Generation X: Tales for an Accelerated Culture* are the *Iliad* and *Odyssey* of this brave new postmodern world, just as the CD-ROM hit *Myst* may be to interactive media what *The Great Train Robbery* was to narrative in film. Other authors— Bruce Craven, Mark Leyner, K. S. Haddock, Mark Kriegel, Poppy Z. Brite— echo Douglas Rushkoff (1994a) when he says, "We are the media generation." In *Media Virus* (1994a), *Cyberia: Life in the Trenches of Hyperspace* (1992), and *The GenX Reader* (1994b), Rushkoff argues that Generation X is defined by the experience of being truly children of the media. GenXers have an interactive, interpersonal sensibility about technology more than a passive attitude of consumption. The American mediascape "is more than a mirror of our culture; it *is* our culture" (1994a, p. 20). To Rushkoff, trends that seem very different are all part of the same social movement: "Raves and psychedelics and computers and role-playing games and chaos math are all part of a single society impulse toward more consciously designed and experienced reality" (Puckett, 1995, p. 14). Nesting in the gaps of metamedia, Rushkoff suggests, "Just as ecologists now understand the life on this planet to be part of a single biological organism, media activists see the datasphere as the circulatory system for today's information, ideas, and images" (1994a, p. 7).

As the cyberculture of high technology emerges still further, video games may prove to be an important training ground for that development.

Why Are There Video Games?

What do we learn about participation with media by examining human interaction with electronic video games?[2]

Video games are a precursor of the on-line age of Internet and universal information access and interaction, the age of the hacker cowboy. A massive industry thrives on this semiprivatized interaction with a machine. What are the attractions and implications of the fast-growing world of video games? Many skills not involved in traditional television reading are called for: hand-eye coordination, immediate sensory feedback, active suspension of normal timespace, godlike control of a universe, perception of complex patterns and choices, manipulation of representational violence, and others. Many challenges are posed for parents, schools, and children by these games. Video games significantly represent a new age in human-machine interfacing. "Virtual reality" games increase the total immersion of the ritually participating subject into a prepared media environment.

A typical video game places you in front of a screen with a joystick and buttons to control the action. You may compete alone with the machine or against an opponent. The goal is to work your way through a set of obstacles, challenges, and opponents to reach a series of destinations. Initial success may propel you to a new level of the game, a level with more complexity and some difference in rules. Your score is compiled based on a formula for timing and reflexes, successful evasion tactics, outmaneuvering and outfiring opponents, and collecting tokens, prizes, or tools along the way. Successful completion of levels with creativity, speed, and calculation rewards you with exciting victory graphics and triumphant music. Success leads to still higher levels of video gaming, until you become William Gibson's joystick riding super-cowboy of cyberspace from the classic cyberpunk text, *Neuromancer* (1983).

Will all media culture at some point in the future become a cyberculture of exotic technologies and human adaptation? Exploring video games in the context of media culture points to new modes of encoding and decoding information, of creating meaning structures, and of representing reality in a ritual activity. To assess the cultural place of video games we begin by asking, where have video games come from and where are they leading?

History and Growth of Video Games

Video games represent a major advance over the unidirectional flow of television. McConnell (1990) notes "the TV went one way—toward us and over what it had to tell us, we had precious little control" (p. 256, used by permission). In effect, interactive games and entertainment lifted the potato off the couch and inserted the viewer into the action on the screen.

Video games were dynamic improvements on previous game forms and on previous television viewing. Older board games required the participants to create all the interaction, whereas video games added visual movement and sounds (Walker, 1993). Board games such as *Monopoly* and *Clue* tended to teach young people to develop strategy, think and plan ahead, be patient, play fairly, take turns, and follow written directions. Video games are based instead on classical conditioning theory; the sights, sounds, and colors are reinforcers. They are fast-paced and entertaining. They teach some of the same abilities as older board games yet they reduce, without necessarily eliminating, the interpersonal interaction. Many video games teach "cooperative" skills but in a different manner than board games.

Video games bring together computing, narrativity, and graphic art. Their history begins with the simple table-tennis-like game of *Pong* (Kinder, 1991). The coin-operated *Pong* was the first successful totally electronic video game in the United States. It was designed in 1971 by electrical engineers who then formed the immensely successful corporation named Atari. Atari released the game in 1974 and sold more than 10,000 units, with another 90,000 copies sold by other manufacturers. In 1976 Warner Communications acquired Atari and the next year introduced the first successful home package, the Atari Video Computer System. In 1979 the first *home* video game boom began. By 1982, U.S. video game income was $9 billion per year, with $8 billion from coin-operated machines and $1 billion from home games. This income compares favorably with that of the entire Hollywood film industry at the time. Atari's *Asteroids* game alone earned some $700-$800 million in its top year, more than the box office of any motion picture in history.

From 1983 to 1985 the video game market in the United States crashed in a glut of poorly designed games, but it was soon rescued by Japanese initiatives. In 1983 in Japan, a hundred-year-old Kyoto-based firm named Nintendo introduced its Famicon, a home video game system. Nintendo quickly beat out Sony and Matsushita in Japan and achieved a 33 percent penetration of all Japanese households. Nintendo's seven million users considerably outnumbered the four million personal computers then in use in Japan. In 1985 Nintendo cured the American video game recession by introducing Nintendo with a $30 million campaign. Within 5 years Nintendo controlled 80% of the United States market.

In the 1990s Nintendo and Sega battled each other in the high-stakes video game product and marketing wars. By 1989, Nintendo of America reached total sales of $5 billion a year, giving it a 20% share of the entire U.S. toy market and a presence in one of every five U.S. homes. The keys to its success were a sound graphics computer with expanded memory that could sell for between $80 and $150 and a continuously expanding line of new software for the system. David Sheff's grandiose history of Nintendo, *Game Over: How Nintendo Zapped an American Industry, Captured Your Dollars, and Enslaved Your Children* (1993), recounts an anecdote that illustrates for what high stakes the video game industry competed. By 1990, highway hijacking of new video games was a problem in Japan. When the new Super

Nintendo Entertainment System was to be released that year throughout Japan, the company created Operation Midnight to covertly distribute the program to retailers. One hundred trucks secretly and successfully dropped off their shipments without the knowledge of most Nintendo employees and especially of the mob rings who could steal the merchandise and sell it on the black market. All systems were sold by the third business day and another 1.5 million orders were taken. A total of two million systems were sold within 6 months, and over four million within a year.

By 1990, Nintendo of America still led Sega in the multi-billion dollar U.S. video game business. By 1992, 28 million Americans over the age of 18 were playing Nintendo. One in three U.S. children reported having or having had a Nintendo system. Nintendo reported that 35% of the original players of the Nintendo Entertainment System were over 18 years of age, as were 46% of the original players of its portable sister program Gameboy. For the newer, more advanced and expensive Sega CD system, some 70% of those who played were 18 or older. *Super Mario Brothers 3* had grossed $500 million following its release in 1990, more even than *E.T.* or *Jurassic Park* or *Batman*. Sales and rentals of video games approached $13 billion by 1993 and were predicted to reach $21.5 billion by the end of the decade (Elmer-Dewitt, 1993).

By 1994, Sega had edged ahead of Nintendo, buoyed by the success of its supercharged Genesis System. In 1994, first-week sales of $50 million for *Mortal Kombat II* surpassed the movie opening sales of $40 million for *The Lion King*. Sega and media giants Time Warner and Telecommunications, Inc. were combining to put together the Sega Channel as a premium service on cable. In the mid-1990s, Americans were spending $3 billion a year on video game cartridges alone, and some 40 million video game systems were being sold worldwide. CD-ROM was challenging the cartridge-based systems of Sega and Nintendo and promising a new generation of video games. New game systems from Panasonic, Philips, Pioneer, and others offered not only games but audio CDs, electronic versions of books and musical instruments, and software that used sophisticated animation and video (Shaffer, 1993, p. 108, reprinted by permission of *Forbes* magazine © Forbes, Inc., 1993). Virtual reality also moved toward the home as Sega developed a Virtual Reality helmet and games. Because fiber optics can beam limitless quantities of data around the world at nearly the speed of light, its application was greatly expanding networking game opportunities.

The growth of video games illustrates the development of new expressions of media culture. A new combination of technologies suggests a new application, public response is positive, more and better options are developed, giant corporations absorb the innovators and shoulder their way forward, vast marketing, promotions, and distribution systems extend and standardize the products and practices, yet newer technologies begin to compete for parts of the pie and the cycle starts over again.

Attractions and Benefits of Video Games

Like other expressions of media culture—sports, aerobics, music, and so forth—video games are a mixed bag of positive and negative representations, practices, and values.

On the positive side, the *educational* benefits of video games lie in their ability to develop skills in thinking, strategy, and quick reflexes. When you interact with a game, you assimilate "information about structure and strategy," according to MIT researcher Sherry Turkle (White, 1992, p. 12, used by permission). Then when the game is mastered, "there is learning about how to generalize strategies [to other games]." In the process, Turkle says, "there is learning how to learn" (White, 1992, p. 74). Psychologist Patricia Greenfield finds that children need a variety of skills in today's multimedia world (Wood, 1990, p. 12). These include skills taught by video games: an understanding of visual and spatial relationships, the decoding of dynamic graphics, and a comfort level with trial-and-error learning. These skills can now be learned interactively rather than by traditional observation or by reading directions. Video games can increase spatial and hand-eye coordination, develop decision-making processes, and improve playing ability. The social benefits of video games are especially strong for children who are not athletic or outgoing. Video games do not necessarily isolate individual players; they can "foster communication and cooperation between players, leading to a joint effort to succeed" (White, 1992, p. 74).

Medical benefits of video games include helping visually impaired people improve their eyesight and develop improved hand-eye coordination and reaction time. Video games help treat such problems as "lazy eye" in young children. Anxiety and side effects from chemotherapy treatment have lessened as the result of video games. The electronic games have even helped in the rehabilitation of brain disorders and improvement of reaction time, fine motor control, visual scanning, multidirectional movement tracking, and other skills.

Video games in hospitals have been found to help children cope with fear and stress. Deborah Fingerhut found that "the games can be educational, they can help with eye-hand coordination and, more importantly, Nintendo is a normalizing experience for kids. Since most kids have a machine at home, when they play they can forget they're in the hospital." The majority of children in Long Beach Memorial Medical Center reported to Fingerhut that they had access to Nintendo or another game system (Adams, 1992, p. E1, used by permission).

Video games resemble traditional ritual in their ability to transport the player into a *liminal* crossing over into a new sensation of time and space. "When you interface with the computer, you interface with truly instantaneous time—or as nearly instantaneous as lightspeed can be—and regular time is thereby suspended. You blink less; you don't get hungry or thirsty as fast as you would, say, reading a book, just because for the 'time' you're playing 'Super Mario,' you are in a kind of sempeternity" (McConnell, 1990, p. 256). Carl Holmgren (in Potts, 1992, p. F1) finds video games an important element in the study of liminality. Players turn on their video games for the purpose of changing how they feel about themselves, about their lives, and about their jobs. Playing a video game transports players into a created world of new space and time rules where they play an active role with immediate feedback and rewards. Video games not only take one across a liminal threshold, they contain immense utopian possibilities in the best tradition of fantasy, science fiction, and adventure in a form rich in both stylization and seeming realism.

Limitations and Problems of Video Games

On the negative side, the charges against video games are numerous. "American kids who have video-game machines already play, on average, nearly 1.5 hours a day. For many parents, the problem is not what their children are doing on their Nintendo systems, but what they are not doing while locked in Mortal Kombat—reading books, playing outdoors, making friends" (Elmer-Dewitt, 1993, p. 67, used by permission). Christopher Geist (in Potts, 1992, p. F1) recalls that parents had similar fears about comic books, rock music, television, and other media popular among youth.

Video games offer preordained scenarios instead of offering flexibility and exploration, warns Eugene Provenzo (1992). He notes, "When children write, they can create infinitely rich micro worlds—worlds only limited by their imagination. In the computer-based environment of video games, at least as currently designed, potential to create such micro worlds is much more limited" (p. 56).

These accusations of time taken away from other activities and of preprogrammed pleasure are the stuff of traditional media criticism, whatever the medium. Likewise, the accusations of dangerous levels of violence and narrowly sexist gender roles recall decades of debate over television and movies.

Violence in Video Games

Despite the variety of educational and psychological benefits, the thematic content in video games contains violence that may have harmful effects.

According to *Computer Magazine,* in the one in three American homes with video games, children spend up to 40 hours a week playing, and roughly 80 percent of the games have violence as a theme (Milloy, 1991, p. D3). Critics worry that video games encourage isolation, addiction, and sociopathology as players kill enemies in large numbers. Experts find that video game violence is emotionally stimulating, appears socially acceptable, and shares the same screen format as television news. Distinctions about the reality of the violence become blurred (Supplee, 1990, p. A3). UCLA media consultant Carole Lieberman notes that the U.S. Army uses Nintendo games to prepare soldiers for combat in a way that fosters detachment from real death and its consequences (Milloy, 1991, p. D3).

As many as 71% of the video games licensed by Nintendo have violent-action levels high enough to be harmful to children, according to the National Coalition on Television and Violence (Wood, 1990, p. 12). In the early 1990s, however, Nintendo attempted to maintain a strict rule about the type of violence in their games: no graphic violence and no blood. With their control over who made games for their system, that rule carried great influence. Sega of America developed a self-imposed rating system for its games, a rating system that Nintendo condemned as "a self-serving way of tolerating sex and violence" (Brandt, Gross, & Coy, 1994, p. 38, used by permission).

Mortal Kombat, designed at Williams Bally/Midway in Chicago, generated great controversy after its release in 1993 because its more photographic visual realism was combined with graphic violence. A solid punch sends animated blood flying, a loser knocked off a ledge lands impaled on a spike, a still-pulsing heart is ripped out by hand, and an opponent's head is torn off and held up victoriously with the spinal cord dangling from its neck. Successful in arcades, the gory game was released by Acclaim Entertainment for the home market on infamous "Mortal Monday," September 13, 1993, with a $10 million media blitz. The sequel, *Mortal Kombat II,* countered the violence with clever twists. When warrior Kitana punches deadly Shang Tsung, gooey blood spills out; when she throws razor-edged fans, more blood splatters. Then a voice, deep and menacing, calls out "Finish him!" With the right controller moves, suddenly and without warning, Kitana hands Tsung a cake decorated with candles and the word "Friendship" flashes on the screen. Other surprise moves include offering a present wrapped with a big bow, using a weapon to cut paper dolls, or turning your opponent into a baby. Whether this attempts to counter the violence or is only a clever new incongruity in the game, *Mortal Kombat* illustrates the worst of the violence that concerns critics. Such critics fear that games make life such a cheap commodity that death is only a blip on a screen or a colorful flash of gore (Dolbee, 1994, pp. E1, 4).

One of Sega's CD-ROM based games, *Night Trap,* triggered controversy over its depiction of teenage girls at a pajama party who are abducted by zombies. Zombie violence included sticking a claw-like appendage against their victim's neck. The game was banned in England for anyone under 15, and Toys R Us in Britain and Canada refused to sell the game. Finally, under pressure from the U.S. Congress and children's advocates, Sega pulled the game off the market (Brandt, Gross, & Coy, 1994, p. 68).

A more general criticism is stated by Eugene Provenzo (1992): "The lone individual setting out on a quest is not a new theme in Western culture, but such tales usually are leavened with pathos or tragedy. . . . Video games lack [any] moral counterweight" (p. 56). Provenzo's content analysis of video games finds recurring themes of gender stereotyping, aggression, and violence. One study found only 2% of video game characters were active women, 6% were damsels in distress, and the remaining 92% of games had no women characters (Provenzo, 1992, p. 56). Later games incorporated more Amazon types as participants, a dubious improvement. Researcher Robert Kubey wonders whether society should label as approved behavior having children spend endless hours blowing up simulated people (Supplee 1990, p. A3).

Gender, Video Games, and Hacker Culture

The world of computers, video games, and on-line interaction has been dominated by men. Research indicates this and a glance at the demographics of computer engineering majors, e-mail chat groups, and video game parlors confirms this. Women are not absent but their presence is far less than their 52% of the general population would warrant. The resulting sex-role stereotyping, masculinization of pleasure, and antifemale patriarchy severely restricts the value and potential of video games as positive contributors to a healthy, balanced media culture.

Sex-Role Stereotyping. Although 30% of Nintendo users are women, video games are generally designed to appeal to men, most particularly to the prime market of boys aged 8 to 14. Girls are less comfortable with game formats that reward competition, control, and a penchant for destruction, according to Kubey (in Supplee, 1990, p. A3). Psychologist Patricia Greenfield (in Wood, 1990, p. 12) finds that video games separate men into active roles and women into passive roles. Men slay dragons and drive race cars whereas women are depicted as maidens rescued or destroyed. Peggy Charron of Action for Children's Television finds, in the world of video games, that girls are second-class citizens (in Wood, 1990, p. 12). Video games, like Saturday morning television and toy stores, show a much greater sexual division defined by particular gender traits than has ever existed before, according to Susan Willis (1987, p. 404). Marsha Kinder (1991, p. 9) finds "traditional gender roles are increasingly reinforced rather than transgressed" in the software of video games, television programs, and popular movies.

Masculine Pleasures. Are the pleasures offered by video games gender specific? Gillian Skirrow (1986) argues that to women "video games are particularly unattractive since . . . they are about mastering a specifically male anxiety in a specifically male way" (p. 138). The software and its marketing articulate the cultural meanings of video games through a set of masculinized images. Popular forms that appeal to boys dominate the marketing, principally action, adventure, travel, horror, and science fiction with a strong emphasis on technology as the solution to narrative problems.

Feminine Resistance to Hacker Culture. These tendencies also suggest why the computer in general "has primarily come to be seen (and used) as a masculine technology," according to David Morley (1994, p. 113). From the first interest in computers among male electronics enthusiasts to the controversial computer hackers who break encryption codes to enter computer systems or inject viruses, men have predominated in computer applications, according to studies in Britain, France, and the United States.

Sherry Turkle (1988) studied the seeming rejection of computers by highly able female students at MIT and Harvard. She found not computer phobia but computer reticence, which she characterized as "wanting to stay away, because the computer becomes a personal and cultural symbol of what a woman is not" (p. 41). Hackers find pleasure in the protective security of abstract formal systems in computing as opposed to the ambiguities of interpersonal relationships, creating "a flight from relationships with people to relationships to the machine" (p. 45). Turkle also finds hacker culture characterized by a concern with winning and with risky learning strategies of plunging in first and trying to understand later, concerns identified with masculine cultural traits. Women are inclined to reject computers for the same reasons they are distanced from science and mathematics: they are gender coded in ways that compromise women's sense of femininity. The machines of computing and the software of video games are perceived as mediated through a heavily masculine culture. Turkle concludes that women use their rejection of computers "to assert something about themselves as women. Being a woman is opposed to a compelling relationship with a thing that shuts people out" (p. 50).

The general computer culture of "hackers," on-line computer gurus, and video game aficionados calls up more than the notion of playing one game or drawing on one electronic data/interaction source. The texts and technologies are heavily interrelated.

Intertextuality and Video Games

Intertextuality occurs with video games and means that any video game is read in relationship to other texts circulating in our culture. Thus, both violence and sex-role stereotyping in video games interact with television programming, movies, music lyrics, advertising, conversation, and the other discursive practices of our culture.

Marsha Kinder (1991) argues that intertextuality, a topic that will reappear in chapter four, creates a restrictive sense of narrative, of what a story is, of how it is organized, and of how it can be used or varied in response to different problems. For the very young especially, narrative has a special status in the integration of affect, cognition, and action. A child learns by trial and error constrained by the properties of the larger family system. Infantile monologues from the crib will inevitably be maps of the parents' larger maps. This combination of voices of authority with one's own voice is called "reenvoicement." Kinder brings this all to bear on her exploration of "how television and video games teach children to recognize and recombine popular narrative genres and thereby facilitate intertextual reenvoicement" (p. 23).

The reading of video games occurs within the larger context of television and popular culture discourses. Kinder warns,

In being positioned in the home and in assimilating earlier narrative forms such as movies, novels, comic books and cartoons, the television medium shapes the infant's entry into narrative. Also by appropriating functions that once were performed by what Althusser considers the most powerful ideological state apparatuses of earlier eras—the family, the education system, and the church—the television medium has become the most powerful ideological state apparatus in this late phase of postindustrial capitalism. (p. 37)

When *Teenage Mutant Ninja Turtles, Muppet Babies, Super Mario Brothers,* and their intertextual cousins exhibit similar tendencies and assumptions— about gender, about violence, about problem-solving, about people—these become reenvoiced in the youthful viewing subject. Kinder concludes that these powerful vehicles create the self as a "gendered commodity." She writes, "The newly emerging subject comes to perceive himself or herself as a gendered commodity around which a whole commercial nexus is organized—just like Garfield, the Muppet babies, and other TV personalities with whom the child is led to identify" (p. 38).

The popularity of video games from the age of 7 or 8 is explained by Jean Piaget's theory of child development, according to Kinder (1991, p. 8). At this age, "concrete operations" are organized by the child in the form of operational groupings of thought concerning objects that can be manipulated or known through the senses. Patricia Greenfield (1984) found that all the children she interviewed, who were between ages 8 and 14, were unanimous in preferring video games to television because they offered active control. Greenfield concludes, "Video games are the first medium to combine visual dynamism with an active participatory role for the child" (p. 102). Because of this innate psychological attraction for young people and the formative power of active involvement, the likelihood is very great that video games will have significant effects on a child's construction of narrativity, gender, self, and society.

New and improved video game technology and Hollywood crossovers accelerate the process. Mass market films such as *Cliffhanger, The Last Action Hero,* and *Wayne's World,* as well as Warner Brothers cartoons, are marketed also as video games. Movie scripts in development are now routinely screened for game potential. Hollywood scriptwriters, stars, and directors have been recruited to produce the increasingly realistic next generation of video games. Hollywood agents help their clients share the wealth of high-tech Silicon Valley. By 1994, the movie business, making some \$5 billion a year, was beginning to integrate with the video game business, which was making almost \$10 billion a year and was growing exponentially through new technologies and marketing (Fleming, 1994, p. 45).

Ritual participation in media in the form of video games offers much to consider and debate. At the first major academic conference on video games, underwritten by Nintendo, the conference chair Christopher Geist commented, "I don't believe anyone ever expected video games to have such a fundamental effect on our society in so many areas. [They] have become an integral part of the fabric of American life, changing the way we think, the way we learn, and the way we see the future" (in Sheff, 1993, p. 301).

Summary: Ritual Theory and Participation in Media Sports, Aerobics, and Video Games

Through ritual the media user acts out a relationship to the technology and texts of media culture. The experience is active to the point where John Fiske can speak of a "producerly" reading of media texts; the reader seems to coproduce the meaning along with the author-producers of the text. We are each of us "co-authors" of our media experience. This co-authorship becomes obvious in the active role of ritual fans, video game players, and aerobic dancers.

As a media activity, ritual participation in viewing a media sport, doing aerobics, or playing a video game shows some common characteristics: nonverbal participation, multisensory involvement, visual feedback, coordinated reflex responses, and sequences with embedded patterns. Each exhibits gender and age bias, though in different directions, with viewing sports appealing primarily to men, video games to younger men, and aerobics to women. The differences between these activities as media rituals are striking. In aerobics one is more directly involved in full-body motion, group activity, social reinforcement, longer-term membership (as opposed to single-game play), and developed adult activity. Ritual participation in media sports is less complete than either video games or aerobics because it does not offer physical, kinetic activity except as incidental to viewing, reading, or hearing sports. Sports viewing may be social and verbal and multisensory but it does not involve the viewer in the action by working a proactive joystick or by jumping and stretching. Interactive barroom games that allow viewers to guess at upcoming plays make sport viewing more active, but the guessing does not affect the outcome in the way joystick riding does in video games.

Especially with video games and aerobics, participation with media does not happen only passively and "in the head." These ritualized media experiences include physical participation in addition to the cognitive and emotional reactions that sports and other "finished" media texts generate. But all experiences of media culture in varying degrees entail active ritual participation and mythical perception, even experiences performed silently and in isolation. For example, in the modern era, reading has become "privatized" and is engaged in silently by lone individuals. But even reading was previously associated with more active social contexts, as Elizabeth Long records in her study of the history of women's reading groups, "Textual Interpretation as Collective Action" (1994). Reading news, listening to records or the radio, watching television, and most other media reception originally took place in group settings and was associated with social interaction. Even such isolating devices as the Walkman place the listener into contact with others through sound, either recorded or broadcast live. Reading a bestseller, watching a soap opera, tuning the car radio, or surfing the Internet each inserts us into mythic participation in ritual activity.

We are physical, social beings, and an emphasis on "ritual" teases out the many ways in which our relationship to media texts and technology is also physical and social. This relationship is invariably active cognitively and emotionally, or we are not decoding the text. Sport and video games tend to replicate the patriarchy and aggression of dominant culture. Aerobics can lead to a gendered commodification of the participating subject. But all significant media use gets us involved and invites us to enter into a dynamic interaction with texts and technology. Recent advances in technology have increased the interactive participation of subjects. The television screen once offered only a passive choice among several scheduled network programs. Now it offers choices from among 50 or 100 channels of cablecasting with the option of VCR time shifting and extensive choices in rented or purchased tapes. The same screen also hosts interactive video games. Cyberculture can be accessed as "read only" if one wishes, but it also offers interaction in ways not available to readers of printed texts. Teleconferencing and community access cable programming invite participation. Increased interactivity does not guarantee true diversity in media offerings, but it does make passive uniformity among audience members far less likely.

If we recall Hall's original encoding-decoding model, we note that he places the meaning structures of decoding within a relationship of frameworks of knowledge, relations of production, and the technical infrastructure. This moves our concern beyond reception and ritual participation to consideration of the political economy that structures media culture. Underlying power relations around gender, race, ideology, and politics shape both the encoding process within media organizations and the decoding process within individual and group receivers. These dynamic elements beneath sports, aerobics, or video games are the subjects of later chapters here.

Does "ritual participation" explain media culture and solve our original problem? Is it the solution? The telltale clue? Certainly it contributes importantly to accounting for our relationship to media experiences, but it leaves many other issues unresolved. How do participants receive and interpret messages? What qualities do texts of media culture possess in form and content? How do corporate power and hegemony condition the entire process? Do gender, race, ideology, political economy, history, or ethics always play a role? Our investigation into the moments and problematics of media culture must continue beyond ritual participation.

Notes

1. I am grateful to Dr. Lorna Francis for her clarifications of the industry background and teacher qualifications in aerobics.

2. I am indebted to Loren Kling, who interrupted his work as a video game tester (yes, he got paid for that) long enough to gather materials for this section on video games, thus proving that an electronic hacker can also master the print medium.

EXERCISES

Chapter Two

Exercise A. RITUAL ETHNOGRAPHY. Select a group media experience on the scale of either a group of friends or a larger public event. What might a foreign anthropologist notice about ritual participation in this event? Interview and observe those involved in it. How do participants externally express in behavior, gesture, clothing, speech, and other ways their identification with it? What meanings are expressed? Does the experience appear more female or male oriented? Are participants affluent or indigent? Is it just an entertainment diversion for them, or is it more than that? Does it perform any of the ritual functions listed in Figure 2.1?

Exercise B. SPORTS MEDIA. Compare the different ways people follow sports by attending in person or through a media representation such as reading a newspaper or magazine, listening to the radio, or watching television. Which is most informative? Which most involving? Which do you personally find most satisfying? How do these sources interact for the typical sports fan? When and why do sports fans wear special clothes, wave banners, join in cheers, and otherwise express themselves externally?

Exercise C. AEROBICS AND VIDEO GAMES. Observe and interview persons participating in an aerobics class or a video game or a similar activity. Note the body language of participants—posture, movement, sounds, comments, and so forth. Ask participants what they like about the activity, how often they participate, when, with whom, and what it all means to them. Note differences in male and female participants in addition to ethnic, class, and age differences.

Exercise D. PATRIARCHY. Summarize the feminist critique of hegemonic male sports culture. Trace its history. Note current expressions of it that you witness. How can sports be made more fair and beneficial for everyone?

Exercise E. VIDEO GAME VALUES. Select one or several video games and analyze the gender of figures in it and the degree of violence and aggression in it. What mental and motor skills are involved? What kind of people appear to play this game? What does this game seem to emphasize, reward, and highlight most? What cultural values do these tie in to?

Exercise F. RITUAL THEORY. Contrast ritual theory to a bullet model of communication. Identify examples of people ritually participating with the media text they are accessing. Are there any media experiences that do not involve some degree of ritual and myth? What aspects of media culture does "ritual theory" help explain and clarify?

3

Reception Theory:
Sex, Violence, and (Ms.)Interpreting Madonna

What do I think when I hear "Madonna"? Well, I should be struck by Catholic religious images, but I'm not. I picture the sassy, crotch-grabbing, blonde on MTV.—*Male, 21*

The second suspect to be interrogated in the mystery drama of media culture is *reception theory*, the study of how we as subjects perceive and interpret the texts of media culture. When you see the name "Madonna" on the page, what do you first think of? What image first pops to mind—an icon of the mother of Jesus or a visual of an outrageous media celebrity? When you read about or see or hear the pop star Madonna, do you enjoy it or detest it? Should media of film, television, music, magazines include portrayals of sexuality? Of violence? How *do* we receive media texts?

Reception studies examine the manner in which texts are received by the audience, whether while reading a romance novel (Radway, 1984), interpreting a broadcast from the BBC (Morley, 1980), reading a classic of German literature (Iser, 1978; Jauss, 1982), watching a live media event (Dayan & Katz, 1992), or encountering any other form of media text. A discourse accessed through any medium becomes personal discourse and contributes to our conception of its "meaning." As reading subjects, we may attribute any number of different meanings to the text. "The meaning of a film is not something to be discovered purely in the text itself but is constituted in the interaction between the text and its users" (Abercrombie, Hill, & Turner, 1980, p. 17).

An obvious and sometimes humorous example is our frequently idiosyncratic understanding of song lyrics. The daily ethnography of public life, the newspaper, occasionally features examples of this. The Rolling Stones refusing to be your beast of burden is mistakenly taken as "I'll never leave your pizza burning." The Beatles famous girl with kaleidoscope eyes becomes "the girl with colitis goes by." (I wondered for months why the Bee Gees sang of this "bald-headed woman" which, of course, was really intended as more than a woman.) Johnny Rivers's "Secret Agent Man" became "Secret Asian Man" for one fan, who said, "Even today when I hear it on the radio, I could swear he's singing 'Asian' instead of 'Agent' " (Salm, 1993). Others report hearing "Don't be cruel, two-hearted shrew" in Elvis's song about a heart that's true. The Police's "Canary in a Coal Mine" became "Mary in a coma." Jimi Hendrix's famous effort to kiss the sky was used by Gavin Edwards in the title of his book on this subject, *'Scuse Me While I Kiss This Guy and Other Misheard Lyrics* (1995). Obviously what people often interpret as the images and subjects of song lyrics are not those intended by the writers and performers. This simple misunderstanding points to complications in our relationship to media culture and its texts and icons.

The Many Madonnas

One media icon of the past decade who has generated conflicting "readings" and substantial academic debate is a woman from Detroit named Madonna Ciccone who, shorn of her last name and sometimes her clothes, is the famous, or infamous, "Madonna." Madonna first emerged as a pop singer on records and radio in the early 1980s. She moved quickly into elaborate music videos, major concert tours, and then movies, always with maximum exposure through magazines, newspapers, and any other medium possible. Self-promotion and a canny business sense accompanied her through various visual incarnations: "thrift shop chic" (Subjic, 1989, p. 33) in *Desperately Seeking Susan* and her albums *Madonna* and *Like a Virgin*; a "Marilyn Monroe" look in the *Material Girl* video and *Dick Tracy*; in a tight bustier or cone-shaped bra, with shorts, in the early 1990s world tour documented in *Truth or Dare*; in hair pulled back in a bun and in a business dress for news interviews and her role as *Evita*; in nothing at all in her hitchhiking shot in Miami; and in various other transformations. She knowingly manipulates her image, mixing feminism and postmodernism with a hunger for attention through outrage.

Rolling Stone called Madonna "the world's most famous woman" (Zehme, 1989, p. 51). *Women's Review* labeled Madonna "the most successful female solo pop performer ever" (Garrat, 1986, p. 12). Her 16 consecutive top-five hits are second only to Elvis. She tied with then-President Bush for second place as "the most popular public hero" in 1991; only Mother Teresa topped her, but she beat out Jesus, who tied Julia Roberts for fourth. Analysts around the world have composed numerous scholarly studies about her (see Schwichtenberg, 1993a), making a virtual academic cottage industry of Madonna research to go with the innumerable critiques in the popular press. Norman Mailer (1994), with typical understatement, pronounced Madonna our greatest living female artist.

How do people "receive" Madonna and what does she "mean" to them? In this chapter, we employ Madonna as a case study with debates over her sexual representation and pop star role. The quotations cited throughout are from a series of open-ended classroom surveys over a three-year period in the 1990s.[1] With Madonna, one finds reactions decidedly mixed. Some judgments are unrelentingly negative.

What does Madonna make me think of? Belly button (or lower), untalented, inept, ignorant, bi-sexual, hussy, has-been chick.—*Male, 24*

Sex, blonde, Hollywood. Emptiness, vulgarity, uneducated, has no style.— *Female, 42*

I don't believe her music or her "image" portray anything "positive" about our society. What she does and what she stands for is almost always in poor taste.—*Female, 21*

She is what's wrong with our society—people like her that are vulgar, immature, crude, and only out to get very rich off our stupidity.—*Female, 22*

Many responses to Madonna are positive and some are ambivalent.

Madonna is a double-edged sword. She is loud, opinionated, and does not put up with a man's world. She is the boss. On the other hand, she makes sex look too easy. It's not. AIDS is out there, and in her videos I don't see a condom being pulled out. She shows stupidity by doing it.—*Female, 20*

She is doing exactly what she wants and is getting paid obscene amounts of cash. I do not enjoy her work as much as I respect risks she takes. She is self-determined and yet she is a sex object. She is a paradox. She is in charge, yet she is a slave to record company profitmaking. Again a paradox.—*Male, 21*

What's It to You? The Purpose and Focus of Reception Studies

Reception studies help us explore media culture by analyzing the complex, varied, and intriguing ways that readers decode and interpret the texts of media. This approach contrasts with traditional media "effects" research based in the bullet transmission model. Without the benefit of reception studies, media research has tended either to assume total conformity of audiences to media messages, as in the traditional "hypodermic needle" myth of media effectiveness, to assume stubborn resistance to influence, as in the "limited effects" theory, or to settle for a noncommittal middle ground of "mixed effects." The first view sees media as totally effective—Madonna's sexuality converts the audience into sex fiends—and the second as generally ineffective—Madonna's exhibitionism is insignificant. One problem with such "effects" research has been a simplistic notion of an unambiguous message, whether effective or ineffective, and an equally simplistic notion of measurable behavioral effects. Behind the effects debate is often the stereotype of the audience member as a passive, inert cultural dope, a stereotype that ritual theory (in Chapter 2) helps to dispel.

Even at face value, audience members are often more alert and critical than behavioral effects research implies. Two female respondents analyzed Madonna as follows.

> Madonna is an extremely provocative and sexy woman. She likes to express herself in the most interesting ways. In concerts and with her music she exposes herself and her beliefs. I believe that what she does is a good thing. Many people are afraid of being themselves and hide behind a masquerade. Madonna gives people the incentive to free their desires to be and do what they want. Madonna is contemporary and definitely determined. She makes her own decisions and is more a leader than follower.—*Female, 21*

> When I think of Madonna, I'm intrigued because she is constantly changing her image and doing something to ruffle someone's feathers. She's entertainment. She's up on shock value, and I fall victim to that aspect of her.— *Female, 22*

These are self-conscious articulations that do not show up on forced-choice survey questions or measurements of audience size.

The encoding-decoding model of Stuart Hall gives theoretical force to the application of reception studies to media culture. The model is positioned against the one-directional flow and passive reception of the old transmission effects model (Hall, 1994, p. 253): The sender originates the message, the message is unidimensional, and it affects the receiver's behavior. Against this, Hall positions a model that suggests that both creating and receiving the message are not as transparent and one-dimensional as that. He notes, "the message is a complex structure of meanings" (p. 254). Meaning is not fixed but is multilayered (polysemic) and multireferential. Madonna may position herself as both a good girl and a bad girl in a music video, and audience members may respond to different aspects of that message and in different ways. Semiotics and structuralism, along with the ideas of Althusser and Gramsci, make it possible for Hall to identify complexities in the media text and in how people receive and interpret media texts.

In reception analysis, Madonna's text is appropriated by the reader/ viewer/listener as a meaningful discourse and is meaningfully decoded. For Hall (1980, in During 1993, p. 93), "it is this set of decoded meanings which 'have an effect,' influence, entertain, instruct or persuade, with very complex perceptual, cognitive, emotional, ideological or behavioral consequences." In particular, individuals in different positions in the social structure in terms of class, race, or sex will have access to distinct codes and subcultures useful in decoding and interpreting texts. For example, in our survey of 168 university students (81 men made up 50.9% of the sample; 78 women made up 49.1%), we asked: "What meaning does Madonna have for you?" Although close to 28% of both men and women tended to see her meaning in reference to music and show business, more women (30% of the total sample) than men (21%) saw her meaning first in reference to "individuality." More men (38%) described her meaning in terms of a bad girl creating bad popular culture than did women (24%). Not surprisingly, on these questions and others, gender seemed to make a difference in decoding and evaluating Madonna. Gender, economic class, racial self-identity, and other social positions play a role in our decoding of media texts.

Reception studies is the umbrella term used by Janet Staiger (1992, p. 7) to group three strands of reader-centered interpretation. These reader-centered theories comprise the intellectual roots for reception analysis of experiences of media culture. One strand, "reception aesthetics," originated in Germany with the work of Hans Robert Jauss and Wolfgang Iser in the phenomenological tradition of Edmund Husserl to examine the decoding experience. A separate strand, "reader-response criticism," emerged in the work of Stanley Fish, Jonathan Culler, Norman Holland, and others who have examined the reader-text interaction in general. A third strand, "reception theory," has been variously used to designate readings borrowed from or combining the German tradition and reader-response criticism. To avoid confusion among these strands, Staiger suggests the generic label *reception studies*. Whereas ritual participation in the preceding chapter referred to active responses to a text in media culture, reception studies try to explain the decoding of the text, and textual studies in the next chapter try to elucidate the text itself. Thus, reception studies are not interested in Madonna's biography and performances in themselves but rather in what audiences make of those Madonna texts.

Reception studies rely on literary theory and social science, and mark a shift in fundamental emphasis from earlier literary theory. The classical-humanist paradigm (Holub, 1984, p. 2) resulted in a preoccupation with the *author,* particularly in nineteenth century Romanticism (Eagleton, 1983, p. 74). The scientific revolution of historicism and formalism led, by the time of World War II, to New Criticism, with its exclusive concern with the *text.* Only in recent decades has there emerged a marked shift of attention to the *reader.* Each emphasis has had its narrowly exclusionary advocates. In the first period, the high culture of literature was seen by some critics as solely dependent on the author's background, intent, and aesthetics. In New Criticism, nothing outside the text was of major importance; the author was dead as far as interpretation was concerned, and the reader's task was to tease out the complexities buried in the text. Now in reader-response theory, Stanley Fish finds only reader interpretations, and the text disappears. He admits that even his own detailed interpretations are not more correct than others, only perhaps more interesting.

The degree to which we "fill gaps" in the texts we encounter is a major issue in reception theory. Robert Allen (1992) summarizes reception theory through the idea of gap filling: "Gap filling is the process by which the imaginary world suggested by words in the text is constructed in the mind of the reader" (p. 104). We read the words, generate images and impressions, compare the text to other texts, and draw from our own experiences. Our doing so will vary with our culture, our group experiences, and our individual psychology. Viewers from different cultural backgrounds filled gaps very differently as they watched *Dallas,* the soap opera about Texas oil millionaires. Like studies of British soap operas *Brookside* and *Eastenders* (Root, 1986), *Crossroads* (Brunsdon, 1981), or *Coronation Street* (Dyer et al., 1981), the studies of *Dallas* found that women filled the gaps most effectively in these soap operas (Ang, 1985) and that interpretations of the show varied widely, particularly among different ethnic groups—Israeli, Arab, Russian, American, and others (Liebes & Katz, 1990).

Reception studies gain power from recent emphasis on how every media text is many-layered, or *polysemic.* Because each text is polysemic, whether it is a soap opera, a Madonna video, or a news narrative, it has many possible messages that may be extracted from it. Reception studies examine how individuals select from among the possible messages buried in the text and made available to readers.

The encoding-decoding model calls attention to reception, even as the model attempts to hold in balance all the stages in the process of media culture. The meaning cannot be "read off" straight from textual characteristics, but the text is important. The author or production unit does not wholly determine the meanings generated by text and reader interaction, but the creative production process is important. Both production and text serve to privilege specific readings and meanings, as we see in the following section. In the reception view, Madonna as originator of her texts initiates a discursive process. The texts of her songs, music videos, concerts, films, books, and television appearances generate a discourse. Her "wannabes," detractors, and disinterested readers interact with her texts and generate meaning. This last step is the arena of reception studies.

Pornography and Violence in Media Culture

She's not like a virgin, very fake and unbelievable: sex with every race and
every gender. She had a good start but screwed it all away with drugs and sex.
Some concerts she was said to be obscene.—*Male, 21*

She's not doing anything to hurt anyone on purpose; if persons are hurt or
offended, it most likely is a problem with themselves, and they have the choice
not to expose themselves to Madonna's material and actions.—*Male, 20*

The issue of how texts are received and interpreted is at the heart of many
debates over media culture. One of the most widely debated is, does television violence cause subsequent antisocial behavior and, because of this,
require federal regulation? What motivational role do violent texts in television, films, song lyrics, news shows, and other media play in inspiring
drive-by shootings, gang violence, domestic violence, sexual abuse, serial
murders, school violence, substance abuse, and similar social destruction?
Well-publicized incidents suggest there is a direct connection. President
Reagan was shot in 1981 by John Hinckley, Jr., who apparently was imitating
the Robert De Niro character in the movie *Taxi Driver* in an attempt to attract
Jodie Foster's attention. A half-hour after seeing *The Burning Bed* on television, a Milwaukee man imitated it by burning his estranged wife to death.
Several dozen deaths from playing Russian roulette with a loaded handgun
were reported in the days immediately following national cablecasting of
such a scene in *The Deer Hunter*. Two teenagers were killed and another
critically injured (in separate incidents) when they lay down between high-
way lanes at night in imitation of drunken college football players in the 1993
film, *The Program*; the scene was removed from later prints of the film. Two
serious Ohio fires were apparently inspired by *Beavis and Butt-head* in 1993.
Natural Born Killers was banned in Britain and Ireland because of alleged
copycat murders in the United States and France. How direct is the connection between media violence and subsequent behavior?

Another controversial question is, what influence do sexually explicit
materials have on readers and viewers? Are present rating systems and
warnings adequate? Does pornography, however defined, contribute to the
breakdown of families, rape and spousal abuse, teen pregnancy, gang-bang-
ing, sexual dysfunctions, fetishism, neurotic and psychotic sexual episodes,
and the overall disintegration of society and traditional values?

For decades media industries and public officials in many countries have
wrestled with these issues and their policy implications. Media industry
spokespeople deny connections between texts and subsequent behavior—
despite that connection being the basis for the billions of dollars spent on

advertising in their industries—and pledge that self-regulation is the only proper way for media texts to be modified. Politicians, pressed by public demands to do something about social disintegration, periodically threaten greater restrictions on media texts, especially violence on television or, more recently, pornography on the Internet. Advocacy groups mount advertiser boycotts and letter-writing campaigns to sway policy. And everyone wants simple, clear, unambiguous conclusions from media research—conclusions, of course, that support their side.

We regularly encounter popular indications that media have an effect, even positive effects. For example, the American tabloid *The National Enquirer,* under the headline "Can We Learn From Media" (March 8, 1994, p. 3), reported that a 5-year-old had saved her 2-year-old brother's life by performing a Heimlich maneuver that she had learned from watching Robin Williams do the same in the film *Mrs. Doubtfire.* The girl, Kristen Joosten of Bellmore, New York, then called 911 for further assistance, as she had learned to do from television.

To explore media sex and violence, it is helpful to include the findings of behavioral research along with the concerns of less behavioristic reception studies in general. Behavioral research has the advantage of close measurement of the outcomes of exposure to media content and the disadvantage of implying uniform cause and effect stimulus-response conditioning when the reality of how we receive media texts is far more complex than that.

Violence Research. What research offers instead of simple answers is qualified and complex responses that point in certain directions but do not dictate policy. For decades, we have known that *there is a connection between exposure to violent messages on television and subsequent antisocial behavior.* Many different kinds of research reported in numerous journals and reviews and periodically summarized by the United States Surgeon General (e.g., 1971) and other reviews (Comstock, Chafee, Katzman, McCombs, & Roberts, 1978; Murray, 1980; Tan, 1985) confirm a causal connection. The research is reliable and largely agrees—the violence of Rambo and the Mighty Morphin Power Rangers can create problems. In general, the social learning theory of Bandura (1968, 1973) is confirmed, whereas the catharsis theory of Feshbach (1955, 1969) is rejected, with its fantasy that vicarious violence will eliminate the impulse toward actual violence.

Television violence is of particular concern for three reasons. First, television is the most pervasive medium in modern societies. Television comes right into the home, its content is frequently violent, especially in programs children are likely to watch, and research has established its negative consequences. Second, research has found that children can learn aggressive acts simply by observing them once, and that realistic media violence that is "rewarded or justified by the story" is especially likely to elicit viewer aggression. Third, repeated exposure to media violence desensitizes audiences to violence and, following such desensitization, emotional arousal of anger or frustration facilitates aggressive responses. Of course, exposure to one act of media violence does not automatically cause violence, any more than smoking one cigarette causes lung cancer. But just as there is a significant correlation overall between smoking and lung cancer, so there is between heavy viewing of media violence and later aggression.

Two complications, however, frustrate those who accept the media-violence connection and who would like to ban violent content as a result. The first is the difficulty in weighing how exposure to media violence interacts with other potential causes of violence. Access to weapons, victimization by violence at home, joblessness, mental or emotional illness, peer pressure, and any number of other factors interact with media exposure to motivate any specific destructive act. In the United States much more than in Canada or Great Britain, for example, interactive systems of violence inducement range from the abundance of handguns to violent plot solutions in media to absence of compensating social experience. As an outcome of this system, violent crime is endemic and the United States has record numbers of its population in prison. From 1970 to 1992, the rate of persons incarcerated in the United States per 100,000 jumped from around 110 to 455 (Associated Press, 1994). Even apartheid South Africa, in second place in the world for prison population, had only 311 per 100,000 in prison. Two years later, the state of California's incarceration rate was estimated at 626 per 100,000, compared to South Africa at 355 and Russia at 335 per 100,000 (Gunnison, 1994). This overabundant violence in America, of course, has many causes. But some researchers estimate that perhaps 10% of the violence can be traced to media influence.

The second complicating factor is that research results do not point to any one specific public policy or law as a solution. One may wish, for example, for self-policing on the part of media decision makers. Or one may propose any number of government actions, from increased funding for less violent and more prosocial public broadcasting to V-chips and serious ratings systems for television, music, film, and all public media. Or one may discourage any pressure toward restriction or self-restraint, trusting in the mechanisms of the marketplace and individual choice, however imperfect the results. In the United States, First Amendment protections of free speech and press make it extremely difficult for the government to censor specific media content and broadcasters have been reluctant to self-police. National comparisons give hints about successful and unsuccessful policies, but research as such is better at identifying problems than solutions.

Pornography Research. Concern over the relationship between media exposure and sexual mores is widespread. India's Bombay-based movie center, sometimes dubbed Bollywood, faces frequent scrutiny. When films and song lyrics turned sexier to compete with MTV beamed into India via Rupert Murdock's Star satellite, there were calls for censorship and tighter standards from India's Central Board of Film Certification. Films with sexy characters and themes offered seductive camera angles of bodies and double entendres, backed by songs that asked "What's beneath the blouse?" or repeated "Sexy, Sexy" more than 100 times to a disco beat (Moore, 1994). The British Board of Film Censors, created by the film industry early in the century, took on official governmental functions after 1984 when it was made responsible for passing on all video features in addition to theatrical releases. In a more conservative era, the head of the British Censorship Board in 1937 was proud that there was not a single film showing in London at that time that dealt with any of the burning questions of the day (Perry, 1994).

As a whole, the results of research on pornography are less conclusive than those on violence. The results are generally relative to the kinds of measures chosen by researchers. Explaining this, Daniel Linz and Neil Malamuth (1993) identify three conflicting approaches and sets of findings. The "conservative-moralist" position cites research (Zillman & Bryant, 1982, 1984, 1986, 1988) that connects pornography to negative *attitudes*. Experiments find that extensive exposure of college students to pornographic films correlates positively with attitudes favoring increased acceptance of nontraditional sexual practices, decreased punishment for rapists, increased acceptance of premarital and extramarital relations, and decreased endorsement of marriage as an essential institution in society.

In contrast, the "liberal erotica" approach cites research that finds "no harm" and no increases in delinquency and criminal behavior resulting from pornography. The research cited uses measures that tend to measure not attitudinal but *behavioral* change. The 1970 U.S. Presidential Commission on Obscenity and Pornography found pornography generally harmless. Correlational studies of pornography and rape in comparisons country-by-country (Kutchinsky, 1991) and state-by-state (Baron, 1990; Baron & Strauss, 1984) yield ambiguous and inconclusive results, with increased availability of pornography correlating with sometimes increased and sometimes decreased instances of rape. In at least one study, institutionalized rapists and pedophiles reported less exposure to erotica than the general male population (see Gray, 1982); the theoretical explanation was that erotica may instruct viewers about normal sex, a subject about which rapists and pedophiles lack understanding. In other studies, the effects of heavy doses of pornography reversed those of light doses. Through "excitation transfer," highly erotic and disgusting portrayals may facilitate aggression among angry persons and persons predisposed to aggression (Tannenbaum & Zillman, 1975), but mildly erotic and pleasant arousal helps distract normal subjects away from an angry state and the use of violence (Donnerstein, Donnerstein, & Evans,

1975; White, 1979). These slight or even benign effects of pornography buttress a liberal tolerance of the circulation of obscene materials.

Finally, one "feminist" approach (there are also other contrasting feminist approaches) opposes pornography as encouraging violence against women. This position is articulated most militantly by Andrea Dworkin and Robin Morgan in the slogan: "Pornography is the theory, rape is the practice" (see Ross, 1993, p. 234). Catherine MacKinnon blames pornography for "rape, mental and physical abuse, murder and attempted murder, illegal drug use, [and] attempted suicide" (Miller, 1995). Andrew Ross notes that the philosophical argument of Women Against Pornography (WAP) is that "patriarchal oppression is *systematic* and *all-inclusive,* and that it is exercised universally and transhistorically" (Ross, 1993, p. 233, emphasis in original). Dworkin argues that "men love death" and "men especially love murder" in her essentialist argument that male sexuality is naturally rapacious and gynocidal whereas female sexuality is naturally nurturing (Ross, 1993, p. 233). Opponents of this extreme view are numerous, including Nadine Strossen, president of the American Civil Liberties Union, whose book *Defending Pornography: Free Speech, Sex, and the Fight for Women's Rights* (1995) argues that censorship will ultimately work against women and feminists.

Some respondents accuse Madonna of being a sex object and falling within the feminist critique of pornography as anti-women.

She does her best to dehumanize her gender for the sake of money.—*Male, 33*

She uses sex to exploit herself and women.—*Male, 28*

She is exploiting the age-old exploitation of women and revelling in a mock "whoredom" that she perpetuates for financial shock value.—*Male, 22*

But many feminists defend Madonna, and details in the representation of sexuality can make all the difference. For example, men who are more likely to commit rape are aroused more by sexual aggression carried out *without* the woman's consent; men less likely to commit rape are equally aroused by scenes of consensual and nonconsensual intercourse (Malamuth & Check, 1983). What critics conclude is that a culture of subordination, discrimination, and aggression against women is reinforced and activated by *violent* pornography. Distorted representations of female responses to rape have consequences as well: Men exposed to scenes of rape in which the victim eventually became aroused were found to perceive a second rape scene less negatively and to consider it more normal than were men who had first been exposed to scenes of rape in which the act was abhorred by the victim throughout (Malamuth & Check, 1980). In addition, men who maintain traditional sex role attitudes are more likely to be influenced by pornography than men who are less sex-typed and more androgynous (McKenzie-Mohr & Zanna, 1990). Research on women's reaction to pornography has found subjects most disgusted by objectification, dominance, and penis worship and least disgusted by explicit and mutual sex scenes (Cowan, 1990). The degree of violence associated with the sexuality is important. Women who are shown sexually violent films, but not those shown sexually explicit nonviolent films, become less sensitive toward the victim in a mock rape trial (Krafta, Penrod, Donnerstein, & Linz, 1992). Desensitization occurs for both men and women.

From the preceding, a conclusion emerges that suggests media violence is a substantial problem and media pornography, except when accompanied by violence, less of a problem. Hong Kong kung fu movies may cause problems for more people in more ways than Madonna. These, of course, are averaged responses showing trends. They do not explain how these connections between media portrayals and human behavior actually work for any one subject. Any individual can respond in a wide variety of ways to any media text. Against the averaged responses of behavioral social psychology, reception theory relishes and explores this variety.

Reading Media: Text, Reader, Context, and "Meaning"

When we encounter a media text, whether violent, pornographic, or noncontroversial, we do three actions almost simultaneously. We read, we comprehend, and we interpret. *Reading* means that there is a text made up of visual or aural symbols from which meanings can be constructed; there is a reader who is capable of constructing meaning from the text; and there is interaction between text and reader. We perceive the symbols in the text and, if they make sense to us, we *comprehend* them by placing them in some kind of "frame." We then *interpret* them by relating the sense of what is going on to what the author seems to intend and to extratextual points of reference. These are not actually separate activities, except logically. As Steven Mailloux notes (1977), "we interpret as we perceive, or rather perception is an interpretation" (p. 418).

Madonna's controversial 1990 music video *Like a Prayer* has many levels of possible reading, but, for straight perception and comprehension, it is not confusing. The narrative shows a black man accused of a murder he did not commit, and it shows Madonna worshipping in front of a black male saint in the church. In the disputed description by Ramona Curry (1990), the statue "is thus moved to life and first blesses and later erotically kisses Madonna as she is sprawled on her back on a pew" (p. 26). In the process, Madonna, in a tight dress, dances in front of burning crosses and eventually seeks a kiss from the black man who leans over her. In the end, the black male character is set free and the statue returns to its sacred place. We "read" the church, the statues, the dress, the kiss, the figure of Madonna, and the other dancers. We "comprehend" the video as constituting characters in a specific setting and sequence. We "interpret" it all as a single narrative story.

From this process of reading, we achieve meaning. Meaning, in this sense, is not something put in the text by the author, but something we construct in the reading of it: "reading is not the discovery of meaning but the creation of it" (Mailloux, 1977, p. 414). Terry Eagleton makes this point more vividly (1983): "Meanings of a text do not lie within them like wisdom teeth within a gum, waiting patiently to be extracted" (p. 89). The competent reader is able to pull all the parts of a text into a single, unified meaning or experience. Still, the "meaning" of Madonna's *Like a Prayer* video is not simple. Ronald Scott (1993) notes the complex and historically resonant depictions of race and religion at work in the video. He places the meaning within the context of the powerful history of the black church and the unrealized potential of the mass media for altering prevailing stereotypes about blacks. For him, the black statue was not moved by sexual motives but by compassion to help a person in trouble. Madonna's dress and dance as such do not erotically move the statue because, in Scott's analysis, the statue never looks over her body or gazes lustfully; instead the statue maintains neutral, unemotional facial expressions throughout. And the kiss, although sensual, is ambiguous and for Scott connotes Madonna's choice of a harmonious resolution of the story against the backdrop of the destructive burning crosses of the Ku Klux Klan. The kiss is presented too close up to say that Madonna is "sprawled on her back" as Curry described. But Scott does not claim that his interpretation was Madonna's intent in making the video. For our comprehension, her actual intent and influence are irrelevant. What Scott receives from this video is that it advocates "the positive role of the black church in the lives of all it touches" (p. 73).

Exactly what dominates our particular construction of meaning from a text has been divided by Staiger (1992, p. 35) into text-activated, reader-acti-vated, or context-activated reading.

Text-activated reading emphasizes that the text exists and sets up what the reader will do. Text-activated readings by Metz, Eco, and the semiologists assume the reading is constituted by the text with its social and literary conventions, and that meaning or significance is dominated by the signs and codes in the text for the reader to interpret. The text-activated reader of pornography takes the sexual representations very literally and might be especially swayed by whether the victim of a portrayed rape is represented as finally succumbing to pleasure in the rape, making such a portrayal especially dangerous for that viewer. The "text-activated" reader of Madonna includes the classic "wannabe." This reader is eager to know everything about Madonna and what Madonna thinks she is doing. Madonna's text itself has meaning.

> Her music means a lot to me because for many years I've enjoyed listening to her. Ever since I can remember I've always had her to listen to, so losing her I guess would be a loss.—*Male, 23*

Reader-activated reading argues that the text exists, but the reader, as an individual, can greatly redo or appropriate that text. In the more radical reception theory of Norman Holland or David Bleich, the reader is constituted by social and literary conventions or psychologies and the meaning or significance is not in the text but in the reader's interpretation. For example, subliminal sex in media, in the controversial interpretation of Wilson Bryan Keyes, triggers powerful subconscious responses in the viewer of ice cubes in a magazine liquor advertisement. The viewer finds sexual organs, orgies, and other imagery in what in itself appears image-free and neutral. Viewing a Madonna video, a professional dancer may be looking for new moves, a pubescent male may be looking for flesh, a young rock musician may be seeking ideas for a music video, or a conservative evangelist may be looking for material to condemn. Each of them places their personal concerns ahead of those of the text itself.

Context-activated reading assumes that the text and the reader are equally significant in creating meaning. In the context-activated works of Stuart Hall or Tony Bennett, the historical context is very significant for the interaction. Meaning or significance occurs in the contextual intersection between text and reader, an intersection that occurs in a historical context and may relate to other historical contexts. This is the healthy, well-adjusted person reading either pornography or violence in media. Such people are able to keep these subjects in context and not be overly swayed by any one representation. Of course, many viewers do not have that balance, particularly ones who subject themselves to heavy diets of violence or pornography.

The extensive analyses of Madonna in *The Madonna Connection* (Schwichtenberg, 1993a) take care to "contextualize" Madonna's place as a provocative figure in a fragmented, postmodern entertainment world. Thus, in the context of historical suppression of expressive women, Madonna is an admirable feminist. Yet in the context of commercial exploitation, Madonna is a rip-off artist and master tease. And further, in the context of the professional media, Madonna is a sophisticated businesswoman. In a fully contextualized reading, all of the many aspects of Madonna are included.

All three kinds of readings of the film *Truth or Dare,* the 1991 documentary of Madonna's "Blond Ambition" tour, have been analyzed by Deidre Pribram (1993). First, the "text-activated" reader finds the film a useful source for understanding how and why the text of Madonna's concerts are as they are. This wannabe gets behind the scenes through the documentary. Second, the "reader-activated" responses emphasize subjective value judgments and include popular press characterizations of her tour: "The Shameless One Stages a Raunchy, Revealing Self-Portrait," "a natural-born exhibitionist exhibits herself," and "a touching, vulgar, erotic and revealing documentary" (Pribram, 1993, p. 190). As hyper-active readers, the tabloid press predigests the projected responses of its audience. Third, a "context-activated" reaction includes Pribram's own reading of the film in reference to feminist reception of Madonna as a postmodern persona. Sexuality, power, gender ambiguity, performance, control, and simulation are central to *Truth or Dare* in the context of feminist struggle within patriarchal society.

If the text is complex, how simple is the subject reading it? French reception studies shift away from the German sense of a unified reader incorporating coherent meaning from a text and move toward the sense of a decentered, textualized reader. For Gadamer's and German reception theory, understanding occurs when our "horizon" made of historical meanings and assumptions fuses with the horizon within the work itself. In the text, instead of leaving home, Gadamer notes, we "come home" (Eagleton, 1983, p. 72), implying a preexisting unified reader identity. But for Barthes and French theory, the plurality of the texts is extended to the reading subject as well. The "I" becomes not a unified center from which meaning and interpretation emerge but is instead marked by dispersion and plurality. Barthes (1974) observes: "This 'I' which approaches the text is already itself a plurality of other texts, of codes which are infinite or, more precisely, lost (whose origin is lost)" (p. 10). In this way, a single subject, "I," may react to Madonna differently at different times and even to different aspects of Madonna in contradictory ways. Eagleton (1983) sees this theoretical difference stereotypically as German rationalism against French hedonism, with the latter caught up in an exuberant dance of language and delight in textures. For French decentered subjects, both text and reader are indeterminate and carry us away from home in what Barthes describes as a kind of readerly orgasm.

Whatever the medium, reception studies posit an active reader, whether centered or not, generating meaning from the perception and interpretation of a directing but indeterminate text. On CD or tape, in video or film, live or recorded, put on a pedestal or in the gutter, only "I" can discover what Madonna means to me.

Who Wins? Preferred, Negotiated, and Oppositional Readings

Many debates have revolved around the question of the alleged "passivity" or, alternatively, the "opposition" of the reader as he or she constructs meaning from a text. Elitist theories of both right and left until mid-century tended to regard audience members as cultural dopes. Conservatives wanted to protect audiences from brutal culture and to lead them to finer things. Radicals wanted to free audiences from commercial exploitation and repressive messages in mass culture. In either case, and in much media theory and research, audience members were assumed to be inactive recipients of messages from radio, television, advertising, music, newspapers, movies, and all media. Literary theory and cognitive psychology have attacked this assumption at its heart and rejected the crude behaviorism that supported it. People do not take Madonna in a passive way; they react! The reactions of what is now called "the active audience" may be accepting, rejecting, or mixed, as we see in reactions to Madonna.

In a general sense, a media discourse may be decoded from three hypothetical positions outlined by Hall in his presentation of the encoding/decoding model (1980). The *preferred reading* accepts fully the intended coding that was placed in the text by the producers and reflects the dominant ideology. This is the "dominant-hegemonic" position and it operates within the dominant code. Consider reactions to the Vietnam War as an example. When American news and entertainment programming drew on Cold War categories and images to represent the Vietnam War, there were implied negative judgments about Communism, North Vietnam, and the Vietcong, and the preferred reading was that the Communist (North) side was evil and the procapitalist (South) side good. Initially, both American politicians and the press presented the war in this way and the preferred public reading was acceptance.

The *negotiated reading,* identified by Hall, contains a mixture of acceptance and rejection of the dominant code and the preferred meaning encoded into the text. The negotiated reading usually accepts the larger frame provided by the dominant code but makes exceptions to it. A negotiated reading of the Vietnam War emerged within the American public over time. People still accepted the overall opposition to Communism but concluded that this war was not worth the cost in lives and dollars.

The *oppositional reading* decodes the message in a totally contrary way within an alternative frame of reference. This response understands the dominant and intended preferred meaning encoded by the media production but interprets the message in a globally contrary way. An oppositional reading by radical antiwar activists found the prowar messages of Presidents

Johnson or Nixon to be nothing more than empty propaganda defending an indefensible war in a wrong-headed larger cause. Oppositional reading interpreted the United States losing the war in Vietnam as a result of its being on the wrong side.

"Negotiated readings are probably what most of us do most of the time," in Hall's view (1994, p. 265). This is because, on the one side, a perfectly transparent reading, in which the decoding by the reader perfectly corresponds to the encoding or preferred discourse, is not usual. Each of us brings our own quirks and subjective associations to the text. On the other side, a perfectly revolutionary reading that systematically pulls from the text the opposite of what the encoders intended is also not usual. One may interpret the exercise of law and order as oppression and injustice, but it requires rare effort and attention in addition to political savvy to read all uses of police force in an oppositional way. In the negotiated and most frequent reading, we are "boxing and coxing" with the text, in the words of Hall, rather than accepting or rejecting it whole.

Fiske argues for *resistant readings* in his interpretation of "the popular." Popular resistance to domination is *always* present in the popular, according to Fiske. He has expanded the definition of oppositional and negotiated decoding to include all active consumption of popular culture. He explains, "popular culture is made by subordinated peoples in their own interests out of resources that also, contradictorily, serve the economic interest of the dominant. Popular culture is made from within and below, not imposed from without or above . . . ." (1989a, p. 2). The opposition may take the form of direct resistance or less direct evasion. In Fiske's reading, the female fans of Madonna *resist* the patriarchal meanings of female sexuality, and surfers at the beach *evade* social discipline with its ideological control. "Resistance," Fiske notes, "produces meanings before pleasures" whereas "evasion is more pleasurable than meaningful" (p. 2). Both are oppositional.

Celeste Michelle Condit (1991) has warned against overestimating the power of these resistant readings of a polysemic text. In a study of how viewers read an episode of the television series *Cagney & Lacey,* she found opposing interpretations based not on the perception of the text but on the evaluation of it, in this case as either for or against abortion. She found that both pro- and antiabortion leaders had "read" the text of the episode *in the same way.* But one liked it and the other did not. This means that judgments of the text, not comprehension, were the source of disagreement. The conflict was not over the multiple layers of embedded meaning proposed by the text, those "polysemic" differences encoded in the narrative. Rather, the disagreement was over values, the "polyvalent" responses to the text by the different readers. This qualifies Fiske's implication that the polysemy of texts *always* generates oppositional interpretation, as if every casual viewer were engaged in stubborn debate with the screen. Gitlin (1986) cautions that we not confuse casual surfing of cable channels with facing down the tanks in Tiananmen Square. Overstating audience "resistance" and "evasion" in reading the popular is quite possible. There are couch potatoes out there who generate very little meaning beyond what the media text gives. As an alternative, the terminology of preferred, negotiated, and oppositional readings, with an emphasis on the negotiated, offers balance.

Which Are the Preferred Readings of Violence, Sex, or Madonna?

Madonna does what she wants to do. For example, while in Canada the officials didn't want her to perform "Like a Virgin" on her Blond Ambition tour. They said it was against the law to touch yourself in public, but she did it.—*Female, 26*

Madonna knows exactly how to play the media system. She, as a woman, is taking herself to the outer limits. She's very risk taking and has a lot of nerve and I admire that in her. She's a self-determined person yet also presents herself as a sex object by expressing her open sexuality.—*Female, 22*

She has been testing some boundaries, and I always like that. Why not shake up those people in Kansas?—*Female, 25*

There's nothing left to shock us with. What's next? X-rays?—*Female, 21*

She thinks she's in charge but I think it is the public. When the public stops caring, it won't matter if she is walking nude with a bone through her cheek.— *Female, 25*

Placing readings of Madonna in the schema of preferred, negotiated, and oppositional readings is a bit difficult. Her own relationship to the dominant culture is an uneasy one, sometimes oppositional, other times accommodating. As a result, one form of opposition to Madonna is itself based in acceptance of the preferred, dominant conservative culture and reading. Other forms of opposition to Madonna may oppose her but also oppose those larger social norms. Likewise, accepting the "preferred" reading of Madonna as proposed by Madonna herself may take several forms. One may accept her because she appears to reject society's norms, or one may accept her because she doesn't seem to have deviated too far from what is seen as society's norms. But of course, as many of our quotes from students about Madonna indicate, the "negotiated" reading that accepts some and rejects other aspects of Ms. Ciccone is the most common.

On the more general questions of sex and violence in the media, there are also contradictory decodings because the encoding is ambiguous. Is dominant media for or against sex and violence? Media entertainment content in drama, talk shows, and news, especially during ratings periods, is saturated with sex and violence. The dominant discourse encoded into the media culture is approval of violence to resolve conflict and of sex to sell goods and motivate other activities. Yet the puritan tradition is strong enough to oppose explicit portrayal of nudity and sexual acts in most English-speaking countries today, except in clearly identified adult vehicles. Somewhat differently, violence is roundly condemned and bemoaned in society even as it flourishes in media. Therefore, the preferred encoding of media culture would appear to be proviolence and prosex, despite words and warnings to the contrary.

What then are the preferred or oppositional decodings or readings of these overarching messages of sex and violence? The preferred or conventional reading accepts media violence in the United States, except for the most graphic forms coming into the home on television. The preferred reading in Great Britain and Canada accepts many more limits on violence. The preferred reading in the United States of media sex likewise accepts it but rejects explicit portrayals, except with restricted access as in private viewing or the NC-17 rating. Curiously, the greater acceptance in America of violence over sex seems to contradict the behavioral research evidence on effects. Once again, the most common reaction is a negotiated reading that simultaneously accepts and rejects selected elements of the dominant encoding of sex and violence. The difficulty in pluralistic, democratic societies is to then determine public policies that accept complexity and find a balance between dominant preferences and oppositional rights.

How do young people read Madonna as a whole? Often in contradictory ways. For example, I asked 70 university undergraduates whether they "approve" or "disapprove" of Madonna. (They were not part of the larger survey.) More men were negative, with 19 disapproving, 16 approving, and 8 in between. More women were positive, with 11 approving, 8 disapproving, and 8 in between. In the total group, exactly 27 approved and 27 disapproved, with 16 in between. With many in this group, the first image that comes to mind with regard to Madonna involves sex. Even those who approve of her acknowledge that they think first of "slut" or of pointed cone bras and lingerie. The semiotic excess spilling over from Madonna leads Fiske (1989a) to speak of her image "not as a model meaning for young girls in patriarchy, but a site of semiotic struggle between the forces of patriarchal control and feminine resistance, of capitalism and the subordinate, of the adult and the young" (p. 97).

No one doubts Madonna's ability to market herself as this "site of semiotic struggle."

The woman is a marketing genius! I don't think her music is fine. She looks like a whore. But, hey, can she sell!—*Female, 22*

When I think of Madonna, I think of a marketing genius. She knows exactly what the public wants of her. Madonna means the ability to look into the hearts of the consumers and present them with something that they want but normally do not receive. For example, the explicit costumes and gestures they receive from viewing her. I think it's the voyeur quality that sells.—*Male, 25*

Madonna is a performer who has been incredibly successful by scandalizing and exposing herself. She does what every performer does, but takes it to an extreme. Madonna is a businesswoman. She knows what sells, what people want to see, and what will cause a commotion. She takes this and uses it to her advantage.—*Male, 20*

Madonna is a very smart business woman who worked very hard to get where she is today. I feel she is very intelligent, gets what she wants when she wants it, and serves as a positive role model for those striving for the top. I feel that too many people are jealous and that is why they are so negative toward her.—*Female, 24*

The marketing thrust of Madonna and all of media culture has qualities of hegemony and domination and plays a role in the way we read media texts.[2] In light of this, an emphasis on context-activated reading sees encoding taking place within the circuits of production in capitalism and decoding taking place within the circuits of consumption in capitalism. The dominant system's encoding serves to privilege certain readings, but decoding makes variations on those readings. Dominant capitalist encodings of violence, sex, or Madonna propose them as acceptable vehicles for moving commodities and enriching the privileged but is less comfortable with them as sources of pleasure or opposition in their own right. Preferred readings accept that, oppositional readings oppose it, and negotiated readings navigate between the extremes.

The Power of "Interpretive Communities" in Media Reception

I hang out with a lot of people who almost idolize and worship Madonna, so I hear only good things about her. Negative media attention doesn't get a second look by my peers.—*Male, 20*

One of my friends is a huge Madonna fan—read all the books, etc., and passed down the info. She may be biased because she likes her, but I think I have taken it into account.—*Male, 21*

Some of her songs are cute and catchy, but neither me nor the people I hang out with ever talk about her.—Male, 20

I am positive toward Madonna. Why? Because everyone hates her so much, which in turn makes me like her a lot more.—*Male, 22*

All the preceding relate their reactions to Madonna to group membership. Subjects do not live in social vacuums when they read media texts. Early cultural studies may have oversimplified by implying that class, race, and sex were the dominant variables determining how a person will read a text. True, minimum-wage workers, the unemployed, non-whites, and women have prima facie motivations toward oppositional readings that rich, white management men do not have. But empirical studies of how people actually decode a television program or romance novel indicate a more complex, less predictable set of responses that sometimes reflect social positioning by race, sex, and class and sometimes do not. As Hall notes, "your readings arise from the family in which you were brought up, the places of work, the institutions you belong to, the other practices you do" (1994, p. 270).

In "Women's Genres," Annette Kuhn (1984) distinguishes between the individual spectator and the social audience of cinema. The individual spectator is constituted by cognitive and psychic relations to the cinematic text but the social audience has the added dimension of a group experience and the interpretive strategies available to members of that group. Film viewing is considered to be a complex act of decoding from visual-aural cues in narrative, mise-en-scène, cinematography, acting, music, special effects, and other filmic codes. Yet talking with friends about a film, reading reviews, seeing ads and previews for it—these and more add extratextual cues that influence our personal reading of the film. Film, because it has historically been written about as an art form, is seen to have complex individual and group readings. Television, in contrast, because it has been considered largely to be a business, is seen to have passive and inactive readings, and audiences have been studied primarily in the aggregate to provide ratings for advertisers. Reception studies attempt to retain the best of both by wedding the active viewer of film with the social audience member of television.

Feminist awareness is the most clearly documented instance of decoding strategies developed by and available within interpretive communities. Radway's (1984) influential, groundbreaking study, *Reading the Romance*, found a group of women who unself-consciously used romance novels to create a space for themselves that was outside the patriarchal culture of their daily lives with its routines of raising children, homemaking, and work. Their group experience around a particular bookstore was decisive in maintaining that negotiated reading of what romance novels can do. Likewise, Linda Steiner's (1991) study, "Oppositional Decoding as an Act of Resistance," examined the "No Comment" section of *Ms.* magazine. That section quotes sexist items in the general press and then holds them up for critical examination and humor within the *Ms.* context. Like the romance reading group, the "No Comment" section creates an interpretive community that facilitates oppositional and negotiated readings by individual female subjects.

Interpretive communities often direct our reading of media culture. In the preceding chapter, for example, membership in interpretive communities played an important role in ritual participation and enabled the "acting out" of textual readings in sports viewing, aerobics classes, and video games. For Madonna readers too, interpretive communities are influential. Studies of Madonna by Patton (1993), Henderson (1993), and Schwichtenberg (1993c) read her contribution from within the interpretive communities of gay and lesbian culture. They find densely coded references with rich meaning for gays and lesbians in Madonna texts. Many feminists have written extensively of Madonna in her role as a text that poses a feminist question (see Kaplan, Mandziuk, Pribram, & Morton in Schwichtenberg, 1993a), that is, they read her from within a feminist interpretive community. As a postmodern star, Madonna challenges many cultural conventions (Rogers & Real, 1994). Madonna's independence and iconoclasm toward the dominant patriarchal and restrictive culture suggests oppositional discourse, especially for those with access to feminist interpretive strategies assisted by interpretive communities. Many survey respondents saw Madonna within a feminist perspective:

Madonna is a feminist in the true sense. She goes beyond all typecast gender roles. She is powerful and exploits sex rather than it exploiting her.— *Female, 23*

She provides a strong female role and has done more for females as stronger characters than most anyone.—*Male, 21*

Madonna has changed the culture among the 13- to 20-year olds. I feel she is not a great role model for children, although she has acted out what men have been acting out for years. She's a slut, but she is mocking men in an abrasive way.—*Female, 28*

Madonna is a strong woman, ballsy, chameleon. I think of her as clever, talented, ground breaking, a feminist and manipulative of the media for her own ends.—*Female, 26*

Terry Eagleton (1983) notes certain moments and places in history when culture becomes newly relevant, "charged with a significance beyond itself" (p. 215). This is when interpretive communities emerge and exert influence. He identifies four such culturally important moments in recent history. First, those struggling for independence from political and economic imperialism become aware of the political power in culture. Second, the women's movement concerns culture directly both as a site where oppressive discourse can be deciphered and as a place where it can be challenged. Third, the "culture industry" marks an area where traditional sensibility is challenged and democratic control is being fought for. Fourth, working-class writing opens up culture by breaking from the dominant relations of literary production and offering community and cooperative publishing in addition to alternative social values.

Reception theory incorporates the experience of these communities as it also incorporates the power of the unconscious and the findings of empirical studies. Stuart Hall calls for incorporating an awareness of the "unconscious" to balance the earlier preoccupation of reception studies with cognition and strictly mental responses (Hall, 1994). Operating below the consicous cognitive level, the unconscious seeks out the pleasurable response. This fills in an additional aspect of how reception constructs meaning. At the same time, reception studies have benefited from increased empirical work to test and extend theory. These reception studies employ methodologies of ethnography, focus groups, interviews, and self-analysis. Just as empirical research on sex and violence sheds light on our responses to them, and surveys concerning Madonna clarify her cultural ambiguity, so additional empirical studies will interact effectively with reception theory to clarify how we respond to media culture.

Summary

Reception studies examine the way we read and interpret media culture. Our reading may be activated primarily by the text, the reader, or the context. Media messages of sex or violence or Madonna can influence us, but our interpretation of the messages takes many forms. In response to messages encoded by the dominant culture, our reading may accept the preferred meaning or oppose it or find some negotiated mixture. We often take our lead in interpreting media from the interpretive community to which we belong.

In short, reception studies clarify how the decentered subject in postmodern culture constructs meaning from a text, decoding with or against the encoding embedded in the text. Texts suggest, but do not determine, our reading of them and our ritual participation with them.

Are reception studies, then, the solution to our hypothetical mystery, our current cultural crisis? Reception studies open up important dimensions of the problem of media culture today. Yet at this point and by themselves they cannot resolve the mystery, for they must necessarily confine their attention to the work of the reader without explaining the structures of dominance in the encoding infrastructure or the textual characteristics of media messages themselves or other aspects of media culture not directly involved with how texts are received. The following chapters suggest further suspects. Can "textual analysis" solve our mystery by explaining what message content is presented to us in the media and how it is structured? Does the power of "production hegemony" over the making of media culture explain our problem, or can the conflicts over gender, race, history, and ethics resolve our riddle? How do these approaches to media culture interact with reception studies? Whatever the answers to those questions, an understanding of reception studies takes us a step closer to resolving the mystery of media culture in our lives today.

Notes

1. The surveys reported here were conducted in an undergraduate media course during fall semester for three years at San Diego State University. The first survey included 168 students, approximately half from 1991 and half from 1992. The second survey included 70 students from 1993. There were five questions on each survey. (1) When you hear "Madonna" what first comes to your mind? (2) What does Madonna mean to you? (3) Do you think Madonna is an old style exploited sex object or a new style self-directed woman? (4) Is Madonna managed by herself or by others? (5) How much exposure have you had to Madonna? Responses on the last question were in six rows: exposure to Madonna on MTV, radio, movies, magazines, concerts, and other. Each row offered three choices: a lot, some, none. The 1993 sample was asked, in addition, if they approved or disapproved of Madonna.

Demographically, only sex and age were asked of respondents. In general, survey respondents were reflective of national college student demographics with an age range from 17 to 63 but with a concentration in the 20s and a mixture of Latino, African American, and other ethnic groups. Sampling methods and representativeness are not issues because no generalizations to the total population are attempted.

2. The terminology of preferred, negotiated, and oppositional builds from the work of Althusser, Derrida, and Gramsci. The structural Marxism of Louis Althusser (1971) identifies repressive state apparatuses (RSAs), which include the government, armies, police, courts, and prisons; they function on behalf of the dominant class and often through violence or repression. Althusser also identifies ideological state apparatuses (ISAs) of religion, education, families, political parties, and media culture; ISAs are more plural and ideological than the RSAs, which are more overdetermined and direct. The deconstruction of texts and reading by Jacques Derrida

(1976) partially seeks to undermine the control of structures of domination in the manner of poststructuralism. The state apparatuses identified by Althusser can be seen, for example, to propose patriarchal domination by traditional male culture. Deconstruction of texts and readings conveying such patriarchy point out the power relations at work. As noted previously, Gramsci's (1971) concept of hegemony clarifies the exercise of influence by the dominant over the dominated, whether rich over poor, industrialized over traditional, white over non-white, male over female, or any other arena of struggle. Modern hegemony is exercised not by coercion by the RSAs or ISAs through force but by achieving the consent of the dominated. To do this, hegemony marshals the power of media culture in addition to other institutions and forces in society. The result is not absolute domination but a negotiated mix of dominant containment and subordinate opposition. From these we make our preferred, negotiated, or oppositional readings.

EXERCISES

Chapter Three

Exercise A. CONFLICTING READINGS. Select a "controversial" topic in current news and interview a small number of people in-depth about their reading of it. Seek divergent opinions. Where is their information from? How and why do they interpret it? Why do readings (polysemy) and evaluations (polyvalence) vary so much from person to person?

Exercise B. LYRICS. Quiz friends about song lyrics they may have misunderstood. How did their misreading differ from the actual lyrics? How did they find out they were wrong? Does it make any difference how we understand songs? Take one song and identify a text-activated reading of it, a reader-activated reading of it, and a context-activated reading of it.

Exercise C. RECEPTION THEORY. What are the origins and implications of "reception studies" as a critical development? Where do reception studies fit in the traditions of literary theory? Of media research? What does sensitivity to variations in reception add to our understanding of media culture?

Exercise D. STAR RECEPTION. Select a popular star and analyze her or him as Madonna has been analyzed. What does your star mean, both as a text and as received by fans? What different responses can you identify among fans (and nonfans)? Which are preferred, negotiated, or oppositional readings?

Exercise E. NEGOTIATED READING. Pick a favorite expression of media culture and identify to what extent your reading of it may be preferred, negotiated, or oppositional. Define each of those three terms. Do friends in your interpretive community make readings similar to yours? Do you find your reaction to popular topics tends to fall regularly toward the preferred, negotiated, or oppositional decodings?

Exercise F. SEX AND VIOLENCE. How does research evidence on the effects of media violence differ from that on pornography? Do you find the claims of either research tradition plausible according to your common sense and experience? What are the differences between research findings and mere opinion? Trace facts, evidence, and logic employed in popular arguments about media sex and violence.

4

Textual Analysis:
Light Against Darkness in Disney and Film Noir

Mickey Mouse lives as a middle-aged has-been above a dingy bar with Minnie. Donald Duck frequents the same bar. He is working on a road show deal with shady characters in topcoats. Goofy is no longer allowed in the bar after having been caught one too many times shooting up in the men's room. At the end of another day with no calls from the Italian director, Minnie helps Mickey up the backstairs to their tiny, bare apartment.

The preceding is a summary of a text by British playwright Campbell Black. The text is a tragic scenario in the form of a sacrilegious play based on Disney characters titled *And They Used to Be in Movies*. The Disney lawyers have prevented it from being produced and the play has received scant recognition, but it is an ingenious turn on the textual standards for Disney products, reversing them in effect into film noir characters and stories. How can such a text, or any text for that matter, work?

Textual Analysis in Media Culture

Is "textual analysis" the key to unlocking the mysteries of contemporary media culture? What does it mean to consider "the text" of a media experience? The words on the page in this book, the images on the screen of a theater or television set or computer, and the music emanating from speakers are what convey the text. The text is whatever is encountered by the receiver's physical senses in accessing the media presentation. The text is that magical point of contact when one person's or group's creation reaches others, generating from the contact some form of meaning.

The Pleasure of the Text. The attraction of a media experience lies in "the pleasure of the text," as Roland Barthes (1975) dubbed it. We play video games or attend ballet, watch a ball game or read classics, in most cases because we enjoy the experience generated by our reception of those texts. Film study in particular has stressed the pleasurable encounter between spectator and screen, between reader and text. Film critic Robert Warshow (1970) labeled this *The Immediate Experience.* Even those who claim to read the newspaper "to be informed" are usually found also to experience in it pleasure for its own sake (Berelson, 1949). Whether it is sought as art or information or distraction, "the immediate experience" reaches us in the form of a text that comes from the media producer to the receiver who is seeking its pleasures.

The pleasure sought may be joy and light—a Disney touch—or cynicism and darkness—the noir touch. The Disney Corporation has created an abundance of texts in a wide range of media for the greater part of a century. These texts, despite their diversity, tend to exhibit a similarity that makes them identified with "the Disney touch." In a parallel movement in the opposite direction, the cinema style called *film noir* has been with us almost as long as Disney. These film texts reflect a dark similarity of style and emphasis that identify them as film noir (literally "black film," from the French). Despite their contrasting directions, the texts of Disney and film noir have a great deal in common. Each achieved fame as film texts. They share historical and geographical origins in the Hollywood of the Golden Era, namely, Los Angeles in the 1930s and 1940s, and have waxed and waned in popularity since then. Both have recently experienced renewed success, they have singularly distinctive styles, and each has received excellent critical treatment. The studies edited by Eric Smoodin (1994a) titled *Disney Discourse: Producing the Magic Kingdom* and by Alain Silver and Elizabeth Ward (1992) on *Film Noir: An Encyclopedic Reference to the American Style* are exceptional in their critical facility and completeness as examinations of texts in media culture.

Texts employ specific forms and conventions to give shape and purpose to our media experience, and textual analysis explores those devices. We learn a great deal about Disney and noir by asking, what are their differences and similarities in terms of narrative structure, semiotic coding, genre conventions, use of language and discourse, and political economic context?

The central place of the text in the communication experience is illustrated in the introductory figure (Figure 0.1) in this book—Stuart Hall's chart of the media encoding-decoding process (1980). In that chart the component in the top and center is the text, in the form of a television program as meaningful discourse. Social, technical, and cognitive factors contribute to the meaning encoded in the text and the meaning decoded from the text, but the text remains central.

Textual analysis foregrounds a number of elements that traditional media research suppresses. First, in "effects" research the pleasure of the text itself was largely ignored in the search for behavioral effects. Second, "uses and gratifications" studies returned focus to the media experience but in relation only to the psychological or social motivations and rewards for seeking out media. Third, media "content analysis" from the start restricted itself to "the objective, systematic, and quantitative description of the manifest content" (Berelson, 1952), eliminating all the subtle messages only implied by texts. Textual analysis moves beyond these reflections of the old bullet transmission model to seek a richer sense of meaning in media texts of all types. In particular, the opening of media analysis to literary, hermeneutic, and rhetorical forms of study has recovered a sense of depth in texts. Literary theories of "narrativity" consider far more than the mere transmission of "information." Correlatively, an understanding of sign and code systems, genre, formula, convention, discourse, intertextuality, and context opens important and interesting dimensions within the exploration of media culture.

The Disney Text: Utopian Brightness of the Magic (Corporate) Kingdom

The Disney text takes countless forms but the message remains consistent. These forms appear in feature films, animated cartoons, television specials, theme parks, comic books, jigsaw puzzles, dolls, clothing, watches, and virtually any imaginable cultural product. Their message is: Feel happy in seeing good triumph and evil be destroyed. This message is the classic utopian attraction. Happiness is possible by restructuring the world into an ideal form where good and evil are clearly distinguishable, the good is like us, and the evil is identified and eliminated. The narrative texts most associated with the Disney name draw this out. Once upon a time, an attractive hero, often a young person, faces a challenge. He or she is opposed by a villain or villains readily identifiable as evil. The hero attempts to achieve a positive triumph but is thwarted and threatened by the villain. After much travail, the hero overcomes the villain in an outcome that also benefits many other people. And the good people live happily ever after.

From the earliest Mickey Mouse cartoons to the latest spin-offs from summertime animated features, from the simplest text to theme parks in three countries, the overriding Disney message has always been one of comfort and optimism in the midst of life's adversities. The theme parks are, in fact, structured after the manner of a classical utopia (Real, 1977), separated from the world, built to their own idealistic rules, and never-ending in the quest for new means to realize escapist dreams of good triumphant and virtue rewarded. Sir Thomas More's *Utopia,* Dante's *The Divine Comedy,* the utopian farm of B. F. Skinner, and Aldous Huxley's *Island* never came close to being fleshed out with the vividness and participation of the magic utopian kingdom where wishes come true at the hands of Walter Elias Disney, his descendants, and their "imagineers." As Mitsuhiro Yoshimoto (1994) notes, "the theme park tries to create an autonomous, utopian space cut off from the rest of society" (p. 186). The physical separations of sacred Disney from profane freeways (Marin, 1977) are coupled with narrative packaged histories, complete with beginning, middle, and end, to create a "self-enclosed totality" (Yoshimoto, p. 186).

The Disney text has been immensely popular since 1930 (deCordova, 1994) but not consistently so (Gomery, 1994). Since the takeover that put Michael Eisner in charge in 1984, Disney has multiplied itself several times over on a global scale. But the Disney drive for expansion and diversification has never disengaged itself from the varied, but somehow always similar, universal Disney text. Until his death in 1965, Walt Disney, backed by his businessman brother Roy, was the force behind what Richard Schickel (1968) called *The Disney Version,* a version of imagined text that reached all corners of the globe and helped shape several generations of children and families. For two decades after Walt's death, the Disney team coasted on the name but had no creative daring, "poisoned by their own success" (Masters, 1991). The financial gold mines born with Disneyland in 1955 and Walt Disney World in 1971 carried the lackluster Disney films and television of the period (Gomery, 1994).

The first decade of Michael Eisner's obsessive leadership brought a successful Disney cable channel, new theme parks in Asia and Europe, creation of Disney stores and clothing lines, a return to first-class animation, new adult feature films from Disney-owned Touchstone and Hollywood Pictures, and a $9 billion annual revenue (Lewis, 1994). The new film-making subsidiaries produced *Three Men and a Baby* and *Sister Act,* which did not stray all that far from the simple Disney formulas, but also others, such as Paul Mazursky's *Down and Out in Beverly Hills,* Abrahams and Zucker's *Ruthless People,* Robert Redford's *Quiz Show,* or Garry Marshall's *Pretty Woman,* all aimed at a range of mature, even cynical audiences. These films provided income to the larger Disney corporation without tainting the pristine Disney name. The theme parks in Florida, Japan, and France, the first two wildly successful and the third not, were slight but lucrative variations on the original designed by Walt for Southern California (Wilson, 1994).

The quintessential Disney text in all this is bright, upbeat, optimistic, simple, and clever. The text celebrates the "light" side of life, especially family and childhood, if not as they really are, then at least as middle-class people wish they were. The very name "Disney" continues to evoke a naively happy utopia where wishing, dreaming, and magic come true. Echoing the advertising slogans of the theme parks, all Disney products beckon us to enter "the magic kingdom," "the happiest place on earth." Disney products exemplify the way texts tell a story, carry a message, multiply, divide, and conquer.

The Film Noir Text: Darkness
in Content, Style, and Worldview

At the opposite pole from the interminable lightness of Disney texts lies the darkness of film image and story known as *film noir.* First labeled *film noir* by French critics in 1946, the group of films known by this label are a curious American melting pot of historical, social, and stylistic trends. Their literary genesis is the hard-boiled detective novels of Raymond Chandler, Dashiell Hammett, James M. Cain, Cornell Woolrich, and *Black Mask* magazine. Their visual sources are the shadowy, underlit, high-contrast images of German Expressionism in the works of Hollywood refugees Fritz Lang, Robert Siodmak, Max Ophuls, Billy Wilder, Otto Preminger, and others, influenced also by the visual style of Hollywood gangster movies of the 1930s and the look of Italian neo-realism in the 1940s. Noir works in the historical-social context of the suffering and aftermath of World War II with a sense of disillusionment and pessimism absent from most American films. The story line relies on a serious crime investigated by a cynical private detective or police investigator (or sometimes a naive layman caught up in a web of crime) who is confounded by an attractive femme fatale, both operating in a seedy urban underworld of amoral alienation, paranoia, and fatalism.

The classic film noir style thrived from the making of *Double Indemnity* in 1944 to the completion of *Sunset Boulevard* in 1950. Many critics (Schrader, 1972) extend the classic period of noir from *The Maltese Falcon* in 1941 to *Touch of Evil* in 1958. The definitive publication on the style, *Film Noir: An Encyclopedic Reference to the American Style* (Silver & Ward, 1992), extends the high noir period into the 1960s but documents its declining popularity after the middle 1950s and its renewed popularity in the 1980s and 1990s. The heritage of noir continues to the present in neo-noir films such as *The Grifters, Taxi Driver, Silence of the Lambs, Lethal Weapon, 48 Hours, Body Heat, Blood Simple, Basic Instinct, Reservoir Dogs, Seven, Chinatown,* and *Pulp Fiction.*

Worldview, story line, and visual presentation converge uniquely into a single unified whole in film noir. The result is a recurring form in world cinema. As different from Disneyana as gangster rap is from *Sesame Street,* film noir illustrates how media culture constructs variant texts within the larger circus tent of popular communications. Noir is the evil twin of Disney's bright world. Adult, pessimistic, sexual, brutal, and unsettling, film noir stands starkly opposed to the childlike optimism and reassuring puritanism of the Disney text.

Differences between Disney and film noir underscore the point that "the text matters." Reception theories, as we saw in the preceding chapter,

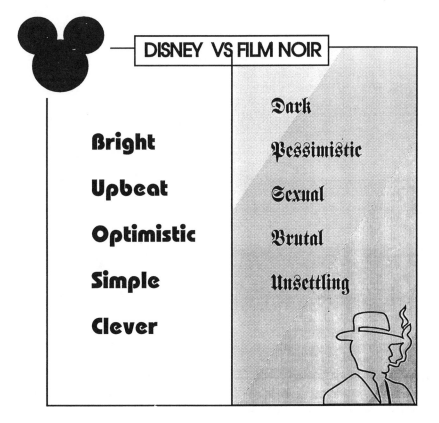

Figure 4.1. Disney texts evoke a naively happy utopia where wishing, dreaming, and magic come true. Film noir texts stand starkly in contrast with adult pessimism and dark psychosocial conflicts.

emphasize the active reader interpreting and constructing meaning from a text, but this does not make the text "endlessly open" to every imaginable interpretation. Even the most inventive readers do not get the same thing from Disney that they get from film noir (see Figure 4.1).

**Narrative Structure in
Media Texts: Storytelling**

Media Form. Texts in art or media take a specific shape or "media form" as a novel or a movie or a statistical table. Form follows function. If the function is to mass market an audiovisual product, the form may be a feature film, a fully visualized narrative story such as Disney's *Beauty and the Beast* or Robert Aldrich's *Kiss Me Deadly*. If the function is to provide cheapness and portability, it may take the form of *Walt Disney Comics and Stories,* complete with Donald Duck and bubble dialogue. For noir, the book form may be a Dashiell Hammett hard-boiled Sam Spade thriller. Recognizing the form and function of a media text is often a major part of what allows us to unpack the meaning loaded into it.

The form of a film, for example, entails a total system that the reader/ viewer/listener perceives. The form is not the opposite of content but rather conveys content. "Film form" is an organizational structure; we know whether we are watching a dramatic or a documentary film (Bordwell & Thompson, 1993). Narrative is one form of media, but there are also nonnarrative forms such as abstract, documentary, or rhetorical media forms. Leni Riefenstahl's documentary *Olympia* (1938) uses many such formalist forms in addition to narrative form. The form sets up viewer expectations by connecting with our previous experiences and by employing conventions and genres with which we are familiar. Degrees of repetition, variation, development, and unity distinguish each particular text and generate feeling and meaning.

The mixture of predictability and surprise in the form helps maintain interest. For example, if we experience the beginning of a media text as "AB," we are motivated to guess that the next unit will be an A, B, C, or something else. If it is an "A" we have "ABA," and the next may become "ABAB" or "ABAC." If the latter, then it in turn may lead to "ABACA" and so on (Bordwell & Thompson, 1993). The line, verse, and chorus structure of most popular songs follows a simple four-bar form that, despite its simplicity, seems capable of infinite variations. The sequential form gives coherence to the text. "Popular" texts feature predictability whereas "avant-garde" texts highlight surprise.

Narrative. "Narrative" is the most common form for media texts to take because stories are fundamental to human life and claim a universal, permanent appeal in their dramatic structure and form. Bedtime stories, news stories, biblical stories, jokes, novels, films—our interactions and entertainments frequently take the form of stories. We recall human history as a story and envision the future as a story. We experience our individual and group existence as a sequential story with its mixture of continuities and changes (Josselson & Lieblich, 1993; Riessman, 1993). Narrative refers to the textual form we call story. Stories exercise social control (Mumby, 1994) and are a major discourse genre for the reproduction of culture and society (Van Dijk, 1993). Story capacity may be more fundamental to humans than is reasoning capacity. Viewing the human as *homo narrans* rather than *homo ratio* emphasizes this against certain foundations of Western thought (Fisher, 1984, 1985) that have long argued for reason instead of storytelling as our fundamental human ability.

Narrative has been defined (Bordwell & Thompson, 1993) as "a chain of events in cause-effect relationship occurring in time and space" (p. 65). The narrative form of the first feature-length animated film, Disney's *Snow White* (1937), sets its time and space in an imagined rural and imperial past. Once upon a time, a chain of events is set in motion, is caused by, the evil Queen's jealousy of the beauty of her young stepdaughter Snow White. The Queen causes her to be taken to the woods to be killed by a huntsman, but the huntsman has pity on Snow White and releases her to escape into the dark woods. Snow White lives for a time happily with the Seven Dwarfs until the Queen, disguised as an old hag, feeds her a poison apple. The hag is chased by the Seven Dwarfs up a mountain where a bolt of lightning hurls her to her death. The Dwarfs mourn at Snow White's side until a handsome Prince gives her sleeping figure a kiss of pure love that awakens her back to life, and all live happily ever after.

In *Snow White* the time and place fix our imaginations with particular images developed in the Disney studios. Each of the actions exists as a step in the causes and effects that move the chain of events. Our identification with characters brings our feelings into play, the uncertainty of outcome creates excitement, and the resolution of the story brings a psychologically satisfying sense of closure at the end. Narrative's dramatic appeal was first charted and explained by the ancient Greeks but is as old as the human race.

Billy Wilder's *Double Indemnity* (1944) is a classic noir narrative film. The film's time and space are urban contemporary America. The chain of events is set in motion by the seduction of an insurance agent Walter (Fred MacMurray) by Phyllis (Barbara Stanwyck) so that he will assist her in murdering her husband and collecting on his accident insurance policy. Walter's insurance colleague Barton Keyes (Edward G. Robinson) suspects foul play and hesitates to pay the insurance claim. Because there is no honor among thieves, Walter mistrusts Phyllis and decides to kill her, hoping to pin both murders on Phyllis's other boyfriend Zachette. But Phyllis mistrusts Walter and the two wind up shooting each other, Phyllis proclaiming her love for Walter as she dies. Walter stumbles back to his office and dictates a confession that he gives to Keyes before he collapses dead on his way to the elevator. *Double Indemnity* offers almost a new template of film narrative, one built on greed, passion, mistrust, and destruction. The script is based on a novel by James M. Cain and co-authored by Raymond Chandler, and the cinematography is by John F. Seitz and the music by Miklos Rozsa, giving *Double Indemnity* as pure a film noir bloodline as any.

Both films' narratives are stories of good and evil, of selfish greed and violence. But their narratives differ. The central characters in *Double Indemnity* are the villains, whereas Snow White is goodness personified. The central characters in *Double Indemnity*, Walter and Phyllis, commit a clever murder, are anxious, and finally propel themselves to destruction. Snow White avoids evil, remains pure, and passively receives a happy ending. Evil is punished in both cases and justice done. But, ironically, in *Snow White* the evil Queen is destroyed and Snow White revived only through magical deus ex machina solutions. In *Double Indemnity* the evil is punished by the narrative progression of psychological mistrust and self-protective destruction, not by outside forces. In this sense, the universe constructed by the film noir text has punishment and justice built into it, whereas the Disney universe has it imposed from outside. Why then would moralistic parents prefer to expose their children to *Snow White*?

The narrative details of the two films, the total systems of form in them, of course, set up the Disney film as "good" popular culture and the noir film as "adult." The characters and context are developed in *Snow White* with a happy, upbeat feeling through songs, the Dwarfs' antics, and Snow White's virtuousness. Only the Queen is evil and, although the woods and lightning storms can be momentarily scary, the bulk of the story takes place in brightly lit, colorful, charming, and attractive sites such as the Dwarfs' cottage and woods. Those visual and aural appeals, together with the happy ending, make this reassuring fare for youngsters.

In contrast, *Double Indemnity* is remorselessly dark, both visually and psychologically. Night-for-night exteriors and moodily lit interiors couple with Walter's depressed flashback narration to convey unremitting danger and negation. Phyllis plays the classic femme fatale ensnaring Walter in her web of evil, an archetypal figure common to film noir and widely reexamined in feminist writings (see Kaplan, 1980). The entanglements are obsessive and doomed. The story, visual style, and overall tone require mature appreciation of life's darker sides, an appreciation that many children, in addition to adults with Disney tastes, find almost impossible to achieve.

These contrasts arise as we generate "meaning in narrative" (Scholes & Kellogg, 1966). Meaning in narrative is a function of the relationship between two worlds: the fictional world created by the author and the real world experienced by the reader. When we say we "understand" a narrative, we mean that "we have found a satisfactory relationship or set of relationships between these two worlds" (p. 82). The "real world" of the reader may be so tawdry that noir makes sense or so cheery that only Disney fits. But we also choose fictional worlds because they do *not* resemble our real world but offer a variation from it, a new and different experience.

Narratives are built around a course of action and characters. Vladimir Propp, in his famous *Morphology of the Folktale* (1968), found characters and their functions essential for narrative. Arthur Asa Berger (1992) traces these through 31 functions that heroes, villains, and others perform in the sequence of the conflict and resolution of the folktale. In more general terms,

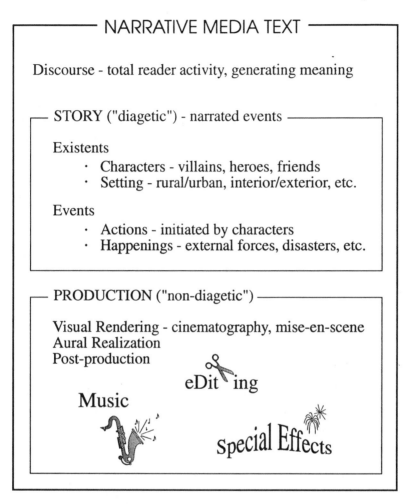

Figure 4.2. Components of the typical narrative text in media, including most films, videos, television shows, novels, and other popular forms.

the structural components of narrative form (Bordwell & Thompson, 1993; Chatman, 1978) in media texts includes the elements in Figure 4.2.

Discourse here is the interaction between the story, how the story is told, the reader, and the meaning generated from the story. *Story* is what is told, the plotline. In the story by Disney, the character of Snow White and the setting of happy forests contrast with the narrated elements in the noir story, the characters of Phyllis and Walter and the dark urban setting. These are the *existents* who experience *events* by taking actions and experiencing happenings in the story, issuing in the final happiness of Snow White and the destruction of Phyllis and Walter. Making these stories into films entails *production,* which renders the stories into a visual/aural form completed with postproduction enhancements. The finished production includes both the *diagetic* elements of all that takes place within the story itself and the *nondiagetic* elements such as titles, credits, and off-screen music that are brought in from outside the story. When Snow White sings, it is diagetic music, happening in the story, but when somber music tolls the fate of Phyllis and Walter in *Double Indemnity,* it is a nondiagetic addition that does not originate from within the story world itself.

Why do media narratives so powerfully attract and hold our attention? Peter Brooks examines this in *Reading for the Plot: Design and Invention in Narrative* (1984). Psychologically, why do we turn the pages? Why is it so difficult to leave a movie early, even a stinker? The answer lies in the dynamics of "the motor forces that drive the text forward, of the desires that connect narrative ends and beginnings, and make of the textual middle a highly charged field of force" (pp. xiii-xiv). We join in the story, our curiosity is aroused, and we want satisfaction. Narrative and discourse dominate the way we relate to each other and to the world. *Narrative in Culture: The Uses of Storytelling in the Sciences, Philosophy, and Literature* (Nash, 1990) argues for the importance of narrative to philosophers, psychoanalysts, historians, scientists, lawyers, economists and numerous others.

Humans live and breathe in stories so that, unsurprisingly, story narratives fill our lives and our media culture. "Narrative therapy" emerged in the 1990s as a method for getting clients to reexamine their life story, find successful passages, and focus on them instead of on their failures. The postmodern idea that we do not so much perceive the world as interpret it combines with the idea that the psyche is not a fixed, objective entity but a fluid social construct. Our story is not set in stone from childhood and our problem or crisis is not our whole life. We can review, revise, and amend our story. Instead of filtering out experiences of hope, resourcefulness, and capability, we can "reauthor" stories to make them do us justice. Because media culture provides our narrative tools and models, it plays an important role in such personal narrative psychotherapy.

Narrative drama has been respected since the time of Aristotle for its psychological power. In that tradition, the first influential theoretical work on film, Hugo Munsterberg's *The Photoplay: A Psychological Study* (1916), emphasized the natural power of film narrative, as art, to first stir the mind and then put it to rest. Christian Metz (1974), in his phenomenology of film, notes "a narrative has a beginning and an ending . . . [and a] basic requirement of enclosure" (p. 17). He then defines narrative as "a closed discourse that proceeds by unrealizing a temporal sequence of events" (p. 28). The narrative progressively chooses one option and closes off other options. Our ABAC sequence runs out as ABACADAEABACADAEBCBDBEAF or whatever until it reaches an end, and the anxiety of the narrative uncertainty is resolved in an experience of psychological and dramatic closure, of resolution, satisfaction, and peace. The causes and effects in time and place reach an end. Popular narratives incline toward a final "and they all lived happily ever after," although in the case of film noir that might read "unhappily ever after." In any case, the events and characters, the discourse and story, come to a resolution.

The visitor to Disneyland experiences a "narrativized space" broken into micronarratives in each land, creating through the movement of the visitor "the thematic coherence of Disneyland" (Willis, 1991, p. 57). The parks function not only as upscale amusement parks but also "as an extension of the cinema" in which "the spectator sees not the two-dimensional image reflected on the distant screen but a three-dimensional image that actively interacts with the spectator" (Yoshimoto, 1994, p. 186). Like Sergei Eisenstein, Walt Disney sensed the fundamental connection between the amusement park and the cinema; Disney revitalized the park by applying to it the narrative principles of cinema. The authorized account of *The Art of Walt Disney: From Mickey Mouse to the Magic Kingdom* by Christopher Finch (1973) notes that each park is designed like a movie lot, using the design skills that go into building film sets and the narrative skills of filmmakers to sequence the events into narratives (p. 393). The Disneyland designers were consciously aware that the park's moving vehicles in the Haunted Mansion, Pirates of the Caribbean, and elsewhere, carried the viewer through the plot like a movie camera (p. 415). In other words, principles of narrativity infuse life into Disney cultural products in all media, not only film or television.

Genre as a Narrative Convention in Media Texts

Narratives come to us in recognizable groupings—westerns, science fiction, comedies, and so forth—for which the French word for type or kind, *genre,* has become the label. Genres are a kind of conspiracy or tacit contract (Schatz, 1981) between author and reader, creators and audiences, for shorthand identification of narrative categories. Northrop Frye's famous *Anatomy of Criticism* (1957) argued that genre was the key to organizing all literature, drawing from the comic, romantic, tragic, and ironic, which roughly parallel spring, summer, autumn, and winter in spirit. Frye drew from New Criticism, which had centered literary theory on the text itself as an aesthetic object, and, in a formalist manner, he then schematized universal genres and modes.

For contemporary media culture, it is more common to treat genre in more specific ways, as historically contingent rather than as the universal forms proposed by Frye (1957). Feuer (1993) points out that critics and media industry workers classify works less in reference to universals of tragedy and comedy and more in reference to specific forms such as television situation comedies or movie screwball comedies. We use these categories as second nature when we browse particular sections in a video rental store: children's, romance, horror, science fiction, mystery, classics, foreign language, comedy, action-adventure, and others.

The value and power of genre awareness is efficiency. With a few brush strokes directors create and we recognize a western—horses, open range, cowboy hats, six-guns, lawmen, outlaws, and simple codes of force and honor. We recognize these signs as demarcating the western, and we anticipate what kind of plotline, conflict, and outcome we are most likely to encounter within it. We know whether we have generally liked this genre in the past or not. We may have our own set of classics in the genre to measure new efforts against. The mainstream standards of John Ford's *Stagecoach* (1939) or Fred Zinneman's *High Noon* (1952) may be our measure, or a revisionist western such as Kevin Costner's *Dances With Wolves* (1990) or Clint Eastwood's *Unforgiven* (1992) may be a personal favorite. Imagine how confusing and incomprehensible or even boring a western might be to a viewer who had never seen or heard of westerns. The show would lack meaningful context, predictable conflicts and structure, recognizable character types, and other familiar elements that virtually any modern viewer knowingly but unselfconsciously brings to an experience of the western genre.

Conformity and creativity fight against each other in the composition of a genre piece. The filmmaker creating a western has a number of givens already determined in advance. But within the given "conventions" of the genre, the filmmaker employs "inventions" that make each film an original entry in the western genre. For example, Michael Mann's *The Last of the Mohicans* (1992) and Arthur Penn's *Little Big Man* (1970) are inventive in portraying Native American life from within its own culture rather than from the conventional stereotype of savages threatening the paleface world. Disney's animated *Pocahontas* is falsely conventional in its invention of a purely mythic version of the Native American maiden. According to anthropologists and literary experts on Pocahontas, the film resists history in favor of popular myth. As evidence, one of the few reliable contemporary accounts describes Pocahontas as a naked 12-year-old with a shaved head, turning cartwheels around the Jamestown encampment to provoke the settlers (Connell, 1995); not exactly narrative imagery proper to a Disney text.

Disney struck it rich with a frontier western genre film in 1955 in the form of a three-part television series, later re-edited for theatrical release, titled

Davy Crockett. The theme song, "The Ballad of Davy Crockett," became a hit along with the television series and several additional Crockett films, making coonskin caps as popular as Mouseketeer ears in the 1950s. *Davy Crockett* told the story of the legendary frontiersman who fought Indians, went to Congress, and died at the Alamo. The show's strong landscape, solid acting, and effective action scenes combined with a typically idealized storyline to appeal widely to American audiences. *Davy Crockett* marries conventions of the western genre with conventions of the prototypical Disney story, clean-cut, uplifting, adventurous in a safe family way. In addition, *Davy Crockett* came along at a time when Disney had just begun a weekly television show and opened Disneyland and was fully exploiting the cross-marketing potential of these media.

The Disney theme parks also use genre effectively, with Frontierland typifying the western, Adventureland the overseas action-adventure genre, Fantasyland the fairy-tale genre of animation, and Tomorrowland a cautious science fiction genre. Disney products, in their quest for a large middle-class market, invariably exploit genre effectively, whether in musicals such as *Mary Poppins* (1964) or documentaries such as *Seal Island* (1949). The genre of animated musical features has been virtually defined and certainly dominated by Disney with some 34 such features from *Snow White* to *Pocahontas.*

Is Film Noir a Genre? Film noir poses a challenge to genre analysis. Although the grouping of movies known as film noir has been labeled a genre in *Hollywood in the Forties* (Higham & Greenberg, 1968) and in *Toward a Definition of the American Film Noir* (Karimi, 1976), most critics deny that noir really constitutes a genre. That film noir is not a genre, in contrast to the Western or gangster film, but instead takes us into the realm of classification by motif and tone was argued by Raymond Durgnat (1970, p. 49) and echoed by Paul Schrader (1972), Robert Porfirio (1976), and others. Schrader notes that noir is not defined, as are the western and gangster genres, by conventions of setting and conflict, but rather by the more subtle qualities of tone and mood (1972, p. 8). He traces noir tone and mood, themes and stylistics to four conditions. First, war and postwar disillusionment left Americans cynical and uneasy. Second, postwar realism in Italian, French, and world cinema countered Hollywood's Depression-era escapism and wartime patriotism, and proved it could attract an audience. A third condition was created when German Expressionism and expatriates contributed the definitive dark, high-contrast lighting of noir. And fourth, the hard-boiled school of American writers contributed preset conventions of heroes, minor characters, plots, dialogue, and themes (p. 10).

From these four conditions arose a distinctive style emphasizing scenes lit for night, oblique and vertical lines, actors not set off from the background, compositional tension, a Freudian attachment to water, fatalistic narration, and a complex chronological order. Recurring in all this was a set of 11 themes identified by Durgnat: crimes and social criticism, gangsterism, being on the run, private eyes and adventurers, middle-class murder, portraits and doubles, sexual pathology, psychopaths, hostages to fortune, blacks and reds, horror and fantasy. Certainly, of course, these elements together constitute an identifiable grouping of films. But the same could be said of Italian neo-realist or French New Wave films, and those are not considered genres.

Nevertheless, a case can be made for film noir as a genre. Foster Hirsch, in *The Dark Side of the Screen: Film Noir* (1981), calls noir "a full fledged genre." He notes, "a genre, after all, is determined by conventions of narrative structure, characterizations, theme, and visual design, of just the sort noir offers in abundance" (p. 72).

The question of genre status for noir resolves itself into how large we draw the circle in our definition of genre. If we make a long list of characteristic qualities necessary to define a genre, few groupings qualify. All films in the genre would have to share characteristic settings, icons, characters, plotlines, themes and motifs, visual designs, moods, and tones. Only the obvious genres would qualify: westerns, science fiction, and a few others. But if we make a shorter list of characteristics necessary for a genre and require only some of them, we can describe more genres and include more varied works in them. Mystery stories, police stories, private detective cases, gangster films, hard-boiled detective stories, drawing room who-done-its, terrorist cases, vigilante or kidnapping or embezzlement stories—all these and more could be called genres or, more precisely, identifiable subgenres of the larger master genre of crime fiction, if we draw the circle that way. Where to draw the circle depends at least partially on the practical purposes of the classifier.

A mixture of genres marks many products of media culture. A western with musical numbers is dubbed a *horse opera*. A continuing melodrama intended to sell domestic cleaners is called a *soap opera* in daytime television or, in the form of a nighttime *Knot's Landing* or *Coronation Street*, a *prime-time serial*. Disney's film and theater piece, *Beauty and the Beast*, blends a childhood fairy tale of a human trapped in the animal body of the Beast with an adolescent rite of passage for Belle and a stage comedy musical. These three genres—fairytale, coming-of-age, and musical—work dramatically together largely due to the exquisite detail in the animation, music, characterizations, and humor. Disney's *Aladdin* reworks the Arabian Nights adventure genre by introducing youthful romance and some stand-up comedy by Robin Williams backed by "A Whole New World" of music. Genre combinations allow interesting mixes of *conventions* from each genre and *inventions* in the crossovers between them.

Genre is a subject of continuous debate (see Grant, 1986) but its basic formulas are clear:

Formula stories like the detective story, the Western, the seduction novel, the biblical epic, and many others are structures of narrative conventions which carry out a variety of cultural functions in a unified way. We can best define these formulas as principles for the selection of certain plots, characters, and settings, which possess in addition to their basic narrative structure the dimensions of collective ritual, game and dream. (Cawelti, 1971, p. 33)

Cawelti calls these *formulas,* but Berger (1992) rightly suggests that "we use the term genre to cover the various kinds of texts that Cawelti sees as formulaic—westerns, spy stories, detective stories, and so forth and understand formulas to involve the various conventions found in various genres and subgenres" (p. 31).

In any case, most of us have a sense of genre that works and enables us to negotiate the classification of narratives into categories of genre and type adequate for our everyday purposes, however simple or complex.

Signs and Formulas in Media Culture

If the texts of Disney and film noir occur as narratives in recognizable genres, what smaller units in turn make specific action and scenes intelligible? How does the reader, viewer, or listener come to perceive a narrative text in a manner somewhat similar to what the author intends? What specific textual devices let us know that the father-son force in the *The Lion King* is "Disneyesque" and the mother, son, girlfriend edginess in *The Grifters* is "noirish"?

Specific signifying practices lead to the construction of meaning in media culture. Within the larger category of recognizable narrative genres, our media culture works through smaller units of formulas, signs, and codes. In flat, two-dimensional drawings within a projected frame of light, when we watch *The Lion King* we recognize the signs on the screen as a young lion and an old lion interacting. Even though cartoon animation does not look very much like reality, children know how to "read" cartoons, with no formal training, well before they can read written words. Preschoolers as young as two are readily sucked into the world of television cartoons, as virtually every modern parent can attest.

Signs and formulas work somewhat like the words in verbal language. An on-screen action is like a word, a film sequence is like a sentence, a full scene is like a paragraph or chapter, and a complete film is like a book. We read this grammar just as the filmmaker unselfconsciously produces it, that is, semiotically. These sign systems are familiar to both the producers who make media products and the consumers who buy them—with the effect that signs and sign systems work as means of cultural communication.

Signs and formulas, like the words that make up the scripts and dialogue of media, are the building blocks in the signifying systems of media culture. For semiotic and structuralist analysis these signs are to be interpreted or "deconstructed" specifically in reference to each other and to their total system. We understand Aladdin, his genie, his clothes, and his ethnicity within a coding system as old as the fables of the Arabian Nights. The outside world of the authors who create texts and the contexts that surround texts are of less interest to semiotic analysis than what is found in the formal structures and codes. The specific sign value of Mickey Mouse exists in his multiple incarnations in classic cartoons, comic books, wristwatches, clothing lines, and general Mousekemerchandising.

A "formulaic" convention employs signs to construct a specific reading and effect that occurs within the larger genre of the work. Take the example of a dramatic reunion between two lovers. Somewhere near the formulaic climax of a film or a television commercial, two people who are madly in love race toward each other to share the narrative's culminating embrace. The formulaic presentation employs slow motion for their running, cuts back and forth between their anxious but joyous faces, and shows it all happening in a well-lit frame with gauzy edges, wind billowing their hair and clothes, and a soaring soundtrack. Anyone caught up at all in the narrative cannot escape the programmed emotions of this formulaic coming together. Each of the signaling devices—slow motion, editing, lighting, acting, effects, sound—contributes to a single, unified effect. The "formula" for creating this climactic scene of lovers uniting comes from a ready-made set of conventions programmed for a specific effect.

Disney films are long on formulas of cute kids or pets and nasty villains, such as the lovable human and canine protagonists and the demonic antagonist Cruella de Vil in *101 Dalmatians* (1961). Similarly, when the brave heart of E.T. ceases, everything about the buildup to the scene and its presentation is calculated to induce tears. In this, the Spielberg touch is reminiscent of Disney. These emotional scenes are comprised of aural and visual signs arranged into a conventional formula to achieve predetermined ends.

Disney signs and formulas are widely recognized. The Disney formulaic textual devices often include a narrative of endangerment and rescue, especially of young and often female characters, whether human or animal. *The Little Mermaid* (1989), *Beauty and the Beast* (1991), *Homeward Bound: The Incredible Journey* (1993), and *Snow White and the Seven Dwarfs* (1937) employ this formula. Combining with formulaic storylines, the Disney animation style follows visual formulas, emphasizing brightly colored, well-lit scenes as dominant, with minor variations in the form of darkly sinister storms and night scenes. Disney characters are given fully rounded figures and flowing shapes that approximate naturalistic movement. Because of this completeness and constant search for improvement, in the 1930s British artist David Low called Walt Disney "the most significant figure in graphic art since Leonardo" (Schickel, 1968, p. 130). Exaggerated as that praise may be, the Disney visual style markedly surpasses the cheap line drawings and jagged movement of low-budget children's television animation, and the Disney style has come to virtually define naturalistic animation in the twentieth century.

Film noir also has characteristic formulas, the dark mirror reversals of Disney's. In a noir film the damsel may be the demon and the innocent hero the victim. Endangerment without rescue, victims facing imminent (self)destruction—the formulas have a seedy predictability against the formulaic lighting and music of wet, lonely streets in the night. Noir formulas occur often as visual motifs (Place & Peterson, 1974). Noir lighting purposely breaks the rules of classic key, fill, and back lighting, most noticeably by reducing the softening effect of fill lights. Lighting angles are changed, often moving key lighting below, above, or to the side of the character. This creates unnatural shadows and strange facial expressions. Interior sets are always dark, with foreboding patterns of shadow lacing the walls, and exteriors are shot "night-for-night" for maximum bleakness, rather than in the usual filtered Hollywood "day-for-night" manner. Wide-angle lenses are employed to achieve depth of field, so that objects at any distance are in sharp focus, giving equal weight to each. Wide-angle lenses also make faces bulge outward in close-up shots, especially in very tight "choker" close-ups of mouth to eyes, a shot favored in film noir. Gregg Toland's cinematography for Orson Welles's *Citizen Kane* contributed to these noir innovations. The mise-en-scène of film noir screen space disorients the viewer with bizarre, off-angle composition and claustrophobic framing devices such as doors, windows, stairways, and shadows. The visual style of noir, in this, stands as a direct descendant of the German Expressionism of *The Cabinet of Dr. Caligari* and *Metropolis.*

The viewer of *Double Indemnity* senses an anxious, troubled, even sinister quality as the narrative of Walter and Phyllis is shown in noir conventions of lighting, cinematography, and mise-en-scène. Place and Peterson conclude: "The 'dark mirror' of film noir creates a visually unstable environment in which no character has a firm moral base from which he can confidently operate. . . . Right and wrong become relative, subject to the same distortions and disruptions created in the lighting and camera work. Moral values, like identities that pass in and out of shadow, are constantly shifting and must be redefined at every turn" (p. 32).

Redundancy and Metaphor as Textual Devices. The texts we read in our cultural products employ varying degrees of *redundancy,* or repetition and mutual reinforcement among elements. Our codes or sign systems may be either restricted or elaborated, either redundantly predictable or complex and less predictable. Restricted codes are simpler and repeat themselves for emphasis. For example, in either Disney or film noir, as an action scene approaches a climax, the film's musical score becomes louder, characters and camera movement more dramatic, and the editing cuts more frequent. In this way, music, movement, the pace of editing, and the story reinforce the unified cognitive and emotional effect of the scene. They become redundant and mutually reinforcing.

A high degree of redundancy marks cultural products aimed at the mass market, the "most popular" culture. In contrast, a low degree of redundancy, with more originality and unpredictability, indicates ambitions toward so-called higher, elite, or avant-garde art. Famed Russian director and film theorist, Sergei Eisenstein, argued against redundancy between sound and image; he wanted the two to create a "collision of opposites" as part of his montage theory of film construction (Eisenstein, 1949). Eisenstein's willingness to combine a jarring image with placid music or vice versa increased the challenge and sophistication of his films. At the same time, of course, Eisenstein employed, in fact virtually created, many standard film conventions, formulas, and redundancies. Strikingly, in Disney, there is a great deal of formulaic redundancy between the mood or tone achieved in the aural-visual style and the mood or tone of the characters and storyline. Noir too seeks its own redundancy between style and content. In Disney, both are light; in film noir, both are dark.

There are many other semiotic devices at work in media texts, including metonym and metaphor. Mickey's image is a *metonym* for the Disney cartoons, that is, it is a part that stands for a whole. The smile on Mickey's face is a *metaphor* for the happiness of Disney audiences and, less obviously, for the happiness of Disney investors, that is, the smile stands metaphorically for something not literally related to itself. Another formulaic metaphor for Disneyland is the image of Mickey's face carved into the flower bed at the entrance of Disneyland, an image that exactly matches the flower beds depicting Lenin's face in old Soviet public parks. John Fiske, in his *Introduction to Communication Studies* (1990), explains additional semiotic devices that make the encoding and decoding of media texts work: categories of signs, analog and digital codes, conventions, aesthetic codes, denotations and connotations, and the ideologies and meanings that result from use of these devices.

Intertextuality in the Media Text

Intertextuality refers to the relationship of one text to other texts. Disney texts and noir texts are densely intertextual, Disney's referring to other

Disney texts and noir's referring to other films noir. The classic Disney texts from the cartoons to the amusement parks employ abundant intertextual devices of style, form, and content. Mickey, Donald, or Goofy may reappear in any Disney medium. The early anarchic Mickey appears in the first sound animation, *Steamboat Willie,* and in the visualization of Dukas's "Sorcerer's Apprentice" in *Fantasia.* Eventually, however, Mickey became much more restrained and statesmanlike, appropriate to an international ambassador for the Magic Kingdom itself. In Campbell Black's satirical play of Disney has-beens on the skids, there are intertextual references to noir settings, conflicts, and tone, just as there are to Disneyana as well. These elements can also give birth to "seriality" in intertextual referencing through sequels, remakes, series, or continuing sagas (Eco, 1985), an intertextual exploitation all too familiar in the *Friday the 13th, Police Academy, Rocky, Star Trek,* and *Star Wars* series, and in virtually any box office hit that has left a crack open for a sequel.

The sophistication of intertextuality in genre interpretation may be far greater than we normally assume, in the view of Jim Collins in *Architectures of Excess: Cultural Life in the Information Age* (1995). Intertextuality enables contemporary viewers to follow complex blends of genre. The "eclectic, hybrid films of the eighties and nineties" such as *Road Warrior* (1981), *Blade Runner* (1982), *Blue Velvet* (1986), *Batman* (1989, 1992, 1995), *Back to the Future* (1985, 1989, 1990), *Thelma & Louise* (1991), and *Forrest Gump* (1994) "all engage in specific transformation across genres," in the words of Collins (p. 131). Technological developments in the form of VCRs and cable movies have created an image-saturated audience ready to deal with increasing self-reflexivity in films through a "sophisticated hyper-consciousness concerning . . . narrative formulae" (p. 133). In Robert Altman's *The Player* (1992), the opening sequence skewers the lame "meets" formula in the writer's pathetic intertextual pitches for a project: "It's *Out of Africa* meets *Pretty Woman.*" Collins also cites the mixture of the pop song genre with the crime genre in the *Blue Velvet* sequence in which the villain Frank (Dennis Hopper) combines the haunting Roy Orbison song "In Dreams" with the terrorizing and beating of Jeffrey (Kyle MacLachlan), which is witnessed by Dorothy (Isabella Rossellini). Popular television programs such as *The Simpsons* employ numerous intertextual references. Episodes feature Homer chasing his neighbor Flanders as though he were the Schwarzenegger *Terminator* character or Side Show Bob stalking Bart and his family as though he were Robert De Niro in the Scorsese version of *Cape Fear. The Animaniacs,* a cartoon show featuring the characters of Bugs Bunny, Daffy Duck, and others as young children, seems to be aimed at the very young but the plots draw heavily from *Citizen Kane, Gone With the Wind,* and other classic films, lending an edge of additional interest and a tone of irony for adult viewers.

A single scene in a media text may evoke multiple genres and intertextual references. Collins (1995) notes this in the scene in *Back to the Future II* in which Marty (Michael J. Fox) practices his draw in the mirror in preparation for his final showdown. He simultaneously evokes the clothing of Clint Eastwood in the spaghetti western *A Fistful of Dollars* (1964), the "Make my day" line of Eastwood as the hard-boiled cop *Dirty Harry* (1971), and the "Are you talkin' to me?" routine of Travis Bickle (Robert De Niro) in the urban psychopath genre film *Taxi Driver* (1976). Appropriated from diverse contexts, the use of these macho poses purposely confuses time and genre. Finally, Collins notes, "the fact that the hero's choices are all cinematic quotations reflects not just the increasing sophistication of the cinematic literacy of *Back to the Future*'s audiences (and the profoundly intertextual nature of that literacy), but also the entertainment value that the ironic manipulation of that stored information now provides" (p. 139). The genre classicists who decry these impurities ignore, in Collins's view, "the possibility that the nature of entertainment, narrative, art, identification may be undergoing significant reformulation due to widespread changes in the nature of information distribution, access and manipulability" (p. 14).

Are Visual Media Read as a "Language"?

Does our media culture operate as a formal "language"? Given its genres, formulas, signs, and redundancies, does a film or motion picture communicate in the same manner as human verbal language?

Writing in the first half-century of film history, screenwriter and theorist Béla Balázs (1952) identified what he called the "language-form" of cinema. This language-form emerged with early films and matured in the 1920s: Filmmakers modified novels, plays, and events into film's unique language-form. Film, however, is not a passive reflection but "adds to" the objects it represents, according to famed critic André Bazin (1967). Reality leaves its fingerprint but is also transformed in the cinematic image.

Film imagery reflects the material world even as the plasticity of the filmed image and the resources of editing enable the filmmaker to create representations that go beyond what exists in nature. This leads to something quite different from verbal language. In verbal language, the word (the signifier) and the object (the signified) are connected only arbitrarily by the conventions of language: The spoken or written word *mouse* has no physical, acoustic, or necessary connection to the small rodent to which it refers. But in film, as Christian Metz (1974) noted, the signifiers of image and sound-track (film words) are physically associated with the signified elements seen and heard (filmed objects) in the film. A film of a mouse looks like the real-world mouse, even in highly stylized animation. In short, film works less like formal verbal language with its arbitrary sign system and more like tactile, nonverbal, proxemic communication through physical similarities, contacts, and distances.

This distinction is developed at length in *Visual Literacy* (1994) by experimental psychologist Paul Messaris. Strictly speaking, many of the interpretive devices in so-called film literacy—the interpretation of a close-up, the editing transition from shot to shot, the camera crane movement up and away in a final scene—Messaris finds are not the result of learning an arbitrary language code but are rather rooted in our everyday visual experience. In intimate moments we see the partner very close in film as in real life. We depart a scene by moving away, whether bodily or carried by the cinematography. We look from more than one fixed angle at interactions in a scene, whether we are living it or watching it on film. The field experiments of Renee Hobbs (1991) in Tanzania found that people never previously exposed to film or video experienced no loss of comprehension when editing, close-ups, or other film conventions were used. The visual conventions of cinema from Lumière through Melies, Griffith, Eisenstein, Welles, Hitchcock, Kurosawa, Bergman, and Bertolucci do not constitute a language proper or even exactly a paralanguage, despite the fact that each employs signs and codes.

Discursive Practice. A better term than *language* for describing how visual media signify is *discursive practice*. Discursive practice, in the writings of Michel Foucault, refers to historically constituted activities such as criminality, mental illness, or sexuality. Each is a discursive practice. In *Tyranny of Discourse* (see Inglis, 1990, p. 197) Foucault argues that the rules and conventions of discourse "inscribe" the discourse in the lives of those who speak, read, and write it. The Freudian, driven sexuality of film noir may employ sexually loaded signs and codes in the semiotic sense, but the sexuality also works as a *discourse,* a speech act governed by social, material, and historical forces that both encourage and prohibit specific practices. The discursive practice of sexuality in film noir is conditioned by repressive puritanism encountering existential hedonism and nihilism, imbued with Freudian libido and Jungian symbolism. Discourse theory also draws from the "deconstruction" of literary works by Jacques Derrida, a practice which goes beyond formal semiotics to find "symptomatic" points in the work that may undermine the apparent logic of the work. With Barthes we find an even greater opening outward of interpretation, a shift from "work" to "text," as Barthes put it. Terry Eagleton (1983) summarizes this important change: "It is a shift from seeing the poem or novel as a closed entity, equipped with definite meanings which it is the critic's task to decipher, to seeing it as irreducibly plural, an endless play of signifiers which can never be finally nailed down to a single center, essence or meaning" (p. 138). This is precisely where "textual analysis" encounters "reception studies" through discursive practices.

A theory of discursive practice applied to what Disney and film noir do, and for what we engage in with them, relates the text and narrative to contexts and social power. The theory of discursive practice takes us back to Stuart Hall's chart in the beginning of this book, which places the television program between structures of power at work in the creation or encoding of the program and structures of power at work in the reception or decoding of the program. This placement is precisely what Eagleton recommends in his classic *Literary Theory: An Introduction* (1983). He concludes that what was "literary theory" should not be restricted to literature proper but must cover a whole field of discursive practices. Moreover, the theory cannot be specifically literary but "is really no more than a branch of social ideologies" (p. 204). This formulation reconnects literary and cultural criticism with the larger contexts of political economy and privileged or marginalized populations. Text and narrative are placed in a framework of struggle for power and for creative expression and market success. These are central issues connecting textual analysis to production hegemony (in the next chapter) and to reception theory (in the previous chapter).

The "discursive practices" around sexuality in the Disney cultural products, since the creation of Mickey Mouse in 1927 and especially since the corporation went public in 1940, cannot be separated from the economic incentive *to sell to a mass, family-based audience.* Disney articulations of sexuality are more constrained than puritanism and resort to a kind of magic in which sexual activity disappears but reproduction continues. Yet this has been coupled at times with extensive use of sexual innuendoes, notably in the *Three Caballeros* and related Latin American Disney films of the early 1940s that grew out of Walt's goodwill trips to South and Central America (see Burton-Carvajal, 1994; Cartwright & Goldfarb, 1994). In contrast, noir discursive practices around sexuality address an adult, experienced audience. The noir classics of the 1940s and 1950s were forced to exploit the edges of the Hayes and Breen censorship offices in Hollywood and the stipulations of the Motion Picture Production Code. These industry taboos against overt sexuality forced noir to resort to indirection—lingering gazes, ambiguously suggestive lines, provocative but approved clothing styles, sensual expressions and gestures, and an overall tone of heavy-breathing passion. The sexual contrast between Disney and noir could not be more pronounced. The difference occurs in the sign, formula, genre, and narrative conventions that construct the discursive practices associated with the texts. Visual media may not operate in the formal manner of abstract verbal "language," but they represent and generate "discursive practices" as influential as any communication known to humankind.

Context and Hegemony in the Encoding
and Decoding of Disney Texts

There are contrasting discourses in Disney and film noir by intent and in relation to social, material, and historical forces surrounding the text. The author and reader share the signs, codes, formulas, genres, and narratives of the text and, in varying degrees, they also share a context that fills in additional meanings and interpretations. As Hall's model notes, the author encodes the text from a particular position within specific frameworks of knowledge, relations of production, and technical infrastructure. The reader decodes the same text from a position also within frameworks of knowledge, production, and infrastructure.

The reoccurrence of dominant racial, gender, and ideological patterns in media culture indicates a symmetry between the attitudes within the larger society in which the media texts circulate and the attitudes within the specific media text itself. The caricature of Native Americans in Disney's *Peter Pan* (1953), the racial stereotypes of the crows in *Dumbo* (1941), the anti-Semitism some saw in the wolf in *The Three Little Pigs* (1933), and the controversial ethnicity of *Aladdin* exemplify Disney's production within a context of biased American cultural values. The more politically correct *Pocahontas* (1995) exemplifies Disney's cautious conformity to changing values in the larger society. As a consequence, Disney's *Pocahontas* avoids the negative stereotypes of "redskin" savages from the western genre but also avoids the historical actuality of Pocahontas. With regard to gender, Disney products even more obviously recapitulate stereotypical sex roles within the dominant society. Minnie Mouse and Daisy Duck are subordinate to Mickey and Donald and play games to attract male attention. Roles as active agents of change are reserved for Disney males; roles as passive flirts or endangered victims are common for Disney females. Watch a Disney Valentine's Day cartoon special and you will see blatant sex stereotyping.

Ideologically, Disney narratives and texts also rearticulate and serve the larger context. One can read a Disney story without thinking about its corporate context, but the very attachment of the label "Disney" to the text immediately connects the story to a specific, well-known corporation. This label is not unrelated to the story's style. Disney's America, the theme park planned in Virginia just 35 miles from the capitol in Washington, DC, was conceived as a 1980s representation of American history—but whose version? The planned Civil War fort, family farm, Indian village, and tribute to baseball could take many forms. Officials claimed that they wanted visitors to feel what it was like to be a Civil War soldier or a slave on a plantation, and yet they also wanted big smiles and "fun with a capital 'F'" (Walker, 1994, p. 36). Authentic history and commercial popularity clearly conflict here. Historians feared that the park would present a sanitized version of the country's evolution. In addition, Prince William County neighbors of Disney's 3,000 acres feared that the urban sprawl would extend into the Blue Ridge Mountains. Government officials feared that tourists would be drained away from the real historical sites in the capital. Disney finally abandoned the project in frustration because of conflicting ideological, environmental, and social pressures. Alexander Wilson (1994) sees a similarly impossible pseudohistory in "The American Adventure" in Walt Disney World: "When FDR or John Wayne or Chief Joseph can be wrenched from their context of opposition and struggle, . . . what we have is a simulacrum of history, a middlebrow impersonation of an epic story that never took place" (p. 128). Wilson sees a parallel failure in the Florida park's EPCOT representation of the future as created by rigid technological determinism: "Indeed, theirs is a future that differs from the present only in its details; it is a future of hierarchy, continued industrialization, enforced scarcity, and a ravished planet" (p. 128).

Disney texts gain much of their identifiability by being encoded within the notoriously tight Disney corporate structure. This structure is controlling, litigious, and profitable in the extreme (Lewis, 1994). The corporation is very protective of its products, practices, and history, as the suppression of Campbell Black's satirical play of Disney characters indicates. Disney texts do not float free of their context but have it subtly embedded in them through corporate control over both production and reception. When readers decode a Disney text, they do so within a context of familiarity with past Disney products and history and within their personal life history.

What does a close textual analysis of Disney's first mixed cartoon and live-action feature reveal? Julianne Burton-Carvajal (1994) charges:

> Blatant sexual punning and predation. Inadvertent homosexual advances. Cross-dressing and cross-species coupling. Reiterative narratives of conquest in which the patriarchal unconscious and the imperial unconscious insidiously overlap. . . . The characteristic fun, frolic and fireworks purveyed in Disney's *The Three Caballeros,* released in 1945 when the studio's national and international fame was at its zenith, are based on all of the above. (p. 132)

To document these charges, Burton-Carvajal examines the nearly two dozen Disney films, both shorts and features, that resulted from three trips south of the border by Walt, his wife, and his staff. The films refigure and appropriate the genuinely Latin American into stereotypes of the seductive-repulsive "other." Consistent with the reading of imperialist ideology in Disney comics in Latin America made by Dorfman and Mattelart in their famous *How to Read Donald Duck* (1975), Burton-Carvajal finds these films to be allegories of "colonialism par excellence. Every story packaged here is a narrative of conquest or of enslavement" (p. 142). Donald constantly chases live-action bathing beauties and other passionate Latin females in pursuit of "celluloid miscegenation" (p. 140). Donald's "phallic inadequacy" in the narrative makes him "a disarmingly inept but no less effective front man for the imperial machine" (p. 145). Recurrent ejaculatory imagery leaves Donald languorously feminized, in contrast to the secure machismo of Joe Carioca and Panchito, Donald's new Latin friends. Burton-Carvajal finds in the narrative "the equation of cultural expression with femininity and cultural exchange with heterosexual conquest and . . . that the female of the species is a willing target of appropriation" (p. 147). Culturally, she finds the Disney Latin American films of the 1940s to be rooted in America's "neocolonizing ambition" revealed in "the perverse dialectic of economic aid, which rewards the donor while impoverishing the recipient" (p. 146). Despite high intentions and creative talent, *The Three Caballeros* "proves the rule of cross-cultural borrowing as self-aggrandizement, of Good-Neighborliness as foil for empire-building-as-usual, of innocent entertainment masking a set of interests and assumptions that are anything but innocuous" (p. 147).

In an equally provocative reading of the text of the Tokyo Disneyland, Mitsuhiro Yoshimoto (1994) finds a very different ideological message. He finds that within the Japanese context, the Tokyo Disneyland, despite its exact imitation of the Anaheim park, is not really an implement of American cultural imperialism because it is not accompanied by any U.S. economic domination of Japan in the conventional colonizing sense. Instead, Yoshimoto finds that the Japanese pursuit of a leisure clearly protected from work and the drive for commodification make the park experience especially attractive to Japanese. Because the park is dehistoricized and decontextualized for the Japanese visitor, it is appropriated into a sense of Japanese cultural hegemony. America is "just another brand name, like Chanel, Armani, and so on" (p. 195) and the park can be incorporated as one more "foreign village," understood "not as a sign of mere Westernization of Japan, but of an imperial expansion of Tokyo's hegemonic culture" (p. 194). American cultural expression coexists with Japanese culture rather than hybridizing it. The Tokyo park reinforces the Japanese sense of native uniqueness. In fact, Disneyland's cleanliness, quality control, and exacting management make it arguably the most Japanese institution in the United States. Tokyo Disneyland, to Yoshimoto, "is in fact one of the most powerful manifestations of contemporary Japanese nationalism . . . [and it] epitomizes the ingenious mechanism of neocultural imperialism of Japan" (p. 197).

Summary

Having made much of the contrasting character of film noir and Disney, it is now necessary to acknowledge a forthright, self-conscious union of the two in the admittedly unusual *Who Framed Roger Rabbit?* (1988). In the middle of the period between his first hit, *Back to the Future* (1985), and his first director's Oscar for *Forrest Gump* (1994), Robert Zemeckis brilliantly blended this impossible concoction in a coproduction for Steven Spielberg and the Disney corporation. In this film we find combined the usually contrasting noir and Disney signs, codes, and systems of narrative formulas and conventions.

The narrative of *Roger Rabbit* tells a noir story of deception, betrayal, and sabotage investigated by a hard-drinking private detective (Bob Hoskins). Set in 1947, it has both the story and various visual elements of classic noir genre or style. At the same time, Roger Rabbit himself is semiotically realized as an animated character, along with the rest of the inhabitants of the stunningly imagined Toontown. Observing standard formulas and conventions, they make jokes and act silly in the best cartoon tradition. The technically impressive integration of signs and codes of live action with signs and codes of animation brings the separate worlds together. Prominent cartoon characters from Warner Brothers and Disney mingle in the Toon population. They suffer from discrimination, ghettoization, and economic exploitation at the hands of the live-action Los Angeleños.

Intertextuality flourishes as the film knowingly refers to numerous cartoon and noir signatures in this genre hybrid. The sexy Toon, Jessica Rabbit, seduces live-action characters in yet more "celluloid miscegenation." The evocation of the actual historical dismantling of the Los Angeles trolley system at the behest of an automobile tire manufacturer is largely lost in the film's convoluted plotting and action. Because of this, the film's implicit critique of Detroit's hegemony effectively disappears behind the conventional villainy of Christopher Lloyd's corrupt police activities, making it ideologically muted entertainment that effectively serves the infrastructural requirements of Disney commerce without disturbing the parallel commodified consciousness of the viewing audience. In the end, and despite its pseudo-liberal critique of the automobile lobby, the discursive practices associated with *Roger Rabbit* reassert the status quo.

In this manner, one can sort through the work of formal analysis, narrative theory, semiotic analysis, linguistic structure, discourse analysis, deconstructionism, poststructuralism, and other sources for additional insights into a textual analysis of media culture. The range of interpretive possibilities, even for the simplest Disney or film noir text, is virtually limitless. Whatever the extent of such textual interpretation, the textual approach has the central advantage of focusing our critical attention on that crucial point of the dialogic encounter between the receiver reading the text of media culture and the creator writing it. Badly used, these tools of textual analysis can obscure or defeat the innate pleasure of the text and confuse its relationship with the larger contexts. Well used, these tools can richly enhance our pleasure in and control over the text.

Does this mean that "textual analysis" solves the mystery of media culture? Is it the culprit? The sleuth? The telltale clue? Certainly it makes an important contribution to our ability to come to terms with specific experiences of media culture, but it leaves many other issues unresolved. How do readers go beyond reception to actively participate with media texts? How do corporate power and hegemony condition texts? Why do culture-specific portrayals of gender, ethnicity, and ideology occur in the ways they do? Our investigation into the problematic of media culture must continue beyond textual analysis.

EXERCISES

Chapter Four

Exercise A. CONTRASTS. Select a Disney cultural product and identify its text, narrative, genre, formulas, signs, and overall discursive practices. Select a movie, classic or recent, from the film noir canon and identify its text, narrative, genre, formulas, signs, and overall discursive practices. Compare and contrast the two as distinct texts in as many different ways as possible.

Exercise B. GENRES. Make a list of popular genres you are familiar with in media culture; which are your most and least favorite? Why? Have you ever avoided a genre and then found out later that you liked it? Have you ever looked forward to a cultural product with great expectation because it was in a genre you like, only to be disappointed with the result? What was the difference? Why are personal tastes in favorite genres so varied?

Exercise C. COMPARISONS. *Genre:* Compare two films or television programs from the same genre. Note the genre "conventions" present in both and the different genre "inventions" in each. *Directors:* Compare two films directed by the same director. Note how each film embodies stylistic and thematic elements present in the director's total body of films. How do the films compare in terms of narrative and style? This comparison is easier for directors who have been written about extensively: Griffith, Eisenstein, Ford, Wilder, Hitchcock, Welles, Kurosawa, Bergman, Fellini, Bertolucci, Scorcese, Campion, Tarantino, Almodóvar, and so forth. *International:* Compare two related films or television programs made in different countries. You even may wish to select a foreign film *remade* by a Hollywood company, such as *The Vanishing, Sommersby, Three Men and a Baby, The Magnificent Seven, Breathless,* and so forth. *Versions:* Compare a film or television program to its origins in a novel, a stage play, a comic book, a true incident, or any other nonfilm version of the story.

Exercise D. TEXTUAL ANALYSIS OF A FILM. Develop a detailed critical analysis of the text of any one film. The following points may be considered.

I. ORIGINS AND PURPOSE

    A. In one sentence, summarize the central plot or theme.

    B. What genre, if any, is indicated by the setting, characters, and so forth?

    C. Who is the intended audience—elite or mass, youth or mature, domestic or international, male or female, and so forth?

    D. What other films has the director made? Does this director have a characteristic style or thematic emphasis?

    E. As relevant, name the writer, producer, studio, and so forth?

    F. Does the film interpret specific human ideas or experiences? What sources of conflict, symbolism, satire, or irony are employed? Is the meaning "referential" to factors outside the film?

II. STRUCTURE

    A. Do the story sequence and film style fit together? Does the overall result have unity, complexity, originality, and intensity of effect?

    B. Does the film build to a climax or use a more circular structure? Is there one turning point or several?

    C. Does time progress linearly or are there flashbacks or flashforwards?

    D. Is the point of view that of one character (restricted) or is it more all-seeing (omniscient)?

    E. Is viewer interest sustained by plot devices, by psychological depth, by special effects, by highly imaginative or realistic circumstances, or by combinations of these elements?

III. FILMIC TECHNIQUES

    A. CINEMATOGRAPHY: What is the visual composition, the film's mise-en-scène?

        1. Is lighting naturalistic, or "noir" with its high contrast, heavy shadows, and unusual angles and framing?

        2. Are close-ups extreme and frequent?

        3. Are establishing shots employed traditionally?

        4. Is color used in unusual ways?

        5. Are unsteady hand-held shots, noticeable pans, truck, crane, or dolly shots, long lenses, or other visual techniques used?

        6. Are the art design, set, costuming, production elements noteworthy?

        7. Are digitized morphing, miniatures, or other special effects used?

    B. SCRIPTING

        1. Is the story taken from another source—a novel, play, story, or so forth?

        2. Is this a sequel or otherwise dependent on other films' successes?

3. Is there effective verbal dialogue or is the film primarily action?
4. Are plot and character developments well set up and plausible?
5. Are any loose ends in the plot all tied up by the end of the film? Are there unnecessary or unexplained scenes or plot shifts?
6. Does the film employ a classical three-act structure?
7. Is there good pacing of development and climaxes?
8. Are the characters well-defined and their motivations clear?
9. Are there paradoxes between the verbal and visual presentations?

C. ACTING

1. What special strengths or weaknesses does the cast bring to this film?
2. Is the acting naturalistic or highly stylized? Does this fit the overall style of the film?
3. Are there particularly telling or powerful performances at specific places in the film?
4. Are there any negative stereotypes (of gender, race, age, nationality, etc.) and could they be avoided?
5. Do central characters interact convincingly; is their chemistry good?

D. EDITING

1. Which scenes are presented through quick cuts or long takes?
2. Is the effect appropriate?
3. Is there montage editing, which combines unmatched shots for special effect or abbreviates the passage of time?
4. Are the rhythm and timing of cuts effective?
5. Is suspense or interest maintained by the editing? Are surprises effectively timed?
6. Does the editing work unobtrusively, not call attention to itself?
7. Is cutting between parallel action effectively done?
8. Is the pace of the film overly tedious or frenetic?

E. SOUND

1. Do the words, sound effects, and music effectively match and enhance the visuals?
2. Is the overall sound of the film quiet or loud? What is the result?
3. Is musical scoring used well to direct the emotional effect of scenes?
4. Is sound used to overlap between one scene and another?
5. Are popular songs used in the soundtrack? Are they natural and effective, or transparently tagged on to create a soundtrack album?
6. Is voice-over narration used and with what effect?

IV. EFFECT

A. Was the film convincing and satisfying? Why or why not?
B. What is most memorable or noteworthy about this film? On first viewing? On subsequent viewings?
C. How was the film received by the public? By critics?
D. Does the film have historic value?
E. How much did you like or dislike this film? Why?

5

Production/Hegemony:
"And the Winner Is . . . Hollywood!"

You live in Rome and want to see a good movie. You jump on your Vespa
and head to the cinema, thinking, "Italy, the home of Fellini, Antonioni,
Bertolucci . . . Great cinema." The local theater is playing . . . Stallone and
Schwarzenegger.

A friend in Sweden, home of Ingmar Bergman, can only find films of Julia
Roberts and Demi Moore.

Everywhere, it seems, once-thriving national cinemas have been supplanted
by Hollywood. How can this be?

The commercial core of media culture leads to a suspicion that "production
analysis" with particular attention to "hegemonic power" actually explains
how media culture works. In this view, sophisticated, well-financed industrial production creates our cultural products and conditions us to want more
from a limited and biased array of manufactured entertainment goods. The
financial rewards of this production enable the controlling transnational
corporations to further refine their power to exploit popular tastes for
commercial profit. Considerations of human need, artistic integrity, ecology,
and truth play second fiddle in this capitalist race for maximized return on
media investment. These issues, from the "great debates" in Chapter 1, still
warrant serious consideration.

The size and profitability of major cultural industries contribute to the
sense that control over production, coupled with hegemonic shaping of
audiences, predominates over everything else. What do we find if we closely
examine media culture in terms of the "production/hegemony" nexus?

Production, Hegemony, and Consciousness

The value of exploring production and hegemony in media culture is
apparent in Hall's encoding-decoding model (see Figure 0.1). The entire
(left) "encoding" side of the model concerns how the media text originates.
The production process precedes and leads to all the other dimensions of

media culture—text, reception, participation, identity—and production is where biased gender, race, or class issues are embedded in cultural products. However, the sequence is not unidirectional and causal in a simple sense. Audiences determine the ultimate success of cultural products, but audiences do not exist in vacuums either. Each dimension of the media culture process conditions and influences the other dimensions.

We explore the *production* of media texts and culture by asking some obvious questions. Who made this cultural product or practice? Under what conditions was it created and with what purposes? Who owns the product and gains financially from its sales? How is the product distributed, and who benefits from it? Are corporate and financial interests influencing other aspects of the process? Is there a competitive environment and a level playing field among all participants? This chapter uses these queries to examine the Hollywood film industry.

The issue of hegemony also calls up obvious questions. We introduced *hegemony* in Chapter 1 as "the power or dominance that one social group holds over another." In hegemony there is an asymmetrical dominance structured by power. This imbalance leads to influence achieved by consent rather than coercion. This undue influence is embedded in widely circulated cultural products and practices.

Certain questions raise issues of hegemony. Does any special group exert decisive and distorting influence over the shape of the cultural product? Are there particular interests that are served and others that are omitted or opposed through this process of production and distribution? Are certain meanings and ideologies favored? Are the controlling individuals and institutions representative of the population in general? Do women, ethnic groups, workers, minorities, and other populations have a say in how they are represented in the product? Beyond the individual product, are the patterns of representation in a set of cultural products biased or distorted as a whole? The crucial, and difficult, issue behind these questions is: What measure or standards of comparison should be used to evaluate the fairness, balance, honesty, representativeness, and justice of the media culture and its products?

These questions explore media culture with reference to any power imbalances in its production processes and hegemonic influence. These are especially important questions and explorations because media are "the consciousness industries" (Enzensberger, 1974) that distribute products whose end result is not just a product but an effect on the consciousness of those receiving it. Just as Detroit makes cars and France makes wines, Smythe (1994) argues that the media make audiences to sell to advertisers. The consciousness of these audiences can be influenced by the texts the media industries produce. As mentioned in the first chapter, *political economy* refers to the study of the power arrangements in society. Studying the political economy of media culture is especially important in a time when culture is being industrialized, information is being commodified, and information, knowledge, and technology are considered to be the bases of wealth, power, and economic growth (Mueller, 1995).

The world dominance of audiovisual products by Hollywood is a classic example of production hegemony. A snapshot of this powerful industry at one moment in time indicates its size and economic power, which have caused great concern on the part of the European Union and others.

A Snapshot of Hollywood, THE Media Industry

A time-capsule portrait of American media industries early in the last decade of the twentieth century underscores their profitability and market dominance. In 1992, the cable television industry reported $25 billion in revenue, up 10% from 1991. The broadcasting industry, both radio and television, reported income of $28.8 billion, up 4% from 1991. The telephone industry reported revenues of $165 billion, up 3.5% from 1992 (U.S. Commerce Department, 1994). In 1993, the recording industry reported an 11% income increase to $10 billion (Hawkins, 1995). Also in 1993, U.S. consumers spent $2 billion on computer software, $5 billion on video games, $5.2 billion on theatrical movies, and $13.2 billion on video movies (Meyer, 1994). Broadway musicals brought in about $1 billion dollars, two-thirds of it in road productions (*Preview,* 1994), approximately what live music concerts brought in.

This thumbnail sketch of only the most prominent media industries adds up to a total of more than $250 billion income in a typical year, that is, a quarter of a trillion dollars, with steady growth potential. A large portion of this economic and cultural power revolves around "Hollywood," the capital of media culture production.

At that same moment in the 1990s, MGM studios were being bailed out of debt and taken over by the banking company, Crédit Lyonnais of France, for an amount of slightly over $1 billion. In contrast, Universal Pictures was projecting an estimated $339 million profit from $640 million gross income for the Steven Spielberg film of Michael Crichton's bestseller *Jurassic Park.* Given that a major studio, any one of the seven or so in Hollywood, typically generates $300 million to $500 million in *annual* operating profit from a slate of 20 or more movies, television programs, and film library licensing agreements, it is apparent that the huge income from *Jurassic Park* was serving Universal well as the film passed *E.T.* and *Home Alone* at the box office. *Jurassic Park's* projected $301 million in expenses included production costs, theatrical marketing, video duplication, support advertising, talent royalties, residuals, interest, and studio overhead. *Jurassic Park's* projected $640 million in income included worldwide ticket sales, videocassette sales, pay-per-view and pay television sales, network television, and basic cable sales (Marich, 1993). Additional product licensing agreements were expected to earn between $100 million and $1 billion for Universal.

Also at that time, Paramount Communications was coming off 1992 revenues of $4.258 billion from its publishing (38%), movies (29.5%), sports, theaters, theme parks, and television stations (16.9%), and television programming (15.4%). But Paramount was trailing Walt Disney Co. and Time Warner, Inc. by about 30% in cash flow for recent years. Paramount had made a bid to buy Time, Inc., in 1989 but lost out as Time instead purchased Warner Communications. This economic weakness led to Paramount's takeover by Sumner Redford and Viacom in 1994. Sherry Lansing, as studio head under Paramount President Stanley R. Jaffe in 1993, was then in the process of giving the green light to eventual Best Picture Oscar winner *Forrest Gump* and was watching *The Firm* bring in excellent summer box office revenues. (Harris, 1993; Welkos, 1993). Lansing, the first woman ever to head production at a major studio, had run Twentieth Century Fox from 1980 to 1983, paving the way for Dawn Steel as president of Columbia Pictures in 1987 and Lisa Henson as head of Columbia in 1993. At this moment, however, despite having produced *The Accused,* which won an Oscar for Jodie Foster and in Lansing's words, "changed the way people thought about rape," she was on the hot seat with feminists for alleged female exploitation in Paramount's *Indecent Proposal* and *Sliver* (Welkos, 1993, p. 32).

In that summer of 1993, one could look around the world and see why so much money and pressure was concentrated in Hollywood—it dominated box offices. By early September the number-one film in Brazil and Brussels was *Sliver.* In Denmark it was *Indecent Proposal.* In Great Britain and Ireland, number one was *The Firm,* and in Holland and France it was *The Fugitive.* And, of course, this was the summer of *Jurassic Park,* which dominated the box office almost everywhere it opened. In film-rich Japan that September, the top-three films in order were *Jurassic Park, Aladdin,* and *The Last Action Hero,* all Hollywood productions. In Australia and Sweden, active filmmaking countries, 9 of the top 10 movies were from Hollywood. In Brazil and Germany, 8 of the top 10 were also American, and even in France 6 of the top 10 were Hollywood releases (Cosford, 1993).

If ever a country dominated a global cultural market, it has been the United States' domination of international cinema in the 1980s and 1990s. In fact, in 1992 the otherwise recession-battered California economy made $8 billion directly in film revenues and an estimated $18.5 billion total when one calculates that every dollar spent by the film industry was worth about $2.30

to the local economy. Of the 480 features shot in the United States that year, 319, or 66%, were filmed entirely or in part in California and 75% of those in Los Angeles, where more than 103,000 people were employed by the film industry (Sims, 1993). Hollywood, California, is unmistakably the production capital of the world film industry.

"Hollywood," less a geographical subcity than a kind of mythical home to the entire entertainment industry of greater Los Angeles, has managed to position itself at the top of the audiovisual production pyramid in the United States and around the world. Hollywood's place in the media structure is clear in Figure 5.1.

Hollywood has concentrated technology, facilities, personnel, and management to produce the majority of programming for television, video, cable, theater, and parts of the multimedia interactive domain. These distribution systems bring in huge returns through direct sales of videos, movie tickets, and pay-per-view, and even more through advertising revenues at local, national, and international levels.

Ideologically, Hollywood is one of the major instruments of the capitalist-consumer status quo. Conservative critics charge it with liberal bias even when its mainstays are *Forrest Gump, The Lion King, Jurassic Park,* and similar forms of traditional middle-class entertainment. Conservative film critic Michael Medved calls Hollywood a one-party liberal state, but liberal activist and chairman of Warner Brothers Records, Danny Goldberg, responds that Hollywood follows the marketplace without regard to ideology (Goodale, 1995). Hollywood's predictable marquee products are order-maintaining, whereas its more off-beat fringes have mildly order-transforming qualities. Hollywood's only revolutionary potential is its capacity to conquer new markets and make even more revenue. This potential concerns some observers, especially those abroad.

Hegemony in the Global
Film Industry: A European View

Hollywood's domination has not gone unnoticed by others. In the 1960s, when television and film made in Hollywood were inundating new markets around the world, there were cries of cultural imperialism, one-way flow, media colonialism, and multinational monopoly. Gradually, strong local and regional growth in the audiovisual sector around the world eroded that domination. But it returned with a vengeance in the Reagan-Thatcher years. The European Union, among others, took notice of the new arrangement. In a document titled only *Report by the Think Tank* (Vasconcelos, 1994), the European Union (EU) assessed the state of European audiovisual industries.

STRUCTURE OF
U.S. FILM/TV SYSTEM

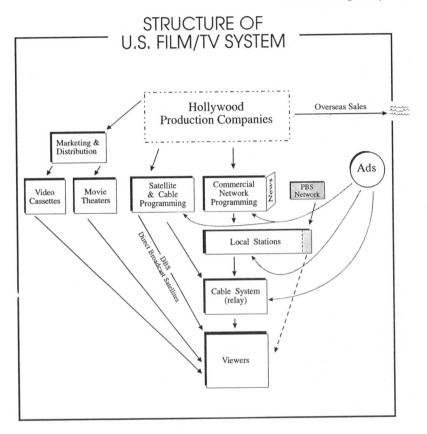

Figure 5.1. The distribution system for Hollywood products reaches consumers through sophisticated technology and commercialized control mechanisms.

In 1994, European film and television audiences represented 54% of the global market and the European industry employed at least 1.8 million people, according to figures in the European Union report. In addition to its economic and employment importance, the audiovisual industry was of crucial sociocultural importance, according to the report. What was at stake, the report warned, was "access to information, to culture and knowledge of the Europeans, in addition to communication between European people" (Vasconcelos, 1994, p. 20). The EU shared the worries of Czech intellectual Antonin Lihen: "Humanity will to a large extent be formed by audiovisual means. Audiovisual practices will invade everything in the coming decades. . . . I do not think any of the cultures in our continents, whether large or small, will be able to develop normally unless their roots are nurtured in the European context" (p. 16). The film and television industries, what the EU calls "the audiovisual industry," is a sector of clear priority and strategic interest to the European community.

In earlier times, the report recalls, until the 1960s, the European audiovisual industry was strong and effectively represented European cultural expression. Cinema as both art and industry flourished: "European cinema was concentrated in two or three major productions centres, the prestige of film stars crossed borders, films enjoyed the public's favour, receipts largely covered productions costs and investors did well" (p. 9). Cinema had reached maturity with its best directors from Europe, America, India, and Japan controlling film narration and establishing the medium as "the seventh art."

Since that time, the European situation has deteriorated significantly. "Over the last ten years, European films have lost 50% of the European movie market in favour of U.S. industry," declares the EU report (p. 17). In 1968, European films had 60% of the European box office and American films had 35%. At the end of the 1970s, the European box office was 50% European and 45% American. "Today the share of the American film industry in the EU is an 80% average—France is the only significant exception—and scarcely 20% for European cinema" (p. 18). Even in France, American films held 55% of the market. In Portugal, Ireland, and Greece, non-American films claimed less than 5% of the box office, and in Germany and Spain 10% (Vasconcelos, 1994).

European receipts virtually disappeared, whereas Hollywood's remained strong. Regular moviegoers in Europe declined in 15 years from 1,200 million to 550 million, with the entire drop absorbed by European-made films. Audiences for European films dropped from 600 million to 100 million, whereas audiences for American films remained stable at 450 million. As a consequence, from 1984 to 1992 annual U.S. film and television sales in Europe increased from $330 million to $3.6 billion, creating an annual trade deficit of $3.5 billion. In an age when the United States expresses great concern about its overall foreign trade deficit, only the combined military-aerospace industry creates a greater trade surplus for the United States than film exportation.

What factors contribute to the American domination of the European film market? For example, is the imbalance caused by an insurmountable language problem in Europe? The mosaic of European languages and cultures has led European producers to think in terms of their own nation and language. Yet American films, either dubbed (85% of the cases) or subtitled, reach a single European-wide market that seems to exist only for American films. "In 15 years European films have largely become money-losers," states the report (p. 23). Investment in production has exceeded total gross receipts within France since 1985 and within Italy since 1986, making those industries net losers.

Is the imbalance caused by concentration of resources and power? The EU report finds evidence of this. One factor mentioned is the move in Europe since the 1960s away from concentration around three major studios in England, France, and Italy: Pinewood, Billancourt, and Cinecittà, respectively. Concern for the expression of cultural and linguistic minorities and for decentralized democracy "stepped up the centrifugal trend of an industry whose economic rationale called for concentration" (p. 24). This resulted in the formation of some 950 European film distributors (p. 37). In contrast, the seven major American film studios (Disney/Buena Vista, Paramount, Universal, Columbia/Tristar, Warner, Fox, and MGM) combine their foreign efforts through the Motion Picture Association of America (MPAA). The MPAA, created in 1945, is protected against legal action for anticompetitive practices as long as its activities are strictly limited to exports. In addition, Universal, Paramount, and MGM distribute jointly through their United International Pictures (UIP) subsidiary, licensed under Dutch law.

This means that U.S. legal restrictions against monopoly practices by the American studios do not apply to their overseas operations. By 1948, within the United States, antitrust actions had eliminated the vertical integration of studios cooperating as an oligarchy and the horizontal integration of one studio controlling its own production, distribution, marketing, and exhibition across the country. But these prohibitions against anticompetitive collusion to drive out competitors do not apply outside the United States. *Blockbooking* in Europe allows American companies to make highly desirable releases available to theaters only if they also book less prominent films, a practice prohibited in the United States. *Blindbooking* schedules films the theater operator has not seen beforehand. These practices are successful especially because of the "blockbuster" strategy that has proven successful since the mid-1970s with films such as *Jaws* and *Star Wars*. The report observes that some forms of blockbuster strategies go back to D. W. Griffith, but "it was not until the generation of Lucas and Spielberg that, through colossal investments in promotion, and the perfecting of marketing techniques, combined with the covering of the planet with thousands of copies, that the blockbusters have become a very sure element indispensable in the strategy of the major studios" (Vasconcelos, 1994, p. 37).

Is the imbalance caused by low visibility for European products? The EU report sees some truth in that. European films face the dilemma that they "no longer have what draws audiences to American films: solid stories, popular stars, production values, full-blown promotion" (p. 26). The growing concentration of attendance on a reduced number of titles, the development of blockbusters, and the reduction in competitive film supply has created a chicken-and-egg problem for Europe. Until the late 1970s, European stars could generate financing and box-office revenues: Sophia Loren, Alain Delon, Romy Schneider, Jean-Paul Belmondo, Catherine Deneuve, Marcello Mastroianni, Jeanne Moreau and a whole host of others. The report notes, "today no European star (except Gérard Depardieu, or Jeremy Irons, whom the public confuses with an American actor) is capable of mobilizing significant investment upstream by distributors" (p. 28). European directors, themselves stars in the 1960s, with only a few exceptions no longer attract European financing. The historic drain of European actors, directors, cinematographers, and other talent to Hollywood has recently been followed by the *story drain,* the purchase by Americans of scripts of films shot in Europe. *Three Men and a Baby, The Return of Martin Guerre, The Vanishing, Breathless,* and others exemplify this trend. European films sometimes reached 7% to 8% of the American market in the 1960s but now reach 1% to 3%. Although American interests have concentrated production and distribution in powerful companies that enjoy real economies of scale, European financing, production, distribution, and marketing have become hopelessly fragmented.

The report concludes: "In the film industry, more than in other economic sectors, the rule is that the power in the market and therefore cultural hegemony are variables of the *quantity* and *dimension.* Whoever only has an atomized parcel with which to act will constantly be at the service of the others" (p. 31).

Is television any better off than movies? European television, although historically much more protected against American domination than film, has been declining. The think tank's report to the European Union notes how the liberalization of European television has contributed to this. New private stations, prevented by the established national public television services from buying what those services produced, turned to American products. The new competition weakened the national public services and worked against the establishment of a continental market for European products. Competition for a maximized audience created a demand for cheap national/international products, which Europe was not producing. The steady increase of satellite and cable television threatened to make the penetration of American products uncontrollable. The report concluded,

This phenomenon was accompanied by a massive consumption of American products (films, but also series, television films, sitcoms and soap operas) which in the case of the films benefited from promotion in cinemas and in the case of television products from prices that in certain instances could be considered dumping: with their cost already recouped in the United States, the

American products were sold to the stations in batches and at absolutely unbeatable prices. (Vasconcelos, 1994, p. 32)

This clearly is what *cultural hegemony* is all about—the domination of one group by another group through media products. A sector of tremendous importance economically, politically, and culturally, the European audiovisual film/television industry, has come under virtually complete domination by American products, from *Baywatch* to Spielberg. Given the rich traditions of art and creative culture in Europe, it can hardly be assumed that some inherent superiority in American audiovisual talent accounts for this. Rather, a fragmented, unfocused set of policies and practices on the European side is overmatched by the large-scale industrial integration and promotion of the American side. With this situation, it is not surprising that American cries for worldwide "freedom of expression" in the form of no distribution restrictions or public subsidies strike Europeans as self-serving and even imperialistic. Why should American firms be allowed to operate in Europe in ways that they are prohibited from in the United States?

One single media event each year celebrates Hollywood's domination of the world film market. The dramatic moment arrives. We hear the familiar words, "The envelope, please." The envelope is nervously opened. "And the winner is . . . ." Overall, of course, the winner is the Hollywood audiovisual industry itself.

Hollywood's Academy Awards Telecast: The World's Longest Commercial

The Academy Awards telecast is the most widely viewed annual media event originating from the United States. The event's 50 million American viewers fall well short of the Super Bowl audience of 130 million, but the Academy Award (or "Oscars") telecast attracts another 200 million viewers overseas in countries where the Super Bowl is virtually unheard of. *Roots* or *Gone With the Wind* may break American television ratings records, but they do not go out live at one moment to the whole world in the way the Oscar telecast does. Even the Olympics and World Cup playoffs, which attract world audiences of a billion or more, do not attempt to repeat themselves every year. The Oscars are a uniquely successful—and self-serving—transnational media event.

Reception study shows that the annual Academy Awards celebration means different things to different people. To the network carrying the event, the Oscar show means an audience of more than 250 million people in 75 countries. To those millions of viewers, the Academy Awards telecast means three hours of celebrities, glamour, and coveted awards—interspersed with tedious walks to the stage, rambling thank-you's, and some obscure prizes. To the movie studio winning a Best Picture Oscar, the award means $20-$50 million in increased box office revenues for that film. To the study of media culture, the Academy Awards means a subject worthy of analysis, a multi-layered televised text produced by transnational corporations and interpreted by diverse persons in many countries. To critical theory, the show means a showcase for hegemony.

The Academy Award telecast powerfully combines the resources of the Hollywood film industry and the American television industry to produce a lucrative "media event." Such media events provide, in the words of Elihu Katz (1980), the "high holidays" of contemporary daily life. Whether a "contest," as in a Wimbledon playoff, or a "conquest," as in a Middle East war, or a "coronation," as in a royal wedding, these events capture the attention of vast populations and elicit collective excitement, celebration, or mourning. The Oscars encompass all of this. They are a contest among films, a coronation of winners, and a conquest over moviegoers by the colossal commercial that is the Academy Awards.

A series of legends confuse our judgments of the Oscars. The Academy of Motion Picture Arts and Sciences is a disinterested, objective body sharing its professional, impartial evaluations, is it not? Television carries this awards event as a public service similar to political conventions and debates, does it not? Members of the public participate and agree on what they like best in this event, do they not? The availability of this service informs the international public by spreading before it the widest possible range of cultural goods, does it not? Europeans and others are as pleased and excited by this event as are Americans, are they not? This is art, not industry, democracy, not autocracy, right? The real question is, to what extent are these legends fact or fiction? What do we reliably know about the Academy Awards, the Oscar-winning films, and the Oscar event?

Different aspects of the Oscar event can be organized under the five steps of the transmission model of the communication process: Who, Says What, Through Which Channel, To Whom, With What Effect? The "who" of the Academy Awards telecast is the academy itself, which produces the show under contract to a television network. The "says what" is the three-hour telecast. The "through which channel" is the television network that transmits the signal from the Los Angeles venue through relays to viewers. The "to whom" is the audience member viewing from home, a pub, or elsewhere throughout the world. The "effect" is any modification of behavior, such as attending Oscar-winning movies or participating in conversations about the awards.

The Oscar event also illustrates how media carry out the three traditional functions of communication in society, as outlined by Lasswell in his early classic (1948/1960).

- Surveillance of the environment (the news function)
- Correlation of the parts (the editorial function)
- Transmission of the social heritage (the education function)

The Academy Awards event surveys the film environment by presenting an array of almost exclusively Hollywood-based stars, films, songs, and attendant glitter as the approved frame of reference for film everywhere. The event correlates the parts by giving awards to those people and films that the Los Angeles-based film industry members consider the most worthy. And the event transmits social heritage by teaching celebrity-watching, filmgoing, humor, art, competition, commercialism, and other values within the dominant hegemonic code of Hollywood.

Who Produces the Oscar Text?
Gatekeepers and Hegemony

Exploring the production/hegemony nexus behind dominant media leads us to ask who creates and distributes the media text and why. In turn, we also sift through what frameworks of knowledge are employed, what social relations play a role in mounting the production, and what technical infrastructures are used.

The power behind the Oscar telecast is the Academy of Motion Picture Arts and Sciences together with the television network carrying the show. The academy names the show's producer—usually a Hollywood industry fixture, such as Jack Haley or Howard Koch or Norman Jewison—in addition to controlling the nomination and granting of the Oscar awards. The producer maintains ultimate control over the entire show, although the network names the television director. Everything in the ceremony is planned with regard to how effective it will be on television in serving the interests of the film industry. The Oscar tradition goes back to 1927, when the Academy was founded, and 1929, when its first awards were presented with extensive newspaper and magazine coverage. For the second awards presentation, in 1930, live radio coverage was added and, in 1953, television.

The economic payoff of the Oscars for the film industry is obvious. The annual awards ceremony funds most of the academy's annual expenses,

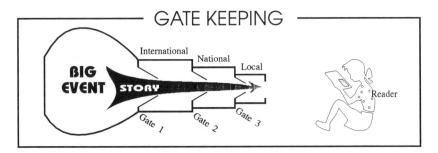

Figure 5.2. Classic gatekeeping by news editors illustrates the information control mechanisms of cultural hegemony through media.

makes profits for the television network, and promotes Hollywood films. The television network pays the Academy millions of dollars for rights to carry the telecast, and the network then makes several times that amount in advertising income. The Oscar telecast serves as a moneymaker all around and serves the film industry in particular on a fundamental level as an inexpensive and widely viewed three-hour advertisement for films.

Who controls the media process?—this is a central question of production/hegemony analysis (see Figure 5.2). The Academy and the television network determine what message goes out to the audience in the classic manner of "gatekeepers" (Breed, 1952; White, 1950).

A *gatekeeper* is the person in the information flow who decides what parts will and will not be sent down the line. For example, a news story may be written in Australia, edited down by Reuters news service, and then further abbreviated in a London newspaper or BBC report. At each step, gatekeeping of information takes place. These decisions are not automatic. They are made according to personal judgments and institutional pressures (Gans, 1980; Hirsch, 1977) and are influenced by organizational, genre-related, and sociocultural factors (Galtung & Ruge, 1965). In the case of the Academy Awards telecast, the Hollywood industry is its own gatekeeper insofar as it decides what the public will see and learn about Hollywood films that year in the Oscars.

Despite Hollywood's international market, the Oscar media event has a narrow geographical base. The first gatekeeper is the Los Angeles film industry. Only about 200 of the 3,500 voting members of the academy live outside the Los Angeles area, and in all 24 categories, except for Best Foreign-Language Film, Oscar nominations are open only to films that have played in the Los Angeles area by the preceding December. The second gatekeeper is the American national television network, and, whereas the Oscars go out to the world, no foreign film award ceremony is beamed back into the United States. This geographical narrowness and one-way flow confirm the charge of cultural hegemony referred to in the previously quoted European Union report. From time to time, British films—*Hamlet, Gandhi, Chariots of Fire*—have earned Oscars, but Hollywood products usually dominate. Even a winning film made in China by an Italian director, *The Last Emperor,* was distributed by Hollywood. The gatekeeping also favors American performers. More than three out of four (76.1%) Oscar-winning performances have been by American actors and actresses; 16.5% have been by British performers; and 7.4% have been performers who were neither British nor American (Levy, 1987, p. 348). The Oscar's gatekeeping clearly serves culturally and economically to benefit Los Angeles-based and American-financed filmmaking above all others.

The Oscars are also affected by social routines among production personnel (Altheide, 1976; Tuchman, 1978) and by institutional alignments in which the interests of media owners or managers indirectly shape the mentality of those they direct and promote (Barnouw, 1975, 1978; Curran & Seaton, 1981; Halberstam, 1979).

How do frameworks of knowledge, relations of production, and technical infrastructure (Hall, 1980) influence the Oscars? One common "framework of knowledge" is shared by producer, director, crew, and cast. This framework establishes that the major challenge is to present a technically and artistically sophisticated product that will have mass entertainment appeal. This is the framework both for the presentation of the Oscars and for the day-to-day work of Hollywood. Deviations from this framework, for example, by introducing overtly political issues, are resisted. The "relations of production" in the Oscars are the industry standard of authoritarian control from top to bottom, with experienced, skilled technicians at every point. The "technical infrastructure" is the seamlessly integrated set of production and distribution technologies that distribute around the world selected sounds and pictures of the event, from prepackaged film clips and dance numbers to movie stars' comments and commercials. This infrastructure includes some 17 cameras, 45 monitors, 15 video decks, numerous items of special-effects equipment, and a worldwide television distribution system.

The resulting telecast is beamed out internationally via satellite in two versions. The full-length live version is distributed to most of the countries receiving the event, whether live or tape-delayed. Another version, a shorter one-hour version, is edited down immediately after the live ceremony and beamed out within eight hours to England and a few other European countries for prime time there. This one-hour version limits itself to the 11 major awards, including, of course, Best Actor, Best Actress, and Best Picture. Both versions are crafted with a well-developed sense of what the Hollywood film and television industry wants.

This process recalls the "industrialization of culture," a process that creates texts that Enzensberger (1974) warns can lead to the "industrialization of the mind" by the "consciousness industry." But although the process resembles industrialization in a mass sense, it is also a kind of culture by consensus, a consensus created not by coercion but by consent. The process operates not by direct cultural dictation but rather by hegemony or indirect influence. Elements that would not serve the interests of the sponsoring bodies—that is, the Academy, the television network, and advertisers—will not appear.

The Resulting Text:
Does It Reflect Its Producers?

The Academy Awards show brims over with stars and glamour, with competition and winning, with high-blown rhetoric and glittery production. Hundreds of millions of people around the world recognize the inset windows of nominees awaiting a decision and the famous line, "And the envelope, please." Any viewer knows the content at least superficially, but what is it finally? What kinds of material dominate the Oscars? Does the show reflect the interests and biases of Hollywood with regard to genre, gender, celebrity, competition, ethnicity, and other values?

A typical 3-hour Oscar telecast spends half an hour showing winners receiving awards but even more time showing celebrities walking on and introducing awards. Almost as much time is given to commercials as to film clips from nominated films. Nearly half an hour of special awards feature career achievement, humanitarian contributions, or scientific and technical contributions. Twenty-five minutes are eaten up by transitions, which include connecting comments made by the host, applause, walks to the microphone, reading the academy rules, and other less-than-memorable moments. Songs and dances include the five songs nominated for an Oscar and take up 26 minutes in the form of production numbers that attempt, Las Vegas style, to liven the festivities. The grandiose opening includes the arrival of celebrities, and the closing includes lengthy credits.

To what *genre* of media content does the Academy Awards telecast belong? The telecast is a mixture of traditional awards banquet, variety show television special, and ceremonial parade. The telecast is contest, conquest, and coronation, in which the Hollywood equivalents of the royal family exercise their symbolic leadership, replete with well-publicized glamour, privilege, and performance of duty. The Oscar's closest genre relatives are the awards shows for the Grammys, Tonys, Emmys, Miss Universe, and so forth. But at the same time as it recognizes individual and collective filmmaking achievement, the Oscar telecast resembles a long, calculated commercial for the Hollywood film industry. In this way, the show's genre fits perfectly the interests of its controlling bodies.

The Hollywood industry's attitude toward gender is also clearly on parade. Glamour and decoration only accentuate sex-role stereotyping. Every man connected with the ceremony must wear a tuxedo, from superstar to delivery truck driver, whereas women must wear extravagantly varied and enticing gowns. Male domination and female stereotypes have served Hollywood throughout its history and are deeply embedded in the culture that Hollywood's hegemony produces and here celebrates.

Men's and women's Oscar-winning roles from 1927 to 1985 have been studied in detail by Emmanuel Levy (1987). The film genres with the most Oscar-winning roles have been the serious drama (59%) and the comedy (15%). Men and women have been equally represented in them numerically, but have differed sharply in age, marital status, and occupation. The second most frequent genre for men's winning roles is the action-adventure, which has provided 19% of all men's Oscar-winning roles but only 6% of women's roles. The women's "equivalent" has been the romantic melodrama, with 14% of the women's roles (19% of Best Actress winners) and not one male Oscar winner. These differences indicate that not only does Hollywood portray men and women differently, but that there are certain types of films regarded as appropriate for men and others for women.

Matching age and marital status with gender reveals further disparities in Oscar-winning roles. Only 16% of men's Oscar roles have depicted young characters, compared to 62% of women's roles. Only 22% of female characters have been middle-aged, compared to 57% of male characters. Of men's roles, 27% have depicted elderly characters, compared to only 13% of women's roles. Movies mention the marital status of women, but not always of men. No reference to marital status occurred for 18% of the men's Oscar roles, but this was true of only 3% of the women's roles. The marital status of *every* Best Actress winner was provided.

Occupations also vary by gender in Oscar-winning roles. Almost all winning men's roles (97%) had identifiable occupations, but only 64% of winning women's roles did. Moreover, men have been portrayed in three times as many occupations as women. The two most frequent occupations among men have been soldier (14%), as in the winning roles of George C. Scott, Jon Voight, Christopher Walken, and Louis Gossett, Jr., and law enforcer (9%), as in the winning roles of Gary Cooper, Rod Steiger, Gene Hackman, and others. Men have also played kings, politicians, judges, lawyers, and priests in winning roles. In comparison, prominent women's roles have been in service occupations, such as teacher, nurse, or secretary, and in entertainment occupations, such as actress, singer, or dancer. The two most common occupations for female winning roles have been actress (15%) and prostitute (12%). As Levy (1987, p. 191) notes ruefully, "at least one out of every three gainfully employed women has been an actress or a prostitute and, at times, both actress and prostitute," as in the case of the Jane Fonda character in Klute. Other women's roles have been in family settings as wives, mothers, and daughters, often characterized by a generous sprinkling of suffering and victimization. Fully 42% of the Best Actress roles have portrayed victims of their spouses or lovers, compared to 2% of the Best Actor roles. Moreover, as Levy (1987) notes: "Any attempt by screen women—until the 1970s—to deviate from their prescribed, stereotypical roles has been consistently and continuously punished . . . from the most extreme sanction, death, to lesser sanctions such as humiliation, ostracization, and relegation to domestic life" (p. 198). Career women are generally dehumanized, as in the case of Big Nurse Ratched, played by Louise Fletcher in *One Flew Over the Cuckoo's Nest,* and the power-hungry television executive played by Faye Dunaway in *Network.* A notable exception occurred in 1977, when four of the five Best Picture nominees were films about women: *Annie Hall* with Diane Keaton, *The Goodbye Girl* with Marsha Mason, *Julia* with Vanessa Redgrave, and *The Turning Point* with Shirley MacLaine and Anne Bancroft.

In Oscar-winning roles, men are recognizable *types,* but women are confined and rigid *stereotypes.* Levy (1987) points to the basic problem this indicates:

> The function of the male types and female stereotypes, from the point of view of dominant ideology, is to keep women in their place, to reward them for accepting their traditional roles and for not challenging the status quo. These screen roles have provided an ideological rationalization much needed to reconcile women to marriage and family life. Comprehensive and all-embracing, these images go beyond the socioeconomic area, providing a mental state of mind, a whole way of life for women. (p. 202)

This is precisely where the hegemonic power of Hollywood over gender role representation has concerned a large number of critics (see Chapter 6).

In addition to questions of genre and gender, an exploration of production/hegemony is interested in the Oscar's textual messages endorsing celebrity, competition, tradition, ethnocentrism, regionalism, and nationalism. The show attracts an audience by presenting a vast number of popular stars (celebrity) and by creating suspense about who will win (competition). Tradition is present in the sense of historic grandeur evoked by film clips of past Hollywood classics and by the honored presence of elderly stars and directors. Ethnically, fewer than 5% of the featured celebrities are non-white, a figure dramatically below non-white proportions in United States and world populations. Regionally, as we have seen, this American celebration represents the narrow Southern California domination of electronic entertainment, a domination that competes with East Coast domination of literary, political, and economic power. In terms of nationality, fewer than one-fourth of the presenters or winners are non-Americans in a media event through which cultural norms are proposed to people scattered throughout the world.

Hegemony Over Audience Reception, Interpretation, and Participation

Does production control over the text of a cultural product affect what is taken away from it by viewers, listeners, and readers? To examine what typical Academy Awards viewers make of the show, 141 randomly selected telephone respondents were surveyed in the four days following an Oscar telecast.[1] The effect of the Oscar on audiences can be grouped around three classic "functions" of media in society: status conferral, enforcement of social norms, and narcotizing dysfunction (Lazarsfeld & Merton, 1948/1957).

The "status-conferral" function can be seen at work with Oscar viewers. Asked to rate on a 5-point scale the importance to them of each of eight motives for viewing, survey respondents rated most highly "to find out the winners" (4.5) and "to see the celebrities" (3.5). After those came "to see the dances and hear the songs" (3.2) and "to see the film clips" (2.9). The lowest-rated motives all received ratings of 2.2 or 2.3: "For the celebrity chitchat," "because nothing else was on," "to be able to talk about it," and "to share time with others." Finding out the winners, the first motive, is all about who has status conferred on them. Seeing the celebrities, the second motive, also concerns celebrities who enjoy high status because of media.

Hollywood films and the Oscar telecast are associated with subtle "enforcement of social norms." The majority (57%) of respondents agreed with the statement "I enjoy the beauty and fashion displayed at the Academy Awards telecast." Certainly films themselves help establish norms of beauty and fashion. When Clark Gable, in the Oscar-sweeping *It Happened One Night,* removed his shirt and was seen to be wearing no undershirt, the sale of undershirts plummeted. The young John Travolta sped along two fashion trends, one for disco attire in *Saturday Night Fever* and the other for western outfits in *Urban Cowboy*; his revival in *Pulp Fiction* proposed an even more extreme postmodern model of fashion.

Certain audience responses to the Academy Awards telecast suggest the passivity of the "narcotizing dysfunction" of media. Two-thirds (66%) of the respondents agreed with the statement "I enjoy watching the Academy

Awards show." But only one-third (34%) agreed with "I look forward to the Academy Awards each year." If this is generally true, then one-third of the audience, or more than 100 million people internationally, do not look forward to the Oscars but enjoy them, revealing in their unplanned viewing a vague sense of acceptance for whatever enjoyable comes down the line, a passive and almost Pavlovian approach to television viewing. Almost two-thirds (64.5%) *disagreed* with the statement "I talk about the nominations with friends before the awards are given," and 44% disagreed with "I usually have my personal favorites picked out before the awards show." These responses indicate low involvement and participation in the viewing event, despite the nearly 3 hours taken up by the event. Heavy, passive television viewing has long been associated with this kind of social disengagement, even to television's being called "the plug-in drug" (Winn, 1975).

The status-conferral function, the enforcement of social norms, and the narcotizing dysfunction indicate mechanisms through which norms proposed in the hegemonic telecast get translated into the lives of viewers.

In addition, the telecast worked for many in achieving its commercial, promotional role. Asked, "are you more likely to see a certain movie because it has won an Academy Award?," 45% answered yes. If a film was merely nominated, 34% were more likely to see it. Fully 77% agreed that "a movie's earnings are greatly increased by winning an Academy Award." Only 3.5% felt winning had no effect on a film's success or an actor's career. A slight majority (50.4%) agreed that "films with larger budgets are more likely to be nominated for an Academy Award." Survey respondents were asked whether they agreed with the statement "the Academy Awards are nothing more than a public relations event for the film industry, in an effort to focus attention on films and increase moviegoing by the public." More than half the sample (55%) agreed with the statement. The strong phrasing "nothing more than" did not scare away respondents; only 27% disagreed with it. Another 18% had no opinion on the statement. Audiences perceive the "hype."

Transnational Hollywood. Despite the preceding, it would be an error to conceive of Hollywood as a simple geographically and culturally homogeneous center that unilaterally imposes its products on the world screen. The transnational complexity and diversity of current Hollywood operations flies in the face of that simplistic conception. Frederick Wasser (1995) notes a turning point when, in 1972, Dino DeLaurentiis moved his film producing career from Italy to Hollywood with an explicitly transnational strategy. By preselling foreign rights to his Hollywood films, DeLaurentiis brought foreign money into Hollywood production. By making films explicitly for the global market and seeing the United States as just another territory, DeLaurentiis reversed Hollywood's strategy, formulated by P. A. Powers in

1920, of recouping investment through the domestic American market with the foreign market merely a supplement. DeLaurentiis produced *Death Wish* (1974) to capitalize on Charles Bronson's overseas appeal and found its domestic success a surprise bonus.

In recent decades, Hollywood has become a center of flexible, opportunistic transnationalism exemplified by vagabond directors such as Bernardo Bertolucci, Wim Wenders, and Ang Lee, whose films are often distributed by Hollywood but made with international financing, shot anywhere in the world, and aimed at global audiences. Even Steven Spielberg shot his Oscar-winning *Schindler's List* in Poland with a largely Polish crew and made Indiana Jones films in Spain. Bertolucci's *The Last Emperor* (1987) won nine Oscars, including Best Picture, for its story of Pu Yi, the last emperor of China, whose life spanned incredible historical changes. *The Last Emperor* was shot in China by an Italian director and cinematographer with British financing; its Oscar-winning music was by Ryuichi Sakamoto, David Byrne, and Cong Su. To define "Hollywood" too narrowly would be a mistake, just as it would be a mistake to ignore Hollywood's dominance over world cinema.

Promotional culture (Lazarsfeld, 1941) is one of the classic labels for the dynamics of the production/hegemony nexus. The promotionally overheated culture, permeated by advertising, marketing, public relations, and every level of promotional activity and incentive, has come to be a central characteristic of the media culture of late capitalism. Media audiences are drawn into this, even though reception theory tells us that individuals respond differently and unpredictably in any given case. The direct power of the Hollywood audiovisual industry over media texts also gives it indirect power over audience textual interpretation and ritual participation. Hollywood's hegemonically produced texts "set limits" and "exert pressure" on the various interpretations that we are likely to give them. Only when these limits and pressures are acknowledged can we give free rein to how receivers interpret in preferred, negotiated, or oppositional ways.

Summary

"If Shirley Temple, who became Shirley Temple Black by marrying businessman Charles Black, had then married Tyrone Power, would she be known as Black-Power?" goes an old joke. In fact, Shirley Temple Black became America's ambassador to Ghana from 1974-1976, foreshadowing Ronald Reagan's ascension to power in the parade of Hollywood before the world—ironic for a child actress whose films featured the most blatant of African American stereotypes.

Hollywood's hegemony over world film theaters is nowhere more clear than in the familiarity with which buffs around the world recognize Shirley Temple, Ronald Reagan, and their movie descendants. Hollywood makes cultural hegemony as much as movies these days.

The importance of examining the "production/hegemony" nexus of media culture is considerable. Without it, one is lost in a plethora of individual cultural products that seem to bear no meaningful relationship to each other or to society. With it, the underlying incentive system, institutional power arrangements, imbalances between nations or groups, and interrelationships of products and profits become much clearer. Key to exploring the hegemonic influence of production control is asking the questions of who makes it, why, in what interests, for whose benefit, with what profits, through what channels, and with what influence over audience interpretations. Hollywood's power in Europe and its Academy Awards event exemplify the concentration and exercise of cultural power in media culture today.

Does this mean that by uncovering the "production/hegemony" aspect of media culture we have solved our original mystery? Not completely, because once again too many other crucial elements of media culture go unconsidered while analyzing production hegemony. Issues from reception theory to textual analysis to ritual participation are only implicitly included in the search for the hidden power interests behind cultural production. But no clue could be more essential to resolving our current cultural crisis than one that uncovers the arrangements of power in cultural production and the exercise of hegemony through media culture.

Note

1. The Oscar survey drew on a random sample of metropolitan residents of a city in the southwestern United States (Real & Hassett, 1981). The 141 completed questionnaires matched the proportions of the adult population of the United States by age, income, education, and other demographic variables. The survey was conducted during the 4 days following the awards telecast by a graduate research team headed by Chris Hassett (see also Real, 1989, chapter 3).

Approximately half of the survey respondents had watched the telecast. Specifically, of the 141 respondents, 71 had *not* watched the telecast, 42 had watched *some,* and 28 had watched *all.* Viewing the Oscars appears to be a pattern over time for most. Those who had not watched had previously watched a mean of only 1.67 Academy Awards telecasts in the past 5 years; those who had watched some had watched a mean of 3.26 shows in the past 5 years; and those who had watched all had watched a mean of 4.07 in the past 5 years. The roughly 50% viewing among the survey population appears a bit lower than the Oscars' 65%-70% share of American television households reported in Nielsen ratings. In any case, its 75 million American viewers places the Oscars close behind the Super Bowl, but this number is only one-third to one-fifth of its total estimated international audience.

EXERCISES

Chapter Five

Exercise A. INDUSTRY. How does exploring the size and nature of the major media industries give us insight into the relationships among cultural production, hegemony, and power? Find out how large these industries are *this year* in various countries in terms of revenues and influence. What are the consequences for media culture of these concentrations of industry power?

Exercise B. HEGEMONY. Review the reasons why the European Union worries about the place of Hollywood films in Europe. How does the sheer scale of Hollywood production and distribution make it difficult for European film industries to function? What is the history of this situation, and what future policies might change that history? Do you think the current situation should change or not? Why?

Exercise C. PROMOTION. Examine ways in which the Oscar telecast functions as a long commercial. How does this massive global telecast serve the interests of the Hollywood film and television industries? How does the political economy of the sources transmitting the Oscars affect their gatekeeping of the message? Why is this international domination of the film world called *hegemony*?

Exercise D. GENDER. Consider the text of the Oscar telecast. What do we see in terms of gender and values in Oscar-winning films and the Academy Awards telecast? In more recent years, the years since Levy's analysis of Oscar winners, how have male and female winners and their roles compared?

Exercise E. TELEVISION. Analyze and critique a television viewing experience in depth. Search out electronic and print sources for *information about* the show to give depth to your analysis. Account for something of the *origins* and *economic importance* of the program you choose.

- When did it begin? Was it a spin-off from another program?
- What company produces and owns the show?
- What network/channel distributes the program?
- What larger corporation (if any) owns the producing company? The distributing system?

- Who advertises on the show (unless it is noncommercial)?
- What is the ratings history of the program (if available)?
- Are items from the program merchandised in other media?
- What sociocultural "meanings" are present in the show?
- How does its production relate to hegemony?

Your analysis may also consider the program's content, visual style, talent and performances, pacing, viewer interest, and "target audience." In general, however, retain a focus on socioeconomic aspects rather than the stylistic emphasis more common in film reviews.

Explain the facts of your selected program, but also go beyond the facts to examine it in depth, not forgetting Stuart Hall's model of the encoding and decoding of programs within specific frames of power, knowledge, and technique.

6

Gender Analysis:
Patriarchy, Film Women, and *The Piano*

The woman on screen is mute. She functions but cannot express herself. In particular, she cannot express her most personal experience in ways readily understandable to others, and especially to men. She suffers in silence for this. She strikes back but cannot explain or defend herself. For this, she is in imminent danger of being destroyed.

This describes a subtle theme in films as diverse as *The Piano, Thelma & Louise,* and *A Question of Silence.*

We each experience life as a particular "gendered subject." We are male or female, just as we are members of an ethnic group, class, and other categories given us by birth and circumstance. What does it mean to be "female" or "male" today in our particular situation and history? What role do media play in determining how "male" and "female" are experienced by us? At midcentury, studies of media and contemporary culture seldom considered gender. In more recent years, nothing has seemed more important than gender in debates on media culture. How does "gender analysis" explore media culture?

This chapter asks whether the various insights provided by feminist criticism are the missing clues that will unlock the mystery of media culture. To explore this question, the chapter brings together a range of feminist thought on a linked sequence of issues moving from female stereotyping/ exclusion in patriarchal Hollywood to feminist theory and filmmaking. In particular, the themes of "female muteness," the "female voice," and the "male gaze" are paramount. Jane Campion's widely acclaimed 1993 film, *The Piano,* provides a jumping-off point for exploring gender issues.

Gender analysis in the exploration of media culture is wide-ranging. This type of analysis examines each and all of the "moments" in the encoding-decoding model. In this way, gender analysis works in combination with explorations of the production/hegemony structures that produce media text, textual analyses of media content, and analyses of reception and ritual participation by viewers, listeners, and readers of media culture. As we have seen in previous chapters, issues of gender arise in exploring Oscar-winning roles in movies, male and female participation in sports and fitness, the content and style of video games, reactions to Madonna, and in every other area of media culture. Because of this wide range of concerns, feminist theory and criticism have been a major source of insights not just about women's portrayals but about all aspects of culture.

Speaking for "the Other." One delicate point arises in these pages. How can one speak for "the other," whether that other is of another gender, race, class, or country? Is not the media experience of males and females, of ethnic subgroups, of privileged and disadvantaged, of young and old, of rural and urban, of North and South, too different to allow any one source to "speak for" these others? The late twentieth century has witnessed a widespread retreat into traditional cultural, ethnic, sexual, and attitudinal divisions, as predicted by Marshall McLuhan against the grain of the desegregating 1960s. Is not a chapter on feminist criticism a bit presumptuous here because it is not written from inside the experience of being a woman?

Consider, however, the alternative. If we cannot attempt to enter empathetically into the experience of others, we become predictable wooden stereotypes. Each person has the potential of all within, and not merely the preconditioning of one. The self cannot be understood except in relation to the other, as George Herbert Mead noted many years ago. The argument really should be reversed; it is urgent that we all attempt to understand and speak with and for the "other" or we can never understand ourselves. Unless men understand feminism, Anglos understand the experience of being of color, experimentalists appreciate the contributions of culturalists, English-speakers understand the "other" who does not use English, and all the other chasms in culture today bridged in both directions, there will be precious little purpose or outcome for intellectual endeavor as we enter a new century. From whatever singular vantage point we start, the first challenge of truly engaging with media culture is to open up to, rather than close oneself off from, the true diversity of media practices and cultural products in circulation among us. Our increasingly globalized media culture demands that we search through the whole and not through only the perspective of one group, region, language, or interest.

Developing Feminist Film Theory

With *The Piano,* Jane Campion became the first woman director ever to win the top prize at the Cannes Film Festival. The film was the first directed by a woman to be nominated for a Best Picture Academy Award. *The Piano* won Campion an Oscar for Best Original Screenplay and won Oscars for

Holly Hunter and 9-year-old Anna Paquin for Best Actress and Supporting Actress respectively, in addition to earning five nominations in other categories. The Writers Guild of America awarded Campion "best screenplay." Had it not been released in the same year as Spielberg's historic *Schindler's List*, which won 10 Oscars, how many additional honors might *The Piano* have won? Yet when Jane Campion was born, a short 38 years earlier, there were virtually no opportunities for women to direct films and no feminist film theory. If *The Piano* marked a turning point in film and gender, it was a point long overdue.

This raises a question crucial to cultural studies and media: In culture, what is universal and immutable, and what can be changed? Maturity, learning, travel, and life in general teach us that a great deal of what we learned early on as "the way things are" was merely the way things were for particular people in a particular time and place. Older people are respected in some societies and rejected in others; light skin may earn status or scorn in different cultures; gays and lesbians may be accepted or ostracized; and the status, roles, and expectations of women and men also vary from culture to culture. As was noted in Chapter 1, culture is less a universal and immutable given to which individuals must conform than it is an infinitely varied construct created collectively by the lives of all those who are part of it.

This principle of cultural mutability has immense consequences for gender. The inherited "patriarchal culture," a culture in which power and opportunity is unevenly distributed in favor of males, can and should be changed. Feminist criticism, together with other struggles of marginalized and oppressed populations, has brought a refreshing sense of change, responsibility, purpose, and struggle back to media studies, helping to reclaim such studies from a potential staleness in the status quo of empiricism and formalism.

The Piano is a 121-minute English-language film with Australian and French financing. In *The Piano,* Ada (Holly Hunter) is a willfully mute Scottish woman sent with her 9-year-old daughter Flora (Anna Paquin) to New Zealand to marry by contract Stewart (Sam Neill), a somber, well-to-do local landowner and farmer. The film has voice-over narration by Ada, but she has been mute, speechless, since the age of six. She plays the piano beautifully and has brought her piano with her. She watches and struggles for her own identity and happiness in a repressive mid-1800s rural and isolated Victorian environment. This symbolic muteness, the lack of female voice, invites the question: What has been the aesthetic loss—in addition to the injustice—caused by the historic muting of women in the making of films and media in general?

In contending with this question, there have been at least two major stages of classical feminist film criticism. First, there was the "critique of images of women," followed by a more complex and comprehensive stage of "reading against the grain" of classical cinema.

The first stage examined, in the words of Judith Mayne (1988), "the pernicious representations of women and their lack of correspondence to women's lives in the real world" (p. 23). Gender analysis indicated that female representations in film consisted of only mothers and sex objects, or even worse, the femme fatale, most strikingly depicted as the classic noir female in *Mildred Pierce* (1945), a woman who is evil, powerful, and seductive.

Molly Haskell and Marjorie Rosen were pioneers in this first stage of identifying female stereotyping in films. Haskell, in *From Reverence to Rape: The Treatment of Women in the Movies* (1974), observed,

> The whore-virgin dichotomy took hold with a vengeance in the uptight fifties, in the dialectical caricatures of the "sexpot" and the "nice girl." On the one hand, the tarts and the tootsies played by Monroe, Taylor, Russell—even the demonesses played by Ava Gardner—were incapable of an intelligent thought or a lapse of sexual appetite; on the other, the gamines, golightlys, and virgins played by Hepburn, Kelly, Doris Day, and Debbie Reynolds were equally incapable of a base instinct or the hint of sexual appetite. (p. ix)

Haskell sees the latter shallow, protected female sustained in following decades:

> The ideal white woman of the sixties and seventies was not a woman at all, but a girl, an ingenue, a mail-order girl: regular featured, generally a brunette, whose "real person" credentials were proved by her inability to convey any emotion beyond shock or embarrassment and an inarticulateness that was meant to prove her "sincerity." (p. 329)

Marjorie Rosen's *Popcorn Venus: Women, Movies and the American Dream* (1973) reached similar conclusions about the negative and restricting portrayals of women in classic Hollywood film. Innumerable studies of gender stereotyping in advertising, television, news, and music have complemented the continuing studies of stereotyping in film (Lent, 1995, pp. 387-397).

The second stage goes beyond this content analysis of stereotypes and underrepresentation to consider them as components in a system of power and representation. In this reading against the grain of male coding, the contradictions of Joan Crawford's portrayal of Mildred Pierce are worked through as "polysemic" or many-layered and capable of conflicting interpretations. Mayne (1988) observes,

If the early stage was concerned with the absence of real female experience from the screen, the later stage would consider how that "absence" might be better understood as repression and displacement. . . . The difference between these two approaches concerns above all different conceptions of ideology. "Images of women" suggests a relatively simple manipulative system of social control, whereas "reading against the grain" suggests a system full of contradictions, gaps, and slips of the tongue. (pp. 23-24)

Teresa de Lauretis (1985/1994) writes of a related contradiction "familiar to anyone even vaguely acquainted with the development of feminist thought over the past fifteen years" (p. 140). This is a contradiction specific to, even constitutive of, the women's movement itself: "a twofold pressure, a simultaneous pull in opposite directions, a tension toward the positivity of politics, or affirmative action in behalf of women as social subjects, on one front, the negativity inherent in the radical critique of patriarchal, bourgeois culture, on the other" (p. 140). This contradiction is similar to one noted by Silvia Bovenschen in 1976 in answer to the question: Is there a feminine aesthetic? She answered, yes and no. "Certainly there is, if one is talking about aesthetic awareness and modes of sensory perception. Certainly not, if one is talking about an unusual variant of artistic production or about a painstakingly constructed theory of art" (de Lauretis, 1985/1994, p. 140).

In this way, the making of women's cinema is pulled in opposite directions. One pull is toward films that give "immediate documentation for purposes of political activism, consciousness-raising, self expression, or the search for 'positive images' of women" (de Lauretis, 1985/1994, p. 141). The other pull is toward rigorous critical work on cinematic techniques within the social technology of film "in order to analyze and disengage the ideological codes embedded in representation" (p. 141) Similarly, Laura Mulvey (1975/1988a, 1981/1988b) identifies two successive moments of feminist film culture: a period marked by effort to change the *content* of cinematic representation and a period concerned with the *language* of representation itself, especially as that language is challenged by the avant-garde tradition. Figure 6.1 summarizes the traditional situation and the critical efforts.

Campion's film *The Piano* performs masterfully in incorporating both stages of feminist film theory. By telling the story from Ada's point of view, the film presents a critique of negative expectations and stereotypes, primarily in the portrait of her uncomprehending husband: "Stewart, the stiff, bourgeois gentleman represents respectability and ignorance" (Bruzzi, 1993, p. 236) about sex and women. But Campion counters this negative content, typical of the first stage of feminist criticism, with the positive new language

PATRIARCHY
IN CLASSICAL HOLLYWOOD FILM

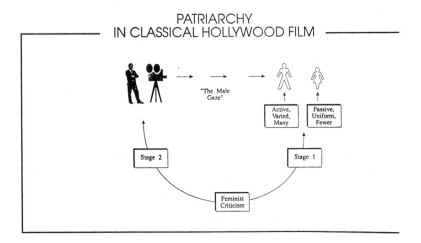

Figure 6.1. Male domination includes the male gaze and female exclusion/stereotypes in the imagery and language of classical film.

of Ada learning to feel, express, and eventually speak. In sexuality and feminist awareness, "Ada and Baines epitomize radicalism and liberation" (p. 236). Campion does not go so far as to resort to avant-garde rejection of narrative and conventional storytelling, but she does present her film in a new language of female representation, the kind called for in the second stage of feminist film theory. The period costumes of cumbersome hoop skirts become a linguistic symbol as Campion shows them constraining and expressing Ada's world. Stella Bruzzi (1993) credits Campion with discovering "a language which articulates a radical opposition to the restrictions imposed on nineteenth-century women through the very means by which those restrictions are usually manifested—clothes" (p. 235).

Robin Morgan finds "an emerging female aesthetic" in Campion's previous film, *An Angel at My Table* (1990). That was the story of New Zealand writer Janet Frame, originally made as a three-part miniseries for New Zealand television. The screenplay was based on Frame's three autobiographies, which describe how she was misdiagnosed as a schizophrenic and spent 8 years in a mental hospital. This attracted Campion, who discovered Frame to be not a mad writer but an ordinary person with a great gift for detail and frankness. Like her first feature film, *Sweetie* (1989), *An Angel at My Table* gave Campion an opportunity to explore the subconscious and the darker side of mind and society. Writing in *Ms.,* Robin Morgan (1991) praises the result:

Separately, Frame and Campion, each with her own merciless eye and generous heart, create work exemplary of an emerging female aesthetic. Together they— and all the women that worked on *Angel*—have given us a film about the daily, quiet suffering of a woman, and the stubborn, quirky means by which she daily triumphs over it. It's an unexpected and unforgettable window into our own lives. (p. 66)

Clearly, a primary task of gender analysis has to do with examining in some detail how women have been represented and can be represented in media culture.[1]

Documenting Women's Absence in Film

In *The Piano* we have a major film directed by a woman about a woman's experience in mid-nineteenth century New Zealand. *The Piano* recounts her cold, lifeless relationship with her well-meaning husband, who is locked into rigid male restraints and expectations. And it reveals her gradual emotional and sexual unfolding as her husband's neighbor and employee Baines (Harvey Keitel) takes an interest in her piano and her. How common is such female-centering in the making of film and culture in general?

The disadvantaged position of women in general is well-documented worldwide. United Nations reports document the striking gender disparity in areas of literacy, health, education, work, politics, and violence. The Fourth World Conference on Women in 1995 addressed these issues. The U.N. Commission on the Status of Women designated, among its goals for 1996, "elimination of stereotyping of women in the mass media" (United Nations, 1991, p. 87).

Gender Disparity in Media Employment. Progress toward the equal employment and portrayal of women in media stems from centuries of struggle that reached watersheds in the United States in the 1960s and 1970s. In 1969, the United States Federal Communications Commission issued rules making it illegal for broadcasters to discriminate against women. Starting in 1971, broadcasters were required to file annual lists of female and minority employees and their job classifications. In 1972, Title VII protections of the Civil Rights Act were extended to private industry in the Equal Employment Opportunity Act, creating the first of a new group of broadcasting professionals, dubbed the "class of '72." This included Lesley Stahl, Jane Pauley, Marcie Carsey, Judy Woodruff, Suzanne de Passe, and others.

Resulting gains were more statistically impressive than real. Assessing the results of Civil Rights, FCC, and EEOP changes, the U.S. Civil Rights

Commission found that between 1971 and 1975 in the top four job categories at stations—officials and managers, professionals, technicians, and salespersons—minority men's employment increased by 42.6%, minority women's employment increased by 80.3%, and white women's employment increased by 89.4% (U.S. Civil Rights Commission, 1977). By 1985, women held 26.7% of the jobs in the top four categories at commercial television stations, up from 21.5% in 1980 (Castro, 1988). However, some 80% of all jobs are listed in the top four categories. The FCC and the Civil Rights Commission agreed that during that period minorities and women did not necessarily make significant employment gains, because many jobs were simply relabeled to move them up into the top four job categories. Differences in real power remained.

In the 1990s, inequities remain in women's directing and management in television. For example, women television news directors earn 34% less, on average, than men, according to the Radio and Television News Directors Association. Women make up just 6.1% of all television station presidents, according to a study by American Women in Radio and TV, Inc., which called that figure "grossly deficient" considering that women constitute 52% of the population and 44% of all employed persons in the United States. The Directors Guild of America (DGA) found that, of the 65,000 prime-time hours aired between 1959 and 1980, women directed just 115. In 1986, women directed 348 of the 3,180 television programs produced in the United States; it is noteworthy that, from this 11%, women garnered 24% of the nominations for DGA directing awards. In 1988, 384 of the 4,684 members of the DGA were women, approximately 8% of the total (Castro, 1988). By 1991, this had climbed to 9.2% of DGA membership.

Women are also distinctly underrepresented in film and television acting, according to figures provided by the Screen Actors Guild (SAG, 1990, 1993). Women represent 43% of the SAG membership, but earn only 34% of income from all SAG contracts. (SAG figures count only the portion of salary for each person for an individual feature or television show up to the $200,000 ceiling for the SAG Pension and Health contribution, established by collective bargaining.) As a consequence, even excluding the multimillion-dollar contracts dominated by men such as Schwarzenegger, Stallone, and Costner, men collectively earn twice as much ($672.4 million) as women ($341.1 million) in the Hollywood production industry (SAG, 1993, p. 1). The worst SAG-documented disparity is in theatrical films, where only 31% of the jobs go to women (up from 29% in 1991), and 69% to men. In television jobs, women get 36% to men's 64%. Television advertising presents the closest equality of all in hiring on-camera principals, with women at 41%, but advertising voice-overs present the worst disparity, with women getting only 19% of the jobs. This last figure is a decline since 1986 from 20%, despite the fact "SAG studies have shown that female voice-overs are equally as effective as male voice-overs" (p. 2). A 1991 SAG report found that although women in general in the labor force earn only 70 cents for every dollar a man earns, among actresses it is 50 cents and among women screenwriters, 63 cents (Infusino, 1991).

Gender Disparity in Media Content. Do on-camera representations of women in television content reflect the employment disparities? Yes, and then some. The restricted portrayal of women and minorities has been identified by scores of content analyses in recent decades. Both women and minorities have been underrepresented in proportion to their numbers in society. They also play a much smaller proportion of leading roles. Furthermore, when women have been presented, they engage in a narrower range of occupations than men and usually exercise less authority, as we saw also in Oscar-winning film roles. More specifically, a sample of 1,365 programs over the 10 years from 1969 through 1978 found men outnumbering women 3 to 1 on prime time (Gerbner & Signiorelli, 1979). Overall trends in media portrayals have not changed drastically from the Civil Rights Commission's summary of the content of 5 years of programming in the 1970s:

> The television world presents a social structure in which males are very much in control of their own lives and are in a position to control the lives of others. Regardless of race, male characters were older, more independent, more frequently portrayed in serious roles, and they held more diverse and prestigious occupations than did female characters. Females were younger, more often unemployed and family bound, and more frequently seen in comic roles. Those who were employed were in stereotyped and sometimes subservient occupations. . . .
>
> The major difference between males and females was the degree to which men were involved in violent action, either as law enforcers or as criminals. Further, women were far more likely to be victims of violence rather than the perpetrators of it.
>
> Female weakness is the complement of masculine control on television and it is seen in an exaggerated form in the portrayal of the nonwhite female. Most nonwhite females were in their twenties, unemployed, and the most likely of all groups to be the victims of violence. The frequent portrayal of the black female as a prostitute illustrates her vulnerability in television's violent world. (U.S. Civil Rights Commission, 1977, p. 40)

In a consistent pattern over time, men continue to outnumber women by 2 or 3 to 1. A 10-year content analysis of television programming (Gerbner, 1993), contracted by SAG and the American Federation of Radio and Television Artists (AFRTA), analyzed 19,642 speaking parts in 1,371 television programs in 8 samples. Women made up one-third or less of the characters in 6 of the 8 samples, that is, male characters constituted two-thirds or more of the total in prime time network drama, Saturday morning drama (mostly cartoons), Fox network drama, cable-originated drama, cable-originated children's drama (including cartoons), and television news. Women were more visible only in daytime serials (45.5%) and in game shows (55.3%), although never as game show hosts (p. 4). Saturday morning children's programming depicts women in less than one-fourth of the human characters' roles (23.4%) and in even fewer of the "major" characters' roles (18%). In news, women constitute 35.7% of those delivering the news but only 20% of those cited as authorities on the news and only 18.1% of those making news (p. 8).

How do age, virtue, and romance factor in with gender in the roles portrayed by women? In their narrative plot roles, younger women but not older women are presented more positively than men. The proportion of "good" women to "bad" women (positively vs. negatively valued) is 5 to 1, whereas the ratio of "good" men to "bad" men is only 2 to 1; but this positive depiction of women reverses dramatically with age. The proportion of "bad" older women is more than 8 times that of "bad" older men. This is on top of the fact that women 40 years old and older receive only 9% of the roles on television and 8% of the roles in theatrical films, whereas 25% and 26% respectively of the roles are played by men 40 and over. Prime-time romance involves more young women than men but more older men than women. Nearly half of women's romances depicted in cartoons occur in adolescence, whereas men's romantic parts occur in greater numbers at all other ages. The television content analysis summarized,

> Women play one out of three roles in prime time television, one out of four in children's programs, and one out of five of those who make news. They fall short of majority even in daytime serials. They age faster than men, and as they age they are more likely to be portrayed [as] evil and unsuccessful. (p. 12)

The SAG/AFRTA report also stresses the important cultural role these television portrayals play. Americans spend one-third of their freely disposable time with television, more than the next 10 highest-ranked leisure time activities put together. The portrayals of gender, race, class, ethnicity, age, and disability reflect society's power structure and affect how we see ourselves and others. Television's representations are damaging; "Minorities are made, not born," in the words of the report (p. 11). Both casting patterns and the narrative fates of characters provide "inescapable images that cultivate conceptions of majority and minority status and the corresponding calculus of visibility, power, and risk" (p. 2). The difficult issue behind this is corporate cultural hegemony:

> For the first time in human history, most of the stories about people, life and values are told not by parents, schools, churches, or others in the community who have something to tell but by a group of distant conglomerates that have something to sell. (p. 1)

What is the historical background of the distorted gender distribution in media culture, particularly in films?

Patriarchal Culture in
the Film Industry: Old Hollywood

When *The Piano* grossed $100 million at the box office worldwide, how unique an achievement was that? Gender analysis is concerned not only with representations of women and men but also with the gendered structuring of power within major media industries and with the access of women and traditionally marginalized groups to the tools and financing of media production in such places as Hollywood.

Few cultural institutions have been as powerful and as exclusively male-dominated as classic Hollywood, particularly from the time of its massive international prominence following World War I to the first tangible effects of the women's movement on it in the early 1980s. Prior to the end of World War I, the early film industry was not centralized in Hollywood and female directors such as Lois Weber were successful within the industry. As films became standard-length products, the 90-minute-or-so feature, and as the star system became dominant, the industry became rationalized in Hollywood, California, in the 1920s in a particularly powerful and patriarchal form. Rampant sexism made the casting couch as important as the screen test for the advancement of women's careers.

A small cluster of male studio executives wielded enormous power. The head of MGM, Louis B. Mayer, was the highest-paid American executive in the Great Depression. During the Golden Era of Hollywood, from the inception of the Talkies at the end of the 1920s to the competition from television in the late 1940s, the studio system was forcefully dominated by the "seven sisters" of major studios, vertically integrated monopolies headed by powerful white men. Studio contracts bound employees in virtual indentured servitude but the money and fame of Hollywood induced acceptance, creating the anomaly of a "conservative labor leader" in Ronald Reagan, president of the Screen Actors Guild. However, the "Paramount decision" by the U.S. Supreme Court in 1947 broke up the vertical monopolies and forced a separation of ownership at levels of production, distribution, and exhibition, although overseas operations could remain monopolistic (as noted in Chapter 5). Throughout its history, male domination of Hollywood was continuous, despite the presence of a few strong female actresses and rare directing efforts by Dorothy Arzner and Ida Lupino.

Ownership contraction in the media industries in the last third of the twentieth century has again restricted diversity in top-level control over Hollywood. Corporate mergers in the 1980s accelerated this trend: "In 1981 there were 46 corporations which controlled most of the business in newspapers, magazines, television, books and motion pictures. By 1986 there were 29" (Williams, 1988). Less than 2% of the television and radio stations in the United States are owned by minorities. Sony Pictures, Disney, Time Warner, and other transnational corporations each control rich mixes of film, television, music, retail stores, real estate, and other synergistic media combinations. Christine Gudorf's study "Gender in the Media: Notes on Profit and Ownership Contraction" (1994) finds the following:

> Ownership contraction in media means that a smaller and smaller number of powerful wealthy white men control the chief avenues of information and consciousness formation in our society. The self-interest of this group opposes any major shift in gender arrangements because this group represents the power and success of the dominant model of gender structuring. (p. 142)

The owners' self-interest "compels them to promote a particular view of gender and gender roles that represents a social construct" (p. 142). In particular, male-dominated media reality becomes structured into "masculine public spheres and feminine private spheres," according to Gudorf (p. 142). The masculine public sphere of politics and business assumes that humans are separate individuals in competition with each other for survival, success, power, and wealth. The feminine private sphere of personal relations, families, religion, and home assumes that humans are essentially social and relational. Male-owned media reinforce this separation and emphasize the priority of the masculine public sphere over the feminine private sphere. Gudorf concludes that media owners protect current gender structures by the following series of practices:

- Reject any responsibility for educating the public; instead provide only what the public is already accustomed to.
- Address products to the composite profile, thus exaggerating similarities and diminishing particularities.

- Minimize the flow of information which stimulates comparisons of gender arrangements either cross-culturally or historically.
- Give women access to traditional male roles, including those in media organizations and representations, to mask the masculinist nature of media.
- Stress "realism" in existing problems such as crime, violence, war, and terrorism, all requiring tough handling by powerful experts.
- Encourage "leisure" escape from work, problems, and the public sphere by marketing leisure products that shape and control leisure time.

Historical tendencies of the American public toward isolationism, extreme individualism, privatization of pleasure, consumerism, and acceptance of the wishes of the dominant class fit nicely with the interests of the media controllers. Gudorf concludes,

> The for-profit nature of the media works to strengthen these tendencies, and the shrinking group which controls the media uses these tendencies to consolidate and preserve its own power. In many ways, the entire process serves the preservation of gender arrangements which benefit the few at the expense of the many. (p. 144)

The muteness of women in media, their lack of voice, and the dominance of the male gaze have risen from and provided crucial support for men's privilege in the patriarchal culture. Men's ownership and control of the means of cultural production has ensured continued reinforcement of restricted options for women and standardized male-oriented conventions in media culture.

Subversive Feminism Within Patriarchal Hollywood. Despite their lack of overt power, women's roles in classic male-run Hollywood cinema were not one-dimensional. Female filmgoers collaborated with female stars to recuperate a female presence and viewpoint despite the overt patriarchal silencing of the female "Other" in classical Hollywood. The subtleties have been nicely teased out by Jeanine Basinger in *A Woman's View: How Hollywood Spoke to Women, 1930-1960* (1993). In Basinger's reading, the women's films of the 1930s, 1940s, and 1950s had a series of contradictory purposes:

- To place a woman at the center of the story universe ("I am a woman, and I am important")
- To reaffirm in the end the concept that a woman's true job is that of just being a woman, a job she can't very well escape no matter what else she does, with the repression disguised as love ("Love is my true job!")
- To provide a temporary visual liberation of some sort, however small—an escape into a purely romantic love, into sexual awareness, into luxury, or into

the rejection of the female role that might only come in some form of questioning ("What other choices do I have?") (p. 13)

These purposes were not usually understood even by those who created them, and they sometimes worked at cross-purposes with one another. An example is the Hollywood tearjerker *To Each His Own* (1946), a film in which Olivia de Havilland won an Oscar for portraying a woman who bears the child of her dead war hero after their one-night stand. She has the baby out of town and then sneaks it onto the porch of her best friend, whose baby has just been born dead; her friend's grateful husband scoops up the baby and places it in his mourning wife's arms. They accept it as a miracle and *ask no questions*. There are frequent absurdities in the plotlines of these films. The heroine proceeds to become a wealthy cosmetics tycoon but her life is presented as a tragedy because she can't mother her son. Basinger (1993) notes, "A crackpot plot becomes the excuse for one woman's life of intense suffering," and adds, "what's astonishing is that these plots work" (p. 6).

These films were overtly system-maintaining but not without subtle subversions:

Women in the audience could watch while their favorite female stars wore great clothes, sat on great furniture, loved bad men, had lots of sex, told the world off for restricting them, destroyed their enemies, even gave their children away. Women could ruin their lives—get free of everything—down at the movie house for twenty-five cents with butter on their popcorn. . . . When the end of the movie came around, the surrogate woman was usually dead, punished, or back in the fold, aware of the error of her ways. Since the stories were so obviously cracked, and since the heroines paid dearly for their unrestrained behavior, it all seemed a perfectly safe form of pseudoliberation for women to enjoy. (Basinger, 1993, p. 6)

Basinger considers these woman's films a "genre" due to their representations of a number of categories: the duality of the women's good and evil sides, women's fashions, female stars, ways of seeing these good/bad women, women's worlds, men and marriage and motherhood, and especially women in a men's world. Basinger concludes by explaining how *Kitty Foyle* (1940), *Smash-Up, the Story of a Woman* (1947), and *The Guilt of Janet Ames* (1947), starring respectively Ginger Rogers, Susan Hayward, and Rosalind Russell, revealed a great deal about being a woman by society's standards. Basinger's conclusion?

A woman's film is one that places at the center of its universe a female who is trying to deal with the emotional, social, and psychological problems that are specifically connected to the fact that she is a woman. These problems are made concrete by various plot developments, and since they are often contradictory, they are represented in the story as a form of choice the woman must make between options that are mutually exclusive. . . . The presentation of the woman's world allows for both an overt indication that women should lead conventional lives and a covert form of liberation in which they are shown doing something else or expressing anger about this need for conformity. (pp. 505-506)

Patriarchal Attitudes and
the Male Gaze: Film Psychology

With moviemaking an exclusively male preserve for generations, the very way that movies view the world has been from a male point of view, the infamous "male gaze." This has been particularly so in the way that movies have viewed women.

The Piano contains several caricatures of the classic "male gaze." Early in the film, shortly after Ada's arrival, Ada's frustrated husband Stewart is reduced to squinting at her through a camera eyepiece as she poses unhappily in her wedding dress. More tellingly, Stewart resorts to peeping through the cracks in the wall and between the floorboards in Baines's house to catch a glimpse of his now erotically active wife. She is with a simpler, cruder, but more sensitive man than himself, and he watches in agony as she does enthusiastically with Baines what she barely managed begrudgingly with him—make love. Traditional Hollywood films were shot from the vantage point of men. *The Piano,* instead, reduces the man from enjoying the dominant point of view to acting as a pathetic voyeur. Also noteworthy is that there is as much full frontal nudity of Baines (Harvey Keitel) in *The Piano* as there is of Ada (Holly Hunter). Bruzzi notes (1993), "Convention is inverted as the man is constructed as a sexual being before the woman" (p. 240).

An in-depth examination of male-dominated filmmaking suggests psychoanalytic origins for the omission and distortion of women's experience in Hollywood films. This is where the feminist critique moves from an analysis of the stereotyped image to the language of representation itself.

In several important essays, Laura Mulvey (1975/1988a, 1981/1988b, 1988c) pioneered the Freudian study of sexism in film. She uses psychoanalysis to explore film's fascination with the "socially established interpretation of sexual difference which controls images, erotic ways of looking and spectacle" (1988a, p. 57). She uses this psychoanalysis "as a political weapon, demonstrating the way the unconscious of patriarchal society has structured film form" (p. 57).

Mulvey attacks the way the dominant patriarchal order has joined pleasure, eroticism, and the image of women: "As an advanced representation system, the cinema poses questions of the ways the unconscious (formed by the dominant order) structures ways of seeing and pleasure in looking" (p. 58). Despite technological changes that have made an alternative cinema possible, Hollywood "always restricted itself to a formal mise-en-scène reflecting the dominant ideological concept of the cinema" (p. 58). Patriarchal film's magic arose "from its skilled and satisfying manipulation of visual pleasure. Unchallenged, mainstream film coded the erotic into the language of the dominant patriarchal order" (p. 58). Mulvey criticizes to eliminate "the interweaving of that erotic pleasure in film, its meaning, and in particular the central place of the image of woman. It is said that analyzing pleasure, or beauty, destroys it. That is the intention of this article" (p. 58).

Film viewing allows a "voyeuristic separation" of the film viewer and the film: "Conditions of screening and narrative conventions give the spectator an illusion of looking in on a private world," allowing the spectator to project "repressed desire on to the performer" (p. 60). Mulvey finds there are

> two contradictory aspects of the pleasurable structures of looking in the conventional cinematic situation. The first, scopophilia, arises from pleasure in using another person as an object of sexual stimulation through sight. The second, developed through narcissism and the constitution of the ego, comes from identification with the screen image. (p. 61)

In the first, viewers are separated from and gaze at the object; in the second, viewers identify with the object as like themselves. Thus, viewers identify either with the one gazing (male) or with the one being gazed at (female).

This self-identification through gaze plays a crucial role in gender representation. Mulvey explains,

> In a world ordered by sexual imbalance, pleasure in looking has been split between active/male and passive/female. The determining male gaze projects its phantasy on to the female figure which it styles accordingly. . . . Women are simultaneously looked at and displayed, with their appearance coded for strong visual and erotic impact so that they can be said to connote *to-be-looked-at-ness*. Woman displayed as sexual object is the leit-motif of erotic spectacle:

from pin-ups to strip-tease, from Ziegfeld to Busby Berkeley, she holds the look, plays to and signifies male desire. . . . Traditionally, the woman displayed has functioned on two levels: as erotic object for the characters within the screen story, and as erotic object for the spectator within the auditorium, with a shifting tension between the looks on either side of the screen. (p. 62)

In this way, the diagetic (within the film) looks by the characters parallel and condition the nondiagetic (outside the film) looks by the film viewers. The active male figure controls and presents the narrative, is its center and point of view, and the passive female figure is an icon, a figure in the landscape around the male-driven narrative.

Mulvey incorporates classic Freudian anxiety in her explanation of men's fears behind these film representations created for the male gaze. Men's insecurity toward women is caused by "her lack of a penis, implying a threat of castration and hence unpleasure" (p. 64). The man's unconscious has two avenues of escape from this castration anxiety: by demystifying and devaluing the guilty object, as in film noir punishment and elimination of the femme fatale; or by disavowing the castration by substituting a fetish object, by turning the represented figure itself into a fetish so that it becomes reassuring rather than dangerous, resulting in the overvaluation of female figures and the cult of the female star. Mulvey concludes, "This second avenue, fetishistic scopophilia, builds up the physical beauty of the object, transforming it into something satisfying in itself. The first avenue, voyeurism, on the contrary, has associations with sadism: pleasure lies in . . . punishment or forgiveness" (p. 64).

The 1954 classic suspense thriller *Rear Window* presents an explicit sense of the film voyeur, a character even called by his nurse (Thelma Ritter) a "Peeping Tom." Alfred Hitchcock, whose women characters were often victimized, presents Jeffries (James Stewart), an injured photographer, sitting immobilized at his apartment window. Many critics have taken the setup of this film to be a metaphor for the cinema. Jeffries is the audience; the events in the apartment block opposite correspond to the screen. As he watches these events, an erotic dimension is added to his look, which becomes a central image to the drama. His girlfriend Lisa, played by Grace Kelly, is of little sexual interest to him while she remains on his own spectator side, but when she crosses the barrier into the block opposite, in effect goes up on screen, their relationship is erotically reborn.

Mulvey finds these psychoanalyzed pleasures and unpleasures deeply identified with the traditional narrative film. "The scopophilic instinct (pleasure in looking at another person as an erotic object), and, in contradistinction, ego libido (forming identification processes) act as formations, mechanisms, which this cinema has played on. The image of woman as (passive) raw material for the (active) gaze of man" (p. 68) then carries this over into the structure of representation, the ideology of the patriarchal order. These cinematic codes must be broken down before mainstream film and its pleasure can be challenged. Criticism must "free the look of the camera . . . and the look of the audience into dialectics, passionate detachment. . . . Women, whose image has continually been stolen and used for this end, cannot view the decline of the traditional film form with anything much more than sentimental regret" (p. 68).

E. Ann Kaplan reinforces this psychoanalytic perspective in *Women and Film: Both Sides of the Camera* (1983). She finds patriarchal myths at the heart of Hollywood films. Central to these myths is the portrayal of "Woman" as the "Other," eternal and unchanging. The theme of masculine against feminine revolves around first, the gaze, and second, patterns of dominance and submission. She writes,

> Our culture is deeply committed to myths of demarcated sex differences, called "masculine" and "feminine," which in turn revolve first on a complex gaze apparatus and second on dominance-submission patterns. This positioning of the two sex genders in representation clearly privileges the male (through the mechanisms of voyeurism and fetishism, which are male operations, and because his desire carries power/action where woman's usually does not). However, as a result of the recent women's movement, women have been permitted in representation to assume (step into) the position defined as "masculine," as long as the man then steps into her position, thus keeping the whole structure intact. (p. 28)

Kaplan cites as examples characters played by John Travolta and Robert Redford. Constance Penley (1989) has also written extensively on the Freudian psychoanalytic dimensions of male film dominance.

Tania Modleski (1991), in *Feminism Without Women: Culture and Criticism in a "Postfeminist" Age,* examines, among other issues, "Lethal Bodies: Thoughts on Sex, Gender, and Representation from the Mainstream to the Margins." The microworld of a film reflects the larger social world outside for Modleski, accounting for "how our (fe)male bodies are used to represent a more macro social and political reality(s)" (p. 135). Her "postfeminist" take on Peter Weir's 1989 film *Dead Poets Society* (with Robin Williams) leads Modleski to relabel the film "Dead White Male Heterosexual Poets Society." To Modleski, it is the repressed homosexuality of upper-class whites that motivates the plot and leads the father of one of Williams's students to demand that his son not play a part in *A Midsummer Night's*

Dream. The boy plays Puck, a "fairy" type of character, anyway. When his father finds out, the boy commits suicide. Gender analysis reveals that men can be victims and perpetrators of the restricted look called the male gaze.

Gender, Domestic Technology, and the Television Gaze

For a variety of reasons, the way gender relates to television tends to be quite different from the way gender relates to film, even to the point of television being associated with "the female gaze" as film is with the male gaze. The male gaze is associated with film, a medium viewed in public away from distractions, whereas the female gaze is associated with television, a medium viewed in a domestic environment and made of a disparate strip of programming, advertisements, promotions, and notices. The filmic male gaze is fixed, controlling, uninterruptible, and the televisual female gaze distracted, obscured, fragmented, already busy (Kaplan, 1988).

Household Technology and Gendered Power. Despite its female gaze, television remains a medium that women cannot easily relax with and enjoy. For women, the viewing site of television is also a work site, more so than it is for men. Domestic duties still command attention even when the woman is at home and the television available. Ann Gray (1992) found that many women do not consider themselves to have any specific leisure time in the home and would feel guilty just sitting and watching television. Men at home do not feel such competition for their attention during television viewing. Charlotte Brunsdon (1981) cautions that power and gender play a role in home television viewing. Insofar as the man in the home directs television viewing, television masculinizes the domestic sphere through the structure of domestic power relations.

In a detailed analysis of a small set of working-class television households, David Morley (1986) found gender differentiation in many aspects of viewing. Power and control over program choice, for example, normally resided with the man in the household, represented particularly by possession of the remote control device. Also, the styles of viewing differed. Men preferred to view attentively, in silence, without interruption, whereas women regarded television viewing as a social activity accompanied by conversation and the performance of at least one other domestic activity such as ironing clothes. Men planned their viewing by checking the printed listings, whereas women had a more take-it-or-leave-it attitude, unconcerned about missing certain shows except, as Morley (p. 153) notes, their favorite serials. Further, despite the hours that women may be reported by surveys to be around a television set that is on, in the opinion of both partners focused attentive viewing is done more by men. Women, however, admit that they talk about television far more than men will admit to. Men are hesitant to admit to too much viewing and talking about television. Talk about television is considered somehow unmasculine, except, of course, in the case of viewing and talking about sports.

Not surprisingly, Morley found that "none of the women operate the video recorder themselves to any great extent, relying on husband or children to work it for them" (p. 158). Why is this? Gender roles and experience direct boys and men toward technological toys such as video games, as we saw previously, but the fact remains that many women regularly use other sophisticated domestic technology. Ann Gray (1992) suggests that women may be employing a "calculated ignorance" to avoid making the operation of the VCR another of their domestic service tasks. Television viewing in the household relates to gender conditioning and domestic power. Morley found that when women indulge in the guilty pleasure of viewing what they really want, they more commonly engage in solo viewing at odd hours, whereas men will more often watch what they like alone even when their partner is there.

Male-weighted values dominate television within the household. Gray notes (1992), "the most powerful member of the household . . . defines this hierarchy of serious and silly, important and trivial, which leaves women and their pleasures downgraded" (p. 252). In Morley's working class homes, men preferred "factual" programs of news, current affairs, and documentaries and women preferred fiction programs. One exception was that women expressed a particular interest in local news but not national news, and also not zany comedies that ridiculed domestic order. Morley notes that other variables, such as class or age, interact with the gender variable, qualifying the preceding generalizations. But across all classes, Gray (1992) found "the female-preferred genres were considered by both women and men to be of a lower order than the male-preferred genres, which texts would always take priority for shared viewing" (p. 252). By combining semiotic analysis of how texts are decoded with the sociology of domestic leisure, Morley, Gray, Lull, and other domestic ethnographers have painted a broader picture of actual television viewing against the crude demographic scratchings by standard television ratings surveys.

Lull (1988, 1990) adds the important clarification that the television gender patterns previously described are culture specific. They predominate in Northern cultures. But the domestic power structure differs from those patterns in Venezuela, China, and India.

Television as Female Gaze. If men dominate domestic television viewing, how is it that television can be associated with "the female gaze"? The distinctions between film and television from a feminist perspective have been developed by E. Ann Kaplan (1988). She asks, "Since feminist film theory evolved very much in relation to the classic Hollywood cinema . . . how far [is] that theory . . . relevant to the different apparatus that television is?" (p. 133). In particular, she finds a "decentred spectator" in television, one who consumes comparatively short segments of different kinds of programming, ads, and so forth. This is the recognized "strip" quality of television, recalling the newspaper sequencing of unrelated serial comic strips. Classic Hollywood film maintains the illusion of real life by following a singular narrative with actors playing other people presented from the conventional camera point of view. The decentered television spectator encounters texts that do not conform to these Hollywood film conventions. In television viewing, there is not a single naturalistic plotline in the diagesis of the text to make it clearly distinguishable from the nondiagetic elements—titles and credits, musical soundtrack, superimposed dates or facts. There is also no single point of view, the anonymous camera observer. Television, and especially music videos, break filmic conventions of narrative, point of view, and standardized viewing.

Kaplan finds by focusing on MTV in particular that we discover television's "studied self-consciousness" playing off classic Hollywood sexism in more knowing and varied ways. In a typical Madonna video, for example, the singer may be playing a film character à la Marilyn Monroe and a nonfilm character who is part of a different storyline that critiques the first. Kaplan lists the many ways that the conventions of the classic Hollywood film are routinely violated in Madonna's music video *Material Girl.* The video recreates Monroe's performance of "Diamonds Are a Girl's Best Friend" from the film *Gentlemen Prefer Blondes* (1953). But in the video, Madonna's place is not singular, as Monroe's was in the film. She is the Monroe figure being imitated, she is the performer as "Material Girl," and she is the star/image/person Madonna, all at once and self-consciously. We move seamlessly back and forth between the stories of these three, breaking narrative conventions and role separations.

In *Material Girl,* the text of the video is itself decentred, a pastiche of different levels of story and character, both related and unrelated, but not separated by Hollywood's standard coding system. The video's view, or "the gaze," shifts likewise between different perspectives and levels of access to the story, unlike the fixed gaze of Hollywood cinema. The unique song-image relationship of MTV facilitates this freedom of visual representation. As a result, Madonna's video articulates "the desire to be desired in an unabashed, aggressive, gutsy manner" rather than "the self-abnegating desire to lose oneself in the male evident in the classic Hollywood film"

(Kaplan, 1988, p. 145). *Material Girl* is postfeminist and postmodernist: "The usual bi-polar categories—male/female, high art/pop art, film/ television, fiction/reality, private/public, interior/exterior—no longer apply to many rock videos, including 'Material Girl' " (p. 146).

The televisual image and viewer are more diverse and fragmented than their film counterparts. Music videos are interspersed with advertisements and promotions and specials which are presented in styles as decentered as the videos, creating one long strip for consumption and to promote consumption. The male gaze is not monolithic here, and the classic Freudian, humanist critique from a feminist perspective does not work as it does with classic Hollywood film. Kaplan (1988) concludes,

> The new postmodern universe, however, with its celebration of the look, surfaces, textures, the self-as-commodity, produces an array of images/representations/simulacra that co-opts any possible critical position by the very incorporation of what were previously "dissenting" images; this makes difficult the processes of foregrounding or exposing gender issues that feminist filmmakers have used. As a cultural mode, postmodernism would eliminate gender difference as a significant category, just as it sweeps aside other polarities. Television, as a postmodernist apparatus—with its decentred address, its flattening out of things into a network or system that is endless, unbounded, unframed and whose parts all rely on each other—urgently requires more thorough examination, particularly in relation to its impact on women. (p. 154)

These changes that television and music videos have brought to the audiovisual world have softened the feminist problem with standard narrative. Narrative, to many feminist filmmakers, "functions to reproduce the patriarchal order" (Cartwright & Fonoroff, 1994, p. 125). Therefore, only avant-garde nonnarrative strategies could effectively distance themselves from patriarchy. But with the breakup of film narrative in the form of music videos, feminists are no longer faced with an either/or choice of narrative or not. Yet the traditional conventions of film plots—action and adventure, strong heroes, resolution by force, and so forth—still indicate how the very language of film has become masculinized in traditional Hollywood.

If Women Ran Hollywood

If women ran Hollywood, Jane Campion's rise might have been quicker and less difficult. Also, if there were not special state-financed programs in Australia to support new young filmmakers, there might be no film director Jane Campion at all. Raised in a theatrical family, Campion majored in anthropology at Victoria University, then bounced around Europe and worked in London for a time on documentaries and commercials. Looking for an art school, she enrolled in the Sydney College of the Arts in Australia where painting and drama led to her first short film, *Tissues*. That led her to the state-financed Australian Film, Television, and Radio School, where she made *Peel* (1982), which won an award at Cannes, *A Girl's Own Story* (1984), and *Passionless Moments* (1984). She then joined another publicly subsidized group, the Women's Film Unit, where she made a film on sexual harassment in the workplace. In 1985, she received her first development money for *The Piano* from the Australian Film Commission. Feeling she lacked the confidence and experience to direct it then, she worked on a television film with Jan Chapman, *Two Friends* (1986), and directed *Sweetie* and *An Angel at My Table*.

Had there not been the Australian Film, Television, and Radio School, the Women's Film Unit, and the Australian Film Commission, would there be the much-acclaimed *The Piano* and would Jane Campion be a filmmaker? In these respects, her career bears out the wisdom of the European Union and others in proposing public support for developing alternatives to and competition for Hollywood. Campion is in this sense a product of Australian affirmative action, and the world is richer for it. If women ran Hollywood, her career might have led her to big-time filmmaking sooner, but there is no guarantee of it. She might also now have easier film financing, bigger budgets, more stars, more producing deals, and more demand as a script doctor, but there is no guarantee they would lead to better films.

Women's relationship to the film industry are complex. Successful director Martha Coolidge recalls of Hollywood, "when I first came here in 1976, there were no women directors to speak of. Things are still bad. But they have gotten better" (Infusino, 1991, p. E4). Coolidge found that the first generation of women film executives made it because they were able to think like men without making films significantly better for women. The old-boy network remains a fact of life in Hollywood, and offshore ownership of major film studios by Japanese, Italian, and Australian interests could prove to be less sympathetic to women. Coolidge concludes, "until women are in significant numbers in the industry, we won't see a difference in the kind of films being made or a lot of understanding of women's plight both in the industry and as an audience" (Infusino, 1991, p. E4).

What would an alternative Hollywood look like, one not run by men? Julia Phillips and Anne Thompson (1992) have whimsically pointed out interesting possibilities "if women ran Hollywood." They suggest,

Thelma and Louise would live at the end, and get away with it.
There would be a new TV series based on the movie. . . .

There wouldn't be an annual scramble to find five acceptable nominees for the Best Actress ballot. . . .

Linda Hamilton would nab $10 million for a *Terminator* sequel: *Woman Warrior.* As for Arnold: *Hasta la vista,* baby!

Penny Marshall, Randa Haines, and Barbra Streisand would finally get Best Director Oscars. . . .

There would be more big-budget special-effects films starring strong women heroes, from Amelia Earhart and Wonder Woman to Ripley— who wouldn't die at the end of *Alien 3.* . . .

Rain Woman would star Meryl Streep and Nicole Kidman. . . .

Jodie Foster would make $10 million a picture. . . .

In the eyes of the MPAA ratings board, frontal male nudity would be no different from frontal female nudity. . . .

Older male stars would be cast opposite women their own age. . . .

Julie Christie, Jacqueline Bisset, and Faye Dunaway would be allowed to be middle-aged sex symbols. . . .

Studios would have day-care centers. Studio stores would stock Tampax and Pampers. . . .

Lakers games, card tables, and golfcourses would be replaced as power networking centers by baby showers, Jennifer's Nails, and Beverly Hot Springs. . . .

Male executives wouldn't refer routinely to their body parts in story meetings. . . .

After a first offense, a sexual harasser would lose his (or her) coveted studio-lot parking space for a week. . . .

After a second offense, the harasser would lose the parking space, be docked two weeks pay, and be publicly flogged in Army Archerd's column. . . .

After a third offense, the harasser would be forced to do an interview with Howard Stern on *E!,* and be blackballed from the industry. . . .

Pauline Kael would be president of the Motion Picture Academy. . . .

Julia Phillips would eat lunch in this town again. . . . (pp. 30-33, © *Entertainment Weekly* Inc., reprinted by permission)

Successful Female Directors: Exceptions to Patriarchal Exclusion

Jane Campion now has visibility as a filmmaker, but it may be worth identifying a few other female film directors because they receive so little attention generally. Women have shown from the early days of filmmaking that they can direct successful, quality motion pictures. Many female directors have played important roles in the development of motion pictures, although they have almost always been placed in seriously disadvantaged positions in the patriarchal culture of filmdom. Important female filmmakers are listed in *Women and Film: A Sight and Sound Reader* (Cook & Dodd, 1993) and in course outlines in *Multiple Voices in Feminist Film Criticism* (Carson, Dittmar, & Welsch, 1994). Female producers have made great strides in recent years, even inside Hollywood (Ryan, 1995). No brief list can satisfy everyone, but the following women have played significant roles as filmmakers.

Lois Weber. Born in 1881 in Pennsylvania, Weber was an actress who began directing in 1913 and became the highest-paid director of all in 1916. She wrote, produced, directed, and occasionally starred in films and formed her own successful company, Lois Weber Productions, in 1917. She made a total of more than 400 films, noted especially for their creative, compassionate response to social problems.

Germaine Dulac. A radical feminist and avant-garde artist, Dulac made *The Smiling Madame Beudet* in 1923. With a rich sense of irony, she manipulated images through superimpositions, dissolves, and slow motion to express the frustrated mental state of Madame Beudet, who is trapped in a stultifying marriage.

Anita Loos. Loos was a prolific and highly regarded scriptwriter who wrote over 100 scripts between 1912 and 1915 and thrived for decades in Hollywood. She wrote important and successful films such as *The New York Hat* (1912, starring Mary Pickford), *San Francisco* (1936), *The Women* (1939), and *Gentlemen Prefer Blondes* (1953), which was based on her 1925 novel. Anita Loos wrote worldly, witty dialogue for assertive women.

Leontine Sagan. Sagan directed the controversial feature *Maedchen in Uniform* (1931), which was eventually banned by Nazi Minister of Propaganda Joseph Goebbels for antiauthoritarianism. The film dealt with, among other things, lesbianism in a girls' boarding school, and forcefully countered fascism with a sensitive humanism.

Leni Riefenstahl. The most famous—or infamous—female director of the first half of the century actually directed a very limited number of films. As an actress, the energetic German starred in mythic mountain-girl films, eventually producing, directing, editing, and coauthoring the successful mountain feature *The Blue Light* (1932). When Hitler came to power, he was impressed with her artistry and commissioned her to make what would become the most famous propaganda film of all time, *Triumph of the Will* (1935); she also directed the much-respected *Olympia* (1938). Roy Muller's three-hour documentary *The Wonderful, Horrible Life of Leni Riefenstahl* (1993) is a compelling portrait.

Dorothy Arzner. Arzner is the only woman editor and director who moved from silent to sound films within the Hollywood system. She directed 17 films from 1927 to 1943. Her films are mainstream but contain a subversive feminism that invited disruption of viewing conventions and "reading against the grain."

Ida Lupino. A successful Hollywood actress, Lupino also managed to work as a screenwriter, producer, and director. Her films tended more toward social issues of the time than feminist issues. She directed *Hard, Fast, and Beautiful* (1951), *The Hitchhiker* (1953), *The Bigamist* (1953), and *The Trouble With Angels* (1966). During this time she was the *only* woman directing Hollywood features.

Maya Deren. The fascinating Deren is called "the mother of the avant-garde film" (Taubin, 1993, p. 94). A poet, journalist, and activist, she made six short experimental films from 1943 to 1958, including *Meshes of the Afternoon* (1943), a meditation on identity, sexuality, and the dislocations of dreams. *The Legend of Maya Deren: A Documentary Biography and Collected Work* (Clark, Hodson, & Neiman, 1985) presents Deren's important contributions.

Agnès Varda. Varda is the female member of the French New Wave. She began filmmaking in 1954, achieved international success with *Cleo from 5 to 7* in 1962, and in her later films became more overtly feminist. During the same period, Mai Zetterling in Sweden and Jeanne Moreau in France starred in and directed films.

Margarethe von Trotta. A German director of features, including *The Long Silence* (1993) and *The Promise* (1994), she mixes rationality and emotion in mature, resonant films. Ruby Rich (1994, p. 40) places von Trotta among the "corrective realists" who use casts and stories aimed at wide audiences and who employ many cinematic conventions but transform the characterizations and narratives to validate feminine concerns, friendships, and activities.

Doris Dörrie. She is the director of *Men* (1985, *Männer,* in German) and a number of other offbeat features with critical perspectives and bizarre characters.

Monika Treut. In Germany, Treut has directed *My Father Is Coming* (1991) and short documentaries, four of which are collected in *Female Misbehavior* (1992). Her films are humorous, disrespectful, and unapologetic about sex or lesbianism. Treut contributed the central Hamburg, Germany, segment to *Érotique* (1995), which opens with Lizzie Borden's Los Angeles segment and ends with Carla Low's Hong Kong segment. A true rarity, *Érotique's* three sexually explicit, female-directed, subtly feminist segments played in first-run multiplexes for a time.

Chantal Akerman. A Belgian experimental feminist filmmaker, Akerman first burst on the scene in 1974 with *Je tu il elle,* a sexually explicit film featuring herself in three set pieces; it was shot within a week on a tiny budget. Her patient, disciplined 1975 feature was prosaically titled *Jeanne Dielman, 23 Quai de Commerce, 1080 Bruxelles.* Running 3 hours and 17 minutes, it has been characterized as a feminist landmark by many for its precise, unglamorized portrait of a middle-class housewife's daily routines as her life disintegrates (Carson, 1994, p. 465; de Lauretis, 1994, pp. 143-145; McRobbie, 1993, pp. 198-203; Rich, 1994, pp. 30-31). Her *Portrait of a Young Girl in the Late Sixties, in Brussels* (1994) is a 60-minute film that follows a 15-year-old through quitting school, roaming the streets, encountering a young Army deserter, and linking up with her girlfriend Daniele. Akerman's *Moving In* (1992) is a 35-minute reminiscence by a man about the laughter of three young women that filled his old house one summer. Self-consciously unconventional, Akerman's films attract extensive comment.

Also among women filmmakers examining themes of female identity and representation are Bette Gordon (*Variety,* 1983) Sally Potter (*Thriller,* 1979, *Orlando,* 1993, a feature film from the novel by Virginia Woolf), Yvonne Rainer (*The Man Who Envied Women,* 1985), and Julie Dash (*Daughters of the Dust,* 1991).

Since 1980, women have had increasing opportunities to direct in Hollywood and have created effective films that are measurably distinctive from male-directed films (see Real, 1989, chapter 5: Gender in Film Directing). Among these female mainstream directors are Penny Marshall, Barbra Streisand, Jodie Foster, Amy Heckerling, Randa Haines, Susan Seidelman, Martha Coolidge, and Penelope Spheeris.

Female Muteness and Solidarity in *A Question of Silence*

One of the more widely discussed films, *A Question of Silence* is a self-consciously alternative feminist film that works from implicit critiques of patriarchy, narrative, and the male gaze. The film serves to "envoice" the near-mute women who form its core.

A 1982 film by Dutch filmmaker Marleen Gorris, *A Question of Silence* is set in Amsterdam.[2] A slow film of subtlety and patience, it masks a profound, mute rage. The film takes one from the familiar to the unfamiliar: from previous definitions of how characters are motivated and self-articulated, from standard (patriarchal) definitions of plotlines and resolution, to something more inchoate and at first ephemeral-seeming but made more unmistakably clear throughout, particularly through the plotline around the efforts of the good, sensitive, dedicated court-appointed psychiatrist.

Carol J. Clover (1993) compares *A Question of Silence* to *Falling Down,* Joel Schumacher's 1993 film in which Michael Douglas plays a character called D-Fens, "the angry white male," who retaliates violently against a frustrating, bureaucratic world. Clover observes that a police officer (Robert Duvall) is able to track D-Fens *and* is able to understand his motivation as a white man committing violence but not taking anything at a Korean grocery store, an army surplus store, and a Whammy burger restaurant. Motivation is key. Clover writes,

> The set-up brings to mind a Dutch film of some years ago, *A Question of Silence* (directed by Marleen Gorris), in which some women browsing in a dress shop suddenly, on the slightest of provocations, join together and beat to death the male owner. The women have never met before; what joins them in common cause is their silence and sudden recognition of themselves as members of the category Woman, and therefore as angry victims of the category Man, of which the crowing shopkeeper seems an exemplary representative. (p. 140)

A more extended analysis of this film appears in Linda Williams's "A Jury of Their Peers: Marleen Gorris's *A Question of Silence*" (Carson, Dittmar, & Welsch, 1994). Williams recalls that in a classic article of feminist criticism, Elaine Showalter describes male and female experience as two overlapping circles; much is shared but beyond the overlap is a small crescent of experience dubbed "a 'wild zone' or 'no man's land' of woman's culture that is entirely off-limits to men" (p. 432). Women know the men's unique crescent area at least through myth and legend; men do not know the women's crescent because so little women's art is known to men. Williams sees *A Question of Silence* capturing that no man's land of the feminine crescent.

The unspoken contradictions between the dominant and the muted come to the fore in feminist art. According to Williams:

> More than any other feminist film of the last decade, Marleen Gorris's 1982 Dutch film, *A Question of Silence,* seems to me to avoid the pitfalls of a facile or utopian feminist revision while speaking eloquently from within the still "muted" experiences of its three women protagonists. (p. 433)

Gorris's film does not go outside the immediate experience of the three women protagonists to propose an explanation or strategy. Still, the sensation of a unique feminine solidarity is unmistakable in the film. The mute solidarity of the female subjects in *A Question of Silence* offers no linguistic, historical, or psychological explanations. This gives the male viewer an experience of what it is like to view as the "Other," a film experience usually reserved for women and ethnic minorities.

Eschewing standard chronological narrative, the key plot event is not presented chronologically up front, although it is central to the entire film. In that key scene, one of the three women is stuffing a dress into her bag and is caught by the smug owner-manager of the boutique. She is a nearly mute mother of three with a harried husband. Instead of complying when the shopkeeper smugly confronts her, she silently stuffs the dress back in her bag and stands defiantly. Two other women come to her silently. As the manager escalates his demands, the three attack him. He falls and (off screen) is kicked and beaten with hangers, ashtrays, and pieces of clothes racks until dead. Four other women in the store silently witness this. Looks are exchanged. All seven leave the store. A conspiracy has been created.

The bulk of the film occurs after this event and takes place around the female psychiatrist's investigation into the women's lives. Despite her sex, the psychiatrist is played with and resisted by the women. Gradually, she realizes that these women will not articulate their motives and self-justifications, but that they are completely real and defensible. The male judges and lawyers in the courtroom assume some form of emotional insanity must be at work. As Linda Williams notes, "the investigation culminates in a hearing on the sanity of the defendants in which the psychiatrist, much to the annoyance of the court, declares the women sane" (p. 433). The three women burst into laughter at the court's reaction to this declaration and the four witnesses, sitting anonymously in the first row of the audience, join in the raucous laughter. Finally, the female psychiatrist, apparently at the expense of her future as a court psychiatrist and perhaps at the expense of her marriage, joins in the loud laughter of solidarity. As all the central female figures in the film share in this rowdy, joyous behavior, they are ejected from the court. They continue laughing while they are led out. The film ends.

Linda Williams compares this film to the 1917 short story, "A Jury of Her Peers." That story, by Susan Keating Glaspell, "has recently joined the canon of feminist literature" and concerns the strangulation murder of a psychologically abusive husband. Women in the kitchen provide an oppositional reading of the events leading up to the murder; they even destroy evidence as they figure it out. Important as its similarities to *A Question of Silence* are, the short story has a central spatial and experiential focus in kitchens and parlors, whereas the Dutch film presents women not able to converge in territory of their own but only mutely able to sense the situation and their choices.

"The film suggests that the most genuinely heroic moment of feminist consciousness consists in a woman's decision to cast her lot with an identity that has not yet been spoken and that cannot as yet speak itself," says Linda Williams (p. 437). Each of the central female characters was part of the "high-heeled army of Furies," as the prosecution calls them as they are led out of the court. The line recalls Aeschylus's *Oresteia,* which features a female chorus sold out in a court of law by a male-dominated goddess. But Gorris's film transfers their rage into the subversive laughter of the defendants. Moreover, it does not create a female-defined happy ending but asks instead "what real judgment of women by women might be" (p. 439). Unlike Glaspell's story, the film does not proceed to that judgment, for "the language of such judgment, it suggests, does not yet exist" (p. 439). Williams concludes,

> The power of *A Question of Silence* as feminist art thus lies in its resistance of all the male paradigms by which female deviance has been understood, in its insistence on the wildness of women's cultural experience and, finally, in its refusal to narrate the positive, utopian identity of women. (p. 439)

Marleen Gorris (1996) acknowledges that *A Question of Silence* "has been controversial all over the world." When her 1994 Oscar-nominated film, *Antonia's Line,* became a success, she noted how interviewers often asked leadingly, "You're not one of those feminists, are you?" To which she happily responded, "Well, yes, I am actually, and why not?"

The Piano is less radical in its style and conclusions. But its theme of muteness is shared with *A Question of Silence.* Ada does not speak, not even when her husband attempts to rape her in the woods only to be prevented by her huge and cumbersome clothes, nor when he chops off her finger to punish her for her affair with Baines. Her frustrations and suffering remain unspoken. But in the clothes she wears and sheds, she is able to express herself. Baines bargains with her to earn her piano back by playing for him. Gradually the piano sessions in his frame house and the negotiations over clothing become increasingly erotic in tone and finally in fact. Ada's sexual responsiveness and her rejection of her husband make her "no longer the passive Victorian woman, acted upon rather than acting" (Bruzzi, 1993, p. 241). In the end, with her husband's consent, Ada and Baines settle down to a new life together in the town of Nelson. There Ada finally chooses to learn to speak again, as she plays her cherished piano with an artificial finger. As Stella Bruzzi concludes, "Jane Campion's *The Piano* is primarily but not exclusively Ada's liberation; it is also the reclamation of women's desires, the sexual personae which the past silenced" (p. 242).

Summary

The world of feature films, reflecting the wider context of all media, offers a set of cultural products and practices that mark patriarchal culture and inspire the feminist response to it. The hegemony of male domination of media culture gives us sexist stereotypes, female underrepresentation and exclusion, the male gaze, and a masculinized language of film representation.

The world of film, owned and directed by men, has undervalued and marginalized women. The male gaze of old Hollywood, from behind the camera and in the audience, objectifies and fetishizes women, leaving women mute and voiceless. Television's more pervasive presence but more fragmented content extends this male film world but opens up its representational patterns. In television also, women are underrepresented and underemployed, and in most homes men dominate viewing patterns and control the remote.

The criticisms of media culture by women have raised fundamental questions about the construction of dominant images, about the language of representation, about psychological compensations, about domestic patterns of power, about economic concentrations of control, and about what truly progressive media culture might be.

Female filmmakers have created a varied body of work that implicitly critiques and explicitly provides an alternative to the traditional male cinema. As women move into more central positions in filmmaking, the overall project takes on new dimensions.

Does this "gender analysis" mean we now completely understand media culture? Have we resolved this mystery? Once again, the answer must be qualified. We have answered perhaps a large part of the mystery, but not everything is explained by analyzing gender relations. Other clues and suspects need exploring at the same time as we study gender and "ways of transcending a polarity that has only brought us all pain" (Kaplan, 1983, p. 206).

Notes

1. In contrast to the film materials focused on in this chapter, the reading of romances by adolescent girls suggests the contours of a nascent female cultural alternative. Because this literature has a substantial history of female orientation, something not found in Hollywood, it is worth considering in some detail to give a more rounded sense of what female media culture has been.

A specific form of "girl culture" was identified in two important works by Angela McRobbie, *Jackie: An Ideology of Adolescent Femininity* (1978a) and "Working Class Girls and the Culture of Femininity" (1978b). These works grew from an in-depth study of girls at a Birmingham, U.K., youth club. These young women are situated in a "culture of femininity" organized around domestic duties, consumption, personal life, and above all, romance. Immersion in romance and beauty routines prepare them for home and family but not for the workplace. McRobbie found that the girls are aware that the idealized version of romance in music and magazines is mismatched with real life, but they still endorse romance and marriage. Economic working-class necessity and the impracticality of being a single working-class woman force their reconciliation to this.

Their lived experience is reinforced by written forms, particularly the magazine *Jackie* (similar to *Teen, Seventeen, Sassy,* and innumerable others in North America and elsewhere). Semiotically, McRobbie found that *Jackie* employs four codes: fashion and beauty, romance, personal and domestic life, and pop music. The magazine's fiction and nonfiction themes involve attracting boys and solving problems inherent in romantic relationships. These texts can give girls some measure of negotiation for power and control, modifying the male-dominated public environment, but they also pit girls in competition with each other for such attraction and control. Sexuality is funneled toward an exclusively heterosexual model and directs these girls toward forms of consumerism and domestic labor required by working-class households.

These themes of early female identity in girl culture in the United States are amplified by Linda Christian-Smith (1990) in *Becoming a Woman Through Romance.* She employs multiple methods of research to examine how teen romance novels fit into and condition the lives of school girls. Teen romance novels are a cultural force; by the mid-1980s romance novels had grown in only 10 years to a half-billion dollar industry. One series, Sweet Valley High, entered the 1990s with more than 26 million copies in print. Christian-Smith combined textual analysis, reader interviews, and historical analysis to explore the content and role of romance fiction among teenage girls.

In her textual analysis, Christian-Smith selected 34 books appearing from 1942—the year of the birth of the teen romance-centered novel with Maureen Daly's *Seventeenth Summer*—to 1982. The books were selected as those most frequently recommended by a number of school selection tools and guides through those four decades. In her study of readers, she worked closely with 75 middle school and junior high students (ages 9 to 15) at three Wisconsin schools. Interviews and observation were combined with a detailed questionnaire. She also employed extensive individual and group interviews, both formal and casual, with all the girls, and recorded her information in extensive notes or tape recordings.

In both the content of the novels and in the way the girls received them, the code of "romance" dominated by structuring emotions as the key to heroines' lives; falling in love and having relations with boys grants meaning to girls' lives. Romance gives the heroine a sense of belonging but also reinforces social subordination. Sexuality is synonymous with heterosexuality, and sexuality defines pleasure, regulates sexual practices, and establishes power relations. The emphasis in romance fiction on beauty "centers feminine consciousness in the body and lays the groundwork for heroines' sexual objectification. Beautification also makes heroines into consumers and establishes consumption as a distinctively feminine activity" (p. 6). The plots favor a feminine personality that is patient and passive against the threat of the "other girl," who is more aggressively sexual and assertive. Girls thus learn to articulate and negotiate an area of life, interpersonal relationships, that boys seldom cope with in any parallel manner, busy as they are with sports, video games, cars, and physical activities. Romance fiction contradictorily "reconciles women to their social subordination while providing an escape from it" (p. 6).

Historically, changes in the novels over the 40 years from 1942 to 1982 served to recode larger social tensions, most notably the domestic, work-related, and political aspects of women's place. Christian-Smith finds that the growth of a massive and relatively uniform teen romance publishing style in the last quarter of the century "parallels the shift in the political climate in the United States to the right-wing positions of Reaganism characterized by traditional perspectives on gender relations" (p. 2).

This parallel between content and context appears in a comparison of the novels in three periods. In period 1, from 1942 to 1959, books such as *Going on Sixteen* (1946), *Sorority Girl* (1952), and *The Boy Next Door* (1956) emphasize domestic themes of heart and hearth to the exclusion of all else. Cleaning, cooking, and caring for children predominate, with increasing attention to the promotion of consumerism. Harmony exists between boys and girls in this period, and uniformity of life and values is pictured across races, classes, and genders. In period 2, from 1963 to 1979, with *My Darling, My Hamburger* (1971), *Very Far Away From Anywhere Else* (1976), *Hey, Dollface* (1978), and *Up in Seth's Room* (1979), the teen romance novels became scenes of struggle with parents and boyfriends regarding sexuality, abortion, sexual orientation, and women working for pay. Romance remains paramount but heroines are more active and questioning, reflecting a dissatisfaction with traditional gender relations and white middle-class femininity. The teen novels of period 3, from 1980 to 1982, lose the sense of struggle and controversy, reverting back to the values and texts of the first period. In *P.S. I Love You* (1981), *California Girl* (1981), *Seven Days to a Brand New Me* (1982), and others, heroines think only of being popular and getting a boyfriend. Gender issues, teenage sexuality, working women, and female career plans are conspicuously absent. As Christian-Smith concludes, in the most recent period, woven into the hearts and flowers of romance stories "is an accompanying discourse that a woman is incomplete without a man, that motherhood is women's destiny, and that woman's rightful place is at home" (p. 2). Although the world of teen romance is a largely female world, the progressive potential of its representations has been to a great extent "recuperated" and turned back by larger forces in the culture.

Popular fiction relates to historical contexts, Christian-Smith notes, not as a representation of reality but as a particular construction of meaning: "For romance fiction, this involves offering readers particular gender, class, race, and sexual identities that maintain the social order, instead of challenging it" (p. 126).

Popular culture is the "area of negotiation" between dominant and opposing cultural forces (Bennett, Mercer, & Woollacott, 1986). The struggles of young romance readers represent feminist concerns with "the politics of the personal" in which everyday life and consciousness take on a political character. Young women's lives and leisure are dominated by fashion, romance, popular music, soap opera, videos, and other cultural products produced by large corporations. "It is important to continue struggling against such interests along with seeking new spaces for competing cultural practices," says Linda Christian-Smith (p. 142); "Gender, class, race, age, and sexuality are not immutable categories in teen romance or anywhere else, but cultural constructs that are produced and can be transformed" (p. 143). Media representations of gender are important in culture. Michael Apple, in the introduction to *Becoming a Woman Through Romance,* writes, "popular cultural forms matter because of what they themselves do and what people do with them" (p. xiii). A similar point is made by Dorothy Hobson in *Crossroads: The Diary of a Soap Opera* (1982): "At stake in the struggles and contestations over these meanings are not only textual representations of femininity and gender relations in particular cultural commodities, but also their place and significance in the lives of the actual women and men who consume, use, and make sense of them in the contexts of their daily practices and social relations" (quoted in Christian-Smith, p. xiii). Linda Christian-Smith concludes,

The struggle for girls and women, then (whether they are feminist or not), over the gendered meanings, representations, and ideologies in popular cultural forms is nothing less than a struggle to understand and hopefully transform the historical contradictions of becoming feminine within the contexts of conflicting sets of power relations. The process of becoming feminine involves not only the unequal gendered power relations between men and women, but also those of class, race, age, and sexual orientations. (pp. 3-4)

The place of women in media culture becomes more marginalized as we move from romance literature to mainstream film and television.

2. *A Question of Silence* is available from alternative video stores, but low-definition video and white subtitles without drop shadows make viewing less than ideal.

EXERCISES

Chapter Six

Exercise A. An "essentialist" position that says culture and gender are immutably fixed "as is" conflicts with the constructivist definitions of culture and gender favored in this book. Why does this distinction have major implications for the position and future of women in media culture?

Exercise B. What is the difference between the critique of the representational images of women and the critique of the language of representation? Do you find the argument for a specifically "male gaze" persuasive? If so, how do you view its consequences and alternatives? Is the development of positive female alternatives to the stereotypes or the critical analysis of current inadequacies of more interest to you?

Exercise C. Conduct your own gender analysis of a television program, a film, and several commercials. How many men and women are in the cast? How many in major roles? What are their ages? Their occupations? Are they good or bad characters? Are they romantically involved and is their marital status indicated? Do they succeed or fail in the end? How does what you find compare with the real world? From this study and your general viewing experience, do you find the figures in the SAG surveys accurate?

Exercise D. Why are ownership patterns of media important to issues of gender? Who owns media today? What connections are there between men's media ownership and the representation of women?

Exercise E. Seek out one or two films made by feminist filmmakers and view them with friends. What distinct qualities do you detect in them? What are the unique strengths and weaknesses of the film(s) in your judgment?

Exercise F. Select a book of feminist film criticism. These may be of three kinds: (1) general books applying feminist criticism to media; (2) feminist theory books touching on film, video, music, or other media; (3) specialized studies of one filmmaker or one genre or one movement. (In the Dewey Decimal System sections PN 1993 to PN 1998 contain many of these works.) Avoid popular nontheory books, such as star biographies or collected movie reviews. Compose a careful review of the book using the following guidelines.

A. BOOK IDENTIFICATION

At the top of page 1, list publication information on the book: author, year, title, place of publication, publisher.

Example: Diane Carson, Linda Dittmar, & Janice R. Welsch (Eds.). 1944. *Multiple voices in feminist film criticism.* Minneapolis: University of Minnesota Press.

B. INTRODUCTION

Prepare the reader for the book review to come. Introduce the topic, its importance, the book's focus. Why read this book?

C. CENTRAL THEME

In one sentence, all in capital letters, summarize the central theme of the book. The main clause of the sentence should state the book's primary thesis. The subordinate clauses and phrases in the sentence should indicate supporting evidence and arguments employed to explain the primary thesis.

Example: *MULTIPLE VOICES IN FEMINIST FILM CRITICISM* CONTAINS 36 ESSAYS FROM A VARIETY OF PERSPECTIVES OVER THE PAST TWO DECADES WITH AN EMPHASIS ON PSYCHOANALYTIC, LINGUISTIC, HISTORICAL, AND TEXTUAL ASPECTS OF FILM, INCLUDING SIX ACCOUNTS OF TEACHING FILM, AND WITH AN EMPHASIS ON GENDER-FOCUSED SCHOLARSHIP AS DIRECTLY GERMANE TO WOMEN'S SOCIAL IDENTITY WITHIN PATRIARCHY.

D. AUTHOR

Identify the author. What other books or essays has she or he written? What positions has the author held? How does the author's background and expertise qualify her or him to write on this subject? Are there any institutional or personal biases evident?

E. CHAPTERS

Every chapter in the book should be summarized in one paragraph each. (If there are more than eight chapters, discussions of several chapters may be combined.) In this way, if the book has six chapters, you will write six paragraphs, one about each chapter. If the book has 15 chapters, you may wish to summarize these in 6 to 8 paragraphs.

F. EVIDENCE AND REASONING

What justification does the author provide for positions taken in the book? Are there specific examples of films or videos to illustrate the ideas, to justify the generalizations made about film theory? What other sources or facts are provided to back up ideas in the book? Is the focus primarily historical or comparative, or more abstract and conceptual? Are there positions the book is arguing against?

G. EVALUATION

Spend some paragraphs critically evaluating the book. Indicate what you believe are its strongest points and its weakest points. State what you find are the book's most important contributions and what you learned from it that seems most valuable.

7

Historical/Ethical Interpretation: Reconstructing the Quiz Show Scandal

He stands in the isolation booth sweating profusely. He wears the ill-fitting suit and sidewall crewcut ordered by the producers. He thinks loathingly of the privileged Ivy Leaguer in the challenger's booth. He knows the answer to the easy question, but the fix is on. Herb Stempel must sacrifice himself as ordered in front of 50 million Americans. The producers, the sponsors, and huge television profits have deemed it must be so.

The most notorious illusion in American television history is achieving its greatest success.

The popular understanding of history plays a crucial role in political decision making, in legal and economic affairs, in education and domestic life. From history we learn what works and does not work and who we are as human beings. In providing what we need from the past, how do history and media culture interact?

Is "historical interpretation" the secret key that can unlock our understanding of media culture? After all, historical analysis can incorporate all theories and methods. As Nicholas Garnham observes, it is in some sense the *only* discipline.

Two distinct questions arise here because, at once, media affect our historical understanding and history affects our media. The first question is: What are the standards of truth when media represent history? More specifically, are there different standards of truth for different media genres, ranging from scholarly written history to the slippery reenactments of docudrama? Robert Rosenstone's collection, *Revisioning History: Film and the Construction of a New Past* (1995) foregrounds such questions. The second question is: What are the lessons history offers for our media practices and ethics? For example, are there blind spots and suppressed alternatives in the ways we structure and operate our media culture, as Robert McChesney (1994) proposes in his challenging reexamination of the origins of telecommunication regulation in the United States? In examining these two questions, can historical interpretation pry open the meaning and significance of media culture and its relationship to the rest of human life?

To examine history's relation to media culture, we here explore the famous American television quiz show scandal of the 1950s.[1] From 1958 to 1960, this scandal was investigated and publicly exposed. Surprisingly, in the 1990s, more than 30 years later, a feature film, a book, a television documentary, a play, and other re-creations have attempted to redefine, in very different versions, that embarrassing time in the middle 1950s when quiz shows dominated network television and ratings, only to explode in a series of rumors, hearings, and eventual criminal prosecutions. Specifically, Robert Redford (1994) directed and produced a film on the scandal, Richard Greenberg (1994a) wrote a play on it, Julian Krainin (Krainin & Lawrence, 1992) produced a historical documentary on the scandal and its aftermath, and Joseph Stone (Stone & Yohn, 1992) published an account of his 4-year investigation of the scandal as assistant district attorney for Manhattan. Add in chapters on the quiz show scandal in Richard Goodwin's book, *Remembering America* (1988) and in David Halberstam's book, *The Fifties* (1993), and you have an amazing explosion of interest over a scandal that had spawned only two major studies (Anderson, 1978; Weinberg 1962) in the preceding three decades.

The depth of current popular concern over that dark chapter in media history suggests an infatuation bordering on obsession, an infatuation that ties the midcentury quiz shows to a variety of historical and cultural trends central to media culture at the end of the century. By what standards of truth should "docudramas" like Redford's film be judged? Was the quiz show "scandal" a preview of numerous scandals to come, from the Profumo scandal to the Gulf of Tonkin to Watergate, Iran-Contra, and beyond? Does the ambition to win, or the "merchant mentality," as Redford calls it, spiral out of control in personal and corporate life when little public regulation and no ethical constraints counter the hunger for profit? How deep does ethical confusion run in the "postmodern" media culture as it enters the twenty-first century? In short, what historical and ethical "meaning" can the quiz show scandal possibly have today?

The quiz show scandal and debates over its representations take us down into the heart of central concepts in media analysis. Many of these appeared in earlier chapters but here include the following:

- truth versus deception—fact and fiction in media representation
- media events—their nature, power, and meaning
- political economy—competition for ratings and profit
- genre conventions—accepted standards of truth
- law and media—how society regulates and polices representations
- ethics and media—right and wrong in media practice
- postmodernism and the relativity of values

As a method for exploring media culture, historical analysis asks: What are the earliest and most accurate records of an event? Relating this to media culture means asking first, how do media accounts measure up against accurate records? Second, what do the lessons of accurate history tell us of the present and future? How can we track down physical evidence, information, versions, and fugitive records effectively, and how do we work through their lessons and consequences for the present?

Deception in Media Culture:
How the Quiz Shows Did It

All the new versions of the quiz story cover the basic territory of the scandal, though with quite different emphases. In general, all agree with prosecutor Stone (Stone & Yohn, 1992) that the quiz debacle was a scandal, "which, because it involved television, ranks only after the Watergate and the Iran-Contra affairs in terms of the furor and national soul-searching it would bring about" (p. 4). Robert Redford (in Wakefield, 1994, p. 28) agrees and feels the quiz scandal was the end of American innocence and marked the decline in American morality. Now, Redford says, such deception and lying to the public would not even raise eyebrows, but it helped create an atmosphere conducive to the bigger lies and scandals in Vietnam, Watergate, and Iran-Contra.

The conspiracy included celebrities and producers, contestants and staff. Together they conspired successfully to captivate the American public and set television ratings records from 1955 to 1958 by rigging *The $64,000 Question, Twenty-One, Dotto,* and other now-infamous quiz shows. Ordinary people became Warholian celebrities overnight with their 15 minutes of fame in the form of publicity tours, awards, endorsements, and meetings with dignitaries. And without question, the most famous and tragic victim, or villain, was a modest and attractive young Columbia University instructor, Charles Van Doren, son of poet and professor Mark Van Doren and member of an unusually prominent literary family among the intellectual elite in America. Van Doren's defeat of Herb Stempel on *Twenty-One,* his subsequent fame and fall, are central dramas in the movie, the play, and Goodwin's and Halberstam's chapters.

The scandal, like the quiz shows themselves, was an emotion-filled American soap opera of the 1950s, wrenching people from rags to riches only to leave them in final ignominy. America was enjoying a time of affluence and empire-building but the cozy Norman Rockwell pictures were edged with the insecurities of anticommunism, the Cold War, and atomic threats. Narrow conformity and suppressed problems internal and external to the United

States resided side-by-side with postwar self-confidence and ambition. "Get rich quick" has long been part of the American dream. Was it perhaps excessive free market profiteering in the 1990s that brought America's attention back to those thrilling days of yesteryear when the quiz scandal erupted?

The first major television quiz show, the famous *$64,000 Question,* came on the air on Tuesday, June 7, 1955, and by July was the top-rated program with an estimated one-third of the American populace viewing. Other quiz shows soon followed. In the next two years, the five top-rated weekly television programs were sometimes all quiz and game shows. Sponsors and networks saw profits soar, making the payment of quiz prize money well worth the investment. Goodwin (1988) reports that when *The $64,000 Question* was playing on Tuesday nights, it was difficult to get a taxi in New York and theater owners complained about the drop in Tuesday attendance. With its fifty million viewers, a successful quiz show could even compete regularly with *I Love Lucy.*

The mechanics of quiz show rigging were both simple and clever, according to all the re-creations of the debacle. Suspense was maximized and outcomes prearranged with a kind of mock innocence. The "control" began with picking contestants who were attractive and preferably, but not necessarily, competent. They would then be warmed up in "playback" sessions in which trial questions were asked; if they answered incorrectly, they would be given the correct answer. For contestants selected to defeat their rivals on the air, these same questions would be used on the show. The controllers also taught contestants how to close their eyes and bite their lips as they paused before exploding with the answer. Contestants were instructed how many points to go for and, as needed, when to lose.

Quiz show controllers could even reduce constestants' winnings. Because in some shows when a tie occurred, the dollars rolled over to the following week, and because losing meant deducting whatever was at stake from those carried-over winnings, a contestant could win tens of thousands of dollars over a period of many weeks yet walk away with far less. In Stone and Yohn (1992), we learn of one contestant, Martin Dowd, on *Tic Tac Dough* who had been promised $10,000 in winnings but had accumulated posted earnings above $40,000. Rather than let them reduce his winnings to the prearranged amount, Dowd double-crossed his controllers, threw a match, and left the show with $19,700 (Stone & Yohn, 1992, p. 190).

Quiz show rigging ran deeper and wider than we sometimes like to admit. The film and play are less explicit on this than the written accounts and to some extent the PBS documentary. Successful "control" techniques had been pioneered 20 years earlier with the radio show *Quiz Kids.* By 1957, fully 47 network half-hour periods were filled with quiz shows of varying degrees of handling, coaching, and rigging. Dan Enright, producer of *Twenty-One* and the famous Stempel-Van Doren showdown, also produced with his partner Jack Barry three other quiz shows for NBC. In Krainin's documentary Enright recalls that, when the first *Twenty-One* aired undoctored, it was a boring failure and the sponsor threatened cancellation; but careful casting, control, playback, and stage direction—*rigging*—saved it and moved it up to challenge *I Love Lucy* in the ratings. Enright, with his on-air sidekick Jack Barry, came as close as anyone to being the mastermind behind the quiz show rigging and, as the scheme unraveled, behind the cover-up. But many others were involved as "controllers" of quiz contestants, and still more knew that quiz shows were being influenced for maximum entertainment and ratings effect.

The profits for sponsors were enormous. In the first 6 months of *The $64,000 Question,* Revlon sales jumped 54 percent from $33.6 million to $51.6 million, and in the next year to $85.7 million, according to figures reported by Halberstam (1993). The company's earnings jumped an incredible 250 percent-plus in the short heyday of the famous show. Geritol's profits were not so dramatic, but it is likewise clear in films and writings that Geritol made an excellent return on its television advertising. Who was not convinced in the 1950s that this glorified patent medicine "cures tired blood," whatever that means?

The huge success of the deceptive quiz shows turned them into a "media event" (Dayan & Katz, 1992), a high holiday of media culture. They were live events with the dramatic appeal of major sports competitions that attract "deep fans," as we saw in Chapter 1. The shows achieved a hegemonic domination of public attention. People viewed in active, ritualized ways and experienced vicarious excitement through the myth-laden event. The quizzes emerged in a short period of time as among television's first major events. They competed with comedy hits, variety musicals, wrestling, serials, the World Series, and live drama for television audiences, ratings, and profits. They arrived on the scene soon after the General MacArthur Day parade in Chicago in 1951 (Lang & Lang, 1953) and the coronation of Queen Elizabeth and the American political conventions in 1952, the first televised media events to be closely scrutinized. Quiz shows were dominant media events in the first decade of mass television. The stakes were high, the profits almost unimaginable, the deception easy, and the temptations nearly irresistible.

But the lucrative arrangement began to unravel in August 1958, when Edward Hilgemeier's proof of quiz show rigging caused the immediate cancellation of *Dotto,* opening the scandal floodgates and sending everyone scurrying for cover.

Policing Media Culture:
Uncovering and Covering Up the Quiz Scandal

As was the case in Watergate and so many other scandals in the age of modern media, the cover-up rather than the original misconduct created the greatest damage. After all, quiz show rigging was not illegal at the time! As the story unfolded, the real-life quiz show melodrama moved from a tale of rags to riches in the first act to a crime thriller in the final act, complete with murky legal maneuverings, a sensational confession, and ambivalent results.

The riggings system began to unravel only after a few disgruntled losers, including Hilgemeier and Herb Stempel, went to the D.A. and the press in 1958. A grand jury was convened to see if larceny, extortion, or other crimes between producers and contestants had occurred. The deception itself was not illegal, but when witnesses denied the use of controls, they perjured themselves, an act which, unlike anything they may have done on the air, *was* against the law.

The tangible outcome of the investigations was minimal, despite extensive press coverage of investigations and hearings. The PBS documentary calls the consequences of the scandal "wide-ranging," but the consequences were more symbolic than tangible. Two grand jury investigations in New York resulted only in perjury charges against one producer and 18 contestants, including Van Doren. Stone emphasizes the irony that only those contestants who recanted their earlier lies and finally told the truth were convicted, although only of misdemeanor and not felony perjury. As Stone and Yohn (1992) note, the legal and political context meant that "small fry were being prosecuted while the big shots, who had benefited most from quiz rigging—producers, advertising men, and sponsors—were getting off scot-free" (p. 296). Unexplained to this day is the story behind the sealing-away of the first grand jury report ("quashing the presentment") by the presiding judge, although both Goodwin and Stone and Yohn note that Judge Schweitzer was forced to resign in the early 1970s amid charges of corruption and had apparently bowed to pressure from the quiz show riggers to seal the hearings and prevent further prosecution.

The Congressional hearings in Washington that came between the two New York grand jury investigations resulted only in a 1960 law that made quiz show rigging illegal, a classic case of locking the barn after the horse is stolen. Dan Enright, the key figure in the quiz show rigging, was investigated by the FCC. After several years, his Florida radio license was revoked, only to be later restored with the agreement that Enright would immediately sell it. Enright paid an extraordinary amount of legal fees during these years (more than $200,000 in 1950s dollars), but not without results.

Given the influence over the quiz shows exerted by Revlon, Geritol, and the other sponsors, following the scandal the networks took direct control of programs away from sponsors. But all in all, precious little policy change or punishment resulted from a scandal that fraudulently earned contestants hundreds of thousands of dollars, the networks and the producers millions of dollars, and the sponsors tens of millions of dollars while flamboyantly deceiving a nation. The law broke up the quiz show scheme but did little to punish the true culprits. The quiz show scandal was a classic case in which the political economy of vast profitmaking made it possible to avoid, delay, and subvert true justice. The transcript of the Washington hearings (Congress, 1960) contains considerable debate about remedies for television deception, but the broadcasters' demand for First Amendment free speech protection largely carried the day and stayed any broader legislative or regulatory action.

Who Knew and When Did They Know? The nature of accountability in the making of media culture extends broadly. The 1959 Congressional hearings on the quiz show scandal foreshadowed later hearings by underscoring the question of how high up the chain of command the blame extended. As in the later Watergate and Iran-Contra hearings, many asked, "Did the president know?" Investigators Stone and Goodwin both conclude that network executives knew, the film version implicates the president of NBC Robert Kintner, and the transcripts of the Washington hearings provide tantalizing offerings on both sides of the innocence question.

By most accounts, specific advertising executives played more overt roles than did network executives in the scandal. In the film *Quiz Show,* the head of Geritol, sponsor of *Twenty-One,* is played with suave menace by director Martin Scorsese. The PBS documentary focuses on the head of Revlon cosmetics, Charles Revson. The documentary features interviews with producers who describe how Revson would duck in and out of meetings with demands that particular contestants be kept on or be "stiffed." He judged Dr. Joyce Brothers to be incompatible with Revlon's concept of cosmetics and demanded she lose, but she foiled this plan by knowing boxing so well that they failed to stump her.

Did television executives know of the deceptions? No direct, firsthand, incontrovertible evidence was ever uncovered of such knowledge. But virtually all the knowledgeable producers and investigators point toward a wider circle of guilt reaching to the top. The *Quiz Show* film makes this explicit in an early scene in which NBC President Robert Kintner (who was not actually with NBC at the time of the incident in the film) supports the sponsors' request to get rid of a contestant by telling Enright, "You're a producer, Dan. Produce." The actual Washington testimony by Enright, Al Freedman, and others associated with *Twenty-One* carefully protects the network. The feature film script by Paul Attanasio explains why these tarnished producers took the sole blame: The public has a short memory but corporations never forget, and these men wished to work again in television. The defense of employers by corrupted employees is a suspect defense.

The Washington hearings, in parts of the transcripts that generally did not make it into the movie or other recent versions of the scandal, provide at least three authoritative accounts by experienced quiz show handlers about the rigging. These accounts occur in Enright's testimony, Freedman's testimony, and especially Shirley Bernstein's testimony. Leonard Bernstein's sister was the de facto producer of *The $64,000 Challenge* and affirms that the use of controls was generally known in the television industry. She also affirms that the use of bank vaults for storing questions was intended to create a "false impression" and the deceit was "deliberate." In addition to being quietly implicated in the scandal, Bernstein was a victim of the gender discrimination of the time: Revlon, the sponsor, refused her the title of producer because they did not think it was appropriate to have a woman producer for their show.

The pious disclaimers of network presidents occur in hearings that were full of lawyers' requests to discuss items "off the record" and executive claims that no direct orders were given to lie to investigators. Enright, in particular, sounds like Colonel Oliver North at the Iran-Contra Hearings—without the medals and the choir-boy style—as he accepts responsibility and protects everyone above him with the military "need to know" principle implicit to avoid recriminations. Yet even Enright admits, in his Congressional testimony, that anyone in the radio-television industry for 20 or 25 years would have to be "very naive not to understand that certain controls have to be exercised" (Congress, 1960, p. 252). Freedman testifies that it was not necessary to instruct him about controls when he took on the role of producer of *Twenty-One* "because when you assumed the role of producer of a show of this nature, you assumed that these are necessary controls that have to be done, and you are not told in black and white" (Congress, 1960, p. 217). These statements by Bernstein, Enright, and Freedman imply that it would have been virtually impossible for top network executives not to know about the rigging.

Another compelling question in the hearing transcript is, *when* precisely did network executives become concerned?

NBC President Kintner defends the network's innocence by insisting, "there is no question but National Broadcasting Co. was taken by Barry and Enright" (Congress, 1960, p. 1029). Robert Lishman, chief counsel of the committee, pursues the question. He has Kintner repeat his assertion that he had no reason to believe there was collusion prior to August 1958, when *Dotto* was suddenly canceled by CBS because contestant Edward Hilgemeier showed to the press, the FCC, and investigators a registered letter proving that another contestant's preshow notes exactly matched her correct answers recorded on the kinescope of the May 20 telecast.

Counsel Lishman then points out a *Time* article dated April 22, 1957, more than a year before these hearings. That article was titled "The $60 Million Question" and opened with the line, "Are the quiz shows rigged?" The article named a large number of network shows suspected of rigging and concluded, "the producers seem to be able to control virtually everything except their own fears of losing their audience." Lishman also cites an August 20, 1957 feature in *Look* magazine titled, "Are TV Quiz Shows Fixed?" Kintner baldly claims ignorance of those stories. Counsel Lishman and various committee members are understandably incredulous that NBC never had reason to suspect the quiz shows might be fixed. Congressman John Bennett of Michigan acerbically notes that "NBC was something less than diligent in trying to get to the bottom of these rigged quiz shows" (Congress, 1960, p. 1053) and finds it strange that a grand jury and a congressional committee could find out a truth about NBC that had eluded the network itself. Congressman Walter Rogers of Texas notes that 2 years elapsed before the networks took an interest in the rigging and only then when it appeared "they were going to get caught anyway" (p. 1060). Finally, it was Frank Stanton, president of CBS, whose disingenuous line is echoed in the film script. Asked about the *Time* article, Stanton replies, "I was on a trip out of the country" (Congress, 1960, p. 1054).

The political economy of the quiz shows, the backdrop for the scandal, was based of course in a competition for audience ratings, "share of the audience," and advertising sponsorship based on those ratings. At stake were millions of dollars in corporate profit. The drive to make all television programming profitable was already becoming total and was dominating every network decision. The plutocracy of three commercial television networks dominating the attention of the American public created returns on investment in broadcasting that for several decades surpassed almost any other form of stable financial investment in the United States. This may be the heart of what Robert Redford calls "the eternal struggle between ethics and capitalism" (Auletta, 1994, p. 46) that enticed him to make a film "parable" out of the quiz show scandal. The money to be made in television created temptations to think only of profit and to assume that ethics and public service were adequately served if enough audience and profit were created.

Conflicting Media Versions
of the Scandal: How They Compare

The genealogy of recent versions of the quiz show scandal is complex and interesting. Thirty years after the scandal, the whole sad episode had been relegated in most literature to passing references to a temporary spate of deceit of no great significance. Earlier, Meyer Weinberg's book *TV in America: The Morality of Hard Cash* (1962) had examined the scandal as one of a series of failures of public regulation, and Kent Anderson's book *Television Fraud: The History and Implications of the Quiz Show Scandals* (1978) had carefully recounted the events and studied America's self-perception through the case. But neither book generated great attention or altered the general sense that the quiz show scandal was relatively trivial.

Washington investigator Richard Goodwin (1988) was the first to prominently challenge this industry-serving orthodoxy and revive interest in the scandal. His chapter on the quiz show investigation became the basis for Redford's film 6 years later (1994). In the meantime, Krainin's documentary (Krainin & Lawrence, 1992) arose independently as an outgrowth of Krainin's negotiations with Charles Van Doren on another project. Simultaneously, Halberstam (1993) chose to dedicate a chapter to the scandal in his book on the 1950s and prosecutor Stone (Stone & Yohn, 1992) developed his account of the entire investigation. Playwright Greenberg (1994b) was interested in the subject in the 1992 documentary and, like others, used Kent Anderson's earlier book for background.

The numerous 1990s media versions of the scandal are far from identical. They borrow from each other but also from many magazine and newspaper articles from the time of the scandal. Despite what they share in common, these recent reconstructions differ strikingly in what might be called "genre conventions."

Genre Conventions: Relativity in Media Depictions of Truth. Genre conventions can make a great difference in how history is constructed in the popular consciousness. The Hollywood docudrama version of *Quiz Show* was accused of using "deception" because it rearranged the chronology and reduced the number of people involved in the scandal. Joseph Stone, author of the definitive legal and investigatory book on the scandal, condemned the film as "a tawdry hoax" in a report by Richard Bernstein (1994) in the *New York Times.* Al Freedman, Enright's assistant and the man dubbed the "fall guy" for the networks, accused Redford's film of oversimplification and of making moral judgments appear easier than they had been in reality. He maintains, according to Bernstein, that "ironically, the film is fixed. It is even more rigged than the show it portrays" (Bernstein, 1994, p. 21). Can that be true?

That question suggests that in the unique "conventions"—or standards accepted by audience and producer alike—of particular genres not all media truths are created equal. *Genres,* as we saw in Chapter 3, are those media products marked by an obvious similarity in form and content, such as westerns, science fiction, news, sitcoms, or sports. Are there sliding standards of objectivity, truth, and fairness that are proper to each of these genres of media representation?

Audiences have a well-established ability to distinguish between the characteristics of different genres. Generally, we identify a genre easily and without thought, as when we pick a show by surfing the cable channels. But there are times when the genre label may be more difficult to apply and the conventions implied by it harder to rely on. Orson Welles proved this in 1938 with his little Halloween prank of presenting a fictional invasion from Mars as if it were an actual news event. Using a "news" genre format for a work in the "fantasy" genre blended contradictory standards of truth framing, news and fantasy. Welles intended the show to be fantasy; confused listeners took it to be news. Anxiety, panic, and eventual outrage resulted (Cantril, 1940). News, history, and documentary are *nonfiction* genres, whereas most comedy and drama are *fiction*. Problems arise when fiction and nonfiction are combined in that hybrid genre called "docudrama."

No account of history or news can be absolutely "objective" and "complete" without being also exhaustive, endless, and, as a consequence, boring. What did each participant in this news event eat for breakfast? Where did they buy the blouse they are wearing? Every version of an event must be selective. What kind of truth, then, do the necessarily less-than-complete actual accounts carry? Each of the accounts of the quiz show scandal belongs to a distinctive genre with its related standard of truth. One of the jobs of historical interpretation in media culture is to answer the question: What kind of truth is proper to each media genre?

Actual Record: The Hearings Transcript. The actual transcript of the Congressional hearings in 1960 on the quiz shows is a 1,156-page printed and bound record of the actual words and documents presented by witnesses at that time. The standard of truth sought for and expected from such a record is very high. No summaries or omissions or deletions are expected; the transcript should present only the words spoken and the documents presented. Moreover, no interpretive framework describes the setting or explains the background of any of the material. On American television today, C-Span attempts to parallel the transcript standard by presenting Congressional debates in their entirety without comment.

Scholarly History: Kent Anderson's Book. In 1978, Greenwood Press published Anderson's well-researched and -documented book *Television Fraud: The History and Implications of the Quiz Show Scandals.* Written in the third person, it carefully footnotes all facts and quotes and carries a bibliography, index, and appendices that contain transcriptions from the kinescopes of *Twenty-One* and *Dotto.* The standard of truth on those is absolute. But the book also does what a good history and analysis should do: it explains and interprets.

Anderson's book places the entire episode in the context of television at the time and draws on David Potter's critique of advertising's effect on values. The book's interpretations appear honest and perceptive, but they move beyond the simplistic level of truth presented in a transcript of public proceedings. As a narrative account of what happened, Anderson's book stands the test of time well and earned him an acknowledgment at the end of the credits in Redford's film.

Political History: Goodwin's Chapter. Richard Goodwin's book, *Remembering America: A Voice From the Sixties* (1988), describes his role in Kennedy's New Frontier and Johnson's Great Society as a young Harvard law graduate. His description of those heady years is prefaced by a chapter on his role as a special consultant to the House Subcommittee on Legislative Oversight, the body that held the quiz show hearings. Despite his tender years and inexperience, Goodwin was the one who found the item in the *New York Times* about the grand jury presentment being quashed and won permission to go to New York and request its unsealing. Goodwin's personal experience, which included a complicated friendship with Charles Van Doren, whom he was investigating, became the basis for Redford's movie *Quiz Show.*

Goodwin's book is written in the first person, recalling conversations and events in which he participated. He describes trips to New York to get the grand jury information and to question participants. He describes how the victimized Herb Stempel would arrange meetings, call Goodwin, and even visit Goodwin's home unannounced. Stempel, according to Goodwin, was motivated by a fear that Van Doren "his despised adversary might escape. And he was right to be apprehensive. Van Doren almost got away. I wanted him to" (p. 51). Goodwin's friendship with the newly famous Van Doren was curious for an investigator, to say the least. Later, Goodwin was surprised to see that the quiz show producers returned to television and was convinced that ranking corporate executives had known about the rigging. "I believed then, as I believe now, that they knew; must have known—from Stanton and Kintner and Revson down" (p. 62).

Clearly, there is a difference between the standards of accuracy in a transcript and the standards of truth in Goodwin's recollection and impressions. Goodwin's purposes in writing were political. He wanted to correct and revive the hopes of the Kennedy years. Yet his account does not appear untrue, merely impressionistic. Other versions might seem quite different. Many of Goodwin's details appear in Redford's film, which is discussed later in this chapter.

Legal History: Stone's Book. In contrast to Goodwin's brief account, the more central investigator of the quiz show scandal, Joseph Stone, with co-author Tim Yohn, has written an elaborate and painstakingly documented account of the legal progression of the investigation and prosecution. The book's 349 pages are culled from a draft manuscript three times that long and provide the most complete insider and legal view of the entire episode yet published. Stone and Yohn's book, *Prime Time and Misdemeanors:*

Investigating the 1950s TV Quiz Show Scandal—A D.A.'s Account, is a sober but spellbinding behind-the-scenes account of the quiz show rigging scheme, the two grand jury probes, the circus-like U.S. Congressional hearings, and the eventual criminal prosecution of Charles Van Doren and a score of others for perjury.

Like Goodwin, Stone (Stone & Yohn, 1992) employs a first-person narrative at times but also includes all the other legal and public issues and events connected with the case. Stone wants to set the record straight by getting as much as possible out in the open about the law, deception, events, and people involved. Stone draws from all previous accounts but goes well beyond them in tracing the investigative and legal evolution of the scandal.

Stone was motivated by the lack of serious, complete accounts of the scandal, accounts going beyond Goodwin's "breezy" reminiscences and including the insider perspectives lacking in the 1962 account and the 1978 book on the scandal. In particular, Stone wanted to correct "the trivializing of the affair, perpetuating the myth that the quiz show rigging really hurt no one" (Stone & Yohn, 1992, p. 10). Stone sees the quiz show scandal as part of today's ominous trends. For example, the attraction of winning huge amounts of money with little effort has spawned state-run gambling backed by television advertising; prosecutor Stone regards these policies as a recipe for disaster in an age when money-making is glorified and government regulation diminished. Finally, whereas Goodwin's account fills in the Washington context, Stone and Yohn's book details developments in New York City. Only the combined efforts of New York and Washington investigations working in tandem could crack the amazing wall of silence protecting the quiz shows.

Prosecutor Stone was continuously amazed by the number of people who perjured themselves, even when they were explicitly warned in advance that the confession of rigging would not subject them to criminal penalties but that lying to the grand jury would. His decades of big-city prosecution of hard-bitten criminals paled against this. Stone writes, "nothing in my experience prepared me for the mass perjury that took place" (Stone & Yohn, 1992, p. 7). Stone's boss Frank Hogan, the New York district attorney, reported to the press that of the 150 people who testified, perhaps 50 told the truth. Contestants and quiz show employees were so tightly integrated into the closed circle of rigging that they repeatedly perjured themselves to protect their own reputations and the myth of honesty in quiz shows.

When compared, Goodwin's (1988) and Stone and Yohn's (1992) accounts differ more in their relative emphasis than in their facts. Goodwin acknowledges the New York work directed by Stone and praises Stone personally, but focuses on Washington and his own experiences. Stone, in turn, found Goodwin bright, aggressive, and astute but also ambitious and mercurial.

Stone and Yohn's book seeks to maintain a higher standard of completeness and documentation than Goodwin's account, but it lacks Goodwin's political and personal liveliness. The standard Stone and Yohn maintain is similar to that of Kent Anderson's scholarly book on the subject.

As a consequence, Stone and Yohn's book, not Goodwin's chapter, stands as the more authoritative legal and investigatory record of the quiz scandal. In fact, if there is one true injustice in the feature film reenactment of the scandal, it is the omission of Joseph Stone's painstaking investigative work in favor of Goodwin's briefer but more glamorous role.

Journalistic Documentary: Krainin's Program and Halberstam's Chapter. The popularity and rigging of the shows is vividly documented in the one-hour 1992 PBS documentary *The Quiz Show Scandal,* written and co-produced by Julian Krainin in *The American Experience* series. Curiously, that historical documentary originated in Krainin's effort to have Van Doren narrate a series on the history of philosophy. Because Van Doren had never spoken publicly of the scandal since his 1959 confession, PBS suggested to Krainin that, before creating the history of philosophy series with Van Doren, he first clear the air with a documentary on the quiz show scandal. Van Doren initially agreed to participate but later backed out. Ironically, in the end Van Doren was the only important living participant who refused to participate in the PBS documentary.

Despite his absence, the quiz show story is effectively told as what the narration calls a "morality play" on the "unprecedented potential for deception" in the new era of television and the violation of trust "in an age we still like to think of as innocent." Playwright Richard Greenberg was inspired to develop his theatrical presentation after accidentally viewing the last 15 minutes of that documentary.

Krainin's documentary follows the conventional format and standards of historical documentary. Kinescopes of the programs are intercut with new interviews with the principals. Voice-over narration emphasizes the trust and power of television in that era. The selective emphasis is on the actual rigging, with firsthand accounts from producers, announcers, and contestants, with little attention to the investigation that so preoccupied Goodwin and Stone. No restaging of events is included; only actual audiovisual records and interviews are employed.

Krainin's version was the first to get many participants to speak in public about the affair. Stempel and other contestants, Enright and other producers, investigators Stone and Goodwin—all went on the record and reflected on the experience. The result effectively surveys the national experience of the 1950s quiz scandal. The hoopla, the rigging systems, the behind-the-scenes manipulations, the public's infatuation with the show, and the collapse of the system are all present in Krainin's authoritative recounting. Scenes of the actual programs and recollections by the producers and the "quizlings," as Art Buchwald dubbed them, give a heightened sense of truth and reality to the scandal.

The 24-page summary of the quiz show story in David Halberstam's *The Fifties* (1993) quickly and authoritatively reviews what happened. Standards of journalistic truth are maintained by the use of documented sources and precise statement. Halberstam's summary includes the story of Krainin's failed negotiations with Van Doren concerning his participation in the documentary. Halberstam employs many of the same details and witnesses as Krainin and follows a standard of journalistic truth similar to that in Krainin's documentary, but Halberstam provides verbal detail and interpretation beyond that which can be presented in a television hour. There is little that is unique in Halberstam's version but much that is important. His version is the classic journalistic "first draft of history."

For Halberstam, the most powerful lesson of the scandal was its demonstration "that television *cast* everything it touched: politics, news shows, and sitcoms. The demands of entertainment and theater were at least as powerful as substance." This theme is picked up in Redford's film and Greenberg's play, which show the quiz show producers and sponsors recruiting, selecting, and rehearsing the competitors to be put on the air. The public took as reality what was contrived, and the television industry thrived.

Theater Drama: Greenberg's Play. Dramatic representations have always been understood to be free of the literal constraints of historical research and documentary presentation. Shakespeare's historical plays are imaginary, at times whimsical, revisions of actual historical personages and events. *Camelot* is hardly drawn from eyewitness accounts of life at King Arthur's court. Shaw imagines the life, events, and dialogue of the Maid of Orleans in *Saint Joan* in a way no historian could justify; the voice of spirits reflecting after death can be heard only in fictionalized drama. The fictionalized dramatization, of course, provides the power of visualization and the sensation of being present at the events being depicted. Dramatizations go beyond the facts to seek deeper meaning in the historical events thus fictionalized. Playwright Richard Greenberg (1994b) approached his version of the quiz show scandal with the idea, "the facts of history are less expressive of underlying truth than the drama you can make of it."

Greenberg's play, *Night and Her Stars*[2] (1994b), shares with Redford's film the license and burden of dramatic or docudrama invention, in contrast to the limiting literalism of documentary representation. Both Redford and Greenberg appear to have had available all the historical sources. Both docudramas evoke the times and center on a triangle in which two points are made by the personal dramas of Van Doren and Stempel. But, whereas Redford completes the triangle with Goodwin the investigator, Greenberg completes it with Enright, the mastermind who drew them into the scandal and left them victimized.

Greenberg uses Enright as what he calls "the fulcrum" of his play. For Greenberg, the dramatic attraction of the events resided in the period atmosphere, the mass deception, the high-level soap opera, and the challenge of scripting "reality-based" media in a society that is titillated by the sight of winners and losers being blown up into larger-than-life heroes and villains (Greenberg, 1994b). He was struck that, for Stempel, making $25,000 was argument enough for rigging the shows, but for Van Doren, idealistic appeals were necessary to convince him that his appearance would promote the world of education and the teachers of America. Dan Enright admits in the 1992 PBS documentary, "and frankly, we induced him to do it by convincing him that . . . it would help glamorize intellectualism."

Enright's "genius" captivated Greenberg.

> He was incredibly insightful about the time he was living in, sensitive to the popular myths of the day. He was gifted at his work, a visionary, and I try to suppress this note of admiration that creeps in. But television was new and undefined at the time; it had no prohibitions. Enright was able to put a spin on anything to achieve his end. I was attracted by his bravado and daring. He transformed Herb Stempel into a villain. He was later eaten up with remorse apparently, but he brilliantly manipulated people. He had tremendous psychological insight. (Greenberg, 1994b)

The play's plotline resembles that of the Redford film in portraying the events culminating in the Washington hearing. But instead of beginning with Goodwin the investigator, Greenberg opens his play with a Whitmanesque soliloquy by Enright on radio, television, quizzes, advertising, and giving people a hero. Situated in a quaintly modernistic 1950s, *Night and Her Stars* conveys the timelessness of human venality and opportunism, whereas Redford's film points toward recent political and corporate scandals. The play provides a stylized and impressionistic portrait of the captains of the new mass entertainment industry and their enthusiastic, if compromised, loyal subjects, both contestants and viewers. The final reconciliation between the chastened, guilt-ridden Charles Van Doren and his remarkable father provides its touching ending.

Several times the play asks, what was life like before television? To Greenberg, who was born in the late 1950s, television did not cause the 1950s but it certainly demarcated the era. Greenberg (1994b) is concerned with television in what he calls the McLuhanesque sense: "It is the central nervous system of society. What was its early formation like?"

Film Docudrama: Redford's Film. Quiz Show, produced and directed by Robert Redford for Disney's Hollywood Pictures, was not a big box office winner but did receive laudatory reviews throughout the country. The New York Film Critics Circle voted it the best motion picture of 1994. In some reviews and in newspaper and magazine features the movie also generated a great deal of criticism about docudrama accuracy.

"Docudrama," the retelling of history through dramatic reenactment, has a rich and controversial history in films. In 1915, D. W. Griffith's racist tract *Birth of a Nation* wrapped its distortions in emotion-provoking copies of historic photos and source citations and was lauded by Washington legislators, justices, and even Woodrow Wilson, who was alleged to have said, "it is like writing history with lightning." In 1941, *Citizen Kane* was cautious enough to employ fictitious names in its roman à clef on the life of William Randolph Hearst.

The nature of a "New History film" is described by Robert A. Rosenstone (1995):

> The premise: the visual media are a legitimate way of doing history—of representing, interpreting, thinking about, and making meaning from the traces of the past.
>
> The approach: the historical film must be seen not in terms of how it compares to written history but as way of recounting the past with its own rules of interpretation.
>
> The films: traditional costume dramas and documentaries are less important as history than a new kind of film, made all over the world—one that seriously deals with the relationship of past to present. (p. 3)

The new history films include *Hiroshima Mon Amour* (France), *Night of the Shooting Stars* (Italy), *Memories of Underdevelopment* (Cuba), *Repentence* (Soviet Union), *The Home and the World* (India), and many others that confront serious issues in an effort to understand the legacy of the past and that grow out of communities that see themselves in desperate need of historical connections. Questioning traditional forms, the filmmakers create new ones, in the words of Rosenstone, "abandoning 'realism' for other presentational modes, mixing genres, blurring the distinction between the documentary and the dramatic film" (p. 5). Rather than presenting economic data or chronological facts on Nazism or colonialism, these films resurrect the emotional ambiance of those periods that lie like a dark shadow across contemporary consciousness. The challenge in viewing these films is "to understand history in the visual medium, this past that is somehow different both from fiction and from academic history, this past that does not depend entirely upon data for the way it asserts truths or engages the ongoing discourse of history" (p. 13). Redford's *Quiz Show* combines these interests with those of the classic docudrama.

The classic popular docudrama on television or film revisits history through the experience of *imagined* individuals: *Winds of War, The Holocaust, Shogun, Gone With the Wind.* More exacting is the portrayal of *real* individuals in history: *Gandhi, Patton, Malcolm X, Franklin and Eleanor.* *Roots,* arguably the most influential of American docudramas, was presented as the latter, the story of real individuals in the person of Kunta Kinte and his descendants, but was accused of being the former, a fine yarn of imagined individuals. Oliver Stone's hotly debated docudramas sometimes emphasize the "drama" at the expense of the "docu" in *JFK, Nixon, The Doors, Born on the Fourth of July,* and others.

Redford's *Quiz Show,* like Greenberg's play or *All the President's Men* or Stone's films, places itself in the most exacting category of docudrama, one in which real names, places, and incidents are portrayed. *Quiz Show* reduces a drawn-out, convoluted historical episode to classic docudrama, distilling and personalizing the complex events into the story of three people—the investigator from Washington, Richard Goodwin; the flawed hero, Van Doren; and the disgruntled commoner, Stempel. Is this film about deception itself deceptive, as charged by some?

Criticisms of the Redford film *Quiz Show* revolve around charges that the film "dissects the scandal by taking great pains with small details but great liberties with large facts, such as who the real heroes were and how the scam unraveled," according to Jan Herman in the *Los Angeles Times* (1994, pp. F1, F24). Richard Bernstein (1994, p. H21) in the *New York Times* worried that because the film paid such scrupulous attention to getting the small details right, moviegoers would be misled into believing the larger issues were also right. Howard Rosenberg of the *Los Angeles Times* found it ironic that a movie so judgmental about the TV industry's dishonesty in the 1950s should itself play so fast and loose with the truth for the sake of putting on a good show (Leo, 1994). Dan Enright's son Don (Herman, 1994, p. F5) even accused the movie of being rigged and fixed, just like its television counterparts.

Were the makers of *Quiz Show* attempting to deceive or were they working within the established boundaries of docudrama? Screenwriter Paul Attanasio, investigator Goodwin, and director Redford all have explained at length why incidents were modified for dramatic effect. For example, Dave Garroway did not walk onto the *Twenty-One* set to hire Charles Van Doren, but soon after his quiz appearances, Van Doren did sign a contract to do the *Today* show. Likewise, Goodwin was actually told that he was being overly squeamish about subpoenaing Van Doren with the words "not having Van Doren testify is like doing Hamlet without Hamlet," although the words were spoken to him by Supreme Court Justice Felix Frankfurter, for whom

Goodwin had been a clerk, and not by Goodwin's wife, as the film shows. Attanasio summarizes by saying, "my responsibility is not to make a documentary; my responsibility is to remain true to the characters and the events, while making a dramatic story out of it" (Laurence, 1994, p. E1).

The Redford film uses dramatic license in two obvious ways. First, chronologically, the film makes the quiz show run of Van Doren and the investigation by Goodwin appear to occur simultaneously. In fact, Goodwin first became involved only several years after Van Doren's run on *Twenty-One*.

The second license the film takes is in creating "composite characters" who stand in for several real people. In particular, the film makes Richard Goodwin *the* investigator of the quiz shows when the historical record unmistakably shows that Joseph Stone, the New York assistant district attorney, played a much more major role in the overall investigative activities. By eliminating Stone and expanding Goodwin's part, Goodwin is made a composite of all investigators, as Stempel, Van Doren, and a few others are made composites of all the contestants on the shows. The *Twenty-One* show is made a composite of all the rigged quiz shows, just as it was to a large extent in the actual Washington hearings. In addition, the network executives are made into a composite represented by NBC President Robert Kintner, who was not even with NBC in 1956 at the beginning of Stempel and Van Doren's historic duel; he joined NBC in January 1957 and became its president in July 1958.

Is the film wrong to distort the chronology and create composite characters, as some have argued? This question addresses the standard of truth proper to the docudrama genre and issues of ethics, deception, and the merchant mentality behind media production in America.

In response to Freedman's charge that the film is more rigged than the show it portrays, it is especially noteworthy that the movie producers readily explain the departures from history that they have made. This is in marked contrast to the quiz show producers, who publicly claimed that their shows were not rigged, when that was a palpable lie. The makers of *Quiz Show* go to great lengths in many press interviews to explain exactly what standards of truth and drama they are employing.

If time sequence is "adjusted" and characters "combined" in the Redford film, the locations, casting, characterizations, and plot details make every effort to compensate by seeking historical accuracy. The "feel" of New York City in the 1950s is one of the film's achievements, and the film cast creates credible, nuanced performances. Fiennes gives Van Doren a charming, subtle ambivalence, mixing innocence and guilt; Fiennes's previous success as the Nazi commandant in Spielberg's *Schindler's List* adds to the viewer's subtle sense of mistrust in Van Doren's seeming virtue. The portrayals of Enright and Stempel in the film make understandable what Enright admitted many years later in the Krainin (1992) documentary: "I bear tremendous guilt to Herb Stempel."

After examining the many charges against the film, Ken Auletta in the *New Yorker* (1994) concluded, "in fairness, Redford's movie does stick to the essential truth of what happened" (p. 48).

In the genre of docudrama, changes are permissible unless they distort the *essential* truth. If Redford's imposition of dramatic structure here is a form of "dishonesty," as John Leo (1994) argues, one could likewise squash virtually all of the many generally admirable television and film docudramas. More subtly, the subtext of a few of the attacks on *Quiz Show* seems to be one of discomfort with the film's critical stance toward television, corporate greed, and capitalism. Such criticism is a backlash against the implications of the history, not the truthfulness of the story. That concern may be worth debating head-on, but it certainly does not make the film a false or dishonest docudrama.

Figure 7.1 summarizes the differing qualities of historical reconstructions. No reconstruction is the event itself, and many affect the popular understanding of history. The reconstructions that often affect the public understanding most, docudramas, are the ones furthest from the factual details. If both historical scholarship and fictionalized docudramas are healthy and honest, their differing proximity to the historical event in the past and the popular understanding in the present will pose no problem. But if the docudramas are irresponsible, public perceptions may be manipulated and distorted. Not only average citizens but policymakers may be affected. For example, President Ronald Reagan was often said to have an understanding of American and world history drawn exclusively from movies and not from books. The influence of media culture, in such cases, is no small thing. Similarly, the lessons one takes away from the quiz show scandal can vary widely depending on the version of the scandal that one knows and believes.

The Dramatic Center of the Quiz Scandal: Van Doren Versus Stempel

The personal drama and conflict of supposedly ordinary people give the quiz show story a dimension attractive to the dramatist. Both the Redford film and the Greenberg drama reduce 5 years of quiz shows and investigations into the dramatic contrast between long-time *Twenty-One* winner Herbert Stempel and his challenger, Charles Van Doren. The versions by Krainin, Halberstam, and Goodwin likewise make the Van Doren-Stempel confrontation a centerpiece. Their contest obviously makes for good storytelling and understandably propels the central drama for stage and screen. The contest is one worth recalling.

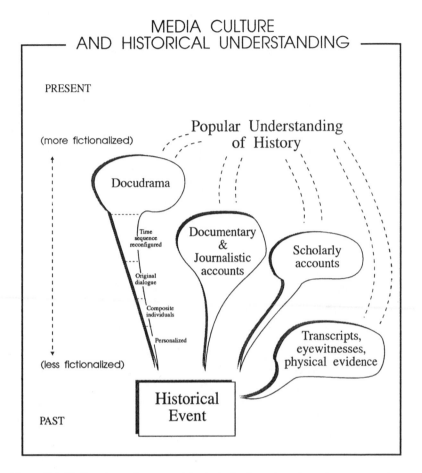

Figure 7.1. Media culture plays a crucial role in the formation of popular understanding of history, as in the 1950s TV quiz show scandal.

Stempel is the *common man,* a self-taught working-class New York Jew with phenomenal recall, doggedly accurate but lacking charm and charisma. After first making him something of a GI blue-collar folk hero, Enright then recast Stempel as a contestant you love to hate, with his unflattering haircut and ill-fitting clothes. At the opposite extreme, Van Doren is *superman* and *the boy next door,* an intellectual's hero, an Ivy Leaguer with graduate study in astrophysics, mathematics, and literature at Cambridge, the Sorbonne, and Columbia, but also a charming and self-effacing nice guy. Greenberg describes Van Doren as "graceful, brilliant, virile, and deserving" (Greenberg, 1994b). He was "proper" America's answer to both the controversial Elvis and the soon-to-come Sputnik. He was the genuine goods from a quality background. His father Mark and uncle Carl were famous men of letters, and his mother Dorothy a successful novelist. The tall, thoughtful, diffident, good-humored Van Doren contrasted sharply with the short, ill-dressed Stempel, the perfect match-up for the Enright production team and for writers of plays or films.

The Redford film, like the Greenberg play, uses the match-up of Stempel and Van Doren to examine issues of ethnicity and class in America: the Jewish Stempel against the gentile Van Doren, with the Jewish but elitist Goodwin as mediator and foil. The America of melting-pot egalitarianism and populism runs aground on the shoals of privilege and breeding: Van Doren's attractiveness snuffs out Stempel's rise. Goodwin, like Enright, finds it easy to renounce the working-class ethnic genius in favor of American quasi-royalty. Some criticism of the film implied that Stempel was being made into a Jewish stereotype in John Turturro's portrayal. Rather, the quota and casting tastes of early television are simply being revealed and, if anything, his portrayal of Stempel makes the man more sympathetic and likable than was the case in any other account of the scandal.

On the air, the conflict between Van Doren and Stempel builds across the nation as they play to ties for a few weeks until Stempel is forced to miss a question about the film *Marty,* particularly galling to him because it was one of his favorites. Then Van Doren wins and goes on for a total of 15 weeks to win $129,000 by the end. (Draconian taxes at the time let him take home only about $28,000, according to Halberstam.) He makes the cover of *Time* and receives 2,000 letters a week and 500 marriage proposals. His Columbia students put up signs directing visitors to "the smartest man in the world." After his quiz show run ends, within weeks NBC signs him to a 3-year contract at $50,000 per year as a "cultural correspondent" to do 5 minutes of poetry, or whatever, daily on Dave Garroway's *Today* show. In both film and play, Van Doren plays a knowing Faust to Enright's seductive Mephistopheles.

But while his star is shining brightly, Van Doren comes under questioning from Assistant D.A. Stone and Washington staff member Goodwin. Van Doren himself, in a striking after-the-fact letter to his investigator and friend Goodwin, refers to the fable in which "the stag loved the hunter who killed it." These fellow Ivy Leaguers seemed to genuinely like and respect each other as they warily circled. *Quiz Show,* the film, builds its story line around this hunter/hunted relationship between Goodwin, the investigator, and Van Doren, the suspect. Parallel story lines in the film simultaneously trace Goodwin's progress as the hunter with Van Doren's progress as the hunted who is also America's brilliant poster boy.

If the movie had instead stuck to history and followed the strung-out chronology of competition and prizes . . . pause . . . charges in the press . . . pause . . . grand jury . . . pause . . . Washington investigation . . . pause . . .

confession . . . pause, it would clearly have been dramatically less interesting than Attanasio's clever parallel-action script. What the Goodwin/Van Doren time-shifted parallel story lines provide is classic suspense around the hunter-hunted theme.

The dramatic public culmination of the quiz show debacle came on November 2, 1959, in a crowded hearing room in Washington, when Van Doren read his now famous confession: "I would give almost anything I have to reverse the course of my life in the last three years. . . . I was involved, deeply involved, in a deception" (Congress, 1960, p. 624). Although frequently taken as cheap melodrama, Van Doren's confession has qualities of classic Greek tragedy, with the tragically flawed hero unrelentingly moving toward the denouement of his sad fall, confrontation, and self-realization. The Redford film captures this in Ralph Fiennes's emotional reenactment. The words are close to verbatim from Van Doren's actual text, though like much of the film they are reordered and abbreviated, incorporating elements of his posthearing press conference and his actual famous testimony. The film's adjusted time frame forces Van Doren (Fiennes) to say "in the last year" instead of "in the last three years." The Greenberg play uses the same sad confession but culminates in the reconciliation between Charles and his famous and sensitive father. In a touching finale, Charles speaks of shame and even of hating the sound of his own voice. He hesitantly opens himself up a crack and his father tightly hugs him.

The film's final on-screen statements, the chapter by Halberstam, and especially the broadcast documentary make clear the sad long-term legacy for Van Doren and Stempel: Van Doren becoming a virtual recluse and Stempel a minor city employee. In contrast, by 1978 Jack Barry's and Dan Enright's successful careers in television included producing *New Tic Tac Dough* for CBS, with Jack Barry back as host. On that show, Navy Lieutenant Thom McKee won $312,750, the all-time quiz show record. Al Freedman, after fleeing to Mexico and then testifying before Congress, spent a long professional career with *Penthouse* publications.

Historical Analysis and
the Lessons for Media Culture

And, now, for the $64,000 question . . . what are the lessons of the quiz show scandal for media culture and life today?

Standards of Truth. The first lesson has to do with the standards of truth when media represent history. As the multiple versions of the quiz show scandal illustrate, different genres have different standards of truth. But each has a standard of truth. Actual records, as in the transcripts of quiz show hearings in Washington, have the most absolute and restrictive standards:

nothing more than a verbatim record is allowed. Scholarly histories can place these records in context and attempt to clarify them, as Kent Anderson's book on television fraud does. Political history, legal history, and journalistic accounts retain factual accuracy but go beyond that to interpret the events and seek their meanings for political judgment and ideology, for police and judicial practice, and for immediate historical implications. Writings by Goodwin, Stone, and Halberstam, in addition to the documentary by Krainin, illustrate these purposes and the standards of truth sought for them. But theatrical and film/television accounts of history have much broader latitude in the form known as *docudramas.*

The standards of truth in docudramas include several important deviations from historical verisimilitude. Docudramas can *personalize* the experience of history, presenting it through the experience of individuals even when dialogue and private experiences by those individuals must be imagined. Docudramas can create *composite characters* who singly represent the experience of several characters but do so consistently with the real-life actions of those several characters. Docudramas can *rearrange chronology* for dramatic effect, in effect improving on the progression of history to increase viewer/reader/listener interest. These deviations are not deception. They are accepted as part of the docudrama genre by producers and consumers of historical materials. And, importantly, these standards can be violated in obvious ways, as in, for example, *The Birth of a Nation,* in which antisegregationists are demonized and the Ku Klux Klan depicted as fighting for goodness and virtue. In such characterizations, the personalizing and composite characters are false to their historical sources and the chronology is not only rearranged but falsified. In contrast, a close examination of the docudrama film *Quiz Show* finds it defensible by such standards.

The challenge of historical analysis in media culture includes assessing carefully and with external research data the historical and genre appropriateness of media presentations.

Healthy Skepticism. A second lesson has to do with the lessons for practice today. Specifically, in this case, what are the lessons of the quiz show scandal for media production and consumption in our own time?

The lesson for media consumers is blatant: Do not take at face value what one finds in the media. The powers of deception are much greater and the tests for validation much more difficult when receiving media than when receiving interpersonal messages from those we encounter face to face. Viewers of television and film should be especially critical toward implied historical truths in docudrama, just as viewers of quiz shows should have been skeptical at the implied honesty of the contestants, questioning, and context of those shows. However, by applying standards of genre expectation and by observing media sources over time, one can develop a limited sense of trust in specific media sources.

Historical Awareness. A third lesson for historical interpretation of media has to do with developing a sense of history in general. For example, most of the recent versions of the quiz scandal associate it with other events occurring in 1950s America. The plugola scandal had revealed that popular radio disc jockeys were given generous kickbacks to feature certain songs. Wrestling, with its campy spoof of honest competition, was television's first big sports success in Japan and in America. Anticommunism justified anything, suburbia thrived, fast food was born, and cigarette advertising paid for much of television. Since that more clear-cut but mildly deceptive time, Vietnam, Watergate, and other American disillusionments suggest that the quiz show scandal may have been an initial confrontation with the postmodern dilemma explored in the next chapter: The "modern" belief in permanent progress rooted in reason, science, and efficiency is giving way to the "postmodern" belief that society's condition is one of superficiality, consumption, irony, and normlessness.

This lesson implies that in looking at the quiz show scandal today we are looking for something of ourselves that we began to lose when we first handed over popular consciousness to the custodians of television entertainment and commerce. For them, winning in ratings games and elsewhere became not a goal but an obsession, an excuse to cut corners, a justification for ignoring principles of honesty and fairness. Into this postmodern black hole, the actual record of the quiz show scandal sent a loud and clear wake-up call: What is legally allowable and commercially successful may still be *unethical.*

Ethics and the Merchant Mentality. Another lesson, then, learned from the quiz show history calls for developing a sense of history that includes a sensitivity to ethical questions and that does not sacrifice all innocence to commercial forces. In virtually every interview about *Quiz Show,* Redford emphasized two points: there was a loss of innocence in the form of ethical consensus and a replacement of ethics by a merchant mentality.

The quiz scandal was a turning point for Americans, in Redford's judgment. To *Rolling Stone* he said, "What the film tries to illustrate is simply that this was the beginning of a loss of innocence. . . . The effect was shattering. Then, historically, we go right down the line with the deaths of J. F. K., Bobby Kennedy, Martin Luther King and then Watergate, Irangate, BCCI and S&L, and then [Sen. Robert] Packwood and O.J. Simpson. . . . And now we're in a place where we just sort of shrug" (DeCurtis, 1994, p. 76, © Straight Arrow Publishers Company, L.P. 1994. All rights reserved. Reprinted by permission). Redford's goal is to highlight the loss of innocence as a way to shed light on present circumstances. He clarifies, "You know, the quiz-show scandal of the '50s, that's not what this is about. It's about that scandal being the genesis of where we are now. *That's* the scandal. So that would be a hope, that we just look at where we are now. I couldn't ask for more than that" (p. 98).

The lesson of the quiz shows concerns themes that Redford "had been wanting to touch for quite a while: greed, the manipulation of truth and the fact that our lives are controlled by merchants. The merchant mentality dominates my industry, and I've wanted for some time to get at something that would illustrate that" (DeCurtis, 1994, p. 74). He wanted the film to be provocative in raising questions about the way we live in our society: "Is this moral ambiguity that we're in going to lead to no morality at all? Is the issue of ethics going out of our culture? Are we going to find some way to express our outrage, or are we just going to continue being numb?" (p. 74). Redford criticized the merchant mentality in an interview with the *Los Angeles Times.* He maintained that ethics and shame do not exist anymore because corruption has become a way of life (Gelmis, 1994, p. F5).

Ethical Standards. The film offers a moral center in the character of Goodwin; it addresses and counters "the decline in American morality" which began with the quiz scandal. In fact, Goodwin himself (1988) disagrees with writers who argue that the quiz shows mark the beginning of America's loss of innocence. To Goodwin, it was the presence of a sense of innocence, the ability to feel indignation and outrage, that fueled the 1960s. The innocence was injured but not destroyed or there would have been no sit-ins, no marches, no 1960s.

Underlying all the lessons from the quiz show scandal is the sense of violated standards. The story is not only about greed and seedy exploitation but also investigation, confession, and the reassertion of accepted standards of truth and morality. *Quiz Show* features the violation of ethics under merchant impulses *and* it emphasizes that the violators were caught and punished. *Quiz Show* examines wrongdoing and rightdoing, the hunted and the hunter, the violation of ethics and reassertion of ethics. In essence and in Redford's descriptions, it is a morality play for our time.

Regulatory Protection for Potential Victims. The quiz show scandal was in danger of being remembered as a victimless crime, prosecutor Stone (Stone & Yohn, 1992) reminds us. No villains were locked up or voted out of office. But, he insists, the real victims were "the television audience" and certain permanently scarred contestants. Underscoring the effectiveness of advertising on the quiz shows, Stone reminds us that "in fact, scores of millions of dollars flowed . . . [away from] fifty million people as a result of their watching the shows, thereby enriching manufacturers, broadcasters, advertising agencies, as well as program packagers and a score or more of contestants" (Stone & Yohn, 1992, p. 320). The rigging was legal but it was a gigantic fraud with a huge number of victims. Stone, a long-time Republican, argues that one lesson learned from the quiz show scandals is the need for vigorous public oversight and regulation. This echoes the point made by McChesney's (1994) historical analysis of broadcast regulation that, left to their own priorities, commercially based media often exclude options for serving the public and exploit opportunities for self-serving gain. For our own time, this tempers the wishful expectation that the next technology just around the corner will solve all our problems without any need for public oversight and regulation or noncommercial alternatives.

Beyond Laws and Profits. Another lesson to learn from the quiz show scandals is that moral decision making necessarily takes us beyond consideration of only legal and economic outcomes. Lying and misrepresentation are impermissible even when lawful and profitable. Goodwin, in *Quiz Show,* laments in the end that they caught the small fry but did not "get television" itself as the culprit, did not expose its lust for money and improve its programming. But the film "gets" television and film in a broader sense; both have social consequences and deserve the harshest criticism when they fail to live up to their responsibility. We are interested in the quiz show scandals because we fear we may be reliving them at any time.

Media Ethics Today. Entering the world of the 1950s scandal can be stimulating but also unsettling, unsettling because it is all too familiar. In addition to the familiar sound of the cant rationalizations, the reexamination is unsettling because the situation today appears demonstrably worse—the explosion of tabloid television, the reduction of news to ratings scrambles, the bastardization of political dialogue in sound bites, attack ads, and talk radio scapegoating, and the glorification of duplicity.

Looking back, would television executives today acknowledge, as they readily did then before Congress, that providing national television programming is a "sacred national trust"? As Newton Minow has noted, his farewell speech as head of the FCC, the speech that became memorable for calling television a "vast wasteland," was actually intended to raise the issue of "public service." The "sacred trust" and "public service" of providing media culture becomes more important over time, as media technologies become ever more a part of daily life and necessary tools for all of us.

A final lesson to take from the quiz show scandals is that ethical failing is wrong no matter how much fame it may generate in a sensationalist era. Van Doren's long life of hiding out in apparent shame and ignominy appears quaint today. John Leo (1994) suggests that Van Doren would now be instantly refurbished on *Geraldo,* and perhaps turned into a Senate candidate like Oliver North. We would be likely to see a bidding war between *Hard Copy, A Current Affair,* and *20-20* for his true story, not to mention a round of talk show appearances. His agent would keep him before the public until he became a respected Nixonian elder statesman. Shameless behavior today is too profitable to resist. But Van Doren's deception destroyed not his fame but his life. The fame and notoriety of serial murderers, vicious dictators, and other psychopaths can never be confused with virtue.

There are many more lessons that might be teased out of the story of the quiz show scandals of the 1950s, but these are enough to illustrate the work of historical/ethical interpretation in exploring media culture. A concern for discovering historical and ethical truths adds interest and meaning to our explorations of media culture.

Summary

The ethical questions raised by the quiz show rigging might be reduced to simplistic levels: a small group of production personnel devised a system of cheating to increase dramatic appeal and ratings. They sucked contestants into the plot by winning their consent. They were caught. Case closed? Not at all.

History offers insights into not only where we came from but also who we are and what we are becoming. Ethical dilemmas of the past suggest numerous lessons for the present. As the saying goes, those ignorant of history are doomed to relive it. Moreover, media reconstructions of the past call up a number of problematic issues, particularly ones involving genre, honesty, and truthfulness.

As we noted in the beginning, many critical areas of media culture are highlighted in the search for truth in the quiz show scandal:

- truth versus deception—fact and fiction in media representation
- media events—their nature, power, and meaning
- political economy—competition for ratings and profit
- genre conventions—accepted standards of truth
- law and media—how society regulates and polices representations
- competition—America's obsession with winning
- ethics and media—right and wrong in media practice
- postmodernism and the relativity of values

The many recent versions of the 1950s scandal give us unique insights into what happened and who was responsible. The books, chapters, documentary, film, and play can help us understand what America was then and hint at what we have become since in our hunt for shared truth, meaning, and purpose.

Does "historical/ethical analysis" solve the mystery of media culture for us? By itself, perhaps not, but it certainly provides important clues. As we find ourselves positioned in the curious postmodern condition of the present—a condition explored in the following chapter—an understanding of history and ethics may not be a luxury for those who can afford it but a necessary survival skill for anyone who would thrive within the confusion that is contemporary media culture.

Notes

1 This chapter is heavily indebted to Dick Pack for suggesting the study, gathering a great deal of the information, editing materials, and publishing my account of the quiz show scandal in a rather different version as the cover feature in *Television Quarterly* (Real, 1995).

2 *Night and Her Stars* premiered at the South Coast Repertory Theater in Costa Mesa, California, in 1994 and played in a revised version at the Manhattan Theater Club in 1995.

EXERCISES

Chapter 7

Exercise A. HISTORICAL TRUTH. Select a controversial event in history—an event in a war, a major independence struggle, a political scandal, a famous life, a labor conflict, or any other debatable historical episode. Seek out presentations of it in various media formats and genres—a critical scholarly history, popular textbook, movie or television docudrama, theatrical play, novel, short story, poem, and so forth. Specify the similarities and differences among the versions. Which is more true? Which more interesting? Can you find misrepresentations or deceptions? What does all this say of the reconstruction of history, especially in the popular consciousness? Is there a single true version of history?

Exercise B. HISTORICAL FABLE. Examine the preceding variations from the viewpoint of hegemony and political economy. Who has vested interests in seeing that the historical event has a particular moral associated with it? How have historical interest groups maintained different versions of the history? How do the priorities of the dominant social forces tend to direct a preferred reading of the history, especially of a nation's history as presented to its youth? What truth is there in Napoleon's saying "history is a fable agreed upon?"

Exercise C. ETHICS. Identify the specific moral issues at stake in the quiz show scandal. How many people may have compromised themselves in different ways in this scandal? How did narrow self-interest dictate the behavior of contestants, quiz managers, sponsors, and executives? What lessons can you find for media producers and consumers in the quiz show scandals?

Exercise D. MEDIA DECEPTION. Compare the specific deceptions in the quiz show scandals with what might be possible today in television deception. If the same deception could not occur in the same way, what other kinds of deception today are possible in game shows, talk shows, magazine feature programs, news, docudramas, and similar places? How might the drive to maximize profits lead to unethical deception? What kind of "truth" do we expect today from advertising and promotional efforts? Evaluate a hypothetical scenario in which an individual is faced with an ethical choice between profit-making and safety or environmental concerns. How should such decisions be made?

8

Postmodern Aesthetics:
MTV, David Lynch, and the Olympics

Three friends make their own music video by listening to Bobby Vinton's "Blue Velvet" as they watch slow-motion close-ups of Olympic athletes in competition.

The athletes' bodies flex, stretch, leap, bend, in exaggerated, random movement.

The music soars with pop feelings of heartache, nostalgia, longing.

The pastiche combination works for the threesome for a few moments. Then they flip over to watch the ads on regular MTV.

Postmodernism lives!

This chapter examines the meaning of the transition from classical to modern to what has been called the *postmodern,* from ancient aesthetic roots to scenes like the one above. Media culture has become indistinguishable from "the postmodern condition." Can "postmodern aesthetics" uncover the central characteristics of media culture, solving our original mystery? Does an understanding of postmodernism in all its dimensions bring together ritual, reception, text, hegemony, gender, and history to unearth the final clues and suspects in a grand resolution of our questions of media culture?

Within media culture, the curious style of MTV, of David Lynch and Quentin Tarantino films, and of the televised Olympic games share a quality named *postmodern.* Each is a blended hodgepodge, or *pastiche,* which has replaced the coherent message and unified style of traditional works of art and culture. In this chapter, we explore the postmodern qualities of media culture by pasting together postmodern elements found in music videos, in *Blue Velvet* and *Pulp Fiction,* and in the media-hyped summer and winter Olympic games. Jane Shattuc (1992) has captured the postmodern connection between *Blue Velvet* and MTV:

From their candy sweet scenes of picture postcard America to the scenes of horrific sexual violence, David Lynch's *Blue Velvet* (1986) and "Twin Peaks" are indisputably postmodern. An ironic celebration of America's commercial culture has replaced the high art or critical sensibility of Bauhaus architecture, Surrealism, and the abstract expressionism of the 1950s. The sense of this movement is contained not only in *Blue Velvet* and "Twin Peaks" but also in . . . MTV videos. In all these works a playful ambiguity . . . [displaces] the monolithic "truth" of the artist's vision in traditional art. Indeed, postmodernism is often heralded as the realization of a long-sought-after goal for many intellectuals: the unification of the popular-based forms of mass culture with an aesthetic distance, or, in Fredric Jameson's words, "an aesthetic populism." (p. 73)

When we use postmodernism as a vehicle for exploring media culture, we note certain characteristics of the specific media experience—a sense of irony, bald commercialism, a playful ambiguity, nostalgic blend of past and present, disparate art styles, a lack of absolutes, and more—and connect these characteristics with the broader currents and style of postmodernism. Doing this requires a sharpened sense of what postmodernism is in all its ambiguity and elusiveness. Fortunately, the often confusing literature on postmodernism has collectively laid out the central qualities usually associated with postmodernism. These range from broad historical influences, the culmination of several centuries, to specific stylistic devices in the form of pastiche, intertextual borrowings, abrupt transitions, and fragmented relativism. What do quirky films and stylized music videos, globally merchandised competitions and pop-star athletes have in common? At once primordial and playful, pillaging genres and conventions, cynical and willfully naive, believing nothing but accepting anything, what is this new aesthetic and paraphilosophy?

Defining Postmodernism: The Elusive Present

Competing definitions of postmodernism, drawing from architecture, aesthetics, history, literature, sociology, critical theory, and elsewhere, have made the label ambiguous and controversial. Here we take *the postmodern* to include the following qualities.

1. The domination of the style of pastiche in art, architecture, and overall aesthetics, a style that juxtaposes unlikely combinations of styles borrowed from past cultural products, as Jameson (1991) explains.
2. The breakdown of the grand narratives, particularly the metanarrative of science as universal human problem-solver, as Lyotard (1984) has argued so compellingly.

3. The centrality of communication technologies in providing global access to a culture of mass reproduction and *simulacra,* or copies of which there is no original, in the view of Baudrillard (1983).
4. The consumer culture of late capitalism in which the puritan ethic of production has been replaced by the commercial ethic of conspicuous consumption (Featherstone, 1990).
5. The fragmentation of sensibility into discontinuous forms of knowledge and culture (McGowan, 1991) in which anchored meanings and permanent principles are absent (Foucault, 1980a, 1980b). This fragmentation includes a culture marked by excess and overload and an art marked by absence, deconstruction, minimalism, and decoration, together with a personal and social life dominated by the pleasure principle, relativism, privatism, and a schizophrenia that dips in and out of different personalities (Bauman, 1988, 1992), just as postmodern art creates pastiches from different styles.
6. An inability to resolve from within postmodernism the dilemmas that postmodernism describes so forcefully, as Best and Kellner (1991) and many others have lamented.

Each of these characteristics of the postmodern condition has its expression in the phenomenon of the (post)modern Olympic Games and in music videos and films such as *Blue Velvet* and *Pulp Fiction.* These specific celebrations of media culture today, in turn, both reflect and extend the postmodern condition, testing the assumptions and shedding light on particular aspects of postmodernism. Because they have a history nearly coextensive with the twentieth century, the Olympic games make an especially useful frame for characterizing the historical changes contributing to postmodernism.

Pastiche as THE Style of Postmodernism

Jameson (1991) describes our media and art as engendering "the well-nigh universal practice today of what may be called pastiche" (p. 16). *Pastiche* is the combining together in one work of the disparate styles and content characteristic of what would normally be presented as quite different artistic eras and messages. High classical combines with art deco and neo-impressionism in the architecture of a single building. One art design may quote from high art of the past such as the "Mona Lisa" and from a pop art comic strip of the present. No period or style of art is too sacred or remote to be borrowed from and quoted, from the textured roughness of primitive art to the slick glass surfaces of modernism itself. E. Ann Kaplan (1988) and others note how this pastiche style occurs in our experience of the dominant medium of the postmodern era, television. The strip of programming juxtaposes programs, advertisements, promotions, and credits in an array of formats from news to comedy, from cartoons to music videos to sports to movies. The pastiche effect is multiplied as the viewer channel surfs by remote control, making the sequence of television viewing an array of images that would seem a bewildering jumble to those conditioned by previous cultures.

Pastiche in Music Videos. A leading expression of the postmodern (or "pomo" to the cognoscenti) pastiche style is the commercial 24-hour music video channel that encompasses the world, the original "Music Television," MTV.

In a milestone event for postmodernism, on August 1, 1981, MTV went on the air a little after midnight with the Buggles's pseudo-prophetic song "Video Killed the Radio Star." Serge Denisoff (1988) calls MTV the third breakthrough in American music broadcasting, following the birth of "Top Forty" radio with Todd Storz in 1955 and the advent of "free form" or "progressive" rock with KMPX in San Francisco in 1967. This first all-music television network by the middle 1990s was reaching an estimated audience of 249 million homes in 88 countries (Zagano, 1994). MTV's outreach includes MTV Europe in English, MTV Brazil in Portuguese, MTV Internacional and MTV Latino in Spanish, MTV Asia in English and some Mandarin, and MTV Japan in Japanese.

Music videos exemplify the complex textual strategies that create the pastiche of current media culture. Whether a music video employs the style of a live, in-concert video or the style of a narrative film or some mixture of the two, as most do, the resulting videos knowingly appropriate other audiovisual media of all kinds, are self-reflexive and ironic in their portrayal of stars and stories, use montage strategies, and intertextually cross-reference themselves (Gow, 1992; Kaplan, 1988). The off-angle, active camera of music videos is also found in "The Real World" of MTV documentary programming and in advertising. Many traditional distinctions of narrative and persona are blurred (Rogers & Real, 1994) and, as Kaplan notes, advertising and entertainment become one and the same. The music videos, watched for their own sake, also promote the sale of music in the same manner as an advertisement; alongside this, the advertisements prepared for MTV often affect the odd-angle or star-based style of the music videos. In the beginning, MTV was a unique stylistic breakthrough for television presentation. In the words of Joe Gow (1992), "video 'auteurs' drew upon their backgrounds in film and advertising in attempting to create aesthetically engaging clips that might effectively promote the musical recordings of the artists featured in them" (p. 36).

The resulting pastiche of music videos is full of contradictions. They convey a liberal spirit of great freedom at the same time as they serve the conservative economic needs of a major corporation, MTV's parent Time Warner. Does the commercial institutionalized distribution system for MTV determine what the music video texts will say? Andrew Goodwin (1992) suggests that textual meanings cannot be "read off" the institutional context, but "the organization of the music and media industries sets clear pressures and limits, partly due to the essentially promotional rhetoric of the music video clips" (p. xviii). MTV presents itself as unconventional, innovative, youth-oriented, very hip and cool, and above the crassness of business, but it is the result of strategic, massive global marketing (Banks, 1995). Traditionally marginalized "others," such as women and people of color, have had only problematic access to mainstream promotion through music videos (Lewis, 1990), and yet in MTV, many rap and female artists have achieved their greatest successes. Music videos are often dismissed as adolescent trivia or attacked as antisocial, but it is clear that viewers learn about romance, personal identity, and politics from them (Bennett & Ferrell, 1987). In a world where social relationships are breaking down, music videos encourage viewers to constantly recreate their identities, according to Patricia Aufderheide (1986), thus creating a curiously postmodern solution to a postmodern problem.

In short, the pastiche of music videos in media culture today is an inherently postmodern phenomenon. Joe Gow, in his review of studies of music video, summarizes (1992), "the popularity of music video in general and MTV in particular signals the emergence of a new, 'postmodern' sensibility" (p. 39). The pastiche style of art, the breakup of traditional categories, and the consumer culture of late capitalism are hallmarks of both music videos and postmodernism.

Postmodern Pastiche in the Olympic Games. The Olympic events lend themselves to a pastiche style. They are not a single sport or event as in the World Cup or Super Bowl. The Olympics are many events occurring simultaneously. Nationalist interests dictate that although Great Britain may prefer equestrian events, India prefers field hockey and team handball. When a national broadcaster buys Olympic rights, the host broadcaster provides a clean video-audio feed from each event, to which the national service may add its own commentator and may transmit live or edit and transmit on a delayed basis. Olympic coverage is "designer" television, in which the original event becomes customized for each different audience, which in turn receives its own pastiche of events. The Olympic ideal of uniting the peoples of the world around a single experience becomes fragmented and nationalized as it is converted for local use. Because of this, John Lucas (1992, p. 42) argues against playing the national anthems for winners. National anthems are played more than 400 times during the Summer Games, creating a pastiche of fragmented nationalism.

Television imposes its own order on the Olympics and viewers make sense of the games, but the Olympics are clearly a pastiche of cultural artifacts in the Jameson sense. For example, Olympic symbolism and mythology combine the mystique of the ancient Greek games with the modern games in the Olympic torch, its relay and its ceremonial lighting, and in other symbols. The grand reliance on tradition to anchor what the Olympics are and mean may sound rather like Jameson's (1991) warning, "the producers of culture have nowhere to turn but to the past: the imitation of dead styles, speech through all the masks and voices stored up in the imaginary museum of a now global culture" (pp. 17-18). This historicism results in "the random cannibalization of all the styles of the past, the play of random stylistic allusion, and . . . the increasing primacy of the 'neo' . . . [in the] new spatial logic of the simulacrum" (p. 18). The fast-paced Olympic television presentation of multiple events with on-screen graphics and announcer commentary is the opposite of the classical coherent, single-authored, focused artistic experience. Underlying this postmodern presentation is the commercial incentive to maximize viewing audience by promotion and titillation, by superlatives and historical allusions, by giving the audience what it expects but in an even fancier form than it had hoped.

In the case of the Olympics, as with MTV, we see a characteristic borrowing and quoting from other periods, styles, and texts in the manner of pastiche. Why does contemporary media culture resort to this borrowing and fragmentation? Does postmodern fragmentation stem from and reflect a larger breakup of coherent traditions and values from the past?

Postmodernism and the Breakdown of the "Grand Narratives" of Modernist Ideology

The style that gave rise to MTV, David Lynch, Quentin Tarantino, and the pastiche eclecticism of postmodernism was many decades in the making. Postmodernism is the result of long historical and ideological shifts, initiated especially by the disintegration of the consensus around modernist beliefs in progress and science, the "grand narratives" of the modernist era. Because of their long history, the Olympic Games provide a revealing portrait of the historical evolution from modern to postmodern. The century-long run of the modern games, beginning in 1896, coincides with the intellectual birth of postmodernism, just as the millennium of continuous ancient games from

776 B.C. to 393 A.D. coincided with the intellectual birth of modernism in classical Athenian Greece.

How have the so-called "modern" Olympic Games managed to become "postmodern"?

The Breakdown of Modernist Olympic Ideology. The Olympics have explicitly modernist roots. The intellectual formulation of "Olympism" as the quasi-official ideology of the modern games is firmly rooted in nineteenth-century modernism. The modernist framework of Olympic ideals dominated the rhetoric of the Olympic movement from the first Athens games in 1896 until Pierre de Coubertin's death in 1937 following the Berlin games. The classical Greek ideals, as revived at the time, dramatically attracted Coubertin and those who helped him restore the ancient games. The mental and physical development of the sovereign individual and the cumulative advancement of humanity were at the heart of the modernist worldview and the modern Olympic movement. As Duncan Petrie (1992, p. 1) has pointed out, it was

> an essentialist cultural tradition rooted in Judeo-Christian religion, Roman law, Greek ideas on politics, philosophy, art and science, and all refracted through the Renaissance and the Enlightenment. This tradition . . . promotes itself as being characterised by ideas of high culture, autonomy and liberty, and is frequently contrasted with the cultural traditions of "others," be they Asia, Africa . . . or in more recent times, America.

Coubertin, the classical modernist, dreamed up the modern Games. Throughout his career, Coubertin applauded the nineteenth-century revival of athleticism, crediting it with being a teacher of morals and of health. He wrote, "There are not two parts to a man—body and soul; there are three—body, mind and character; character is not formed by the mind, but primarily by the body. The men of antiquity knew this, and we are painfully relearning it" (Coubertin, 1967, pp. 6-7). The development of character was key to the development of society for Coubertin: "Healthy democracy, wise and peaceful internationalism, will penetrate the new stadium and preserve within it the cult of honour and disinterestedness which will enable athletics to help in the tasks of moral education and social peace as well as of muscular development" (p. 9).

The revival of the Olympic Games was to Coubertin not an isolated phenomenon "but the logical consequence of the great cosmopolitan tendencies of our times" (p. 10). These tendencies included the invention of the railroad and telegraph, "bringing into communication people of all nationalities" (p. 10), and achievements in art, industry, science, and literature, achievements celebrated in universal exhibitions, assemblies, and conferences of the day. Coubertin credited Thomas Arnold and the vigor of Victorian England with rediscovering "one of the most characteristic principles of Greek civilization: To make the muscles the chief factor in the work of moral education" (p. 11). Architecture too should be cast in a classical Hellenistic mold to attract visitors and to "inspire in them the respect due to places consecrated to noble memories or potent hopes" (p. 22).

Here we have the characteristic tenets of classical modernism—the rational, perfectible individual, progress, science, technology, high art, and moral improvement. With reason and technology, humankind can conquer obstacles and achieve happiness. The high hopes of Renaissance humanism, the industrial revolution, the theory of evolution, universal education, and urbanization all came together in the modernist dream of creating an efficient, abundant life for all, one periodically celebrated in the modern Olympic Games. The modern Olympic Games were conceived and developed under the zeitgeist of high modernism, the worldview that believed science, reason, and progress in the classical Renaissance manner would bring humankind increasing health, prosperity, and well-being. The end of the nineteenth century found Baron Pierre de Coubertin preaching the modernist gospel of classical values as the intellectual and mythical foundation of the modern games.

Since then, much has changed. Communication technology and television money have transformed the modern games into the preeminent global event of postmodern culture. At the end of the twentieth century, the modern Olympic Games celebrate their centennial in a dramatically different form than they had at the beginning or in their original incarnation in classical Greece. The current games are media extravaganzas in which huge amounts of television revenues fuel drives for audiences, commercial endorsements, national rivalries, world records, and a universally accessed event in which half the world's population is directly joined by technology. During the middle portion of the twentieth century the Olympics changed, marking the historic shift from modern to postmodern.

Current postmodern theory contrasts sharply with the modernist and classical Olympic view. Postmodernism claims that there is no longer any consensus around modernist-defined historical conditions, human goals, and driving ideas. Against the original well-articulated modern Olympic ideal, Jean-François Lyotard (1984) notes simply the demise of the modernist worldview and prospect. A countryman of Coubertin and the leading articulator of postmodernism, Lyotard ascribes the end of modernism and its replacement by postmodernism to the breakdown of the grand narratives of nineteenth century science, reason, and progress. In their place has risen a sense of limits, of relativity, of varied styles and goals, of skepticism about progress and perfectibility. Architectural theory had already been forced to recognize the end of the modern movement (1910-1945), which had sought nothing less than "a last rebuilding of the whole space occupied by humanity" (Lyotard, 1993, p. 171). With the abrogation of the modernist hegemony of Euclidean geometry, "there is no longer any close linkage between the architectural project and socio-historical progress in the relation of human emancipation on the larger scale" (p. 171). The modernist architectural ideal of progress through rationalism and freedom has given way to an appreciation of pastiche or *"bricolage*: the high frequency of quotations of elements from previous styles or periods (classical or modern)" (p. 171).

Postmodernism, however, goes well beyond the architectural arena. As Lyotard observes, "One can note a sort of decay in the confidence placed by the last two centuries in the idea of progress . . . in the certainty that the development of the arts, technology, knowledge and liberty would be profitable to mankind as a whole" (p. 172). In Lyotard's judgment, too many signs point in the opposite direction: "Neither economic nor political liberalism, nor the various Marxisms, emerge from the sanguinary last two centuries free from the suspicion of crimes against mankind" (p. 172). The development of technosciences can increase disease in addition to fighting it, can destabilize human populations in addition to protecting them. The unified style of modernism, like its inspiration classicism, gives way to the eclectic relativism of Lynch's *Twin Peaks* and MTV's hyperkinetic wash of images.

Blue Velvet and the Breakdown of Modernist Tradition. In place of classical modernist values, postmodernism sets a knowing reliance on familiar images and appearances, a nostalgic rummaging for markers of identity and meaning. Postmodernism offers a nostalgic, depthless image or simulation of the "real" without reference to actual historical detail or reality. Jameson argues that the postmodernism of David Lynch's 1986 film *Blue Velvet* typifies this ahistoricism with "its odd 'synthesis of nostalgia-deco and punk' and its refusal to connect to a historical period" (Shattuc, 1992, p. 76).

Blue Velvet is notably postmodern in its juxtapositions. Ask what one word a viewer associates with the film and you get words such as *surreal, bizarre, expressionistic, sadistic, creepy, "underneath," unique,* and *mesmerizing.* Reviewer readings of it found "the film is either high cinematic art or it is trash" (Denzin, 1991, p. 74). *Blue Velvet* was Lynch's fourth film, following the brilliantly bizarre *Eraserhead* (1978), the commercially successful adaptation of the well-written play *The Elephant Man* (1980), and the exotically unsuccessful *Dune* (1984). In *Blue Velvet,* just behind the facade of a picture-perfect middle American town, a young man, Jeffrey (Kyle

MacLachlan), with the help of his schoolgirl friend, Sandy (Laura Dern), unravels a mystery involving a kinky nightclub singer, Dorothy (Isabella Rossellini), and a sadistic kidnapper, Frank (Dennis Hopper).

The film opens with the blue skies, red roses, and white picket fences of Lumberton. Firemen wave from their truck, school guards help kids cross the street, and Bobby Vinton's "Blue Velvet" fills the air. Dad is watering the lawn when suddenly he is seized by a stroke and falls to the ground, his dog yipping around him and the hose spurting. Then, strikingly, the camera zooms down into the grass and under it to ugly, fighting insects whose buzzing roar gets louder. Likewise, the film digs under the surface of the seemingly tranquil town. In the end the film returns from "underground" to the idyllic backyard barbecue of the same family, with an (obviously mechanical) robin sitting and singing as all seems once more picture-post-card perfect.

Blue Velvet exemplifies postmodern pastiche by blending genres in the best self-reflexive and intertextual manner. The mystery theme owes a debt to Hitchcock. The teen coming-of-age theme combines with romance. The exploitive sadomasochism of the noir B-movie stands against the Disneyesque morality tale of good versus evil. The film carries a potentially subversive alternative vision of America but conveys no message. *Blue Velvet's* visual motifs include an image of fire. The fire images are inserted as what Eisenstein would call an intellectual montage; in one scene, the screen cuts from a violent love scene to the roar and flame of a match in extreme close-up. In the film's central segment, crime and sadistic sex and violence take place amid dark, eerie shadows, which give way in the end to idyllic scenes in rich, saturated primary colors. The sound design is equally impressive, with roars and buzzes and heavily reverberated 1950s pop songs. Despite its controversial subject, *Blue Velvet* won David Lynch an Oscar nomination for best director.

Many critics loved the postmodern stylishness of the film, but not all. Rex Reed (1987) called it "one of the sickest films ever made." Reed argued,

> Violence, graphic sex and nudity, sado-masochism and every perversion known to man follow in bountiful supply, accompanied by plenty of lurid camp, eye-rolling acting, idiot dialogue and off-key choruses of "Blue Velvet" . . . I haven't the vaguest idea what Blue Velvet is about, except the desecration of a pop tune I danced to the night of my senior prom . . . the brain-damaged garbage department. . . . Bring a barf bag. (p. 152)

In direct opposition, Nash and Ross (1987) placed the film among the all-time greats of cinema history:

Every so often in the history of film a picture comes along and knocks the critics and public into a state of shock with its originality and its demand to be recognized . . . *Un Chien Andalou* . . . *L'Avventura* . . . *Psycho* . . . *Last Tango in Paris* . . . *Taxi Driver* . . . . This year, David Lynch has brought his "disease" of dark mysteries before the public, exploring the connections between sex and violence, light and darkness, and good and evil. (p. 34)

Richard Corliss (1987), in *Time,* loved the way Lynch "stocked his movie with artifacts from every decade of postwar America; it could be taking place now, then or never" (p. 154).

Other critics were captivated and bothered by the film's Freudian psyche and symbolic richness. The National Society of Film Critics named *Blue Velvet* best film of the year and Lynch best director. John Robert Kelly (1987) praised it, saying, "As the spectators travel metaphorically 'in one ear and out the other,' Lynch explores the inner psyche, a terrain he depicts with an honesty and bemusement rarely encountered in American films" (p. 114). However, both Steve Jenkins (1987) and Simon Cunliffe (1987) find profound complications in the depictions of male sexual aggression and the presentation of women's bodies, commodified and packaged for consumption by the male gaze. Yet Jenkins says *Blue Velvet* makes Lynch "the most provocative and inspired director in the American mainstream" (p. 147). James Hoberman (1987), in the *Village Voice,* calls the film "Archie and Veronica in the Twilight Zone or the Hardy Boys on Mars" but adds, "there hasn't been an American studio film so rich, so formally controlled, so imaginatively cast and wonderfully acted, and so charged with its maker's pyschosexual energy since *Raging Bull*" (p. 156). The extremity of the reactions to *Blue Velvet* reflect the extremity of its style and story, making it postmodern par excellence.

Blue Velvet, along with Lynch's other work, reflects the breakdown of the grand narratives and geometrical precision of classical modernism. In their place, we find nostalgia, camp, narrative originality, stylistic virtuosity, and a parody of Freudianism and film genres of the past. What Coubertin lost in the passing of modernism, Lynch found in the arrival of postmodernism.

Postmodernism and Communication Technologies

Saturation by technologies of communication is a characteristic feature of the postmodern landscape. The explosion of technologies in recent decades accelerated the shift from modernist consensus to postmodernist fragmentation. The technologies of media culture are the hyperactive nervous system of postmodern society. We create the technologies, and then they create us, McLuhan warned (1964). Cyberpunk literature is only an extreme image of the freewheeling digitized, imaged, on-line existence that increasingly occupies real daily life under postmodernism. The decentered subjects of David Lynch films and music videos ricochet through life, wired and impulsive. Within this plugged-in environment, the greatest concentrations of electronic technology in the history of the world have not been the Gulf War, despite its popular characterization as the Nintendo war, nor the space launchings, with all their futuristic accouterments. Rather, the now-biennial Olympic Games attract the most breathtaking display of our technological capacity to capture, refine, and transmit messages of all types to all places.

In recent decades, more media personnel than athletes have been officially accredited to attend the Games. Opening and closing ceremonies have become big-time show business without equal in media culture. The athletic competitions occurring in the Games are overlaid with promotions, commercial interruptions, sponsor logos, celebrity chasing, abrupt transitions, and entertainment packaging emblematic of what protopostmodernist Guy Debord (1970) decried as "the society of the spectacle."

The International Olympic Committee's (IOC) media policies have been directed by the goal of making the Games available "to the widest possible audience." Although this dictates against reducing television coverage to a pay-per-view event, it has reinforced the incentive to cooperate with commercial television, film, radio, newspaper, magazine, and other media sources to consistently expand the "spectacle" aspects of this global media event. The most advanced video, audio, and textual processing occurs in overwhelming abundance in the Olympic Games, even in arctic conditions like those of the 1994 Lillehammer Winter Olympics. In 1936, Leni Riefenstahl took 2 years to edit her 4-hour film record of the Games; in 1960, CBS flew tapes from Rome to New York to squeeze in some delayed same-day coverage. Today, simultaneous events from widely dispersed venues are instantly relayed to broadcast centers and digitized, rearranged, and transmitted in quite different versions to different national audiences through a complex array of cameras, video decks, editors, signal processors and compressors, microwave relays, satellite feeds, and related technologies, all backed with massive managerial, legal, and economic systems. Science-fiction fantasies of technology's capabilities become real as media consumers everywhere access the competitions and entertainments framed as Olympic spectacles. In addition to the television technology, data and text transmissions speed off to print media, and the record-keeping and coordination of the Games themselves are made possible by massive arrays of computerized technology and organization.

This is precisely the technologically saturated environment that Jean Baudrillard (1983) describes as the postmodern world of *simulacra,* or simulations and representations, a world made up of copies of which there is no original. Walter Benjamin's (1969) famous essay on "The Work of Art in the Age of Mechanical Reproduction" anticipated the problem facing the IOC: How do the Olympics maintain their integrity as a work of human creation in the context of endless media manipulation?

Postmodernism and the Consumer Culture of Late Capitalism

The characteristics of late capitalism have been a driving force in creating the world of postmodernism, with the breakdown of the modernist ideology of Coubertin's early modern Olympics and the rise of Lynch's nostalgic eclecticism. The changes from the aristocratic but idealistic modern games to the pragmatically profit-centered postmodern games illustrate the nature of late capitalism, described by Fredric Jameson in his widely debated analysis of postmodernism.

Jameson (1991) places us in a period called *late capitalism,* a period that Jameson says can also be referred to as " 'multinational capitalism,' 'spectacle or image society,' 'media capitalism,' 'the world system,' even 'postmodernism' itself" (p. xviii). His position is indebted to Adorno, Horkheimer, and the Frankfurt School of critical theory. Jameson emphasizes that this conception of postmodernism "is a historical rather than a merely stylistic one. . . . I cannot stress too greatly the radical distinction between a view for which the postmodern is one (optional) style among many others available and one which seeks to grasp it as the cultural dominant of the logic of late capitalism" (pp. 45-46). Jameson argues that "culture is today no longer endowed with the relative autonomy it once enjoyed" (p. 48). For those suspicious of postmodern jargon, Jameson concedes, "I occasionally get just as tired of the slogan 'postmodern' as anyone else, but . . . I wonder whether any other concept can dramatize the issues in quite so effective and economical a fashion" (p. 418).

The economic history of the modern Olympic games exactly follows the trajectory of what Jameson calls late capitalism. Aristocratic privilege, not commercial sponsorship, sustained the Olympic movement in its well-documented first decades, with no patronage more generous than that of Coubertin himself (Guttman, 1992; Lucas, 1980, 1992; MacAloon, 1981). But when the games after World War I began to gather momentum as major international events, with increasing press coverage and general recognition, the "old boy" network of support became increasingly supplanted by other forces. Cities spent more to host the games, reaching an apex with the Berlin games in 1936 (Mandell, 1971), and competitors came more frequently from outside the leisure class, creating tensions of race and class that were captured in *Chariots of Fire,* a 1981 film about the 1924 Paris games.

With public and commercial support becoming more prominent in the modern Olympics, the nature of contemporary capitalism took on increasing importance relative to the games. This was not only evident in the Cold War battles of Western capitalism against the state capitalism of the Soviet bloc, but also in the more general trend toward expanded fundraising and commercial sponsorship, inclusion of the former European-controlled colonies, and the increased visibility of and income from Olympic television coverage.

With the release of Leni Riefenstahl's two-part *Olympia* film (Graham, 1986) and experimentation with television at the Berlin games, the intrusion of the moving image into the Olympics began. This increased in midcentury with the 1956 Melbourne organizing committee being the first to sell television rights to the games (Lucas, 1984). Because broadcast networks in the United States and Europe boycotted the rights sale, Olympic programming in the United States consisted of only six prerecorded half-hour programs presented on a scattering of independent stations. But the principle of commercial Olympic television had been established and the Olympics would never again be the same.

Perhaps no single force has contributed more to the "postmodernizing" of the Olympics than television coverage in general and television rights fees in particular. They have created a new relationship between the public and the games at the same time as they have brought the dynamics of late capitalism (Mandel, 1975) into the Olympic movement. With a parallel drive, MTV brought commercialism to the image and the sound of popular music.

The television rights fees for the summer Olympics have increased several hundredfold in the second half of the twentieth century. The U.S. commercial networks have generally paid 50% to 75% of the total Olympic revenue from television rights and production costs. In millions of dollars, the fees paid by U.S. television are shown in Figure 8.1 (Lucas, 1984; Lucas, 1992; Quindt, 1995).

Paralleling the summer Games, the winter Olympics in 1986, 1990, and 1994 brought in more than $300 million each in television rights sales. In 1995, NBC bought the U.S. television rights for the winter Games in 2002 for $545 million dollars and in the year 2006 for $613 million, giving NBC coverage of the first five Olympics of the new century.

In the 1960s, television revenues quickly replaced Olympic ticket sales as the principle source of income from the Games. In 1960, television provided

Figure 8.1. Television plays a major role in the communication, commodification, and postmodernization of the Olympic Games.

only 1 of every 400 dollars of the cost of hosting the summer Olympics. In 1972, 1 of every 50 dollars was provided by television; in 1980, 1 of every 15 dollars; and by 1984, 1 of every 3 dollars of Olympic host costs were paid for from television revenues (Real, 1989).

The Olympics' immersion in the world of television exposure and rights fees has been followed by rapidly increasing commercial sponsorship of the Games and teams themselves. The 1984 Los Angeles Games pioneered this approach, even selling rights to one company to bill itself as the "Official Olympic Specimen Carrier" because it transported the urine samples of athletes to laboratories. Television exposure and commercialization prepared the environment for this additional corporate commercial sponsorship. The Olympic Program (TOP), formed in 1982 by the IOC, has combined with the marketing consortium International Sports and Leisure (ISL) to sell corporate sponsorships at a level approaching a 50-50 split with income from television rights. TOP contracts with Coca-Cola, Eastman Kodak, 3M, Ricoh, Matsushita, *Sports Illustrated,* Visa, and U.S. Postal Express in 1992 brought in more than $120 million to the IOC (Lucas, 1992, p. 79).

The Atlanta Games in 1996 set records by selling more than $1 billion in corporate Olympic sponsorships. Ten Worldwide Sponsors paid up to $40 million in money and services, 10 Centennial Olympic Partners also paid $40 million, and 20 regular Sponsors paid up to $20 million. The Worldwide Sponsors' payments went to the International Olympic Committee, and payments from the other two were shared by the U.S. and Atlanta committees. The sponsors spent these amounts for rights to use the Olympic torch logo, five rings, and Olympic name. In 1996, sponsorship worth $179 million was paid to the IOC by one transnational corporation alone, the Coca-Cola Company based in Atlanta (Lucas, 1995).

The intrusion of late capitalism's commercialism into the Olympics through television and sponsorships signals the economic shift from the modern to the postmodern Games. Echoed by hundreds of other critics, British historian Steven Barnett (1990) warns, "The Olympic Games could be hijacked by an obsessively competitive American television industry, whose money will eventually corrupt completely the original spirit" (p. 134). Already the capital produced by the postmodern era's media has carried the Olympic movement through two major financial crises since World War II. First, having been near bankruptcy the decade before, the IOC officially declared in 1970 that all television revenues belonged to the IOC rather than, as previously, to the host city. The IOC, however, returns 60% to the host city, reducing that to 49% in 2004. Second, when Teheran's was the only other bid to host the 1984 Games, the IOC was forced to accept the commercially sponsored 1984 Los Angeles plan without the usual guarantee of public monies. Both commercial turns proved so lucrative to the IOC that Olympic leadership is now as attuned to economic progress and success as it is to athletic achievement. These commercial changes, combined with Olympic hostage-taking and boycotts made attractive because of the Olympics' media prominence, led Jeffrey Segrave and Donald Chu in 1981 to conclude, "the politicization and commercialization of the modern Olympics have reached such a crescendo that few could deny that the idealistic intentions of the Games have become increasingly immersed in a sea of propaganda" (p. 363).

Technologies of communication have made possible the incredible media outreach of the Olympics, bringing with it the increasing commodification of the Games. *Commodification* reduces the value of any act or object to only its monetary exchange value, ignoring historical, artistic, or relational values. In addition, commodification has a fetishistic quality in which the commodities, because they represent commercial advantage, take on a bloated psychological importance to the individual or group. The postmodern Olympics have in recent decades become a virtual circus of commodity values and fetishes. Corporate logos and sponsorship abound, Olympic memorabilia multiply, merchandising and marketing preoccupy officials, shoe sponsors become powerful decision makers, promotions begin months before the Games and continue into the media presentation, and Olympic leaders and the public learn to accept this commodification as if it were part of the (post)modern Olympic credo.

How have postmodern technology, capitalism, and commodification changed the Olympics? When the 1984 opening ceremony featured 84 pianos playing Gershwin, Alan Tomlinson (1989) was led to conclude, "televisual images do linger on; and those of the Los Angeles Olympics of 1984 can only be said to owe more to the spirit of Liberace than to that of Coubertin" (p. 7/9).

In short, the postmodern culture of late capitalism links the commercial incentive of the producers of the Olympics with the conditioned pastiche tastes of the Olympic consumer in a spectacle of nationalistic technological representation.

Late capitalism also provides a comfortable home for Lynch and MTV. One of the curiosities of David Lynch, whose oddness is hinted at by the fact that his most conventional film is *Elephant Man* (1980), is his comfort with capitalism and Americanism, even his stated fondness for Ronald Reagan. Lynch celebrates the America of Detroit cars and picket fences, the consumer society. Lynch's take on Americana in his television soap opera *Twin Peaks* and his Cannes prize-winning *Wild at Heart* (1990) work similarly, even down to their *Wizard of Oz* and Elvis Presley motifs. MTV's global satellite distribution, like the Olympics, tailors itself to regional variations while celebrating a particularly hip version of capitalist commodification. MTV's survival is the result of not only its originality as a vehicle for musical and video creativity, but also its heavy initial capitalization by Warner Communications and ambitious satellite and cable distribution systems. Ideals of modernist human progress are less apparent in Lynch's films or MTV's videos than the consumer commodification of late capitalism.

Postmodern Fragmentation and Relativism

Postmodernism is known for its fragmentation of sensibility into discontinuous forms of knowledge and culture (McGowan, 1991). The search for "information" digitized into bits rather than for coherent knowledge or focused understanding characterizes postmodernism and media culture to-day. Postmodernism contrasts with the rational individualism of classical print culture, a founding principle of the modernist project. Under conditions of postmodernism, our rational decision making, carefully anchored mean-ings, and permanent principles are replaced by undirected social trends and the exercise of power through historical, institutional forces, as Michel Foucault (1980a, 1980b) and the poststructuralists have argued. Postmod-ern culture is marked by a depthlessness in which appearance is all. Media offer simulacra that simulate a reality but remain at a surface level because there is no longer substance behind the image.

The resulting culture is marked by excess and overload but offers an art of absence, of deconstruction and minimalism counterbalanced only by decoration. Little is said, but much is assumed and implied. Within this postmodern environment, personal and social life becomes dominated by private pleasures and encourages a schizophrenia of multiple personalities (Bauman, 1988, 1992). The individual too becomes a postmodern pastiche of disparate styles.

This anarchist spirit in postmodernism is expressed well in Larry McCaf-fery's "Tsunami . . .," the introduction to the collected stories in *Avant-Pop: Fiction for a Daydream Nation* (1993). Describing the avant-pop (A-P) contributors, he says they are far from counterculture wimps:

> I mean, A-P guys are hardened professionals—a new breed of pop-cultural demolition artists, cultural terrorists who've put in their hours of training in front of the boob tube with all regular zombies so they can know the enemy's terrain, the pop figures who live there, the local lingoes. (p. 16)

What mutual goals and strategies did this group share?

> The A-P family's attack-plan relied on the use of concentrated bits of aesthetic disruption to blast through the cocoon of habituation imprisoning most Ameri-cans (a cocoon mostly composed of dangerously addictive pop cultural stereo-types, clichéd attitudes, reductive role models, and narrative formulas that the media was passing out to people like the Brits did with Opium to the Chinese). Once gaining entrance, the A-P gang hoped to rescue the badly malnourished creative imaginations. (p. 21)

The purpose of A-P, to McCaffery, is to introduce conventions and violate them to show there are other options, to "find openings in the system that will let the wind blow back your hair" (p. 30).

Music videos exploit the anarchy, fragmentation, and relativism of post-modernism. A music video can start to tell a narrative story, cut to live performance, suggest a different story, show the musical performers watching or participating in the stories, cut back to the stories, create a metastory that reflects on stories and performance, show more performance but in a different setting, and end the stories or not. Images in a music video can be unusual or oddly juxtaposed. Continuity, valued in conventional feature films, is not necessary. The presentation can be both whimsical and serious, creating ironic distance. Conventions of film and television can be indulged in and then violated. The rules are made to be broken—except the rule that the performer(s) must be presented in some form. The result of watching uninterrupted MTV for a period of time is a kind of delirium of simulacra and appearances, accompanied by aural satiation. Elements of culture are deconstructed, the art is minimalist, but the decoration can be endless. Depthlessness and fragmentation are not failings but goals, to create a different order of meaning and purpose. Music video style is virtually the definition of postmodern.

Postmodernism is closely associated with the avant-garde in art and shares the history and tradition of the avant-garde in the twentieth century. Elements of postmodernism have been developing throughout the century and not only in recent years. Lyotard (1984) argues that postmodernism developed from within modernism and is not merely its successor. Avant-garde works of Cézanne, Picasso, Kandinsky, Klee, Mondrian, and others were, in a subtle Freudian way, a working-through of modernity by itself. Within postmodernism, many classical distinctions, between the mainstream and the avant-garde, between "high" art and "popular" culture, disappear, as documented in the famous traveling exhibit of the Museum of Modern Art, *High and Low: Modern Art, Popular Culture* (Varnedoe & Gopnik, 1990).

Diversity Among Olympic Participants. The fragmentation and relativism of postmodernism finds curious expression in the Olympic Games. The original patriarchal and imperial unity of European-American white male domination of the games has fragmented into a multicultural but imperfect diversity.

Just as postmodernist art developed within modernism, cultural diversity forced itself on the Olympics as the resolution of a number of contradictions between the original Olympic ideals and current practices. As Allen Guttmann (1992) emphasizes, "it has taken nearly a century for some of the internal contradictions of Olympism to be understood and partially eliminated (and for other problems, like commercialism and drug abuse, to have arisen)" (p. 4). In the turn of the century's early modern Games, Olympic ideals of universal human unity and progress were contradicted by nationalism and the Games' exclusion of women, the working class, persons of color, and the Third World. Then, progressively, the Olympics came to adopt those viewpoints that Lyotard describes as leading to the demise of modernism and the emergence of postmodernism, in the form of a more diverse but qualified view of human ideals and potential. The Olympics became more diverse in ethnic and gender diversity but were forced to reject the classical model of one single, universal, perfectable human type.

The first modern Games in Athens in 1896 featured neither women nor athletes from outside Europe and North America. As Adrienne Blue (1988) notes, "No one wanted women at the Olympics" (p. 1). In 1900, women were allowed to compete in the Paris Games, but by 1912 women still numbered only 57 of the competitors compared to 2,447 men (Guttman, 1992, p. 33), who together represented 26 nations, primarily in Europe. At recent summer and winter Games, the percentage of female athletes has been slowly improving but remains at only about 25% of the total participants (Blue, 1988, p. ix; Hargreaves, 1994, p. 220).

Those from other than European Caucasian cultures had even slower entry to the Games than women. At the original 1896 Games, only a Chilean and an Australian participated from countries outside Europe and the United States (Guttmann, 1994, p. 124). The 1904 St. Louis Games were so suffused with white racism that they featured Anthropological Days, in which sideshow non-whites competed in unofficial Games, to the embarrassment of Coubertin and others appalled by the crudeness of the American organizers (p. 25). In 1908, white athletes from Australia and South Africa became the first medal winners from outside Europe and North America. The 1912 American team featured an African American, a Hawaiian, and two Native Americans. In 1920, the first Olympic medals for Asia and Latin America were won by Japanese and Brazilian athletes respectively (Henry & Yeomans, 1984, p. 108). Even today, amid the rich national costumes of the more than 190 nations competing, a small core of advanced nations dominates the winning. As Allen Guttmann (1992) notes, the Olympics remain dominated by the imperial powers of Western civilization: "Since winning, rather than simply taking part, has continued to attract the world's attention, the men and, especially, the women of Africa, Asia, and Latin American have been left to play ancillary roles on the Olympic stage" (p. 171). The IOC itself has always been dominated by Europe and the United States (Guttmann, 1994, p. 133), currently with 93 male and 6 female members (Lucas, 1995), and has yet to be headed by a president from outside Europe and North America. The limited diffusion of leadership in modern sports and the Olympics is a case of cultural hegemony (Guttmann, 1994, p. 178).

This means that the Olympic movement has moved away from its narrow European and Caucasian origins but has only imperfectly embraced the multicultural, postpatriarchal global populace. The simple Eurocentric, patriarchal values of modernism have been displaced only by the relativistic, fragmented condition of postmodernism, which remains considerably short of a fully developed, widely accepted new ideology, value system, and worldview.

The issue of "amateurism" in the Olympics further illustrates this shift away from classical modernist consensus. The Olympic Congress of 1981 in Baden-Baden, Germany (Lucas, 1992, p. 74), took the first decisive steps to dissolve the old "pure amateur code" and open the Olympic door to professional athletes. This has dramatically escalated the celebrity character of the Games, as in the 1992 American basketball "Dream Team." The dissolution of the amateur code has also removed some of the charade of subsidies and trust funds for athletes and has explicitly brought the games into the big-money world of professional athletic salaries and endorsements.

The Olympics today reflect the postmodern "culture of excess." Alongside an "art of absence," in which traditional standards of quality and artistic technique disappear, the postmodern culture of excess rewards extremes of size, flamboyance, self-promotion, consumption, fame, and extravagance. Latin American critics of the Olympics (see Reyes Matta, 1986) have charged the Games with "gigantism" that poor countries must watch from the sidelines. The fixation on quantitative records in the Olympics and elsewhere as measures of success contributes to this Western mechanical emphasis on fragmented, relative values and excess. The use of performance-enhancing drugs in the Olympics comes from a mentality directly opposed to that of Coubertin's oft-cited exhortation that the important thing is not to win but to participate. The West has transformed sports, in the words of Guttmann's book title (1978), *From Ritual to Record.*

The fragmentation of once-absolute standards and ideology, the acceptance of multicultural pluralism and relativism, and the drive to quantitative excess are distinguishing characteristics of both the recent Olympic Games and the postmodern condition. At the same time, the Games have assumed an imperial role by extending to diverse cultures the conflict-based deep structure of modern sports and an attendant set of Western structures of space, time, knowledge, nature, and relationships (Galtung, 1982). A standardized universality in sports reduces diversity in culture, even as it "enables everyone to play the game" (Guttmann, 1994, p. 188).

The postmodern qualities of fragmentation and relativism are not hard to find in music videos and the Olympics. They are also apparent in the films of David Lynch and in the films associated with Quentin Tarantino, whose work has achieved a kind of instant-cult classic status similar to Lynch's.

Postmodernism in Pulp Fiction. In 1995, *Pulp Fiction,* written and directed by Quentin Tarantino, won the grand prize at the Cannes Film Festival.

Tarantino, for 5 years a clerk in a video store, had managed to sell his script for *True Romance* (1993) and then direct the controversial but respected *Reservoir Dogs* (1992). He wrote the original script for *Natural Born Killers* (1995) but removed his name from the credits as it increasingly became Oliver Stone's movie. Despite these achievements, and script doctoring and cameo appearances in other films, it was *Pulp Fiction* that catapulted Tarantino to prominence.

Pulp Fiction celebrates postmodern pastiche. The movie shows not one story, in the traditional Hollywood mold, but three interwoven stories. *Pulp Fiction* draws its inspiration from the lurid, cheaply printed (*pulp*) magazines of the 1930s and 1940s but sets its story in present-day Los Angeles, blending past and present. The movie injects knowing intertextual references to films and pop culture, such as having John Travolta participate in a dance contest, which recalls for many viewers his *Saturday Night Fever* role. *Pulp Fiction* rejects straight chronology, brilliantly slipping back and forth among the three stories and eventually interweaving them all. The language, drugs, and violence in the movie are strong but also so stylized as to be almost parodies of themselves. The movie's plays on genre references make it alternately a gangster film, a satiric comedy, a buddy movie, and more. In overall tone and style, *Pulp Fiction* is as relentlessly postmodern as *Blue Velvet.*

The film introduces us to a pair of verbose hitmen (John Travolta and Samuel L. Jackson), a young couple making a career change from holding up liquor stores to holding up restaurants (Amanda Plummer and Tim Roth), and a double-crossing prizefighter on the run (Bruce Willis). The hitmen's intimidating mob boss (Ving Rhames) has an exotic but drug-addled wife (Uma Thurman). Tarantino borrowed from novelists the trick of having the main character in one story go on to be a supporting character in the next story. His idea was to take the oldest situations in the book and give them a new twist. One mob hitman has to take the boss' wife out for an evening, and she winds up overdosing. The boxer is supposed to throw a fight but wins instead and finds himself in a weird death struggle with the boss. The hitmen do a morning hit but run into cosmetic complications with a car splattered with human remains. Eventually the hitmen encounter both the boxer and the couple holding up the restaurant. Throughout, the dialogue is rich and a bit offbeat. The stories intertwine until, in the words of Tarantino, "you feel like you've seen one movie, a movie about a community of characters" (Homolka, 1995).

Other postmodern qualities in *Pulp Fiction* include pop iconology and commodification, a sense of late capitalism in the mob business, and use of the communication technology to make the film appear seamless. The film had a 500-day shooting schedule and used 70-odd sets around Los Angeles, including Jack Rabbit Slim's diner, which was built in a warehouse in Culver City. The big-name cast and overlapping stories created scheduling problems, but the complex narrative structure of the final edit achieved a striking level of unity and coherence. The film creates an engrossing viewing experience, even though it exhibits postmodern depthlessness and simulation. The message of the film is nonexistent, except as a romantic search for a vague something, as in one hitman's conversion away from killing. In this the film relates less to recognizable normal human life than to other movies and a fictionalized world of nice-guy gangsters.

An unexplained postmodern puzzle in *Pulp Fiction* is the briefcase that is periodically opened with its back to the audience, its contents exclaimed over. Dan Homolka, on the QT web site (1995), notes that this is clearly a "McGuffin," in Hitchcock's words, an object that is not meant to be explained but that works as a mysterious plot device. Nevertheless, the web site developed a list of guesses about what could be in the briefcase: the Palme d'Or from Cannes, an Oscar, gold bricks, heroin, pure evil (to tie in with the 666 lock combination), the Holy Grail, the Ark of the Covenant, the diamonds from the *Reservoir Dogs* jewel heist, a portable TV, a Royale with cheese, Chiclets, or the cocaine from *True Romance*. Such speculation indicates the kind of cult status that *Pulp Fiction* achieved almost immediately.

Pulp Fiction's play on surfaces, its quotation and borrowing, and its anarchic originality place Tarantino alongside David Lynch as Hollywood's leading postmodern auteur. Fragmentation, relativism, depthlessness, intertextuality, ironic parody, and all the other characteristics of postmodernism are seldom used so effectively.

Sources of Renewal Against Postmodern Negations

Today the artist must confront himself. Faced with a society that has lost the very idea of meaning—the market is the perfect expression of nihilism—the artist must ask himself to what purpose he writes or paints. [This] is the one question that counts. (Octavio Paz, 1993, p. 4)

This, admittedly, is the difficulty with postmodernism. Postmodern analysis thus far has proven effective at *describing* trends and problems and identifying their underlying unity. Postmodern analysis has shown far less promise for *prescribing* productive alternative directions and solutions. For many, postmodernism acts like a medical diagnosis of what is wrong with the patient, but many also want a prescription and cure. Whether a cure is needed is a fundamental question, but postmodernism by definition is not a finished period or style but a transitional, relative condition. Postmodernism comes after the modern (*post*) and will give rise to something more independent, as was the case in the Renaissance, the Reformation, the Enlightenment, and Modernism. What will emerge is not yet clear; it may already have emerged but remains as yet unnamed. Still, what we call *postmodern* is a given today; it is not a choice to be ignored or wished away. Nor is it a full cultural solution which needs only to be celebrated. Postmodernism is a condition to be worked through, a site of struggle, a style of media culture to be relished yet improved (see Figure 8.2).

The negativism of postmodernism has been elaborated on by, among others, Steven Best and Douglas Kellner (1991). They particularly decry the individualism, nihilism, and pessimism of the extreme postmodern theory of Baudrillard (1983), Kroker and Cook (1986), the early Lyotard, some Foucault, and poststructuralism. Best and Kellner find it unjustifiably immobilizing "that most postmodern theory rejects macropolitics and the modern projects of radical social reconstruction" (p. 282). They argue that "extreme postmodern theorists have abandoned politics for an avant-gardist posturing that is bloated with cynicism and opportunism" (p. 284). In this vein, Norman Denzin (1991) finds the postmodern cultural texts of Lynch's films *Blue Velvet, Twin Peaks,* and *Wild at Heart* ultimately "take conservative political stances, while they valorize and exploit the radical social margins of society" (p. 79). He warns, "these, then, are dangerous texts. Politically barren, they reproduce the very cultural conditions they seek to criticize" (p. 80). Against such charges, MTV's bow to occasional political reporting and get-out-the-youth-vote are commendable but transparent attempts to modify its "avant-gardist posturing" that overwhelmingly endorses self-indulgence over commitment. Negative extremes of individualism, nihilism, pessimism, and posturing, all of which can be found in postmodernism, leave it vulnerable to a variety of criticisms.

Many feminists have reservations about postmodernism because of its weakness in justifying standards for judgment and value. The abuse of women and the absence of political self-awareness in Lynch's films makes them vulnerable to Jane M. Shattuc's accusation of "Postmodern Misogyny in *Blue Velvet*" (1992). Lynch attempts to explain why the character of Dorothy is hit by Frank and by Jeffrey: "There are some women that you want to hit because you're getting a feeling from them that they want it, or they upset you in a certain way" (Shattuc, 1992, p. 85). Shattuc finds this explanation symptomatic of "the disorientation of the postmodern experience where no one is responsible for the meaning behind representation, not even its creator (the director), let alone society" (p. 85). For Shattuc, feminist

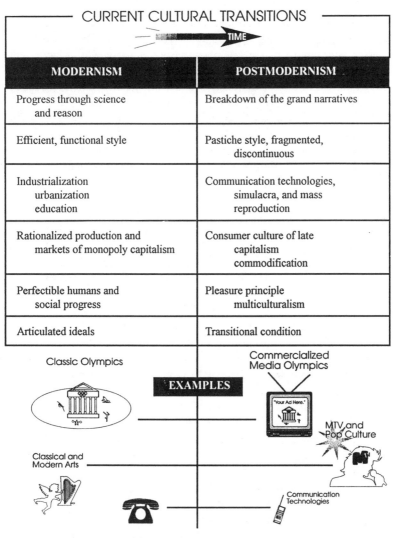

Figure 8.2. The comparative characteristics of high modernism and postmodernism indicate the cultural shift underway at the present time.

commitments conflict with such normless postmodernism. Feminism grows out of a real history of women's domination by men—a history that extreme postmodernism dissolves. Shattuc warns, "by championing commercial postmodernism, feminists could be the newest victims of the patriarchal dominant" (p. 85). She quotes approvingly Susan Suleiman's caution:

> Feminism provided for postmodernism a concrete political edge or wedge, that could be used to counter the accusatory pessimism of a Baudrillard or a Jameson: for if there existed a genuinely *feminist* postmodernist practice, then postmodernism could no longer be seen only as the expression of a fragmented, exhausted culture steeped in nostalgia for a lost center. (Shattuc, 1992, p. 85)

The depthlessness in social analysis, its refusal to perceive social structures—this is postmodernism's central failure for Best and Kellner. They note, "postmodern theory, like some liberal pluralist theory, has problems theorizing macrostructures and seeing how totalizing tendencies, like capitalism or gender and racial oppression, permeate microstructures and the plurality and differences celebrated in the theory" (Best & Kellner, 1991, p. 288). Tarantino's innovative racial casting has been debated in this regard. The film depicts an ideal racial mix. Travolta and Jackson are buddies, one white, one black. Their boss is black, but is married to a white woman. Tarantino's character, the anxious suburban homeowner, is married to an African-American woman. Race appears to be entirely unproblematic. This can be vigorously defended on utopian grounds as modeling an ideal, but can also be criticized, as were *The Cosby Show* and similar upbeat racial representations. The criticism argues that an overdose of such fantasy, however desirable in individual portions, has the negative consequence of falsely convincing the public that racial problems are solved. This naive reading of the social fabric is especially easy within postmodernism because of its readiness to dismiss all but surface and simulacra. If Tarantino is not individually guilty, there may be a kind of collective guilt in postmodern media that portrays a postracial society without recognizing the remaining deeply seated racial antagonisms and imbalances in the real world. Racial oppression on the macro level of society permeates microstructures and requires a theorizing of macrostructures that postmodernism resists.

At the same time, Best and Kellner recognize postmodernism's positive contribution to "the need for reconstruction of society, subjectivity, theory, and culture, and rethinking power and struggle in non-juridical or economistic models" (p. 286). The postmodern critique suggests positive change in culture. Postmodernism can become a source of renewal in society and not merely a self-indulgent attack.

Theories of the physical body and the preservation of utopian ideals offer promise within postmodernism. Postmodernists such as Deleuze and Guattari (1983, 1986, 1987), the early Lyotard, and sometimes Foucault, "privilege the physical body over critical cognition" (Best & Kellner, 1991, p. 287). In MTV, Lynch, Tarantino, and the Olympics, we find reference to the physical instead of only the abstract or the cognitive. This emphasis on the physicality of the body may provide a healthy measure of values over time. In addition, a few postmodernists, such as Jameson or Laclau and Mouffe (1985), argue for the importance of utopian values. These twin emphases on the body and on utopian values are important because they provide standards of measurement for actions and ideals. If media products serve real needs of the body or inspire true utopian ideals, they have value because of that. The body and utopianism suggest such positive measures within postmodernism, belying the negativism associated with much of postmodernism.

In conclusion, Best and Kellner state, "against the postmodern politics of subjectivity and tendencies to aestheticize politics, we would advocate a politics of alliances, a cultural politics, and a strategic politics which combine micro- and macroperspectives and retain a salient place for critical rationality" (pp. 291-292). The critical feminist response to *Blue Velvet* illustrates the value of working from within such cultural alliances. If postmodernism can accept such alliances, they can become forces for renewal.

With these important qualifications, the postmodern analysis offers to MTV, the films of David Lynch and Quentin Tarantino, the Olympics, and the rest of postmodern media culture a more comprehensive and developed frame for interpreting the many otherwise disparate and seemingly unrelated changes and problems infiltrating the once modern and now thoroughly postmodern cultural landscape. (See Figure 8.2.).

The future of culture, postmodern or otherwise, cannot be dealt with apart from the many issues in cultural politics under debate today (see Bérubé, 1994). The elaboration of an adequate intellectual justification for the Olympics and other cultural practices and products is a challenge. Segrave and Chu (1981) summarize the difficulty: "Divorced from the idealistic philosophy of Olympism, however, the Games stand as only another international athletic competition. The spectacle remains but the promise is lost. Consequently, the elaboration of a social-philosophical interpretation of the modern Olympic Games remains at the center of discussions" (pp. 362-363).

The struggle for cultural renewal takes place within and around postmodern media culture today. Lawrence Grossberg (1986) hits the center of many issues in media culture and postmodernism when he reminds us: "The meaning of a text is always the site of a struggle" (p. 86).

Summary

Postmodern aesthetics arise from a variety of forces:

- the breakdown of the grand narratives of science and progress

- the consumer culture and commodification of late capitalism
- global communication technologies
- a pastiche style of simulacra
- fragmentation and depthlessness
- intertextual referencing, relativist values, and ironic playfulness

These characteristics and qualities do not reduce the need for critical analysis and collective sociopolitical action—in fact, they increase it. But they force us to undertake such analysis and action from a grounded and realistic starting point.

Postmodernism accounts for many of the most notable characteristics of music videos and films such as those of David Lynch and Quentin Tarantino. Postmodernism also forces us to reconsider the Olympics and the larger cultural trends they reflect: classicism and classism, the noncommercial Olympic ideal, media technology and Olympics "for the widest possible audience," postwar Olympic growth and escalating costs and media coverage, the model of Los Angeles 1984 and the new *for-profit* Olympics, growth in commercial endorsements and sponsorships, the de-amateurizing of the modern games, the de-Europeanized and postpatriarchal diversity of athletes, and, finally, the possibility of alternative directions for the Olympics under conditions of postmodernism.

Has "postmodern aesthetics" explained all the remaining clues and suspects involved in our original mystery of media culture? Close, but not quite; at least not by itself. But what happens when we combine ritual theory, reception studies, textual analysis, production/hegemony, gender analysis, historical/ethical interpretation, and postmodern analysis? The final chapter examines that strategy.

EXERCISES

Chapter 8

Exercise A. Identify a specific film, music video, or other expression of media culture that you consider to be especially postmodern. What characteristics associate it with postmodernism? Is "pastiche" present? Are there elements of historical change, technology, and commercialism that play a role in shaping it? How does it compare with a classical, unified, traditional work of art?

Exercise B. Summarize the defining characteristics of music videos and MTV. How has commercialism played a role? Technology? What stylistic qualities of music videos are postmodern? Take one specific music video and trace its postmodern aspects. How do text, reception, technology, gender, hegemony, and related factors help to explain what the music video is and how it works in its postmodern setting and style?

Exercise C. List elements that should be included in a definition of postmodernism. Why does the emphasis in definitions of postmodernism seem to be different in different fields—architecture, history, film, and so forth? Which elements of postmodernism are you most comfortable with? Which are you least comfortable with?

Exercise D. Review how the ideals, organization, and rules of the Olympics have changed over the last 100 years. How does the shift in the Olympics reflect the change from "modernism" to "postmodernism"? How has the breakdown of the grand narratives of reason, science, and progress eroded Coubertin's ideals? What changes in technology and media, financing, participants, and scale mark the current Olympics as postmodern?

Exercise E. Take another film by David Lynch or Quentin Tarantino or a similarly postmodern director and consider the film in detail in relation to postmodernism. What stylistic, textual, content, and referential characteristics would lead critics to call this work postmodern?

Exercise F. The consumer culture of late capitalism is closely associated with postmodernism. What characteristics of consumer culture cause this connection? How has the commercial, consumer, and commodity emphasis of that culture, especially through television, affected MTV, cult movies, and the Olympics?

Exercise G. How has an awareness of multiculturalism—of racial, gender, national, linguistic, and other differences—played a role in making postmodernism seem relativistic rather than absolutist? How does postmodernism fit into the culture wars today? Is it politically correct?

Exercise H. What problems are present in the so-called postmodern project? How might postmodernism develop more than a description of present conditions and problems? Are there better analyses of current culture than postmodernism?

9

Conclusions:
Navajos and "Co-Authoring" Media Culture

Navajos gather at the drive-in movie in Gallup, New Mexico. The annual screening of *Cheyenne Autumn* gives them a chance to laugh, hoot, and honk horns at a film that appears serious but is hilarious to them. At this event the Navajos present are co-authoring their experience of media culture.
Tony Hillerman captures this in his novel *Sacred Clowns.*

What does exploring media culture mean? Have we yet solved the mystery of media culture set out in the beginning of this book? Have we put the clues together, assessed the various suspects, and resolved it all? Of course, as is apparent by now, the answer to our original question is not a simple one. The mystery's resolution is similar to the surprise ending of Agatha Christie's 1930s classic *Murder on the Orient Express,* which was made into a film in 1974. In that novel and film, as the Orient Express train steams across Europe, detective Hercule Poirot has a train car full of suspects for a murder that has taken place on the train. Each suspect had motive and means, but which one did it? As he attempts to eliminate suspects and hone in on the one culprit, Poirot discovers that all of the suspects are guilty. They all ritually joined together and stabbed the victim, a most unusual variation on the usual plot conventions of the mystery genre.

In a similar manner, it is the collective value of all of the methods of analysis introduced in these chapters that enables us to understand and take charge of our media culture. Each method contributes to the solution but does not work best alone. Any one tool or method of analysis—reception, text, ritual, hegemonic, gender, and others—may in itself create marvelous insight into a product and experience of media culture. But only by employing a combination of such tools can we begin to explore completely the range of meaning and effects in any one media experience and in the totality of media culture.

Triangulation through many methods working together from different vantage points enables us to generate a fully rounded appreciation and critique of our experiences with media culture. *Triangulation* locates an unknown point, as in navigation, by forming a triangle and calculating from the two known vertices the third unknown vertex. In much the same way, triangulation in media analysis starts from several starting points, rather than only one, to work toward explaining yet unknown aspects of the media experience. Triangulation shines a flashlight into the nooks and crannies of how media work and how culture is expressed. In that light, any meaning can be uncovered and our potential control over our own media culture is maximized.

Co-Authorship of Media Culture

To emphasize the responsibility that both producer and consumer of media culture share, the label co-authorship is proposed here. The idea of proposing a practice of media co-authorship is to draw on the best of media scholarship and to reintegrate media theory and practice.

Co-authorship connects everyday media users with our best critical thinkers. On one side, the renewed sense of an active audience and complex reception strategies gives us reason to stress the active responsibility of the media user. Audience research today supports this, as shown in the work of Morley, Gray, Jenkins, Lull, Fiske, Kaplan, Katz, and others. On the other side, the reality of production hegemony and unequally distributed power and resources make it necessary to stress the responsibility of the creators of media products—artists and corporations—for the meaning and consequences of what they produce. Research on hegemony and production supports this, as shown in the work of Schiller, Garnham, Smythe, Murdock, Curran, Gruneau, Bagdikian, and others concerned with the political economy of media. Co-authorship attempts to summarize the combination. Many researchers examine the media outcome as resulting from the blend of active viewers and powerful industries that we know as media culture. The preceding authors and Hall, Carey, Grossberg, Slack, Downey, Creedon, Jhally, Wenner, Berger, McRobbie, and many others found in the reference list for this book are inspiring examples, each in her or his own way, of researchers engaging in the arduous yet stimulating endeavor of making sense of media culture.

Co-authorship in media culture takes two forms: the "creator co-author" and the "consumer co-author." One initiates the process of generating meaning and the other concludes it.

We are, each of us, a "consumer co-author" of our media experience. We select what media we use, what products from those media we view, hear, or read, how much attention to give each, and what kind of credibility to place in the experience. As a co-author, we have genuine responsibility for the shape of the culture we expose ourselves to.

At the same time, we are only a *co*-author. The other author, the "creator co-author," in the form of media industries that provide us the menu we select from, has also a direct influence on the culture we experience. Creator co-authors may not distribute cultural products of refreshing variety and high quality. Or, more commonly, they may collectively submerge quality products within the huge and heavily promoted mainstream of mediocrity. Creator co-authors may be more interested in making income from me than enlightening me or challenging me. But, whatever the shortcomings, I take from the creator co-authors and shape my own experience of media culture.

The responsibilities of media creators are many, but they are co-authors, not sole authors. Media creators work with the material of the world around us, and that material includes violence, sexuality, and hatred in addition to the more benign aspects of human life. As John Henry Newman observed in the last century, we shall not have a sinless literature until we have a sinless race. The mere presentation of violence, for example, is not irresponsible; it is, in fact, necessary to the larger whole. But it must be presented with an awareness of the co-authors receiving it. Sanitized violence, without consequences and made aesthetically pleasing, is safely offered only to those who can recognize it as that, preferably with cues in the text to remind us that it is sanitized and unrealistic. Likewise, graphic, ugly, gory violence has a place, but for a co-authoring audience capable of processing and managing the message in that form and with that effect. Ratings systems and reviews mediate between producers and consumers, with law and the courts available when these normal sources fail. But responsibility falls first and foremost on the actual co-authors of media culture, both producers and consumers.

Co-authors need to be aware of each other. Creator co-authors must be sensitive to user co-authors and vice versa. Works created for mature, art-house co-authors may become dangerous when other co-authors are invited to participate, in the person of the very young or the emotionally damaged. Serious art deserves no censorship because its co-authors are prepared to contend with its meanings and consequences. Mass-marketed commercial products coming into the home do not warrant the same blanket license, ethically if not legally, because their consumer co-authors are not necessarily capable of receiving, processing, and managing everything at work in them.

Co-authorship lets no one off the hook. The television viewer can complain about programming but cannot finally blame all life's frustrations on it. The glib television executive can note the power of ratings and demographics but cannot pretend to have no choices in or influence over the process. In an age in which blaming others threatens to become a way of life, co-authorship provides balance. We can criticize our co-authors but that does not remove us from the responsibility of co-authorship and the risk of being subjected to criticism as well. There may be exploitive structures and immense manipulation at work, but our ability to read against the grain can never be eliminated. Even under the least encouraging of circumstances, we have at our disposal the "reactive pleasure" that Mary Ellen Brown (1994) finds so compelling in women's co-authorship of soap operas.

Navajo Co-Authorship of *Cheyenne Autumn*

In Tony Hillerman's novel *Sacred Clowns* (1993), Navajo tribal detective Jim Chee is investigating the suspected murder of a Navajo attending a ritual at the Tano Pueblo. As a break from his investigation, he takes a woman he is interested in and a Navajo city-bred colleague to the drive-in movie theater in Gallup, New Mexico, to see *Cheyenne Autumn*. Each year the drive-in plays the 1964 John Ford western *Cheyenne Autumn* (Smith & Ford, 1964) because it is a hit with Navajo audiences. The movie depicts the somewhat shapeless story of Cheyenne Indians struggling back on foot from a new reservation 1,500 miles away, where the government had forced them to relocate. This was director John Ford's last western and his last film shot in Monument Valley on the Arizona-Utah border, a land known as "John Ford country." It had been the site of many of his films, including the flawless classic *Stagecoach* (1939). *Cheyenne Autumn*'s big-name cast features Richard Widmark as a U.S. cavalry officer who deals with the Indians.

Because Monument Valley is legally within Navajo lands, Ford cast Navajos to play the Cheyennes, a fact undetectable to most, but not to Navajos. The "Cheyennes" in the film speak Navajo, dress like Navajos, conduct Navajo ceremonies, are in Navajo country, and are Navajos, but the Hollywood dream factory was undeterred by the equivalent of having Italians play Germans. This casting inaccuracy indicates the traditionally marginalized and stereotyped role that the "Other," Native Americans in this case, plays in Hollywood mythology. The traditional western, largely shaped by Ford himself in *My Darling Clementine* (1946), *Fort Apache* (1948), *She Wore a Yellow Ribbon* (1949), *Rio Grande* (1950), *The Searchers* (1956), *The Man Who Shot Liberty Valance* (1962), and others, treats Indians as an unproblematic plot device in the same class as the shark in *Jaws* or the terrorist in *Speed*. Indians attack settlers, ride horses, and shoot arrows. Sympathetic portrayals by Hollywood had already gone beyond this stereotype at times by mid-century, but in those portrayals the Indians were usually portrayed by white actors, for example, when Jeff Chandler played Cochise in *Broken Arrow* (1950) and *The Battle at Apache Pass* (1952).

Culture, Media, Identity. The issues of culture, media, and identity raised in Chapter 1 are prominent here. Native American culture and identity have been systematically eliminated and excluded in real history and in film. Their actual identity has not been positively secured within the public culture of media for the benefit of either Native Americans or the larger population. Because the public media culture so thoroughly marginalizes them, Native Americans are forced to rely on their own resources to read the culture against the grain. In the way that cultural studies attempts to "historicize" and "contextualize" a case, *Cheyenne Autumn* has its fullest resonance when it is understood within the long tradition of American and Hollywood mistreatment of Native Americans. The Navajo viewing of *Cheyenne Autumn* illustrates how identity interacts with media in our cultural experiences.

Reception Analysis. In receiving the film text, the Navajos watching at the Gallup drive-in manage to "appropriate the text" for their own purposes, recalling the reception studies explored in Chapter 3. Hillerman (1993) provides a striking ethnographic account of this oppositional reading by the Navajos.

Cheyenne Autumn is clearly intended by its makers to be taken as pro-Indian. The Widmark character, the narrator and hero of the text, sympathizes with the would-be Cheyennes and complains about the bureaucratic delegation from Washington. At one point Widmark makes derogatory remarks about the reservation that was forced on the Cheyennes and points at the landscape. Hillerman notes, "since the landscape at which Widmark was pointing was actually the long line of salmon-colored cliffs behind the Iyanbito Chapter House just south of Gallup, this produced more horn honking and a derisive shout from somewhere" (p. 121). The Navajo viewers not only agreed with the judgment being made against government treatment of Cheyennes, they derisively extended it to their own experience.

In the film, Cheyenne leaders speak somberly in Navajo. The film translation indicates that they are speaking of treaties and their people's needs. But the words produce happy bedlam among the Navajos at the drive-in. What the Navajo actors in the film really said in solemn tones generally concerned the size of the colonel's penis or some similarly humorous, disrespectful, and earthy reference. This is oppositional semiotics planted by the actors and read appreciatively by the Gallup-area Navajos. In Janet Staiger's (1992) schema, this is a full context-activated reading of the film that brings in rich history and linguistic detail and goes beyond a merely text-activated or narrowly reader-activated reading. The raucous reception of the text by the Navajos draws on language, geography, history, and a sense of irony to find reactive pleasure in the Hollywood text.

Textual Analysis. Textual analysis from Chapter 4 sheds light on what is contained in the text of the film *Cheyenne Autumn* and in the text of the Navajo viewing described in the novel *Sacred Clowns.*

What the narrative text of the film is actually saying is consistent with revisionist historical accounts that sympathize with Indians over the Hollywood version of "redskin savagery." That is, the film is John Ford's rebuttal to charges that the great western filmmaker exploited his Indian characters and actors. Ford, who was born Sean O'Feeney, was too much the Irish rebel to remain entirely unsympathetic to the Indians he filmed so often. In the film we find Edward G. Robinson playing a sympathetic secretary of the interior who makes reference to the Civil War's important achievement in freeing Negroes from slavery and compares blacks' needs to the needs of Indians. At the time the film was made, in 1964, the African-American civil rights movement was receiving great attention in the United States and undoubtedly influenced the film's text. In effect, in *Cheyenne Autumn* Ford celebrates the autumn of his film career by making the Indians the victims, although he reserves the hero role, perhaps for box office reasons, to Richard Widmark.

If we examine the characters in the film text, we notice that the *Cheyenne Autumn* Indians are stoic, long-suffering, and betrayed. Their leaders are played by non-Native Americans Gilbert Roland and Ricardo Montalban, with Sal Mineo as a young buck. In the end the Indian cause is victorious, but the woodenness of the portrayals leaves the Indians without heroes. The text of the film was greeted without enthusiasm by reviewers. Stanley Kauffmann went so far as to say, "the acting is bad, the dialogue trite and predictable, the pace funereal, the structure fragmented and the climaxes puny" (Halliwell, 1989, p. 193).

However, the text of Hillerman's account of the drive-in viewing offers a reading of the film that goes well beyond Ford's intent. In Hillerman's text, the Navajos break out of the victim role and become insurgent sociologists. They appreciate the genre and conventions of *Cheyenne Autumn* more clearly than most viewers. How could a Native American not? But their actions in Hillerman's text become subversive, referring to present injustices against the Navajo. The Navajos at the drive-in recognize scenes of their own suffering and not merely of the U.S. oppression of Cheyennes.

In the narrative text of the novel, detective Jim Chee wants to watch the film alone with attorney Janet Peete, but Sergeant Harold Blizzard has come along as well. Blizzard is a city-bred Cheyenne who works for the Bureau of Indian Affairs and knows little of the reservation-bred Navajo resistant reading of the culture. Hillerman's text describes the Navajo reactions to *Cheyenne Autumn* but Chee also explains to Janet and Blizzard the background and reasons for the Navajo reception of the movie. In this, Hillerman's account recalls Geertz's famous account (1973) of the cockfight in Bali, even to the point of having a local informant interpreting for visitors.

Ritual Participation. In Hillerman's novelized ethnography, attending the drive-in theater in Gallup, in Navajo pick-ups and cars, becomes a ritual activity of the type explored in Chapter 2. The viewing is a collective experience expressed externally with stylized activities. The Navajo drive-in participants have done this before. Seeing it for the first time, Janet compares it to *The Rocky Horror Picture Show* as a campy ritual event. Chee had hoped Blizzard would not be along so that he and Janet could participate in drive-in movie rituals that go beyond watching the film and talking. Yet he was fully aware that

> talking about the movie during the movie—celebrating the small victory of The People over the white man that this John Ford classic represented—was the reason Navajos still came to see it, and the reason the owner of the Gallup Drive-In still brought it back. (Hillerman, 1993, pp. 119-120)

What better way to celebrate a resistant reading than ritually through horn honking, laughter, shouting, and story telling at a large social center with sympathetic fellow tribal members? The Navajo viewing confirms a particular reading of the text within the "interpretive community" of other Navajos. The ritual participation expresses and confirms their community solidarity and their sense of what being Navajo means. The Navajos are not individually and silently "reading this text against the grain." They are collectively and exuberantly celebrating their shared reading in a set of public, ritualized, and emotionally satisfying acts. Like sports fans, video game players, and aerobics participants they are externalizing and expressing their relationship with the text and its meaning for them.

Production/Hegemony. The historical context and industrial structure of Hollywood, explored in Chapter 5, determined in advance many of the qualities of *Cheyenne Autumn.* The movie would aim for good box office returns; it would be a picturesque narrative with popular romance and action; it would feature popular stars playing sympathetic characters with whom an audience would identify; it would not stray too far from Hollywood conventions or mass audience expectations.

As a result, despite the progressive intentions of the film and the apparent delight of the Navajos in their counterreading, *Cheyenne Autumn* exhibits only an "outsider's" sense of what it means to be Native American. The control of the means of production by John Ford and the Hollywood system was quite removed from Navajo culture and power. The film as a whole comes from an alien culture, the white patriarchal culture of media ownership. This does not imply the presence of a conspiracy, only of a structured, institutionalized concentration of power. Hollywood's industrial values are generally incorporated into the ideological mindset of the filmmakers. Thus, the limitations of Ford's well-intentioned portrayal of Indians illustrate how completely Ford himself was a representative of the Hollywood system of his time. He had shot 30 films before he turned 25, most of them westerns starring Harry Carey. He had made many of the great films of Hollywood's golden era—*The Informer* (1935), *The Grapes of Wrath* (1940), *How Green Was My Valley* (1941)—and eventually produced a unique corpus of strong films in a variety of genres. Yet his final pro-Indian film turned out be one Native Americans could only mock.

The goal of incorporating carefully authentic Native American language, customs, and identity was another generation away for Hollywood. Kevin Costner's *Dances With Wolves* (1990) is in many ways the film Ford seemed to have intended. But Costner went much further by accurately portraying the Dakota Sioux culture, language, and lifestyle (and also went much further by revitalizing the narrative, picking up a Best Picture Oscar that *Cheyenne Autumn* did not come close to winning). Between 1964 and 1990, Native Americans forced Hollywood and the general public to better appreciate how different their lives and national experience had been from the American mainstream. A more sensitive, multicultural Hollywood was willing to try to see Native American experience from the inside, as long as it still made money.

In *Cheyenne Autumn,* the general appearance of Indian culture was adequate for Ford at the time, and the Indian stereotype had served the industry well for decades. As part of Hollywood's hegemony over production and viewer expectations, audiences around the world had long been conditioned to accept Native Americans as savages and enemies, with only a few noteworthy exceptions. *Cheyenne Autumn,* for all its liberal intentions, represented the viewpoint of outsiders sympathetic to Indian suffering and not the Indian experience itself. The Navajos' mocking reaction to the film indicates something of the distance between the dominant ideology conveyed in the hegemonic production of the film and true oppositional culture.

Gender Analysis. Gender analysis, explored in Chapter 6, encourages us to see *Cheyenne Autumn* in terms of the male gaze and of representations of men and women. The Ford film, like most westerns, is a male world of horses and guns and force. The largest female role in *Cheyenne Autumn* is that of a Quaker woman, played by blonde Carroll Baker, who teaches the Indian children and provides a love interest for Richard Widmark. She is strong and independent for her time but also traditional and deferential to males. Her large dresses, form-fitted around her upper body for Hollywood sex appeal, are impractical and make her stand out as a contrast to the buckskin and uniforms of the men. The Cheyenne women are somber, quiet, and busy but remain largely in the background of the film. The male gaze and address are apparent throughout. A particularly absurd and unrelated 20-minute segment especially illustrates this. The segment was eliminated from some prints but was reinserted in the home video version. In it, James Stewart plays a humorously low-key Wyatt Earp presiding over a Dodge City eager to attack the Indians but caught up in dance hall girls, booze, and gambling. The sequence ends with the lead dancer losing her dress and riding off upside down in Stewart's buggy, completing a regression to sexual stereotypes common to westerns and much of Hollywood.

Once again the Navajo drive-in viewing of *Cheyenne Autumn* adds depth. Jim Chee explains that his oldest sister plays one of three Cheyenne shamans shown solemnly praying that the U.S. government would keep its treaty promises. The naiveté of the prayers drew "derisive hoots and horn honkings from the rows of pickup trucks and cars" (Hillerman, 1993, p. 120). Chee further explains that the song they are chanting and accompanying with drums is not Cheyenne. The song was a modification from Navajo Girl Dances, slowed down for solemnity. The Navajos viewing the female Native Americans see through the cardboard representations and, in so doing, largely destroy their potential fetishistic negations of womankind.

Historical/Ethical Interpretation. In addition to entertaining its audience, *Cheyenne Autumn* apparently has historical and ethical goals, the subject of Chapter 7. The film admirably sets out to portray the tragic treks and fatal exclusions of Native Americans that Hollywood had spent so many years not only ignoring but contradicting by painting Indians as villains. The film reminds white audiences of white complicity in a program of genocide against Native Americans. Widmark's commander, who is killed early on, and Widmark's subordinate both carry grudges against the Indians, one passively and the other actively. These characters are made unsympathetic by Ford. The Quaker woman and Widmark's character express care and support for the suffering Cheyennes. They are made sympathetic. The moral of the story is clear: Native Americans have been treated unfairly and deserve better. This is the ethical and historical thrust of the narrative.

But the burden of correcting a negative audiovisual past is far more than this film can manage. The visual media, as Robert A. Rosenstone (1995) reminds us, provide a legitimate way of depicting history and must be seen not in terms of how they compare to written history, but in terms of how they recount the past with their own rules of representation. Television documentary mini-series in the past decade have gone back to original sources—letters, photos, contemporary accounts—to seek the true experience of the frontier in the Western United States of the nineteenth century. But the classic Hollywood westerns may always dominate American and global visions of Native Americans.

As Rosenstone notes, visual media add "vision" to our sense of history, whereas print sources provide "data." Ford's better films were less historically accurate and less sympathetic to Native Americans than *Cheyenne Autumn,* but they generated far more mythic power. More recent treatments of Native Americans in westerns may be progressive, but the cumulative vision of Indians in film remains overwhelmingly regressive. The way history is "revisioned" in film "itself privileges some things, hides others, and conceals as much as it reveals about the past" (Rosenstone, 1995, p. 8).

> Ideas contested on the screen may be narrow or broad, of importance to a minority group in a single community or to a large number of peoples or nations. They may involve a segment of a population or all of it, be part of the discourse of the scholarly establishment or belong to the common consciousness as reflected in the press and the visual media. They may even encompass the unspoken assumptions upon which rests an entire culture or civilization. (pp. 8-9)

The Navajos watching the film in Gallup are aware of the relation of the film to culture and unspoken assumptions. Late in the storyline of *Sacred Clowns,* one of Tony Hillerman's characters refers back to watching the drive-in movie in Gallup. The detectives are stymied in their attempt to solve the crime that took place in the Tano Pueblo community of Navajos. Sergeant Blizzard remarks,

You know, I think maybe all three of us are in the same boat I was in at that
Cheyenne Autumn movie the other night. I couldn't understand why all the
Navajos were hooting and blowing their car horns. Different culture. Different
perceptions. There's probably some Tano Pueblo connection here we just don't
fathom. . . . Different value systems, you know. Hard for us outsiders to
comprehend. (Hillerman, 1993, p. 263)

That humble awareness of difference coincides with effective historical and
ethical interpretation of media culture. The Hillerman novel points up the
positive side of media's use of history and ethics as it gives the reader access
to Navajo life at a level seldom approached by Hollywood.

Postmodern Aesthetics. The ironic reversal of *Cheyenne Autumn* as it is
portrayed in *Sacred Clowns* gives the novel a sophisticated level of postmodern intertextuality. The appropriation of one text or period or style within
another creates the characteristic postmodern pastiche, as we saw in Chapter 8. Hillerman's novels, with their blend of traditional Navajo ways and
contemporary conditions and crimes, contain a subtle postmodernism. Multicultural borrowing and blending are common in postmodernism, and it is
the Native Americans in *Sacred Clowns* who conduct the postmodern intertextual reworking of the *Cheyenne Autumn* text.

In addition, the very ease today with which we grab a copy of the Warner
Home Video of *Cheyenne Autumn* or catch the film on late-night television,
and likewise the ease with which we pick up the mass paperback of *Sacred
Clowns* and then interrelate the two, brings us further into that postmodern
sense of arbitrary juxtapositions, surface associations, replications, and lack
of traditional separations. These would-be Cheyenne and Navajo texts get
jumbled together with others as the commercial system promotes them and
the technological systems relay them. We are increasingly practiced at
dealing with this collective pastiche of media products and practices, but it
is a challenge to work through *Cheyenne Autumn* and *Sacred Clowns* without
an experience of postmodern fragmentation and irony. Today our conditioned
and predominantly unconscious practice at recombining genres, making
intertextual connections, reading against the grain, constructing our own
universe of meaning, and other co-authoring tricks make the most straight-
forward of novels or films into postmodern experiences. These co-authoring
skills also allow us to find our own unique way through the most postmodern
of hypertexts.

Combining the Methods: Constructing the Self. Navajos co-author *Cheyenne Autumn* in a way that contributes positively to their development of
personal and cultural identity. In Hillerman's account, Navajos take the text,
restore what can be salvaged, extend its effect through ritual participation,
and reenvision it within a more realistic and empowering history. In this one
case, they turn culture, consciousness, and history to their advantage.

An additional key to exploring media culture is to combine explicitly the multiple methods of analysis presented here so that each method interacts with the others. Each method has its full value only when related to other methods. The text of *Cheyenne Autumn* has planted in its dialogue, setting, and total sign system Navajo points of reference that trigger the specific Navajo reception and ritual participation. Textual analysis connects with reception study and ritual theory to fully explore these implications. In addition, the Hollywood production system and its hegemonic tendencies connect with the gendered and historicized nature of the text and through it with the preferred readings and the Navajos' oppositional reading. The Navajo readings in turn explain a certain looseness or lack of closure in the text of the film and the production industry behind it. Thus, production/hegemony connects with gender analysis and historical/ethical interpretation.

In the end, despite our ability to take apart separate aspects of media culture—production, text, reception, ritual, hegemony, gender, history—the media product or practice works as a single, unified experience. The product or practice contains within itself all these elements but as one whole that we experience as a unity. As we consider each separate element for analysis, those elements will suggest relations to other elements as central components for the generation of meaning. With each case study we emphasized one specific method or element, but our use of each element also related it to the others.

Recall how each previous chapter worked. Popular music suggests the relationship of media, culture, and identity, but it does so as a gendered, historically situated production of texts that initiate reception and ritual participation within a postmodern condition. Sports fans, aerobic participants, and video game players all ritually participate in media culture, but their rituals are interpretations of produced texts with issues of gender, ethnicity, history, and ethics embedded in them. A textual analysis of Disney and film noir finds those narrative texts reflecting the industries that produce them and the audiences that receive them, generating meaning in interaction with both. Hollywood's hegemonic domination of European and other audiovisual markets connects to particular kinds of texts, reception, rituals, gender, and history with ethical and postmodern implications. Gender analysis of *The Piano* works with regard to its production, text, reception, ritual use, and history, all of which contribute to gender's importance and influence. The television quiz show scandal has historical/ethical meaning because it involves rituals, receivers, texts, and production systems that contribute to meaning in media culture. Music videos, the films of David Lynch and Quentin Tarantino, and the modern Olympic games highlight the postmodern condition in media culture, but they do so specifically with regard to their production, textual, reception, ritualistic, gendered, historical, and ethical qualities. Navajo viewing of *Cheyenne Autumn* illustrates how we co-author the self in media culture so that production, text, reception, ritual, gender, and history work together to form the particular Navajo meaning generated from the experience.

Exploring media culture along all its multiple pathways entails working with particular aspects but always in relation to the larger whole. We are always asking subconsciously: What does this experience of media culture mean to me? But we can also ask explicitly: What can this experience of media culture mean in its totality? Asking the latter question gives us increased comprehension and control of media products and practices. The question shifts control away from producers dictating meanings to users who generate not only preferred meanings but others more useful to them. In short, a critical understanding of media culture and its meaning is empowering.

The broadest questions we can ask today are not unrelated to the media culture that surrounds us. How do humans find happiness? What makes society possible? How can families and communities thrive? What is the value of art or science? Why do we die? What is the meaning of life? How do we relieve suffering? How do we increase our joy and satisfaction? Co-authorship suggests that we cope with those questions in interaction with our media culture.

Co-authorship means that media culture shapes much of the way we frame the questions and also answer them, but we still bring our own unique identity, consciousness, and choice to bear in our struggle with these challenges.

The more we understand media culture—through tools suggested here or elsewhere—and the more we turn media culture to the benefit of ourselves and others, the more control we gain over our lives. Self-determination and democracy are not givens but goals that can be fostered or inhibited by the media culture as it is presently structured. Co-authorship can be frustrating when one really wants to be the sole author, but only hermits actually pursue that option. On the other hand, co-authorship can be exhilarating when one has a strong sense of purpose and a good co-author. We can then hold up for admiration the cultural products that we have co-authored, such as the Navajo reading of *Cheyenne Autumn,* but the long-term reward is the self that is constructed in the process. In brief, the well-guided exploration of media culture has an abundance of rewards.

The Great Whatsit

We ended the first chapter with an unfinished quotation from Paul Schrader about his film noir favorite, what he calls its masterpiece. But we left the resolution of that mystery hanging. Recall that in *Kiss Me Deadly,* Mike Hammer is a small-time investigator, a pulp fiction private eye.

Hammer's case is to find the "great whatsit." In a seedy and sleazy noir environment, Hammer is a midget among dwarfs. Beautiful blondes, U.S. senators, Mr. Big—everybody is after the prize, whatever it may turn out to be. After murders and beatings and seductions galore, what was it Mike Hammer finally found, in the 1953 novel and the 1955 film, that drove such extreme behaviors? Spillane's story takes the whatsit a step beyond the famous Maltese Falcon, that fabled piece of invaluable stone sculpture smuggled down through the centuries and finally into the hands of Sam Spade. Here, in the words of Paul Schrader:

> Hammer overturns the underworld in search of the "great whatsit," and when he finally finds it, it turns out to be—joke of jokes—an exploding atomic bomb. The inhumanity and meaninglessness of the hero are small matters in a world in which The Bomb has the final say. (Schrader, 1972, p. 13):

The "great whatsit" turns out to be nothing less than a volatile, hair-trigger nuclear explosive device. The cataclysmic device, the size of a couple of shoe boxes or "two lunch pails" and covered with hard green metal, combines noir fiction with popular science and our ultimate weaponry, bringing us face-to-face with humanity's ability to destroy itself and its planet.

Media culture is much like the "great whatsit." Important and elusive, powerful beyond imagination, awe-inspiring in its genius, fearsome if abused, media culture is something of a nuclear explosive device in its collective force. By co-authoring our part of it effectively, by using and going beyond the tools suggested in these pages, we may be able to discover and achieve our best future and our best selves. Hans Magnus Enzensberger (1970) called for emancipatory media structures and practices that put power in the hands of the people, that mobilize the masses, that empower and make us "as free as dancers, as aware as football players, as surprising as guerrillas" (p. 27). That is a media culture, and life, worth living.

EXERCISES

Chapter 9

Exercise A. CO-AUTHORSHIP. What does co-authorship of our media experiences mean? Explain how the media creator co-author and the consumer-user co-author share power and responsibility in media culture. How does the term *co-author* suggest that we create our own media culture but from materials not of our own making? Does another term work better for you than *co-author* for indicating our active roles?

Exercise B. CASE STUDY. Select a specific product or practice of media culture, anything from the sexploitation of women in advertising to talk radio to pop music on the Internet. Make it a topic you have a personal interest in. The topic can be from an exercise in a previous chapter. Then investigate your particular product or practice using methods suggested throughout this book.

Look again at the general suggestions in "The Case-Study Method of 'Cultural Exegesis' " in Chapter 1 and at the methods presented in each chapter. Select a combination of these, drawing from analyses of ritual participation, reception, text, production/hegemony, gender, history/ethics, postmodernism, and co-authorship of the self. Your exploration should include an *ethnography* in the form of an exact, detailed record of your topic as it occurs in everyday life, an *exegesis* that delves into your topic's background and implications by searching related library and field data, and *criticism* that interprets and evaluates the meanings and practices generated by your case.

You may wish to present the results of your case examination in some media form—text, slides, video, audio, visual collage, live dramatization, original music, or another medium. This, and all your explorations of media culture, should bring you the critical understanding and enjoyment that come from successful co-authorship.

References

Abercrombie, Nicholas, Hill, Stephen, & Turner, Bryan S. (1980). *The dominant ideology thesis.* London: Allen and Unwin.

Accuracy in Media, Inc. (1993, February 23). Nationwide TV protest. *San Diego Union-Tribune,* p. D-8.

Adams, Emily. (1992, September 22). It's Super Mario to the rescue. *Los Angeles Times,* p. E1.

Adorno, Theodor. (1993). On popular music. In Anthony Easthope & Kate McGowan (Eds.), *A critical and cultural theory reader* (pp. 211-223). Toronto: University of Toronto Press. (Originally published in 1941.)

Agger, Ben. (1992). *Cultural studies as critical theory.* London: Falmer.

Allen, Robert C. (1992). Audience-oriented criticism and television. In Robert C. Allen (Ed.), *Channels of discourse, reassembled: Television and contemporary criticism* (pp. 101-137). Chapel Hill: University of North Carolina Press.

Altheide, David. (1976). *Creating reality: How TV news distorts events.* Newbury Park, CA: Sage.

Althusser, Louis. (1971). *Lenin and philosophy and other essays.* (Ben Brewster, Trans.). New York: Monthly Review.

Alvarado, Manuel, and Thompson, John O. (1990). *The media reader.* London: British Film Institute.

Anderson, Kent. (1978). *Television fraud: The history and implications of the quiz show scandals.* Westport, CN: Greenwood.

Ang, Ien. (1985). *Watching "Dallas": Soap opera and the melodramatic imagination.* (Della Couling, Trans.). London: Methuen.

Aronowitz, Stanley. (1994). *Dead artists, live theories and other cultural problems.* New York: Routledge.

Associated Press. (1994, June 1). U.S. has record number of inmates behind bars. *San Diego Union-Tribune,* p. A-2.

Aufderheide, Patricia. (1986). Music videos: The look of the sound. In Todd Gitlin (Ed.), *Watching television* (pp. 111-135). New York: Pantheon.

Auletta, Ken. (1994, September 19). The $64,000 question. *The New Yorker,* pp. 46-50, 55-56.

Balázs, Béla. (1952). *Theory of the film: Character and growth of a new art.* (Edith Bone, Trans.). London: Dobson.

Bale, John, & Maguire, Joseph. (Eds.). (1994). *The global sports arena: Athletic talent migration in an interdependent world.* London: Frank Cass.

Bandura, Albert. (1968). *Social learning.* Englewood Cliffs, NJ: Prentice Hall.

Bandura, Albert. (1973). *Aggression: A social learning analysis.* Englewood Cliffs, NJ: Prentice Hall.

Banks, Jack. (1995, May). *Does the world want its MTV?: A historical survey of MTV's quest to build a global audience.* Paper presented at annual conference of the International Communication Association, Albuquerque, NM.

Barnett, Steven. (1990). *Games and sets: The changing face of sport on television.* London: British Film Institute.

Barnouw, Eric. (1975). *Tube of plenty: The evolution of American television.* New York: Oxford University Press.

Barnouw, Eric. (1978). *The sponsor: Notes on a modern potentate.* New York: Oxford University Press.

Baron, Larry. (1990). Pornography and gender equality: An empirical analysis. *The Journal of Sex Research, 27*(3), 363-380.

Baron, Larry, & Strauss, M. A. (1984). Sexual stratification, pornography, and rape in the United States. In Neil Malamuth & Ed Donnerstein (Eds.), *Pornography and sexual aggression* (pp. 185-209). Orlando, FL: Academic.

Barthes, Roland. (1974). *S/Z.* (Richard Miller, Trans.). New York: Hill and Wang.

Barthes, Roland. (1975). *The pleasure of the text.* (Richard Miller, Trans.). New York: Hill and Wang.

Barthes, Roland. (1984). *Camera lucida: Reflections on photography.* London: Fontana Flamingo.

Basinger, Jeanine. (1993). *A woman's view: How Hollywood spoke to women, 1930-1960.* New York: Knopf.

Baudrillard, Jean. (1983). *Simulations.* New York: Semiotext(e).

Bauman, Zygmunt. (1988). Is there a postmodern sociology? *Theory, Culture & Society, 5,* 217-237.

Bauman, Zygmunt. (1992). *Intimations of postmodernity.* New York: Routledge.

Bazin, André. (1967). *What is cinema?* (Hugh Gray, Ed. and Trans.). Berkeley: University of California Press.

Benjamin, Walter. (1969). The work of art in the age of mechanical reproduction. *Illuminations* (pp. 219-253), (J. Zohn, Trans.). New York: Schocken.

Bennet, Tony, Mercer, Colin, & Woollacott, Janet. (Eds.). (1986). *Popular culture and social relations.* Milton Keynes, U.K.: Open University Press.

Bennett, H. Stith, & Ferrell, Jeff. (1987). Music videos and epistemic socialization. *Youth and Society 18*(4), 344-362.

Berelson, Bernard. (1949). What "missing the newspaper" means. In Paul Lazarsfeld & Frank Stanton (Eds.), *Communication research 1948-1949* (pp. 111-129). New York: Harper and Bros.

Berelson, Bernard. (1952). *Content analysis in communication research.* New York: Free Press.

Berger, Arthur Asa. (1992). *Popular culture genres: Theories and texts.* Newbury Park, CA: Sage.

Bernstein, Richard. (1994, September 4). For $64,000 what is "fiction"? *New York Times,* Section 2, pp. 1, 20-21.

Bérubé, Michael. (1994). *Public access: Literary theory and American cultural politics.* London: Verso.

Best, Steven, & Kellner, Douglas. (1991). *Postmodern theory: Critical interrogations.* New York: Guilford.

Bielby, Denise, & Harrington, C. Lee. (1994). Reach out and touch someone: Viewers, agency, and audiences in the televisual experience. In Jon Cruz & Justin Lewis (Eds.), *Viewing, reading, listening* (p. 81-100). Boulder, CO: Westview.

Birrill, Susan, & Cole, Cheryl L. (Eds.). (1994). *Women, sport, and culture.* Champaign, IL: Human Kinetics.

Blue, Adrianne. (1988). *Faster, higher, further: Women's triumphs and disasters at the Olympics.* London: Virago.

Bordwell, David, & Thompson, Kristen. (1993). *Film art: An introduction.* (4th ed.). New York: McGraw-Hill.

Boston Women's Health Book Collective. (1971). *Our bodies, ourselves.* New York: Simon & Schuster.

Brandt, Richard, Gross, Neil, & Coy, Peter. (1994, February 21). Sega! It's blasting beyond games and racing to build a high-tech entertainment empire. *Business Week,* pp. 66-74.

Breed, Walter. (1952). Social control in the newsroom. In Wilbur Schramm (Ed.), *Mass communication* (pp. 178-194). Urbana: University of Illinois Press.

Brooks, Peter. (1984). *Reading for the plot: Design and invention in narrative.* Cambridge, MA: Harvard University Press.

Brown, Mary Ellen. (1994). *Soap opera and women's talk: The pleasure of resistance.* Thousand Oaks, CA: Sage.

Brunsdon, Charlotte. (1981). "Crossroads": Notes on soap opera. *Screen, 22*(4), 32-37.

Bruzzi, Stella. (1993). Jane Campion: Costume drama and reclaiming women's past. In Pam Cook & Philip Dodd (Eds.), *Women and film: A sight and sound reader* (pp. 232-242). Philadelphia: Temple University Press.

Bryson, Lois. (1994). Sport and the maintenance of masculine hegemony. In Susan Birrill & Cheryl L. Cole (Eds.), *Women, sport, and culture* (pp. 47-64). Champaign, IL: Human Kinetics.

Burton-Carvajal, Julianne. (1994). "Surprise package": Looking southward with Disney. In Eric Smoodin (Ed.), *Disney discourse: Producing the magic kingdom* (pp. 131-147). New York: Routledge.

Buscombe, Edward. (Ed.). (1975). *Football on television.* London: British Film Institute.

Can we learn from the media? (1994, March 8). *National Enquirer,* p. 3.

Cantelon, Hart, & Harvey, Jean. (Eds.). (1987). *The sociology of sport.* Ottawa: University of Ottawa.

Cantril, Hadley. (1940). *The invasion from Mars: A study in the psychology of panic. With the complete script of the famous Orson Welles broadcast.* (With the assistance of Hazel Gaudet & Herta Herzog.) Princeton: Princeton University Press.

Carey, James W. (1989). *Communication as culture: Essays on media and society.* Winchester, MA: Unwin Hyman.

Carson, Diane. (1994). Women filmmakers. In Diane Carson, Linda Dittmar, & Janice Welsch (Eds.), *Multiple voices in feminist film criticism* (pp. 456-467). Minneapolis: University of Minnesota Press.

Carson, Diane, Dittmar, Linda, & Welsch, Janice. (Eds.). (1994). *Multiple voices in feminist film criticism.* Minneapolis: University of Minnesota Press.

Cartwright, Lisa, & Fonoroff, Nina. (1994). Narrative is *narrative:* So what is new? In Diane Carson, Linda Dittmar, & Janice Welsch (Eds.), *Multiple voices in feminist film criticism* (pp. 124-139). Minneapolis: University of Minnesota Press.

Cartwright, Lisa, & Goldfarb, Brian. (1994). Cultural contagion: On Disney's health education films for Latin America. In Eric Smoodin (Ed.), *Disney discourse: Producing the magic kingdom* (pp. 169-180). New York: Routledge.

Cassirer, Ernst. (1958). *Philosophie die symbolischen formen.* Darmstadt: Wissenschaftliche Buchgesellschaft.

Castro, Janet. (1988, January). Women in television: An uphill battle. *Channels,* 43-52.

Cawelti, John G. (1971). *The six-gun mystique.* Bowling Green, OH: Bowling Green University Popular Press.

Chatman, Seymour. (1978). *Story and discourse: Narrative structure in fiction and film.* Ithaca, NY: Cornell University Press.

Christians, Clifford. (1989). A theory of normative technology. In Edmund F. Byren & Joseph C. Pitt (Eds.), *Technological transformations: Contextual and conceptual implications* (pp. 127-149). The Netherlands: Kluwer Academic.

Christians, Clifford, & Carey, James. (1981). The logic and aims of qualitative research. In Guido Stempel & Bruce Westley (Eds.), *Research methods in mass communication* (2nd ed.), (pp. 354-374). Englewood Cliffs, NJ: Prentice Hall.

Christian-Smith, Linda. (1990). *Becoming a woman through romance.* New York: London.

Christie, Agatha. (1933). *Murder on the Orient Express.* New York: Dodd, Mead.

Clark, VeVe A., Hodson, Millicent, & Neiman, Catrina. (1985). *The legend of Maya Deren: A documentary biography and collected work: Vol. 1.* New York: Anthology Film Archives/Film Culture.

Clover, Carol J. (1993). *Falling Down* and the rise of the average white male. In Pam Cook & Philip Dodd (Eds.), *Women and film: A sight and sound reader* (pp. 138-147). Philadelphia: Temple University Press.

Cole, Cheryl L. (1994). Resisting the canon: Feminist cultural studies, sport, and technologies of the body. In Susan Birrill & Cheryl L. Cole (Eds.), *Women, sport, and culture* (pp. 5-30). Champaign, IL: Human Kinetics.

Collins, Jim. (1995). *Architectures of excess: Cultural life in the information age.* New York: Routledge.

Comstock, George, Chafee, Steve, Katzman, Nathan, McCombs, Malcolm, & Roberts, Don. (1978). *Television and human behavior.* New York: Columbia University Press.

Condit, Celeste Michelle. (1991). The rhetorical limits of polysemy. In Robert K. Avery & David Eason (Eds.), *Critical perspectives on media and society* (pp. 365-386). New York: Guilford.

Congress of the United States. (1960). *Investigation of television quiz shows.* Hearings before a Subcommittee of the Committee on Interstate and Foreign Commerce, House of Representatives. Part 1, October 6, 7, 8, 9, 10, and 12; Part 2, November 2, 3, 4, 5, and 6. Washington: Government Printing Office.

Connell, Joan. (1995, June 23). Historic miss now modern-day myth: Real Pocahontas would never fit the wholesome Disney profile. *San Diego Union-Tribune,* p. E-5.

Cook, Pam, & Dodd, Philip. (Eds.). (1993). *Women and film: A sight and sound reader.* Philadelphia: Temple University Press.

Corliss, Richard. (1987). [Review of the film *Blue Velvet*]. *Film Review Annual* (p. 154). Englewood, NJ: J.S. Ozer. (Reprinted from *Time,* September 22, 1986, p. 86.)

Cosford, Bill. (1993, September 28). Hollywood struts around the world in its summer duds. *San Diego Union-Tribune,* p. E5.

Coubertin, Pierre de. (1967). *The Olympic idea: Discourses and essays.* (John G. Dixon, Trans. & Carl-Diem-Institute, Ed.). Stuttgart: Verlag Karl Hoffman.

Council on Competitiveness. (1993). *Vision for a 21st century information infrastructure.* Washington, DC: Author.

Cowan, Geoffrey. (1990, May). *What is degrading in pornography? Through women's eyes.* Paper presented at the annual meeting of the Western Psychological Association, Los Angeles.

Cramer, Judith A. (1994). Conversations with sports journalists. In Pamela J. Creedon (Ed.), *Women, media and sport: Challenging gender values* (pp. 159-180). Thousand Oaks, CA: Sage.

Creedon, Pamela J. (1994a). From the feminine mystique to the female physique: Uncovering the archetype of Artemis in sport. In Pamela J. Creedon (Ed.), *Women, media and sport: Challenging gender values* (pp. 275-299). Thousand Oaks, CA: Sage.

Creedon, Pamela J. (1994b). Women, media and sport: Creating and reflecting gender values. In Pamela J. Creedon (Ed.), *Women, media and sport: Challenging gender values* (pp. 3-27). Thousand Oaks, CA: Sage.

Creedon, Pamela J. (Ed.). (1994c). *Women, media and sport: Challenging gender values.* Thousand Oaks, CA: Sage.

Cruz, Jon, & Lewis, Justin. (Eds.). (1994). *Viewing, reading, listening: Audiences and culture reception.* Boulder, CO: Westview.

Cunliffe, Simon. (1987). [Review of film *Blue Velvet*]. *Film Review Annual* (pp. 148-150). Englewood, NJ: J.S. Ozer. (Reprinted from *New Statesman*, April 10, 1987, p. 23.)

Curran, James, & Seaton, J. (1981). *Power without responsibility: The press and broadcasting in Britain.* Glasgow: Fontana.

Curry, Ramona. (1990). Madonna from Marilyn to Marlen—pastiche and/or parody? *Journal of Film and Video, 42*(2), 15-30.

Cushman, Thomas. (1995). *Notes from underground: Rock music counterculture in Russia.* Albany: State University of New York Press.

Dayan, Daniel, & Katz, Elihu. (1992). *Media events: The live broadcasting of history.* Cambridge: Harvard University Press.

Debord, Guy. (1970). *Society of the spectacle.* Detroit: Black and Red.

de Certeau, Michel. (1984). *The practice of everyday life.* Berkeley: University of California Press.

deCordova, Richard. (1994). The Mickey in Macy's window: Childhood, consumerism, and Disney animation. In Eric Smoodin (Ed.), *Disney discourse: Producing the magic kingdom* (pp. 203-213). New York: Routledge.

DeCurtis, Anthony. (1994, October 6). Robert Redford: The Rolling Stone interview. *Rolling Stone*, pp. 73-77, 98.

Deleuze, Gilles, & Guattari, Felix. (1983). *Anti-Oedipus.* Minneapolis: University of Minnesota Press.

Deleuze, Gilles, & Guattari, Felix. (1986). *Kafka.* Minneapolis: University of Minnesota Press.

Deleuze, Gilles, & Guattari, Felix. (1987). *A thousand plateaus.* Minneapolis: University of Minnesota Press.

Denisoff, R. Serge. (1988). *Inside MTV.* New Brunswick, NJ: Transaction Books.

Denzin, Norman K. (1991). *Images of postmodern society: Social theory and contemporary cinema.* Newbury Park, CA: Sage.

Derrida, Jacques. (1976). *Of grammatology.* (Gayatri Chakravorty Spivak, Trans.). Baltimore, MD: Johns Hopkins University Press.

Dolbee, Sandi. (1994, February 18). Mortal ethics: Violent game's sequel offers new friendship but opponents aren't impressed. *San Diego Union-Tribune*, pp. E1, E4.

Donnerstein, Edward I., Donnerstein, Marcia V., & Evans, Robert. (1975). Erotic stimuli and aggression: Facilitation or inhibition. *Journal of Personality and Social Psychology, 32*, 237-244.

Dorfman, Ariel, & Mattelart, Armand. (1975). *How to read Donald Duck.* New York: International General.

Downing, Christine. (1988). *The goddess: Mythological images of the feminine.* New York: Crossroad.

Duffy, Mary, & Rhodes, Maura. (1993, December). Aerobics gets real. *Women's Health and Fitness*, 17-18.

Durgnat, Raymond. (1970). Paint it black: The family tree of film noir. *Cinema 6/7*, 49-56.

During, Simon. (Ed.). (1993). *The cultural studies reader.* New York: Routledge.

Dyer, Richard, Geraghty, Christine, Jordan, Marion, Lovell, Terry, Paterson, Richard & Steward, John. (1981). *Coronation Street.* London: British Film Institute.

Eagleton, Terry. (1983). *Literary theory: An introduction.* Minneapolis: University of Minnesota Press.

Easthope, Anthony, & McGowan, Kate. (Eds.). (1992). *A critical and cultural theory reader.* Toronto: University of Toronto Press.

Eco, Umberto. (1985, Fall). Innovation and repetition: Between modern and post-modern aesthetics. *Daedulus.*

Edwards, Gavin. (1995). *'Scuse me while I kiss this guy and other misheard lyrics.* (Chris Kalb, Illus.). New York: Fireside.

Eisenberg, Evan. (1987). *The recording angel: Explorations in phonography.* New York: McGraw-Hill.

Eisenstadt, S. N. (1992). The order-maintaining and order-transforming dimensions of culture. In Richard Munch & Neil J. Smelser (Eds.), *Theory of culture* (pp. 64-87). Berkeley: University of California Press.

Eisenstein, Sergei M. (1949). *Film form: Essays in film theory.* (Jay Leyda, Trans. & Ed.). New York: Harcourt Brace.

Eliade, Mircea. (1961, April). The myths of the modern world. *Jubilee,* 16-19.

Elmer-Dewitt, Philip. (1993, September 27). The amazing video game boom. *Time,* 67.

Enzensberger, Hans Magnus. (1970). Constituents of a theory of media. *New Left Review, 64,* 6-19.

Enzensberger, Hans Magnus. (1974). *The consciousness industry.* New York: Seabury.

Farber, Jerry. (1982). *A field guide to the aesthetic experience.* North Hollywood, CA: Foreworks.

Featherstone, Mike. (1990). *Consumer culture and postmodernism.* Newbury Park, CA: Sage.

Featherstone, Mike. (1992). Cultural production, consumption, and the development of the cultural sphere. In Richard Munch & Neil J. Smelser (Eds.), *Theory of culture* (pp. 265-292). Berkeley: University of California Press.

Feshbach, Seymour. (1955). The drive-reducing function of fantasy behavior. *Journal of Abnormal and Social Psychology, 50,* 3-11.

Feshbach, Seymour. (1969). The catharsis effect: Research and another view. In Robert K. Baker & Sandra J. Ball (Eds.), *Violence and the media: A staff report to the national commission on the causes and prevention of violence* (pp. 461-471). Washington, DC: Government Printing Office.

Feuer, Jane. (1993). *The Hollywood musical.* (2nd ed.). Bloomington: Indiana University Press.

Finch, Christopher. (1973). *The art of Walt Disney: From Mickey Mouse to the magic kingdom.* New York: Harry N. Abrams.

Fisher, Walter. (1985). The narrative paradigm: An elaboration. *Communication Monographs, 51,* 347-367.

Fisher, Walter. (1994). Narration as a human communication paradigm: The case of public moral argument. *Communication Monographs, 51,* 1-22.

Fiske, John. (1989a). *Reading the popular.* Winchester, MA: Unwin Hyman.

Fiske, John. (1989b). *Understanding popular culture.* Winchester, MA: Unwin Hyman.

Fiske, John. (1990). *Introduction to communication studies.* (2nd ed.). New York: Routledge.

Fleming, Charles. (1994, June 27). A marriage made in Hollywood—High tech: Ma Bell exec becomes a talent agent. *Newsweek,* p. 45.

Foucault, Michel. (1980a). *Power/Knowledge.* New York: Pantheon.

Foucault, Michel. (1980b). *The history of sexuality: Vol. 1: An introduction.* New York: Pantheon.

Frith, Simon. (1992). The industrialization of popular music. In James Lull (Ed.), *Popular music and communication* (2nd ed.; pp. 62-79). Newbury Park, CA: Sage.

Frye, Northrop. (1957). *Anatomy of criticism.* Princeton: Princeton University Press.

Funk, Gary D. (1991). *Major violation: The unbalanced priorities in athletics and academics.* Champaign, IL: Leisure.

Galtung, Johann. (1982). Sport as carrier of deep culture and structure. *Current Research on Peace and Violence, 5,* 2-13.

Galtung, Johann, & Ruge, Mari Holmboe. (1965). The structure of foreign news. *Journal of Peace Research, 1,* 64-90.

Gans, Herbert. (1974). *Popular culture and high culture: An analysis and evaluation of taste.* New York: Basic Books.

Gans, Herbert. (1980). *Deciding what's news.* New York: Random House.

Garofalo, Reebee. (Ed.). (1992). *Rockin' the boat: Mass music and mass movements.* Boston: South End.

Garrat, Steven. (1986, March). How I learned to stop worrying and love Madonna. *Women's Review Number Five,* 12-13.

Geertz, Clifford. (1973). *The interpretation of cultures.* New York: Basic Books.

Gelmis, Joseph. (1994, September 13). An icon with a few questions: Redford. *Los Angeles Times,* pp. F1, 5.

Gerbner, George. (1993, June). *Women and minorities on television: A study in casting and fate.* A report to the Screen Actors Guild and the American Federation of Radio and Television Artists. Philadelphia: University of Pennsylvania, Annenberg School of Communication.

Gerbner, George, & Signiorelli, Nancy. (1979). *Aging with television: Images of television drama and conceptions of social reality* (preview report to HEW). Philadelphia: University of Pennsylvania, Annenberg School of Communication.

Gibson, William. (1984). *Neuromancer.* New York: Ace Books.

Gitlin, Todd. (Ed.). (1986). *Watching television.* New York: Pantheon.

Gitlin, Todd. (1995). *The twilight of common dreams: Why America is wracked by culture wars.* New York: Metropolitan, Henry Holt.

Goldlust, John. (1987). *Playing for keeps: Sport, the media and society.* Melbourne: Longman Cheshire.

Gomery, Douglas. (1994). Disney's business history: A reinterpretation. In Eric Smoodin (Ed.), *Disney discourse: Producing the magic kingdom* (pp. 71-86). New York: Routledge.

Goodale, Gail. (1995, June 5). Movies' liberal dose of conservatism: Studios churn out highest portion ever of family movies. *Christian Science Monitor,* p. 1.

Goodwin, Andrew. (1992). *Dancing in the distraction factory: Music television and popular culture.* Minneapolis: University of Minnesota Press.

Goodwin, Richard. (1988). Investigating the quiz shows. In *Remembering America: A voice from the sixties* (pp. 43-65). Boston: Little, Brown.

Gorman, Jerry, & Calhourn, Kirk. (1994). The name of the game: The business of sports. New York: John Wiley.

Gorris, Marleen. (1996, February 15). Interview on *Morning Edition.* National Public Radio.

Gow, Joe. (1992). Making sense of music videos: Research during the inaugural decade. *Journal of American Culture, 15*(3), 35-43.

Graham, Cooper C. (1986). *Leni Riefenstahl and Olympia.* Metuchen, NJ: Scarecrow.

Gramsci, Antonio. (1971). *Selections from the prison notebooks.* London: Lawrence and Wishart.

Grant, Barry Keith. (Ed.). (1986). *Film genre reader.* Austin: University of Texas Press.

Gray, Ann. (1992). *Video playtime: The gendering of a leisure technology.* New York: Routledge.

Gray, Ann, & McGuigan, Jim. (Eds.). (1993). *Studying culture: An introductory reader.* London: Edward Arnold.

Gray, Susan. (1982). Exposure to pornography and aggression toward women: The case of the angry male. *Social Problems, 29*(4), 387-396.

Greenberg, Richard. (Director). (1994a, March 4). *Night and Her Stars.* Premiere performance in the South Coast Repertory Theater, Costa Mesa, CA. A revised version was performed in New York at the Manhattan Theatre Club in 1995.

Greenberg, Richard. (1994b, January 14). Interviewed by Michael Real.

Greene, Graham. (1971). *The third man and the fallen idol.* New York: Penguin.

Greenfield, Patricia Marks. (1984). *Mind and media: The effects of television, video games, and computers.* Cambridge, MA: Harvard University Press.

Gronbeck, Bruce E., Farrell, Thomas J., & Soukup, Paul A. (Eds.). (1991). *Media, consciousness, and culture: Explorations of Walter Ong's thought.* Newbury Park, CA: Sage.

Grossberg, Lawrence. (1986). Reply to the critics. *Critical Studies in Mass Communication, 3,* 86-95.

Grossberg, Lawrence. (1992). Rock and roll in search of an audience. In James Lull (Ed.), *Popular music and communication* (2nd ed.; pp. 148-171). Newbury Park, CA: Sage.

Grossberg, Lawrence, Nelson, Cary, & Treichler, Paula. (Eds.). (1992). *Cultural studies.* New York: Routledge.

Gruneau, Richard. (1983). *Class, sport and social development.* Amherst: University of Massachusetts Press.

Gudorf, Christine E. (1994). Gender in the media: Notes on profit and ownership contraction. In Philip Rossi & Paul Soukup (Eds.), *Mass media and the moral imagination* (pp. 130-145). Kansas City, MO: Sheed and Ward.

Gunnison, Robert B. (1994, July 13). State has highest imprisonment rate. *San Francisco Chronicle,* p. 21

Guttmann, Allen. (1978). *From ritual to record: The nature of modern sports.* New York: Columbia University Press.

Guttmann, Allen. (1986). *Sports spectators.* New York: Columbia University Press.

Guttmann, Allen. (1988). *A whole new ball game.* Chapel Hill: University of North Carolina Press.

Guttmann, Allen. (1991). *Women's sports: A history.* New York: Columbia University Press.

Guttmann, Allen. (1992). *The Olympics: A history of the modern games.* Urbana: University of Illinois Press.

Guttmann, Allen. (1994). *Games and empires: Modern sports and cultural imperialism.* New York: Columbia University Press.

Halberstam, David. (1979). *The powers that be.* New York: Knopf.

Halberstam, David. (1993). *The fifties.* New York: Villard.

Hall, Stuart. (1980). Encoding and decoding. In Stuart Hall (Ed.), *Culture, media, language.* London: Hutchinson. (Originally published as *Encoding and decoding the TV message* [1973]. CCCS Stencilled Paper, Birmingham: CCCS.)

Hall, Stuart. (1985). Master's session. International Communication Association. Honolulu, Hawaii.

Hall, Stuart. (1994). Reflections upon the encoding/decoding model: An interview with Stuart Hall. In Jon Cruz & Justin Lewis (Eds.), *Viewing, reading, listening.* Boulder, CO: Westview.

Halliwell, Leslie. (1989). *Halliwell's film guide.* (7th ed.). New York: Harper and Row.

Hargreaves, Jennifer. (Ed.). (1982). *Sport, culture and ideology.* Boston: Routledge Kegan Paul.

Hargreaves, Jennifer. (1994). *Sporting females: Critical issues in the history and sociology of women's sports.* New York: Routledge.

Hargreaves, John. (1986). *Sport, power and culture: A social and historical analysis of popular sports in Britain.* Cambridge, U.K.: Polity.

Harris, Kathryn. (1993, June 20). Days of reckoning at Paramount. *Los Angeles Times,* pp. D1, D5.

Harvey, Jean, & Cantelon, Hart. (Eds.). (1988). *Not just a game: Essays in Canadian sport sociology.* Toronto: University of Toronto Press.

Haskell, Molly. (1974). *From reverence to rape: The treatment of women in the movies.* New York: Holt, Rinehart & Winston.

Hawkins, Robert J. (1995, April 5). Rock 'n' roll is here to stay. *San Diego Union-Tribune*, p. E7.

Hebdige, Dick. (1979). *Subculture: The meaning of style.* London: Methuen.

Henderson, Lisa. (1993). Justify our love: Madonna and the politics of queer sex. In Cathy Schwicktenberg (Ed.), *The Madonna connection: Representational politics, subcultural identities, and cultural theory* (pp. 107-128). Boulder, CO: Westview.

Henry, Bill, & Yeomans, Patricia Henry. (1984). *An approved history of the Olympic games.* Sherman Oaks, CA: Alfred.

Herman, Jan. (1994, September 9). SCR has dramatic answer to TV quiz. *Los Angeles Times*, pp. F1, F5, F24.

Higham, Charles, & Greenberg, Joel. (1968). *Hollywood in the forties.* Cranbury, NJ: A.S. Barnes.

Hillerman, Tony. (1993). *Sacred clowns.* New York: HarperCollins.

Hirsch, Foster. (1981). *The dark side of the screen: Film noir.* New York: A. S. Barnes.

Hirsch, Paul M. (1977). Occupational, organizational, and institutional models in mass communication. In Paul Hirsch, Peter Miller, & Fred Kline (Eds.), *Strategies for communication research* (pp. 13-42). Newbury Park, CA: Sage.

Hobbs, Renee. (1991). Television and the shaping of cognitive skills. In Alan M. Olson, Christopher Parr, & Debra Parr (Eds.), *Video icons and values* (pp. 33-34). Albany: State University of New York Press.

Hoberman, James. (1987). [Review of the film *Blue Velvet*]. *Film Review Annual* (pp. 154-156). Englewood, NJ: J.S. Ozer. (Reprinted from *Village Voice*, September 23, 1986, p. 58.)

Hobson, Dorothy. (1982). *"Crossroads": The diary of a soap opera.* London: Methuen.

Hoggart, Richard. (1957). *The uses of literacy: Aspects of working class life with special reference to publications and entertainments.* London: Chatto and Windus.

Holub, Robert C. (1984). *Reception theory: A critical introduction.* London: Methuen.

Homolka, Dan. (1995). *Pulp Fiction FAQ.* [World Wide Web]. Available: http://rmd-www.mr.ic.ac.uk/-dan/homepage.html .

Hornby, Nick. (1992). *Fever pitch.* London: Victor Gollancz.

Horne, John, & Bentley, C. E. (1989). *"Fitness chic" and the construction of lifestyles.* Paper presented at the LSA Conference on Leisure, Health and Well Being. Cited in Jennifer Hargreaves. (1994). *Sporting females: Critical issues in the history and sociology of women's sports* (pp. 161 & 310). New York: Routledge.

Hunter, James Davison. (1991). *Culture wars: The struggle to define America.* New York: Basic Books.

Infusino, Divina. (1991, May 5). Screened out: Women in film. *San Diego Union*, pp. E1, E4.

Inglis, Fred. (1990). *Media theory: An introduction.* Oxford: Basil Blackwell.

Iser, Wolfgang. (1978). *The act of reading: A theory of aesthetic response.* Baltimore, MD: Johns Hopkins University Press.

Jameson, Fredric. (1971, Winter). Reification and utopia in mass culture. *Social Text, 1*, 130-148.

Jameson, Fredric. (1991). *Postmodernism: or, the cultural logic of late capitalism.* Durham, NC: Duke University Press.

Jauss, Hans Robert. (1982). *Toward an aesthetic of reception.* (Timothy Bahti, Trans.). Minneapolis: University of Minnesota Press.

Jenkins, Henry. (1992). *Textual poachers: Television fans and participatory culture.* New York: Routledge.

Jenkins, Steve. (1987). [Review of the film *Blue Velvet*]. *Film Review Annual* (pp. 147-148). Englewood, NJ: J.S. Ozer. (Reprinted from *Monthly Film Bulletin*, April, 1987, p. 99.)

Jones, Steve. (1992). *Rock formation: Music, technology, and mass communication.* Newbury Park, CA: Sage.

Josselson, Ruthellen, & Lieblich, Amia. (Eds.). (1993). *The narrative study of lives.* Newbury Park, CA: Sage.

Kaplan, E. Ann. (Ed.). (1980). *Women in film noir.* London: British Film Institute.

Kaplan, E. Ann. (1983). *Women and film: Both sides of the camera.* New York: Methuen.

Kaplan, E. Ann. (1988). Who's imaginary? The televisual apparatus, the female body and textual strategies in select rock videos on MTV. In E. Deidre Pribram (Ed.), *Female spectators: Looking at film and television* (pp. 132-156). New York: Verso.

Karimi, Amir Massoud. (1976). *Toward a definition of the American film noir (1941-1949).* New York: Arno Press Cinema Program.

Katell, David A., & Marcus, Norman. (1988). *Sports for sale: Television, money, and the fans.* New York: Oxford University Press.

Katz, Elihu. (1980). Media events: The sense of occasion. *Studies in Visual Communication, 6*(3), 84-89.

Kelly, John Robert. (1987). *Blue Velvet.* In Frank N. Magill (Ed.), *Magill's cinema annual 1987: A survey of the films of 1986* (p. 110-115). Pasadena, CA: Salem Press.

Kinder, Marsha. (1991). *Playing with power in movies, television, and video games: From Muppet Babies to Teenage Mutant Ninja Turtles.* Berkeley: University of California Press.

Kline, David, & Burstein, Daniel. (1996, January). Elecrosphere: Is government obsolete? *Wired,* pp. 86-105.

Krafta, S., Penrod, S., Donnerstein, E., & Linz, D. (1992). *Sexually explicit, sexually aggressive and violent media: The effect of naturalistic exposure on females.* Unpublished manuscript, University of Wisconsin.

Krainin, Julian, & Lawrence, Michael (Producers). (1992). *The quiz show scandal.* Boston: WGBH-TV, *The American Experience.*

Kroker, Arthur, & Cook, David. (1986). *The postmodern scene: Excremental culture and hyperaesthetics.* New York: St. Martin's.

Kuhn, Annette. (1984). Women's genres. *Screen 25*(1), 18-28.

Kutchinsky, Berl. (1991). Pornography and rape: Theory and practice? Evidence from crime data in four countries where pornography is easily available. *International Journal of Law and Psychiatry, 14,* 147-164.

Laclau, Ernesto, & Mouffe, Chantal. (1985). *Hegemony and socialist strategy: Toward a radical democratic politics.* London: Verso.

Lang, Gladys E. & Lang, Kurt. (1953). The unique perspective of television. *American Sociological Review, 18,* 3-12.

Lasswell, Harold. (1960). The structure and function of communication of society. In Wilbur Schramm (Ed.), *Mass communication* (2nd ed., pp. 117-130). Urbana: University of Illinois Press. (Original work published in 1948.)

Laurence, Robert P. (1994, September 11). When right was wrong—Quiz show cheating made America cynical. *San Diego Union-Tribune,* pp. E1, E11.

de Lauretis, Teresa. (1994). Rethinking women's cinema: Aesthetics and feminist theory. In Diane Carson, Linda Dittmar, & Janice Welsch (Eds.), *Multiple voices in feminist film criticism* (pp. 140-161). Minneapolis: University of Minnesota Press. (Originally published in 1985.)

Lawrence, Geoffrey, & Rowe, David. (Eds.). (1986). *Power play.* Sydney: Hale and Iremonger.

Lazarsfeld, Paul. (1941). Remarks on administrative and critical communication research. *Studies in Philosophy and Social Science, 9,* 2-16.

Lazarsfeld, Paul, & Merton, Robert. (1957). Mass communication, popular taste, and organized social action. In Bernard Rosenberg & David Manning White (Eds.), *Mass culture: The popular arts in America* (pp. 457-473). New York: Van Nostrand Reinhold. (Original work published 1948.)

Lent, John. (1995). *Women and mass communications: An annotated bibliography.* (2nd ed.). Westport, CT: Greenwood.

Leo, John. (1994, October 3). Twisting truth: The $64,000 question. *San Diego Union-Tribune,* p. B7.

Lerner, Gerda. (1986). *The creation of patriarchy.* New York: Oxford University Press.

Levy, Emmanuel. (1987). *And the winner is . . . : The history and politics of the Oscar awards.* New York: Ungar.

Lewis, George. (1992). Patterns of meaning and choice: Taste cultures in popular music. In James Lull (Ed.), *Popular music and communication* (pp. 198-211). Newbury Park: Sage.

Lewis, Jon. (1994). Disney after Disney: Family business and the business of family. In Eric Smoodin (Ed.), *Disney discourse: Producing the magic kingdom* (pp. 87-105). New York: Routledge.

Lewis, Lisa. (1990). *Gender politics and MTV: Voicing the difference.* Philadelphia: Temple University Press.

Liebes, Tamar, & Katz, Elihu. (1990). *The export of meaning: Cross-cultural readings of "Dallas."* New York: Oxford University Press.

Linz, Daniel, & Malamuth, Neil. (1993). *Pornography.* Newbury Park, CA: Sage.

Long, Elizabeth. (1994). Textual interpretation as collective action. In Jon Cruz & Justin Lewis (Eds.), *Viewing, reading, listening* (pp. 181-212). Boulder, CO: Westview.

Lucas, John. (1980). *The modern Olympic games.* South Brunswick, NJ: A. S. Barnes.

Lucas, John. (1992). *Future of the Olympic games.* Champaign, IL: Human Kinetics.

Lucas, John. (1995, March 7). *Television—an integral aesthetic-entertainment/financial thrust of the International Olympic Committee.* Lecture presented at San Diego State University, San Diego, California.

Lucas, Robert J. (1984). *A descriptive history of the interdependence of television and sports in the summer Olympic games, 1956-1984.* Unpublished master's thesis, San Diego State University, California.

Lull, James. (Ed.). (1988). *World families watch television.* Newbury Park, CA: Sage.

Lull, James. (1990). *Inside family viewing: Ethnographic research on television's audiences.* New York: Routledge.

Lull, James. (1995). *Media, communication, culture: A global approach.* New York: Columbia University Press.

Lyotard, Jean-François. (1984). *The postmodern condition.* Minneapolis: University of Minnesota Press. (Originally published in French in 1979.)

Lyotard, Jean-François. (1993). Defining the postmodern. In Simon During (Ed.), *The cultural studies reader* (pp. 170-174). London: Routledge.

MacAloon, John. (1981). *This great symbol: Pierre de Coubertin and the origins of the modern Olympic games.* Chicago: University of Chicago Press.

MacNeill, Margaret. (1994). Active women, media representations, and ideology. In Susan Birrill & Cheryl L. Cole (Eds.), *Women, sport, and culture* (pp. 273-288). Champaign, IL: Human Kinetics.

Mailer, Norman. (1994, August). Like a lady. *Esquire,* pp. 40-56.

Mailloux, Steven. (1977). Reader-response criticism? *Genre, 10,* 413-431.

Malamuth, Neil, & Check, J. V. P. (1980). Sexual arousal to rape and consenting depictions: The importance of the woman's arousal. *Journal of Abnormal Psychology, 89,* 763-766.

Malamuth, Neil, & Check, J. V. P. (1983). Sexual arousal to rape depictions: Individual differences. *Journal of Abnormal Psychology, 92*(1), 55-67.

Mandel, Ernest. (1975). *Late capitalism.* London: New Left.

Mandell, Richard D. (1971). *The Nazi Olympics.* New York: Macmillan.

Marich, Robert. (1993, August 23). Jurassic Park expected to net giant profit. *San Diego Union-Tribune,* p. E4.

Marin, Louis. (1977). *Utopia and ideology: Disneyland.* Paper presented at the University of California at San Diego. (Based on Marin, Louis. [1973]. *Utopiques: Jeux d'espaces.* Paris: Editions de Minuit.)

Marsh, Dave. (1989). *The heart of rock and soul: The 1001 greatest singles ever made.* New York: New American Library.

Martin-Barbero, Jésus. (1993). *Communication, culture and hegemony: From the media to mediations.* (Elizabeth Fox & Robert A. White, Trans.). Newbury Park, CA: Sage.

Masters, Kim. (1991, October 20). Trouble in the magic kingdom. *Washington Post,* p. G11

Mayne, Judith. (1988). The female audience and the feminist critic. In Janet Todd (Ed.), *Women and film* (pp. 22-41). New York: Holmes & Meier.

McCaffery, Larry. (1993). Tsunami: Introduction. In Larry McCaffrey (Ed.), *Avant-pop: Fiction for a daydream nation* (pp. 15-32). Boulder, CO: Fiction Collective Two.

McChesney, Robert. (1989). Media made sport: A history of sports coverage in the United States. In Lawrence Wenner (Ed.), *Media, sports, and society* (pp. 49-69). Newbury Park, CA: Sage.

McChesney, Robert W. (1994). *Telecommunications, mass media, and democracy: The battle for the control of U.S. broadcasting, 1928-1935.* New York: Oxford University Press.

McConnell, Frank. (1990, April 20). Media: Just a moment—the logic of Nintendo. *Commonweal,* pp. 256-257.

McDonald, David G., & Hodgdon, James A. (1991). *The psychological effects of aerobic fitness training: Research and theory.* New York/Berlin: Springer-Verlag.

McGowan, John. (1991). *Postmodernism and its critics.* London: Cornell University Press.

McKenzie-Mohr, Doug, & Zanna, Mark P. (1990). Treating women as sexual objects: Look to the (gender schematic) male who has viewed pornography. *Personality and Social Psychology Bulletin, 16,* 296-308.

McLuhan, Marshall. (1964). *Understanding media: The extensions of man.* New York: McGraw-Hill.

McNamara, Robert S. (1995). *In retrospect.* New York: Times Books, Random House. (Quoted in *Newsweek,* April 17, 1995, p. 46.)

McRobbie, A. (1978a). *Jackie: An ideology of adolescent femininity.* Stencilled Occasional Paper. Birmingham, England: The Centre for Contemporary Cultural Studies.

McRobbie, A. (1978b). Working class girls and the culture of femininity. In Women's Studies Group (Eds.), *Women take issue* (pp. 97-108). London: Hutchinson.

McRobbie, Angela. (1984). Dance and social fantasy. In Angela McRobbie & M. Nava (Eds.), *Gender and generation* (pp. 130-162). London: Macmillan.

McRobbie, Angela. (1993). Chantal Akerman and feminist film-making. In Pam Cook & Philip Dodd (Eds.), *Women and film: A Sight and Sound reader* (pp. 198-203). Philadelphia: Temple University Press.

McRobbie, Angela. (1994). *Postmodernism and popular culture.* New York: Routledge.

Messaris, Paul. (1993). *Visual literacy: Image, mind, and reality.* Boulder, CO: Westview.

Messner, Michael A. (1994). Sports and male domination: The female athlete as contested ideological terrain. In Susan Birrill & Cheryl L. Cole (Eds.), *Women, sport, and culture* (pp. 65-80). Champaign, IL: Human Kinetics.

Messner, Michael A., & Sabo, Donald F. (Eds.). (1990). *Sport, men, and the gender order: Critical feminist perspectives.* Champaign, IL: Human Kinetics.

Metz, Christian. (1974). *Film language: A semiotics of the cinema.* (Michael Taylor, Trans.). New York: Oxford University Press.

Meyer, Michael. (1994, December 12). Fight to the finish—video wars: The world's electronic-game makers battle for ascendancy. *Newsweek,* pp. 56-57.

Miller, Gregory. (1995, February 12). Feminist's defense of porn a bit alarmist. *San Diego Union-Tribune,* p. E5.

Milloy, Courtland. (1991, January 20). Video wars: The next generation. *Washington Post,* p. D3.

Milner, Andrew. (1994). *Contemporary cultural theory: An introduction.* London: University College London Press.

Modleski, Tania. (1991). *Feminism without women: Culture and criticism in a "postfeminist" age.* New York: Routledge.

Moore, Molly. (1994, August 4). Heaving bosoms turn censor's eye to Bollywood. *The Sunday Times* (London), p. 7.

Moores, Shaun. (1993). *Interpreting audiences: The ethnography of media consumption.* London: Sage.

Morgan, Robin. (1991, January-February). Irony and affirmation: *An angel at my table. Ms. Magazine,* p. 66.

Morley, David. (1980). *The "nationwide" audience: Structure and decoding.* London: British Film Institute.

Morley, David. (1986). *Family television: Cultural power and domestic leisure.* London: Comedia.

Morley, David. (1994). Between the public and the private: The domestic uses of information and communications technologies. In Jon Cruz & Justin Lewis (Eds.), *Viewing, reading, listening* (pp. 101-124). Boulder, CO: Westview.

Morris, Meaghan. (1993). Things to do with shopping centers. In Simon During (Ed.), *The cultural studies reader* (pp. 295-319). New York: Routledge.

Mueller, Milton. (1995). Why communications policy is passing "mass communication" by: Political economy as the missing link. *Critical Studies in Mass Communication, 12*(4), 457-472.

Mulvey, Laura. (1988a). Visual pleasure and narrative cinema. In Constance Penley (Ed.), *Feminism and film theory* (pp. 57-68). New York: Routledge. (Originally published 1975).

Mulvey, Laura. (1988b). Afterthoughts on "visual pleasure and narrative cinema" inspired by *Duel in the sun.* In Constance Penley (Ed.), *Feminism and film theory* (pp. 69-79). New York: Routledge. (Originally published 1981)

Mulvey, Laura. (Ed.). (1988c). *Visual and other pleasures.* Bloomington: Indiana University Press.

Mumby, Dennis K. (1993). *Narrative and social control: Critical perspectives.* Newbury Park, CA: Sage.

Munsterberg, Hugo. (1916). *The photoplay: A psychological study.* New York: D. Appleton.

Murray, John P. (1980). *Television and youth: 25 years of research and controversy.* Standford, WA: The Boys Town Center for the Study of Youth Development.

Nash, Christopher. (Ed.). (1990). *Narrative in culture: The uses of storytelling in the sciences, philosophy, and literature.* New York: Scribner.

Nash, Jay Robert, & Ross, Stanley Ralph. (1987). *The motion picture guide: 1987 annual.* Chicago: CineBooks.

Nelson, Mariah Burton. (1994a). *The stronger women get, the more men love football: Sexism and the American culture of sports.* Orlando, FL: Harcourt Brace.

Nelson, Mariah Burton. (1994b, June 22). Violence on and off the field: Sports culture glorifies abuse. *San Diego Union-Tribune,* p. B5.

Newcomb, Horace. (1983). *Television: The critical view* (3rd ed.). New York: Oxford University Press.

Oates, Bob. (1994, May 1). See through the smoke: Don't ban cigarettes, ban cigarette promotion; it's time to throw tobacco out of American sports. *Los Angeles Times,* pp. C3, C9.

O'Connor, Alan. (1990). Culture and communication. In John Downing, Ali Mohammadi, & Annabelle Sreberny-Mohammadi (Eds.), *Questioning the media: A critical introduction* (pp. 27-41). Newbury Park, CA: Sage.

Ong, Walter J. (1981). McLuhan as teacher: The future is a thing of the past. *Journal of Communication, 31,* 129-135.

Ong, Walter J. (1982). *Orality and literacy: The technologizing of the word.* London: Methuen.

O'Sullivan, Tim, Hartley, John, Saunders, Danny, Montgomery, Martin, & Fiske, John. (1994). *Key concepts in communication and cultural studies.* New York: Routledge.

Patton, Cindy. (1993). Embodying subaltern memory: Kinesthesia and the problematics of gender and race. In Cathy Schwichtenberg (Ed.), *The Madonna connection: Representational politics, subcultural identities, and cultural theory* (pp. 81-106). Boulder, CO: Westview.

Paz, Octavio. (1993). *Essays on Mexican art.* (Helen Lane, Trans.). New York: Harcourt Brace Jovanovich.

Penley, Constance. (Ed.). (1988). *Feminism and film theory.* New York: Routledge.

Penley, Constance. (1989). *The future of an illusion: Film, feminism, and psychoanalysis.* Minneapolis: University of Minnesota Press.

Perris, Arnold. (1985). *Music as propaganda, art to persuade, art to control.* Westport, CT: Greenwood.

Perry, George. (1994, August 7). First opinion: Cut and dried? *The Sunday Times* (London), pp. 10, 18.

Petrie, Duncan. (1992). *Screening Europe: Image and identity in contemporary European cinema.* London: British Film Institute.

Phillips, Julia, & Thompson, Anne. (1992, December 18). If women ran Hollywood. *Entertainment Weekly,* pp. 30-33.

Place, Janey Ann, & Peterson, Lowell S. (1974, January). Some visual motifs of film noir. *Film Comment,* 30-35.

The Polity reader in cultural theory. (1994). Cambridge, MA: Polity.

Porfirio, Robert G. (1976). No way out: Existential motifs of film noir. *Sight and Sound, 45*(4), 212-217.

Potts, Mark. (1992, January 25). Mario a big man on campus: Conference studies video game effects. *Washington Post,* p. F1.

Presidential Commission on Obscenity and Pornography. (1970). *Technical reports of the Presidential Commission on Obscenity and Pornography.* Washington, DC: Government Printing Office.

Preview. (1994, June 6). [Untitled note]. p. 2.

Pribram, E. Deidre. (1993). Seduction, control, and the search for authenticity: Madonna's *Truth or dare.* In Cathy Schwichtenberg (Ed.), *The Madonna connection: Representational politics, subcultural identities, and cultural theory* (pp. 189-212). Boulder, CO: Westview.

Propp, Vladimir. (1968). *The morphology of the folktale.* (2nd ed.). Austin: University of Texas Press. (Originally published in 1928)

Provenzo, Eugene F., Jr. (1992, December). What do video games teach. *Educational Digest,* 56.

Puckett, Scott. (1995, January 25). The revolution will be televised: Ideological viruses infect people through media. *The Daily Aztec,* pp. 13-14.

Quindt, Fritz. (1995, December 13). NBC locks up 3 more games for $2.3 billion. *San Diego Union-Tribune,* p. C1.

Rader, Benjamin G. (1984). *In its own image: How television has transformed sports.* New York: Free Press.

Radway, Janice. (1984). *Reading the romance: Women, patriarchy and popular literature.* Chapel Hill: University of North Carolina Press.

Real, Michael. (1975). Superbowl: Mythic spectacle. *Journal of Communication, 25*(1), 31-43.

Real, Michael. (1977). *Mass-mediated culture.* Englewood Cliffs, NJ: Prentice Hall.

Real, Michael. (1989). *Super media: A cultural studies approach.* Newbury Park, CA: Sage.

Real, Michael. (1995, Winter). The great quiz show scandal: Why America remains fascinated. *Television Quarterly, 17*(3), 2-28.

Real, Michael, & Hassett, Chris (1981). *Audience perceptions of the Academy Awards telecast.* Paper presented at the meeting of the International Communication Association, Minneapolis.

Real, Michael, & Mechikoff, Robert A. (1992). Deep fan: Mythic identification, technology, and advertising in spectator sports. *Sociology of Sport Journal, 9,* 323-339.

Redford, Robert (Producer & Director). (1994). *Quiz Show* [Film]. (Available from Hollywood Pictures)

Reed, Rex. (1987). [Review of the film *Blue Velvet*]. *Film Review Annual* (pp. 151-152). Englewood, NJ: J.S. Ozer. (Reprinted from *New York Post,* September 19, p. 49.)

Reyes Matta, Fernando. (1986). Latin American newspaper: Reporting of the Olympic games. In Michael Real (Ed.), *Global ritual: Olympic media coverage and international understanding,* (pp. 194-217). San Diego, CA: San Diego State University, School of Communications.

Rich, B. Ruby. (1994). In the name of feminist film criticism. In Diane Carson, Linda Dittmar, & Janice Welsch (Eds.), *Multiple voices in feminist film criticism* (pp. 27-47). Minneapolis: University of Minnesota Press.

Riessman, Catherine Kohler. (1993). *Narrative analysis.* Newbury Park, CA: Sage.

Robinson, Deanna Campbell, Buck, Elizabeth B., & Cuthbert, Marlene. (1991). *Music at the margins: Popular music and global cultural diversity.* Newbury Park, CA: Sage.

Rogers, Florence, & Real, Michael. (1994). Theorizing postmodern stars: George Michael and Madonna. In Susan J. Drucker & Robert S. Cathcart (Eds.), *American heroes in a media age* (pp. 205-220). Cresskill, NJ: Hampton.

Root, Jane. (1986). *Open the box: About television.* London: Comedia.

Rosen, Marjorie. (1973). *Popcorn Venus: Women, movies, and the American dream.* New York: Coward, McCann, & Geoghegan.

Rosenberg, Bernard, & White, David Manning. (Eds.). (1957). *Mass culture: The popular arts in America.* New York: Free Press.

Rosenstone, Robert A. (1995). Introduction. In Robert A. Rosenstone (Ed.), *Revisioning history: Film and the construction of a new past* (pp. 3-13). Princeton: Princeton University Press.

Ross, Andrew. (1993). The popularity of pornography. In Simon During (Ed.), *The cultural studies reader* (pp. 221-242). New York: Routledge.

Rowe, David. (1995). *Popular cultures: Rock music, sport and the politics of pleasure.* London: Sage.

Rowe, David, & Lawrence, Geoffrey. (1990). *Sport and leisure: Trends in Australian popular culture.* Sydney: Harcourt Brace Jovanovich.

Rushkoff, Douglas. (1992). *Cyberia: Life in the trenches of hyperspace.* New York: Ballantine.

Rushkoff, Douglas. (1994a). *Media virus: Hidden agendas in popular culture*. New York: Ballantine.

Rushkoff, Douglas. (1994b). *The GenX reader*. New York: Ballantine.

Ruttle, Jack. (1989). The symbiotic relationship between television and the Olympic movement. In R. Jackson & Thomas McPhail (Eds.), *The Olympic movement and the mass media: Past, present, and future issues* (pp. 5/3-6). Calgary, Canada: Huford.

Ryan, James. (1995, September 24). And the producer of the movie is. . . . *New York Times*, pp. H13, H22, H23.

Salm, Arthur. (1993, May 10). Public eye. *San Diego Union-Tribune*, p. E2.

Samuelson, Robert J. (1989, September 4). The American sports mania. *Newsweek*, p. 49.

Schatz, Thomas. (1981). *American film genres*. New York: Random House.

Schickel, Richard. (1968). *The Disney version: The life, times, art and commerce of Walt Disney*. New York: Simon & Schuster.

Scholes, Robert, & Kellogg, Robert. (1966). *The nature of narrative*. New York: Oxford University Press.

Schrader, Paul. (1972, Spring). Notes on film noir. *Film Comment*, 8-13.

Schudson, Michael. (1991). The new validation of popular culture: Sense and sentimentality in academia. In Robert K. Avery & David Eason (Eds.), *Critical perspectives on media and society* (pp. 49-68). New York: Guilford.

Schwichtenberg, Cathy. (Ed.). (1993a). *The Madonna connection: Representational politics, subcultural identities, and cultural theory*. Boulder, CO: Westview.

Schwichtenberg, Cathy. (1993b). Introduction: Connections/intersections. In Cathy Schwichtenberg (Ed.), *The Madonna connection: Representational politics, subcultural identities, and cultural theory* (pp. 1-11). Boulder, CO: Westview.

Schwichtenberg, Cathy. (1993c). Madonna's postmodern feminism: Bringing the margins to the center. In Cathy Schwichtenberg (Ed.), *The Madonna connection: Representational politics, subcultural identities, and cultural theory* (pp. 129-145). Boulder, CO: Westview.

Scott, Ronald B. (1993). Images of race and religion in Madonna's video "Like a Prayer": Prayer and praise. In Cathy Schwichtenberg (Ed.), *The Madonna connection: Representational politics, subcultural identities, and cultural theory* (pp. 57-77). Boulder, CO: Westview

Screen Actors Guild. (1990, August 1). *The female in focus: In whose image? A statistical survey of the status of women in film, television and commercials*. Hollywood, CA: Author.

Screen Actors Guild. (1993, June 15). *Employment in entertainment: The search for diversity: A SAG statistical survey of ethnicity, age and gender in film, television and commercials*. Hollywood, CA: Author.

Segrave, Jeffrey, & Chu, Donald. (1981). *Olympism*. Champaign, IL: Human Kinetics.

Shaffer, Richard A. (1993, August 16). Playing games. *Forbes*, p. 108.

Shattuc, Jane M. (1992). Postmodern misogyny in *Blue Velvet. Genders, 13*, 73-89.

Sheff, David. (1993). *Game over: How Nintendo zapped an American industry, captured your dollars, and enslaved your children*. New York: Random House.

Shepherd, John. (1994). The analysis of popular music. In *The Polity reader in cultural theory* (pp. 231-235). Cambridge, U.K.: Polity.

Silver, Alain, & Ward, Elizabeth. (Eds.). (1992). *Film noir: An encyclopedic reference to the American style*. (3rd ed.). Woodstock, NY: Overlook.

Silverstone, Roger. (1991). From audiences to consumers: The household and the consumption of information and communication technologies. *European Journal of Communication, 6*(2), 135-154.

Sims, Calvin. (1993, August 4). In real life, Los Angeles badly needs the movies. *International Herald Tribune*, pp. 9, 13.

Skirrow, Gillian. (1986). Hellivision: An analysis of video games. In Colin McCabe (Ed.), *High theory/low culture* (pp. 128-145). Manchester, U.K.: Manchester University Press.

Slotkin, Richard. (1973). *Regeneration through violence.* Middletown, CT: Wesleyan University Press.

Smelser, Neil J. (1992). Culture: coherent or incoherent. In Richard Munch & Neil J. Smelser (Eds.), *Theory of culture* (pp. 3-28). Berkeley: University of California Press.

Smith, Bernard (Producer), and Ford, John (Director). (1964). *Cheyenne autumn* [Film]. Hollywood, CA: Warner Brothers.

Smoodin, Eric. (Ed.). (1994a). *Disney discourse: Producing the magic kingdom.* New York: Routledge.

Smoodin, Eric. (1994b). Introduction: How to read Walt Disney. In Eric Smoodin (Ed.), *Disney discourse: Producing the magic kingdom* (pp. 1-20). New York: Routledge.

Smythe, Dallas. (1994). *Counterclockwise: Perspectives on communication.* (Thomas Guback, Ed.). Boulder, CO: Westview.

Spillane, Mickey. (1952). *Kiss me, deadly.* New York: E. P. Dutton.

Staiger, Janet. (1992). *Interpreting films: Studies in the historical reception of American cinema.* Princeton: Princeton University Press.

Steiner, Linda. (1991). Oppositional decoding as an act of resistance. *Critical Studies in Mass Communication, 5,* 1-15.

Stone, Joseph, & Yohn, Timothy. (1992). *Prime time and misdemeanors: Investigating the 1950s TV quiz show scandal—A D.A.s account.* New Brunswick, NJ: Rutgers University Press.

Storey, John. (1993). *An introductory guide to cultural theory and popular culture.* Athens: University of Georgia Press.

Straubhaar, Joseph. (1991). Beyond media imperialism: Asymmetrical interdependence and cultural proximity. *Critical Studies in Mass Communication, 8,* 39-59.

Strossen, Nadine. (1995). *Defending pornography: Free speech, sex, and the fight for women's rights.* New York: Scribner.

Subjic, Deyan. (1989). *Cult heroes: How to be famous for more than 15 minutes.* London: Andre Deutsch.

Supplee, Curt. (1990, December 10). Video angst. *Washington Post,* p. A3.

Tan, Alexis S. (1985). *Mass communication theories and research.* (2nd ed.). New York: John Wiley.

Tannenbaum, Percy H., & Zillman, Dolf. (1975). Emotional arousal in the facilitation of aggression through communication. In L. Berkowitz (Ed.), *Advances in experimental social psychology,* Vol. 8 (pp. 150-192). New York: Academic Press.

Taubin, Amy. (1993). The "Alien" trilogy: from feminism to Aids. In Pam Cook & Philip Dodd (Eds.), *Women and film: A Sight and Sound reader* (pp. 93-100). Philadelphia: Temple University Press.

Thompson, John B. (1990). *Ideology and modern culture: Critical social theory in the era of mass communication.* Cambridge, U.K.: Polity.

Thompson, Michael, Ellis, Richard, & Wildavsky, Aaron. (1990). *Cultural theory.* Boulder, CO: Westview.

Tiffin, Chris, & Lawson, Alan. (Eds.). (1994). *De-scribing empire: Post-colonialism and textuality.* New York: Routledge.

Tomlinson, Alan. (1989). Representation, ideology and the Olympic Games: A reading of the opening and closing ceremonies of the 1984 Los Angeles Olympic Games. In Roger C. Jackson & Thomas P. McPhail (Eds.), *The Olympic movement and the mass media: Past, present, and future issues* (pp. 7/3-9). Calgary, Canada: Hurford.

Tomlinson, Alan, & Whannel, Gary. (Eds.). (1984). *Five ring circus: Money, power and politics at the Olympic Games.* London: Pluto.

Trujillo, Nick, & Krizek, Bob. (1994). Emotionality in the stands and in the field: Expressing self through baseball. *Journal of Sport and Social Issues, 18*(4), 303-325.

Tuchman, Gaye. (1978). *Making news: A study in the construction of reality.* New York: Free Press.

Turkle, Sherry. (1988). Computational reticence: Why women fear the intimate machine. In C. Kramarae (Ed.), *Technology and women's voices* (pp. 41-50). London: Routledge.

Turner, Victor. (1969). *The ritual process: Structure and antistructure.* Ithaca, NY: Cornell University Press.

United Nations. (1991). *Women: Challenges to the year 2000.* (U.N. Publication No. DPI/1134). New York: Author.

U.S. Civil Rights Commission. (1977). *Window dressing on the set: Women and minorities in television.* Washington, D.C.: Government Printing Office.

U. S. Commerce Department, Census Bureau. (1994). *Annual survey of communication services* [On-line]. Washington, D.C.: On-line U. S. Government Documents.

Van Dijk, Teun A. (1993). *Elite discourse and racism.* Newbury Park, CA: Sage.

Van Zoonen, Lisbet. (1994). *Feminist media studies.* Thousand Oaks, CA: Sage.

Varnedoe, Kirk, & Gopnik, Adam. (1990). *High and low: Modern art, popular culture.* New York: Museum of Modern Art.

Vasconcelos, Antonio-Pedro (Chair). (1994). *Report by the think tank [on the audiovisual industry in Europe].* Brussels: Commission of the European Union.

Wakefield, Dan. (1994, August 21). Robert Redford—His 50's, then and now. *Quiz Show* takes two guys back to a more innocent America. *The New York Times Magazine,* pp. 26-29.

Walker, Laura Becker. (1993, November 3). What's in a game? *Washington Post,* p. C5.

Walker, Martin. (1994, March). Disney's saccharin turns sour. *World Press Review,* pp. 36-37. (Reprinted from *The Guardian* [London])

Walkerdine, Valerie. (1986). Video replay: Families, film and fantasy. In V. Burgin, J. Donald, & C. Kaplan (Eds.), *Formations of fantasy* (pp. 167-199). London: Methuen.

Warshow, Robert. (1970). *The immediate experience: Movies, comics, theatre and other aspects of popular culture.* New York: Atheneum.

Wasser, Frederick. (1995). Is Hollywood America? The trans-nationalization of the American film industry. *Critical Studies in Mass Communication, 12*(4), 423-437.

Webb, Tammilee (Producer). (1992). Buns of steel [Exercise video]. (Available from Webb International, 2010 Jimmy Durante Blvd., Suite 230, Del Mar, CA 92014.)

Weinberg, Meyer. (1962). *TV in America: The morality of hard cash.* New York: Ballantine.

Welkos, Robert W. (1993, August 22). Every day was high noon. *Los Angeles Times,* pp. 8-9, 29-34.

Wenner, Lawrence A. (Ed.). (1989a). *Media, sports, and society.* Newbury Park, CA: Sage.

Wenner, Lawrence A. (1989b). Preface. In Lawrence A. Wenner (Ed.), *Media, sports, and society* (pp. 7-10). Newbury Park, CA: Sage.

Wenner, Lawrence A., & Gantz, Walter. (1989). The audience experience with sports on television. In Lawrence A. Wenner (Ed.), *Media, sports, and society* (pp. 241-269). Newbury Park, CA: Sage.

Whannel, Garry. (1983). *Blowing the whistle.* London: Pluto.

Whannel, Garry. (1992). *Fields in vision: Television sport and cultural transformation.* New York: Routledge.

White, David Manning. (1950). The "gatekeeper:" A case study in the selection of news. *Journalism Quarterly, 27,* 383-390.

White, Leonard. (1979). Erotica and aggression: The influence of sexual arousal, positive affect, and negative affect on aggressive behavior. *Journal of Personality and Social Psychology, 37,* 591-601.

White, William B., Jr. (1992, March). What value are video games? *USA Today Magazine*, p. 74.

Williams, John A. (1988, April 23). Prior restraints. *The Nation*, pp. 37-41.

Williams, Linda. (1994). A jury of their peers: Questions of silence, speech, and judgment in Marleen Gorris's *A Question of Silence*. In Diane Carson, Linda Dittmar, & Janice Welsch (Eds.), *Multiple voices in feminist film criticism* (pp. 432-440). Minneapolis: University of Minnesota Press.

Williams, Raymond. (1958). *Culture and society: 1780-1950*. London: Chatto and Windus.

Willis, Susan. (1987). Gender as commodity. *South Atlantic Quarterly, 86*(4), 403-421.

Willis, Susan. (1991). *A primer for daily life*. London: Routledge.

Wilson, Alexander. (1994). The betrayal of the future: Walt Disney's EPCOT Center. In Eric Smoodin (Ed.), *Disney discourse: Producing the magic kingdom* (pp. 118-128). New York: Routledge.

Wilstein, Steve. (1993, January 28). Wanna bet on sports? Many do. *San Diego Union-Tribune* (AP), pp. D1, D4.

Winn, Marie. (1975). *The plug-in drug*. New York: Viking.

Wood, Daniel B. (1990, December 3). Nintendo's quest: Staying popular. *Christian Science Monitor*, p. 12.

Wuthnow, Robert. (1992). Infrastructure and superstructure: Revisions in Marxist sociology of culture. In Richard Munch & Neil J. Smelser (Eds.), *Theory of culture* (pp. 145-170). Berkeley: University of California Press.

Yoshimoto, Mitsuhiro. (1994). Images of empire: Tokyo Disneyland and Japanese cultural imperialism. In Eric Smoodin (Ed.), *Disney discourse: Producing the magic kingdom* (pp. 181-199). New York: Routledge.

Zagano, Phyllis. (1994, November 3). Beavis and Butthead, free your minds! *America*, pp. 6-7.

Zehme, Bennett. (1989, March 23). Madonna: The Rolling Stone interview. *Rolling Stone*, p. 51.

Zillman, Dolf, & Bryant, Jennings. (1982). Pornography, sexual callousness, and the trivialization of rape. *Journal of Communication, 32*, 10-21.

Zillman, Dolf, & Bryant, Jennings. (1984). Effects of massive exposure to pornography. In Neil Malamuth & Edward Donnerstein (Eds.), *Pornography and sexual aggression* (pp. 115-138). New York: Academic Press.

Zillman, Dolf, & Bryant, Jennings. (1986). *Pornography's impact on sexual satisfaction*. Unpublished manuscript, Indiana University, Bloomington.

Zillman, Dolf, & Bryant, Jennings. (1988). Effects of prolonged consumption of pornography on family values. *Journal of Family Issues, 9*, 518-544.

Index

About the Author

Michael R. Real is Professor and Director of the School of Communications at San Diego State University. He is the author of *Mass-Mediated Culture* and *Super Media: A Cultural Studies Approach,* and is the editor, for UNESCO, of *Global Ritual: Olympic Media Coverage and International Understanding.* His numerous articles and reviews have appeared in *Critical Studies in Mass Communication, American Quarterly, Journal of Communication, Media Development, Journalism Quarterly, Journal of Popular Culture, TV Quarterly, Quest,* and other academic and popular media, and as chapters in more than a dozen books. He is a member of the International Communication Association, the International Association for Mass Communication Research, and other scholarly and professional organizations.

Professor Real holds a Ph.D. in Communication from the University of Illinois and has directed local, national, and international research projects. He has also produced or hosted a variety of television and radio programming on current issues and for underserved populations. The focus of his work is media, culture, and social responsibility.

Michael Real's home page can be accessed at:

http:/www-rohan.sdsu.edu/faculty/mreal